VENTURES IN CRIMINOLOGY

Contents

PART III. PROGRESSIVE PENOLOGY

PART IV. PHILOSOPHY OF CRIMINOLOGIC RESEARCH

'Not only are we, the general public, often ignorant of the methods by which a scientist works, but many scientists are ignorant of the methods employed in other branches of scientific work. There is no *scientific method* which fits all sciences. Every problem of knowledge has to be attacked with the weapons suitable to it. If we are to explore human nature we must find out the scientific method appropriate to its exploration and that method may not be the same as is suitable for exploring the inside of an atom or even the inside of a human body. . . .

'How does a scientist use his brain to add to knowledge? Most people, including most scientists themselves, imagine that it is a matter of cold, calculated reasoning and nothing else. If we examine the history of discovery and invention we realize at once that this is not so.

'There must, of course, be a trained, reasoning mind as a tool, but much if not most of the work of creative scientific thought is not done by any part of this conscious mind. The crucial part wells up from some unconscious level. Intellectual creativeness is not a conscious act, whether the result is the invention of a steam engine, the making of a poem or the discovery of the principles called Relativity. . . .

'The applied scientific work which occupies the lifetime of most scientific workers is largely concerned with such routine labor as maintaining standards, testing samples and minding machinery. For these purposes exactly the same qualities are required as for any inanimate scientific instrument, namely accuracy, routine, uniformity; for scientific research into unknown things, these too are necessary, but also almost antithetical qualities—adventurousness, imagination, and above all willingness to entertain ideas which may possibly turn out to be wrong—provided the idea is dropped directly it is no longer stimulating. There must be ability to distinguish between the false and the absurd and the latter must be courteously entertained until it is proved to be also the former.

'The beginning of a scientific experiment must always be the asking of a question. Then you set about finding a way of forcing an answer out of nature. But while you are using your existing knowledge and training in this way, you can be sure that the question is echoing in the secret places of your mind and that an ability to listen to some answering voice there is as important to the result as all the hard work you are consciously dedicating to the pursuit.

'Indeed the creative scientist is just one kind of creative artist, and as far removed from the routine worker in a laboratory as the poet is removed from the skilled person who deciphers his writing and makes the poem readable on a typewriter.

'The trouble with all of us when we try to understand scientific work at secondhand is that in the finished work the intuitive creative processes have almost always been carefully hidden by the rational superstructure. This obscures the fact that the scientist also is a creative artist.'

JOHN LANGDON-DAVIES, *Man the Known and Unknown* (1960)

PREFACE

THIS collection of some of our more recent papers is presented for the convenience of students of Criminology who may not have ready access to the journals in which they appear. They have been selected for their timeliness with respect to those fields of thought and endeavor that have been engaging the attention of criminologists and penologists. We have taken liberties with the text of some of the papers, deleting passages that are repetitious of information appearing in one or more chapters. This editing was made necessary by the fact that the papers are not here presented in the order in which they were initially published.

In the first chapter we present a brief review of our major researches, past, present, and future.

Part I considers some aspects of the not always clear issues of etiology.

Part II is concerned with the theory and practice of prediction in the crucial area of sufficiently early identification of delinquents for the purpose of deflecting criminal careers through educative and therapeutic intervention. There is also some discussion of the possible role of the predictive technique in improving the strikingly weak aspects of criminal justice—sentencing and releasing.

Part III provides glimpses into the more promising correctional practices. We think it shows that despite frustrating disappointments in the treatment of the offender, there has been progress—a forward movement reflective of a growing humanitarianism and sobriety of thought on the part not merely of correctional administrators, but of lawmakers and the public generally.

The final part (IV) deals with certain fundamental issues in the study of crime causation—the use and misuse of theoretical constructs, the difference between perceptive and carping criticism, and the role of replicative research in constructing a solid foundation of fact and inference in the study of delinquency. For without such planful and integrated investigation, in which new researches grow naturally out of pre-existing ones, there can be no growth of understanding, but only a continued accumulation of shreds and patches with little rhyme and less reason.

We invite the reader's attention to the chronological bibliography of our writings, which was initially prepared by the Harvard Law School Library under the supervision of Mr Philip A. Putnam,

Assistant Librarian, and somewhat modified for presentation in this volume (pp. 345-64).

Our appreciation is due our assistant, Miss Lillian M. Buller, for handling all the details connected with the assembling and editing of this volume.

We thank the editors of the various journals involved for their kind permission to reproduce the articles. We are grateful also to Martin Secker & Warburg, Publishers, for their permission to reprint a passage from *Man the Known and Unknown*.

Our debt is great to the Ford Foundation and to the U.S. National Institute of Mental Health (Research Grant M-1817) for financial support toward one or another aspect of our research program which made it possible for us to devote some of our time to the preparation of the papers that comprise this volume.

SHELDON and ELEANOR GLUECK

Harvard Law School
Cambridge, Massachusetts
January 1964

CHAPTER 1

Ventures in Criminology

SHELDON AND ELEANOR GLUECK

INTRODUCTORY

OUR interest in problems of delinquency and crime, punishment and correction, therapy and prevention began with the writing by one of us of *Mental Disorder and the Criminal Law*[7], published in 1925. This is a venture into the fog-enshrouded borderland of psychiatry and law. In 1927, *Community Use of Schools*[14] foreshadowed a concern with enhancing the role of schools to take constructive account of parents as well as pupils.

These early engagements of interest were to find their first joint expression in a fruitful series of follow-up inquiries intended to throw light on the product of our correctional institutions.

FOLLOW-UP STUDIES

The first research, published in 1930 under the title *500 Criminal Careers*[26], was designed to determine the effectiveness of reformatory treatment both during and after incarceration. The investigation revealed that some 80 per cent of 510 young adult offenders continued to commit crimes during a five-year post-imprisonment period. This finding attracted wide attention and led to other investigations, which used the same (and sometimes additional) factors in the make-up and background of the offenders, in order to learn more about the recidivism not only of adult but also of juvenile law-violators— 500 female offenders of all grades of felony who were inmates of a reformatory for women (*Five Hundred Delinquent Women*[44]), and 1,000 juvenile delinquents who had passed through the Boston Juvenile Court and had been referred (in 1921–22) to the Judge Baker Guidance Center, a well-known children's clinic in Boston, for diagnosis and for treatment recommendations to the court (*One Thousand Juvenile Delinquents*[45]). The recidivism rate among the women offenders, though lower than that of the male criminals of the earlier study, was quite clearly higher than expected (76 per cent). The findings were even more discouraging among the delinquent boys, 88 per cent of whom committed further acts of delinquency

1

during a five-year follow-up period after contact with court and clinic.

These dismal findings led us to explore larger segments of the life-cycle of the 500 young adult male offenders and the 1,000 juvenile delinquent offenders to see whether and at what stage a reduction in the recidivism rate occurs. This resulted in three further follow-up investigations, incorporated in *Later Criminal Careers*[71], *Criminal Careers in Retrospect*[102], and *Juvenile Delinquents Grown Up*[85].

From these elaborate investigations it became obvious that certain fundamental changes occurred with the passage of the years; there was evident a general reduction of aggressive criminalism during the early and middle thirties, a change for the better apparently attributable to the influences of Father Time and Mother Nature more than to the efforts of the peno-correctional regimes to which these offenders had been subjected. We were led to explain the precipitate drop in recidivism during the thirties largely by the ripening of a delayed process of maturation, the belated fruition of integrative forces that normally follow upon completion of adolescence.[1] This theory has many fundamental implications not only for etiology but for the practical management of the delinquency problem from the points of view of average length of sentence and correctional regimes.

As might be expected, these investigations were attacked in some quarters; but we think it fair to say that their major findings have not been successfully contradicted. It should be pointed out in passing that our various studies did not deal merely with checking on recidivism. For example, *One Thousand Juvenile Delinquents* contributed original material on the relationship between court and clinic; the nature of the recommendations made by the clinic to the court and the extent to which they were carried out; the results of enforcement or non-enforcement of the recommendations; needed reforms in the law governing juvenile court procedure; and other matters. The studies dealing with the adult offenders contained data on the regimes of the institutions involved and on parole administration; the point of view of prisoners and ex-prisoners; data regarding not only the criminal history but also parole and post-parole information respecting the activities of the offenders in terms of their industrial history and economic condition, family life, habits, use of leisure, and other matters. The inquiries contained predictive devices designed for controlled experimental use by judges and parole authorities.[2]

---

[1] We believe that part of the group who ceased their criminalistic activities had lost their energy and drive at an abnormally early period in life. It would have been valuable to have had endocrinologic and psychiatric examinations of these offenders at various stages in their careers.

[2] The various prediction tables developed in the aforementioned works as well as in later researches are assembled in *Predicting delinquency and crime*[212].

These earliest studies, in which the emphasis was on tracing the careers of offenders subjected to society's judicial and peno-correctional apparatus for coping with crime, have had a considerable impact. Upon invitation of the Department of Criminal Science of the Faculty of Law, University of Cambridge (England), they were summarized and to some extent reinterpreted in a volume entitled *After-conduct of Discharged Offenders*[119].[3]

One of the most disturbing revelations of the follow-up studies was that at least three-fourths of the adult offenders investigated had previously been juvenile delinquents. This finding, together with the shocking discovery that almost nine-tenths of the juvenile offender group continued to recidivate during the first five years following the treatment prescribed by an outstanding juvenile court and diagnosis and recommendations by a famous child guidance clinic, led us to focus our attention on the etiology of delinquency.

UNRAVELING JUVENILE DELINQUENCY

IN 1940 we began an intensive and extensive study designed to bring out differences and note similarities between a sample of 500 persistent juvenile delinquents and 500 true non-delinquents. The two groups were matched, pair by pair, in respect of age, intelligence, ethnico-racial derivation, and residence in high-delinquency areas of Greater Boston, as a prelude to their intensive study in several areas that seemed to us relevant. No such large-scale and many-faceted investigation had previously been made.[4] The field of exploration encompassed not only intensive study of the family history and status, the personal and social histories of the delinquents and the control group of non-delinquents, but also studies of the various aspects of their intelligence, personality dynamics, character structure, medical history, health status, anthropometric measurements (for the purpose of determining body structure). The published work[138], resulting from some eight years of investigation, gives ample detail on the reasons for the essential equalization, as between the delinquents and the non-delinquents, of age, general intelligence, ethnico-racial origin, and residence in deprived urban areas; and also the reasons for investigating the complex problem at the various

---

[3] See particularly the clarification of the maturation theory, pp. 78–91.

[4] Compare the works of Dr William Healy and Dr Augusta A. Bronner, especially Healy (1915), *The individual delinquent* (Boston: Little, Brown); Healy and Bronner (1936), *New light on delinquency and its treatment* (London: Oxford U.P.; New Haven: Yale U.P.); Healy and Bronner (1939), *Treatment and what happened afterward* (Boston: Judge Baker Guidance Center). See also Burt, Cyril (1925), *The young delinquent* (9th ed. 1961. London: University of London Press).

levels and by the means we decided upon. The extensive inquiry was carried on with a staff consisting of a psychiatrist who had had long experience in dealing with delinquent children; several trained psychologists with varied practical knowledge in giving and interpreting different intellectual and personality tests; two experienced physical anthropologists familiar with modern methods of anthropometry; several trained and highly knowledgeable social investigators who had had unique opportunity to sharpen their expertise in our follow-up investigations. A methodologic rule of prime importance governed the activities of this team of experts: none of them was permitted access to the others' case reports, this being a precaution to prevent contamination of the findings of one discipline by access to the materials derived by another approach.[5] This planful insulation made it ultimately possible for us to compare various sets of findings and thereby to determine the internal consistency of the work and, to an appreciable extent, the strengths and weaknesses of each participating discipline in contributing to a meaningful conception of the etiology of delinquency. For example, comparison

[5] Although *Unraveling* has had an extensive, varied, and powerful impact on both research and clinical practice, was translated into Japanese shortly after its publication (on the order of the Supreme Court of Japan), and is currently being translated into Spanish, it has not been without its heated critics. For a reply to the objections raised, see Chapter 17 of this volume.

Perceptive and fair criticism is of course always welcome; it is in the best traditions of science. However, it is puzzling to know what to do about criticisms based on misreadings or misconceptions. For example, in speaking of a finding in *Unraveling* concerning mothers who worked occasionally (not regularly) outside the home, Barbara Wootton points out that 'in this group were found 26·6 per cent of the delinquents, but only 14·7 per cent of the controls'. Then she goes on to say: 'From this evidence the Gluecks somewhat surprisingly leap to the conclusion that "whether the matter is approached from the psychoanalytic point of view of the deleterious effect upon the development of personality and character, or simply from ordinary observation and common experience, maternal neglect and careless oversight of children are accepted as major sources of maladjustment and delinquency; and, clearly, the mothers of the delinquent boys, as a group, were much more remiss in the care of their children than the mothers of the non-delinquents" ' (B. Wootton assisted by V. G. Seal & R. Chambers (1959), *Social science and social pathology*, pp. 115–16 (London: Allen & Unwin).)

However, it is not the Gluecks who 'surprisingly leap to the conclusion' quoted, but Barbara Wootton, the critic of *Unraveling*. The pages of *Unraveling* are printed in double columns; what Barbara Wootton has done is to take the factual material in the left-hand column, presented under the heading 'Usual occupation of mother' and jump across to the right-hand column to the discussion under the heading of 'Supervision of children'. This discussion does not at all constitute a surprising leap, but follows logically from the data showing that 'a disproportionately lower percentage of the mothers of the delinquents (7 per cent : 65·2 per cent) gave or arranged for suitable care of their children by keeping close watch over them and providing for their leisure hours, and that far more of the mothers of the delinquents (63·8 per cent : 13 per cent) left their children to shift for themselves or in the care of an irresponsible child or adult.' In other words, Barbara Wootton has confused the comments we make on two different tables in *Unraveling*, Table X–9, Usual Occupation of Mother, and Table X–10, Supervision of Children by Mother (*Unraveling*, pp. 112–13).

of diagnoses arrived at independently by the psychiatrist[6] and the Rorschach experts[7] showed a reassuringly high degree of agreement between the two sets of findings, with only six instances (out of some 1,000 cases) of clear inconsistency (138, pp. 242–3).

From comparisons between the delinquent group and the control group in respect to the subcategories of the 402 factors and traits involved, it was possible to determine the statistically significant differences between them. Much was learned thereby in regard to existing concepts of causal implication, and attention was drawn to areas of significant difference between delinquents and non-delinquents which suggested leads to more intensive inquiries in fields demonstrated to be highly promising for the study of etiology. Among these specialized inquiries may be mentioned *Physique and Delinquency*[176], a correlational integration of body types and traits, many of them criminogenic in the sense that they occurred more frequently among delinquents than among non-delinquents, and 'Working Mothers and Delinquency' (Chapter 3 below). However, *Unraveling* itself contributed much of importance in the way of a description of delinquents which furnished numerous clues for more intensive research in many areas. The tentative summarization of these findings follows:

'The delinquents as a group are distinguishable from the non-delinquents: (1) physically, in being essentially mesomorphic in constitution (solid, closely knit, muscular); (2) temperamentally, in being restlessly energetic, impulsive, extroverted, aggressive, destructive (often sadistic)—traits which may be related more or less to the erratic growth pattern and its psychologic correlates or consequences; (3) in attitude, by being hostile, defiant, resentful, suspicious, stubborn, socially assertive, adventurous, unconventional, non-submissive to authority; (4) psychologically, in tending to direct and concrete, rather than symbolic, intellectual expression, and in being less methodical in their approach to problems; (5) socio-culturally, in having been reared to a far greater extent than the control group in homes of little understanding, affection, stability or moral fibre, by parents usually unfit to be effective guides and protectors or, according to psychoanalytic theory, desirable sources for emulation and the construction of a consistent, well-balanced, and socially normal superego during the early stages of character development. While in individual cases the

[6] Bryant E. Moulton, for twelve years on the staff of the Judge Baker Guidance Center, Boston.

[7] Ernest G. Schachtel and the late Anna Hartoch Schachtel, both trained by Rorschach.

5

stresses contributed by any one of the above pressure-areas of dissocial-behavior tendency may adequately account for persistence in delinquency, in general the high probability of delinquency is dependent upon the interplay of the conditions and forces from all these areas.

'In the exciting, stimulating but little-controlled and culturally inconsistent environment of the underprivileged area, such boys readily give expression to their untamed impulses and their self-centered desires by means of various forms of delinquent behavior. Their tendencies toward uninhibited energy-expression are deeply anchored in soma and psyche and in the malformations of character during the first few years of life' (138, pp. 281–2).

Such, then, were the first broad, yet fruitful, generalizations derived from an intensive comparison of 500 persistent delinquents and 500 true non-delinquents drawn from very similar underprivileged areas of a large urban center. It is obvious from a reading of these generalizations that *Unraveling* has yielded a rich harvest of clues and ideas that call for more intensive exploration. We trust that other investigators will use these suggestive data as points of departure for their own researches.

This brief statement of the major studies we had carried on up to the point of completing *Unraveling* provides the background necessary to an understanding of the further exfoliation of our researches into the etiology and management of juvenile delinquency.

THE NEED FOR INTEGRATED RESEARCH

In comparison with the natural sciences, the disciplines that deal with sociocultural phenomena are underdeveloped. Apart from the fact that the problems involved—unemployment, poverty, crime, psychopathy—carry with them an almost unbanishable freightage of emotional and value judgment, there is the further though more manageable fact that researchers into social problems rarely follow through any consistent and coherent series of investigations. We are convinced that a fundamental reason for slowness in determining the causes, management, and prevention of delinquency and in the development of more successful correctional regimes is that researchers are not generally able to pursue long-term and planful interrelated inquiries. We believe that our long-range studies are among the very few exceptions that prove the rule. Every investigation we have made has grown logically and naturally in steady progression from clues derived from preceding ones. This fact is at long last beginning to be recognized among criminologists and is reflected in a quotation from a review of *Physique and Delinquency* by Professor Hermann Mannheim:

'One of the outstanding features of the work of the Gluecks has, for more than a quarter of a century, been their capacity, unrivalled in criminological research, for systematic and well-planned following-up. For lack of either patience and foresight or financial resources, research in the field of criminology has, more often than not, been of a very casual nature, ending inconclusively at a point when an additional effort might have produced worth-while results. The present volume is a remarkable example of the Glueck technique of a long-term follow-up, in this case of problems rather than, as in most of their previous studies, of individuals. Clearly, some of the findings in their earlier book, *Unraveling Juvenile Delinquency* (1950)—notably the considerably higher rate of mesomorphs in the delinquent group—seemed to be crying out for such further study. As the authors are careful to explain, the fact that this particular biological finding was selected for more detailed analysis was not "animated by any notion of respectful reawakening of the somnolent Lombrosian theory". The choice of somatic factors was merely due to their belief that this was to be "a promising focus of attention", one of several of the features in *Unraveling* which they propose further to explore in future monographs. In the opinion of the present reviewer, this explanation can be readily accepted.'[8]

FAMILY LIFE AND DELINQUENCY

It might be mentioned that in pursuance of the promise held out in *Physique and Delinquency* we have recently completed a long-term analysis of the influence of divisive and unwholesome family conditions on delinquency through their contribution to the formation of certain criminogenic traits; through rendering criminogenic certain other traits which, in the absence of malignant family influences, would be neutral in their impact on delinquency; and through the more direct effect of pathologic home life on particularly vulnerable children. This study is a companion volume to *Physique and Delinquency*, in which the emphasis was essentially constitutional. By assessing the sociocultural involvements in the total etiologic situation, the new study, entitled *Family Environment and Delinquency*[(245)], brings the reader more closely to the etiology of childhood maladjustment that leads to or consists of what in adults would be called crime.

[8] Hermann Mannheim (1957), review in *Int. J. soc. Psychiat.* **3,** 72. See also reviews by Julian Huxley and W. Paterson Brown, ibid. 71–72, 76–78.

In addition to the materials already quarried from the rich source of *Unraveling*, there are a great many data still to be mined and examined. Many facets of these basic materials are still unexplored. Although some aspects will have to be worked over by specialists in such fields as the Rorschach Test and various individual and group intelligence tests, there are many phases of our data that it is our intention personally to subject to more intensive study.

PLANS FOR THE FUTURE

Since this is a summary of our research ventures, it may be of interest to indicate what work we are at present engaged in and what we plan to do within the next few years.

First, we are approaching the completion (to age 31–32) of a follow-up study, begun in 1950, of the 500 delinquents and matched 500 non-delinquent controls who were the subjects of *Unraveling*. Here is a good illustration of the need and promise of extended study of groups of human beings originally examined in boyhood, to note the changes that occur with the passage of time and the vicissitudes of life. The fieldwork on the first segment of the long-term study of these subjects, which deals with the progress of the offenders and non-offenders to age 25, was completed in 1958; and the findings, on a descriptive level, are already in tabular form. The investigation now awaits tabulation of the follow-up of a further segment in the life-cycle to age 31–32. (This was recently completed.)

One of the most promising results to be anticipated from this long-range follow-up study is the opportunity it provides to look more closely at and to elaborate certain fundamentally important clues already derived from our prior investigations. One of these is the role of physical and psychological maturation in the reduction and, in not a few instances, the total abandonment of criminalistic modes of self-expression. Related to this are the changes in the behavior of the delinquents and the control group in many other basic aspects of their life activity, such as family relations, employment, recreation. As already suggested, this has important implications for the field of practical penology and promises to be a realistic biologic-psychologic-sociologic key to the puzzling problem of the most effective length of sentence, with which legislators, judges, and parole boards have thus far not been able to deal effectively.

Another project we have in mind is a systematic comparison of the findings of our various follow-up researches. This is important since these samples were gathered at different times and levels, and it would be revealing to learn to what extent the findings are essentially uniform in respect to the make-up and background of the offenders studied and their response to various forms of treatment, and their development beyond the point of contact with the official agencies of the law. This might be a first step toward a Comparative Criminology, to be enlarged upon by researches in other cultures. The incidence of traits and factors, such as general intelligence, special intelligence, psychiatric diagnoses, health history, family background, age at origin of delinquency, ethnic derivation, and many other characteristics suggested by our researches, would have to be systematically compared to see to what extent the findings in different cultures harmonize and lead to a rational theoretical construct. Differences would also have to be noted and hypotheses thereby arrived at which other researchers might wish to test out on various samples of cases. One important area of comparison involves the concept of maturation, previously discussed, with a further attempt to see whether the age-pattern, as related to the time when delinquent behavior was first noted in childhood, tends to account for the settling down of many offenders during their early thirties.

Another inquiry engaging our attention, and on which we are already focusing, requires a multiple-factor analysis. This grows out of the findings of *Unraveling*, *Physique and Delinquency*, and *Family Environment and Delinquency*. We are here exploring the possibility of an inductive integration of these findings into meaningful patterns or syndromes leading to a typology of delinquents. Any such multiple-trait-and-factor analysis must of necessity be largely experimental, the intercorrelations depending upon various hypotheses with which the raw materials are approached. These have grown out of direct contact with facts and not from purely theoretical speculation or from haphazard experience or scattered information. We hope that by a systematic, widely embracing correlational process it will be possible to arrive at a unifying theory which will integrate relevant information from both a constitutional and a sociocultural matrix. This may well provide a break-through in the quest for definitive explanations of the delinquency phenomenon.

Finally, a few words about prediction studies of which we have already made mention. Over the years, and as by-products of our major lines of research, we have developed some fifty prediction tables for experimental use both in screening children who are especially vulnerable to delinquency and in aiding judges and parole authorities in a more rational choice of action among the alternatives presented by the agencies of the law. Since our researches did not anticipate and were not originally designed for predictive purposes, we regard the work in this field—although more varied and extensive than any other inquiries in the field of prediction—to be only exploratory. The distinctive feature of the set of predictive devices we published in *Predicting Delinquency and Crime* is that it comprises a *system* of statistical prediction based on a wide variety of cases, taken from different sources and analyzed at different times. Thus it permits of reflection upon experience that ranges from very early childhood through the various stages and types of peno-correctional treatment, during a substantial period thereafter, and in certain age-spans in the careers of offenders.

We do not plan to develop any further prediction researches; our interest in this aspect of the work will henceforth be limited in the main to the improvement of the devices already formulated (with particular reference to the identification of potential delinquents), to advising those who seek help in applying on an experimental basis any of our prediction tables, and to accumulating the results of various validation experiments that are in process in the United States, Japan, and France, and other experiments which are being set up elsewhere.[9]

We trust that the reader has by now gained some understanding of the integrated nature of our researches. All lines of inquiry are to a considerable extent interrelated; one study has suggested the next, and the whole is animated by a general plan which has undergone some modification in the light of the development of our ideas upon the impact of the facts. This, we submit, is the method of science.

Only by a systematic approach can the discipline of Criminology move forward from the stage of fragmentary, disconnected bits of information and speculative theorizing not always anchored in fact, toward a more solid, systematized structure of understanding and practice.

In the present volume we present certain occasional papers which reflect our systematic ventures and adventures in the foregrounds and hinterlands of delinquency.

[9] There has been a great deal of confusing discussion of our predictive devices (see Chapter 17 of this volume). We recognize of course that there are several other ways of designing predictive devices than the one we originated; but with the encouragement of a leading biostatistician, Prof. Edwin Bidwell Wilson, we have continued to use our relatively simple method. Some of our tables should prove effective on adequate testing by courts and parole boards; the usefulness of others is more problematical because they are unfortunately based on small numbers and on limited samples, owing to the fact that, as stated in the text, the development of prediction tables was incidental to our major research tasks in the studies from which we derived the tables. We trust, however, that our pioneering efforts in this area will stimulate other investigators to construct more effective instrumentalities based on research designs directed specifically to prediction.

PART I

Some Aspects of Crime Causation

CHAPTER 2

The Home, the School, and Delinquency*
SHELDON GLUECK

READERS of this volume will not need to be reminded that thousands of articles and books have been written on the topic of this chapter. Why then still more?

The reason is to be found in the imperfect status of the social sciences. If a scientist in the field of chemistry or physics were to publish the results of an experiment, he could be certain that his colleagues, using the same careful controls and techniques that he employed, would repeat the experiment and either verify the finding or disprove it. But when it comes to the study of delinquency and crime there is an endless repetition of the same research mistakes, perhaps because the relevant disciplines are as yet greatly under-developed and the subject-matter—human attitudes, motives, and behavior—is very much more difficult. Furthermore, in textbooks on criminology you are likely to find a quotation from some minor piece of superficial so-called 'research' by an inexperienced or obviously prejudiced investigator cheek by jowl with one from a pioneering investigation by original researchers; and both are given equal weight by the textbook writer.

To counteract such weaknesses in criminology every investigator of the problem of delinquency, in publishing his results, ought to be duty bound to render full account of the details of his method of designing the research, gathering, supplementing and verifying the raw materials, defining the terms, statistical techniques and other data necessary for judging the soundness of the work and for permitting parallel research with a view to determining if the results will be similar.

In *Unraveling*[138] we tried our best to do just that. No fewer than seven chapters and several appendices deal with the methods employed in the research and data gathering. It is for that reason that we feel confident that the findings, some of which I shall discuss later, are worthy of serious consideration.

This brings me to another reason why the vast majority of researches in this field are not reliable. They do not include a 'control'

* Address before National League to Promote School Attendance, Boston, 1952.

group of non-delinquent cases with which the delinquents are systematically compared in respect to the various traits and conditions under study. For example, if it is found in a research study that a substantial percentage of delinquents living in a slum area of a city come from homes that are below par economically, we must be cautious about concluding that poverty is a major cause of crime until we compare a valid sample of delinquents with a valid sample of non-delinquents; for it may turn out that a quite similar percentage of boys who are *not* delinquents likewise come from poverty-stricken homes. The same may be said of any other factor frequently stated to be causal of delinquency.

There is a final caution to be observed. Believe it or not, even criminologists, not to speak of legislators and laymen, have not clearly indicated what they mean by 'cause' in speaking of this or that being the cause of delinquency. In recent years, they have made a bow to phrases about the 'complexity of causation' and the 'multiplicity of causes', but beyond this their conceptions are not too clear.

I hope to avoid these weaknesses and I propose to discuss 'The Home, The School, and Delinquency' in a more general causal setting. The specific influences of the home and the school should be considered in the total causal context.

In the research reported in *Unraveling* and in a more popular version, *Delinquents in the Making*[153], we compared 500 persistent delinquents with 500 true non-delinquents, in respect to over 400 factors investigated at various levels: the physique or bodily constitution as determined by anthropologic measurements; the health, by means of medical and neurologic examinations; certain special aspects of intelligence, as determined by the Wechsler-Bellevue test and performance tests; the temperamental and emotional traits and dynamics, through psychiatric interviews; the personality and character structure, by means of the well-known Rorschach Test; the home conditions, school records, and street behavior, through widespread and intensive social investigations.

But before the 500 delinquents were compared with the control group of 500 non-delinquents in these numerous ways, we matched the two sets of cases, pair by pair, equalizing them as much as possible with respect to general intelligence as reflected in the I.Q., ethnic derivation (a delinquent of Italian descent with an Italian non-delinquent, an Irish delinquent with an Irish non-delinquent, etc.), age, and residence in the underprivileged areas of Greater Boston. While it was not too difficult to obtain the needed sample of a thousand cases from the economically and culturally backward regions,

14

it required investigation of a great many additional cases before we could match up 500 delinquent–non-delinquent pairs on the multiple basis of similarity of age, I.Q., and ethnic origin.

The selection and matching of the cases, the various anthropologic, medical, psychiatric, and psychologic examinations and the intensive field investigations all required the collaboration of a considerable group of experts, under our general guidance. We are grateful to them as well as to the Boston school authorities, principals, teachers, probation and parole officers, social workers and others who gave so cheerfully of their time and talents during the ten-year span over which this elaborate research was conducted.

Before discussing some of the major findings, I want to get back to the crucial problem of cause and effect in the social sciences, with particular reference to delinquency.

First, cause-and-effect requires as a basic condition that there be *sequence in time* of the factors presumably related. If, every time (or almost every time) we find factor X to precede acts of delinquency in a substantial series of delinquent boys, and hardly ever in a series of non-delinquents, then we are justified in concluding that these successive events not only follow, but follow *from* one another. Now you would think that it is elementary in this matter of causal sequence not to put the cart before the horse. Yet some professional criminologists do just that. For example, the literature is full of the claim that a chief cause of juvenile delinquency is membership in a gang. Yet we found that the *onset* of persistent misbehavior tendencies among our delinquents was at the early age of seven or younger in 48 per cent of the 500 cases and from eight to ten in an additional 39 per cent, making a total of almost nine-tenths of all the delinquents who definitely displayed delinquency tendencies *long before the age when boys generally become members of gangs*. The leading authorities on the gang recognize that it is essentially an adolescent phenomenon; and Thrasher,[1] who has studied the subject intensively, found that of some 1,200 cases of gang membership investigated in Chicago only 1.5 per cent of the boys were six to twelve years old, while 63 per cent were classified as adolescents. Now it may be that the gang plays a significant role in transforming boy delinquents into adult criminals, but if we keep our definitions clear, we must admit, in the light of such evidence, that gang-membership is not a principal cause in *originating* delinquency.

I should like to make another point about cause-and-effect. 'Cause' requires a *totality* of conditions necessary to the result; it

[1] F. M. Thrasher (1927), *The gang* (2nd rev. ed. 1936. Chicago: University of Chicago Press), p. 74.

is a matter of forces within the individual which tend or press toward innate and acquired antisocial tendencies overbalancing inhibitions within him which tend to draw him back into socially acceptable conduct. Moreover, this required total result may be made up of constituents some of which are also found often among non-delinquents. For example, a typical attitude of *defiance* characterized 50 per cent of our delinquents; but 12 per cent of the non-delinquents also had this attitude, and the very fact that 50 per cent of the delinquents did *not* have it shows at once that it is not defiance alone, or even necessarily, which is involved in that totality of conditions that makes for delinquency.

Furthermore, the *constituents of that totality of forces may well be different* among various classes of delinquents. It is the summation and concentration of them sufficient to make a boy not only once but persistently step across the line of lawabidingness that may be realistically regarded as the causal influence. In the eager but fatuous search for 'the cause' or some specific and exclusive pattern of causes that inevitably and always precedes all forms of persistent delinquency, many criminologists have gone off the track. Persistent delinquency can be the result, not only of one *specific* combination or pattern of factors that markedly differentiates delinquents from non-delinquents, but of each of several *different* patterns. The concept of *plurality of causal combinations* immediately throws light on a host of puzzling problems in the study of crime causation. Just as the fact of a boy's death, although always and everywhere the *same terminal event*, may nonetheless be the result of *various preceding sequences* of conditions, so the terminal event of persistent delinquency may have in its causal pedigree and background a variety of different sequences leading to the same ultimate result of habitual antisocial behavior.

The final point to make about the concept of causation in this field is that we can conceive of cause-and-effect most realistically and with some chance of managing the problem of delinquency if we speak of it in the sense of *high probability* of persistent delinquency. Even the physical sciences, nowadays, state their generalizations in terms not of absolute inevitability in every single instance, but only of high probability if you observe a large enough sample of instances. The statistical method of comparing delinquents, as a group, with non-delinquents, as a group, is not designed to bring out any point-to-point causal sequence that will always and everywhere hold good in each and every case. It is rather intended to disclose whether or not an entire group of lads having one or another well-defined pattern of factors in its make-up and background will much more probably turn out to be delinquent than a group of boys not so loaded down;

or, to put it differently, whether the 'typical' or 'average' persistent delinquent is very likely to be the outcome of such a coming together of specified forces.

In other words, we are concerned with discovering a general relationship between well-defined preceding factors of one type or another and a strong tendency to a specific subsequent course of conduct. Having discovered even such a general relationship, we have at hand much of the crucial information necessary as a guide to experimental programs of prevention and therapy. We can now attack, singly or in closely-knit patterns, those factors which have been found to contribute most frequently and most heavily to the tendency in question.

Where considerable numbers of factors that 'make sense' from the point of view of common experience inside and outside of clinics and schools are found to characterize delinquents far more than non-delinquents, it becomes highly probable that we are dealing with some sort of causal *connection* between the factors and the delinquency, rather than with accidental *coincidence* between them.

— Before closing this matter of causal theory, I should like to point out that many probation and parole officers, teachers, school attendance officers, and others seem to want specific answers to the 'why' of causation; that is, they want to know what the 'ultimate cause' of a child's misbehavior is and how it came about. But the ultimate cause is something like a mirage. The more you approach it, the farther it seems to recede. It may be that some day variations in the way people behave will be explainable in the more ultimate terms of differences in endocrine gland structure and function, or of microscopic or sub-microscopic physico-chemical or electronic phenomena. But even then the researchers will not have the ultimate answer to the 'why'; they will only be able to describe more accurately the 'what'. In the meantime, however, we can reasonably speak of cause-and-effect when we disentangle even the cruder forces at play in inclining persons to one typical course of behavior or another, just as chemistry and physics opened the door to the solution of many problems long before the dawn of nuclear science. The question is, whether such relatively crude and tentative determination of causal relationships in our field leads us closer to an understanding of delinquency and therefore to its management. If it does, then, even though we are dealing with factors which may some day be reduced to more subtle forces and sub-forces, we have made a stride forward in both scientific achievement and the 'know-how' of coping practically with delinquency.

I come now to some of the major findings, to which special interest in home and school factors can give its own emphasis, provided the causal concepts just discussed are borne in mind as well as the fact that particular factors should not be torn out of their general context in the dynamic totality of causal influences.

First it should be mentioned that the systematic comparison of 500 persistent delinquents with 500 non-delinquents yielded an important side-product. It demonstrated that various factors heretofore accepted as strongly causal in most instances of delinquency are in fact not so, because they were found to exist in quite similar percentages among the non-delinquents as well as delinquents. Let me mention but one of the more striking of these complacent or neutral factors. The Rorschach test, given by psychologists in Boston and interpreted 'blind' in New York by other psychologists who were not told ahead of time which boys were delinquent and which were non-delinquent, disclosed that no fewer than 84 per cent of the delinquent boys were plagued by a marked *feeling of not being wanted or loved*. In recent years child psychiatrists have frequently emphasized this as a major cause of delinquency. Yet what are we to say when we find that this same feeling of not being wanted or loved was also found among 88 per cent of the *non-delinquents*? Here you have a vivid illustration of the great value of employing a fairly matched control group.

But, laying aside such neutral factors (and there were some at each level of the inquiry), the way is clear to ask what are the major differentiative factors and how do they weave into a causal pattern of high probability of delinquency?

The data nearest to genetic roots are those dealing with *body form or physique*. Here the most striking finding was the high incidence, among the delinquents, of the mesomorphic, muscular, well-knit dominance in body structure. Further, delinquents as a group have less disharmony in physique, a condition which may well facilitate easy-flowing, energetic behavior. To this should be added a finding that in the majority of delinquents there is evident a growth delay in physical measurements until the age of between thirteen and fourteen, when there is a tendency for a rapid growth-spurt which results in outstripping the boys of the control group. This may be the outcome of the piling up of physiologic tensions (perhaps involving some atypical functioning of the endocrine glands) culminating in the rapid discharge of an accumulated growth tendency which, in turn, may account in some measure for later difficulties of adaptation.

Although it has been claimed that a major cause of delinquency is poor health, we found the health of the delinquents if anything somewhat better than those of the control group. It is, however, significant that a considerably higher proportion of the delinquents than of the other boys had been bedwetters and very restless in childhood, while a significantly *lower* proportion of delinquents showed any typical neurologic abnormalities such as dermographia.

In respect to the *basic dynamics of personality and character* as revealed by the Rorschach test (which projects essentially subconscious tendencies and attitudes), the delinquents as a class were found to be considerably more extroversive, more vivacious, more labile or impulsive emotionally and, correspondingly, less self-controlled, more destructive and sadistic and, in general, more aggressive and adventure-seeking, than the control group of non-delinquents. It should be emphasized that these findings were made by the Rorschach experts without their being told ahead of time which test papers came from delinquents and which from non-delinquents.

There is a cluster of traits, also revealed by the Rorschach test, which may be called emotional attitudes with respect to *authority* and to society's codes. Among these factors which would tend to make 'walking the strait and narrow path' of conventional behavior very difficult, the following were found to exist in marked excess among the delinquents as compared with the control group: hostility, defiance, resentfulness, suspiciousness, social assertiveness, parasitic trends (motivated by a wish to be looked after without effort), narcissistic desires (reflecting a strong thirst for power and status), unconventionality, non-co-operativeness, disinclination to meet the expectations of others, non-dependence upon others and—especially significant to the problem of delinquency—non-submissiveness to authority.

As if this faulty apparatus for legitimate social adaptation were not enough, psychiatric examination disclosed the delinquents as a group to be more stubborn, egocentric, and sensual than the non-delinquents, less critical of themselves, less practical and realistic, and less 'adequate' in general. It was further found that the delinquents are much more conflict-ridden than the non-delinquents, these emotional stresses and strains arising out of a wide variety of situations, such as marked feelings of inferiority, inadequate sexual identification, unsatisfying relationships to father, to mother, and to companions.

Fitting into what has been said regarding the greater energy propulsions among delinquents was the finding that they largely resolve their conflicts by acting them out in antisocial behavior rather than by keeping them bottled up and attempting to cope with them internally, as many non-delinquents were found to do.

19

Since the instruments of adaptive or maladaptive behavior are not merely physical, physiologic, temperamental, and emotional but also, of course, intellectual, we compared the two sets of boys (who had previously been matched by general intelligence as reflected in the I.Q.) in respect to various *constituents* of intelligence. Without going into too much detail, it was found that the delinquents differed from the non-delinquents despite similar I.Q., in that fewer of them had the capacity to approach problems methodically, a trait which bears on the power to reflect upon contemplated behavior and to assess its consequences. Fewer delinquents had verbal ability. The delinquents also tended to express themselves in direct, concrete ways rather than through use of intermediate symbols or abstract ideas.

Character is the result not only of natural endowment but of training. Means of 'sublimation' or of wholesome, or at least harmless, channeling of energy, as well as 'knowledge of right and wrong', are part of the apparatus through which character is expressed. However, a boy does not function in a vacuum, but in a cultural milieu ranging from the intimate, emotion-laden atmosphere of the home to that of the school, the neighborhood, and the general society. The tendencies that nature may implant are both morally and legally neutral. It is the existence of 'thou shalt nots' and laws that color their expression as antisocial, delinquent, or criminal.

For a child to adapt acceptably to the demands and prohibitions of any specific social organization requires the exercise of physical, temperamental, and intellectual capacities in such a way as to conform to the particular values protected by the culture of that society through religion, custom, and law. But modern American culture, especially in underprivileged urban centers, is both highly complex and ill-defined because of conflicting values. The demands made upon the growing boy by every vehicle of modern life are numerous, involved, often subtle, sometimes inconsistent. This is true of the culture of the home, the school, the neighborhood, and the general all-pervasive culture of the times. The child is told that he must be honest, non-aggressive, self-controlled; but on every hand he runs into vivid contradictory attitudes, values, and behavior in an environment that—both in and out of politics—seemingly rewards selfishness, aggression, a predatory attitude, and success by any means. It does not require the wisdom of a Seneca to convince the child, as it convinced that wise statesman, that 'successful and fortunate crime is called virtue'.

The demands made on the growing boy, especially in the underprivileged urban area, require a great deal of adaptive power, self-control, self-management, the ability to choose among alternative

20

values and to postpone immediate satisfactions for future ones—all this in a civilization in which fixed points and agreed-upon values are increasingly difficult to discern and hold to. This means that during the earliest years, when the hard but crucially necessary task of 'internalization' of ideals and symbols of authority is in process, desirable attitudes and behavior standards are not sharply enough defined or are contradictory, leaving a confused residue in the delicate structure of personality and character.

While responses to the complex modern culture differ with the varying constitution and temperament of each person subjected to it, the basic desires of the growing child are similar and imperative. Clinical experience shows that among these are a striving for an assured feeling of security and affectional warmth; a striving for happiness; a desire to be free from too much restraint; a thirst for new experience and for the satisfaction of curiosity.

It is in this connection that the *home climate* becomes of prime importance.

How did the household conditions and parent–child relationships of the delinquents and the non-delinquents tend to facilitate or hinder the process of 'internalization of authority', the taming and sublimation of natural instinctual drives, and the definition of standards of good and bad?

To answer this crucial question requires, first, a consideration of the findings concerning the early background of the parents of the boys; for the parents are not only the products of the biologic and cultural systems in which they were born and reared, but, in turn, the transmitters to their children of their own biosocial heritage.

We found the biosocial legacy of the parents of the delinquents to be consistently poorer than that of the non-delinquents. This was evident in a greater incidence of emotional disturbance, mental retardation, alcoholism, and criminalism among the families from which the mothers and fathers of the delinquents stemmed. Thus, to the extent that the parents communicated the standards, ideals, and behavior patterns of their own rearing to their sons, the social, and partially also the biologic, heritage of the delinquents was distinctly poorer than that of the non-delinquents.

Not only were the grandparents (and close relatives of that generation) of the delinquents more generally handicapped, but a higher proportion of the *parents* of the delinquents than of the non-delinquents suffered from serious physical ailments, were mentally retarded, emotionally disturbed, alcoholic; and, most significant, many more of them had a history of delinquency or criminalism.

Correlatively, there had been less of an effort among the parents

21

f the delinquents to set up decent standards of conduct for the family. They had shown less ambition to improve their status; they had done less planning for the future; and they certainly had been less self-respecting.

But these are not the only ways in which the family background of the delinquent youngsters was less adequate to their proper rearing than that of the non-delinquents. There are other aspects of family life in which the delinquents were more deprived, often markedly so. A somewhat higher proportion of their parents than those of the non-delinquents faced their marital responsibilities without preparation. A far higher proportion of their marriages turned out to be unhappy; more of the homes of the delinquents than of the non-delinquents were broken by desertion, separation, divorce, or death of one or both parents, a large number of such breaches occurring during the early childhood of the boys. Many more delinquents than non-delinquents had step- or foster-parents; and more of them were shunted about from one household to another during their most formative years.

As for the economic status of the two groups of families, despite the fact that the boys were matched at the outset on the basis of residence in economically underprivileged areas, both sporadic and chronic dependency have been markedly more prevalent among the families of the delinquents than among the others. This typical bogging down in the 'lower depths' was found to be partly attributable to the far poorer work habits of the fathers and partly to less planful management of the household income.

It is, however, within the *family emotional climate* that the most deep-rooted and persistent character and personality traits and distortions of the growing child are developed. Here again the delinquents come off much worse than the other boys.

In interpersonal family relationships we found an exceedingly marked difference between the two groups. Thus, a much higher proportion of the families of the delinquents lacked unity and harmony. Family disorganization, with its attendant lack of warmth and respect for the integrity of each member, can have serious consequences for the growing child. It may prevent the development both of an adequate sense of responsibility and of an effective mechanism for the inhibition of conduct that might disgrace the family name. Since the family is the first and foremost vehicle for the transmission of the values of a culture to the young child, lack of family unity may leave him without ethical moorings or convey to him a confused and inconsistent cultural pattern.

Apart from the lesser cohesiveness of the families in which the

22

delinquents were reared, many more of the fathers, mothers, brothers, and sisters of the delinquent group were found to be indifferent or frankly hostile to the boys. A far lower proportion of the delinquents than of the other boys were warmly attached to their parents. Considerably more felt that their parents had not been concerned about their welfare. Twice as many of the delinquents as of the other boys did not look upon their fathers as acceptable patterns for emulation.

The greater inadequacy of the parents of the delinquents is reflected not only in all the respects already noted but in the vital matter of disciplinary practices. In far higher measure than was true of the parents of the non-delinquents, the fathers and mothers of the delinquents resorted to confusing extremes of laxity and harshness, instead of applying reasoned and just disciplinary practices.

So, also, the delinquents' parents were far more careless in their supervision of the children, this often amounting to downright neglect.

In the light of the obvious inferiority of the families of the delinquents as sources of sound personality development and character formation, it is not surprising that the boys were never adequately tamed or socialized, and that they developed persistent antisocial inclinations, even apart from the fundamental somatic and temperamental differences between them and the non-delinquents.

I come now to the group of differentiative factors regarding *school performance and behavior*. But before recounting these, I should point out that there are certain forms of maladapted behavior, in and out of school, which cannot, strictly, be included among the causal pressures to delinquency because, according to our theoretical framework, they are largely *consequences* rather than *causes*. They are nevertheless relevant because they tend, on the whole, to reflect the operation of emotional dynamisms that are frequently also involved in the behavior which the law calls delinquency. For example, school retardation cannot usually be regarded as a factor causal of delinquency although it may well be involved in a 'vicious circle' with delinquency. Yet it does reflect intellectual and temperamental difficulties and abnormalities in early environment and training akin to those which are typically involved in making for delinquency.

These forces and the resulting personality and character traits, their roots sunk deep in early childhood, make themselves evident in such areas as school retardation, school misbehavior, and other types of maladapted or antisocial tendencies expressed in home and street, especially the harmful use of leisure and the choice of undesirable companions.

Here are some of the findings in this connection, stated in actual percentages.

In the delinquent group, 62% of the boys markedly disliked school; in the non-delinquent, only 10%; and it is significant that a substantially lower proportion of the former than of the latter explained their aversion on the grounds of inability to learn or intellectual inferiority, while a far higher proportion of delinquents expressed great resentment at the restrictions imposed upon them by the school routine, or showed a lack of interest, in school work.

Among the delinquents, 44% wanted to stop school immediately; among the non-delinquents, but 7%.

Among the delinquents, only 29% wanted to go on to high school; among the non-delinquents, 68%.

As measured by the scale used in the Boston Public Schools, 41% of the delinquents were two or more years retarded, compared to 21% of the non-delinquents. Wide discrepancies existed also with regard to the number of grades repeated and to placement in special classes. During the last full school year, 41% of the delinquents had to be classified as 'poor' in scholarship, while the incidence among non-delinquents was but 8%.

In a wide variety of types of school misbehavior, the delinquents had a markedly worse record than the non-delinquents, 96% of the delinquents compared to only 17% of the non-delinquents having seriously or persistently misbehaved in one way or another. To cite but a few illustrations of misbehavior manifestations as reported by the most recent teacher, 49% of the delinquents compared to but 13% of the control group were reported to be unreliable; 26% versus 4% were untruthful; 24% versus 7% were disobedient; 22% versus 10% were tardy; 21% versus 12% were attention seekers; 20% versus 8% were markedly disorderly; 19% versus zero per cent stole; 16% versus 3% cheated, etc. It must be remembered that there are many other forms of school misbehavior and that many children committed two or more different forms. In fact, out of over 40 types of maladapted school conduct, the difference in incidence among the delinquents and non-delinquents achieved statistical significance in all but six.

The average age of first school misconduct among the delinquents was nine-and-a-half, or fully three years earlier than among the relatively few non-delinquents who misconducted themselves.

If we look at the nature of the first school misbehavior we find it to have been truancy among 75% of the 478 delinquents who misbehaved and 52% among the 86 non-delinquents who misbehaved.

In fact, no fewer than 95% of *all* delinquents had truanted, two-thirds of them persistently, compared with 11% among the non-delinquents, all of the latter only very occasionally.

Frequent truancy, characteristic of so large a proportion of delinquents, as well as the various other forms of misconduct reflective of temperamental-emotional difficulties of adaptation, reveal a persistent attempt to escape from the restraints of a controlled social situation.

Of other features of the school history I shall just mention one—the adjustment of our boys to their schoolmates. If a boy got on well with other children, was friendly and made an effort to please and hold friends, his relationship was classed as 'good'. Among the delinquents, 46% were so classifiable, among the non-delinquents, 67%.

Turning now to *out-of-school misconduct*, the incidence among delinquents again far exceeded that among non-delinquents. Here I shall not repeat statistics given in *Unraveling*. Let me point out merely that to a much greater extent than the control group the delinquents early acquired the habits of stealing rides, 'hopping' trucks, sneaking into theaters without paying, setting fires, committing various other acts of destructive mischief, bunking out, running away from home, keeping very late hours. Also in marked excess over the others, the delinquents gambled, begged, and began to smoke and drink at a very early age.

In all this there is further evidence of a driving, uninhibited, undisciplined energy propulsion and thirst for adventure on the part of the delinquents. These characteristics are also reflected in the ways in which delinquents typically used their leisure time. Less than half as many of them as of the non-offenders typically spent their spare time at home. Far more of the delinquents preferred to play in distant neighborhoods, to hang around street corners, vacant lots, waterfronts, railroad yards, poolrooms; and gravitated toward the more exciting and unsupervised street trades in after-school jobs. The delinquents also sought vicarious adventure through movies more extensively and frequently than did the control group.

Correlatively, the delinquents were far less inclined than the other boys to supervised recreational activities and far less willing to spend any of their leisure hours in the circumscribed areas of playgrounds. In their choice of companions, also, the delinquents differed markedly from the other boys, almost all of them (in contrast to very few of the non-delinquents) preferring to chum with other delinquents and over half the group (compared to less than 1 per cent of the non-delinquents) having become members of gangs. In far greater measure than the control group, the companions of the delinquents were older boys—possibly indicating a search for temperamentally congenial 'ego-ideals' to replace their own fathers to whom they were not as a rule closely attached and whom they did not admire.

Thus you see that, in their recreational activities and companionships, the delinquents gave further evidence of an inordinate craving for adventure and for opportunities to express restless, aggressive energy tendencies, with the added need of supportive companionship in such activities.

I cannot deal here with other differentiative factors. I should like to emphasize, however, what must already be apparent, that we cannot attribute the end product of delinquency exclusively to any one set of factors derived from the various levels of our exploration. The summation of the major dissimilarities between the two groups of boys indicates, rather, that the separate findings, independently gathered and compared, tend to integrate into an organic dynamic pattern of causation, neither exclusively biologic nor exclusively sociocultural, but evidently deriving from an interplay of somatic, temperamental, intellectual, and sociocultural conditions.

Such a point of view makes both scientific and common sense. Otherwise we are left with serious gaps in the pattern.

If, for example, we resort to an explanation exclusively in terms of somatic constitution, we leave unexplained why most boys of mesomorphic physique do *not* commit crimes; and we do not bridge the gap between bodily structure and conduct. Much falls between somatic constitution and behavior.

If, on the other hand, we limit our explanation to sociocultural influences, we are overlooking the obvious fact that such forces are selective; conditions do not equally affect all persons subjected to them. Our boys did not all choose the same elements in the general environment, or the same types of companions, recreations, and the like. Even in underprivileged areas, the vast majority of boys do *not* develop into persistent delinquents.

Finally, if we limit our explanation to the emotional distortions and unsound character development that result primarily from unwholesome parent-child relations, we fail to account for the fact that many *non-delinquents* show some traits usually deemed unfavourable to sound personality-character development, such as feelings of not being wanted or not being taken care of. We are without an explanation, too, of the fact that many boys who live under conditions in which there is a dearth of parental warmth and understanding nevertheless remain non-delinquent. Nor can we reasonably account for the fact that not a few boys under conditions unfavorable to the development of a wholesome 'superego', or conscience, nevertheless manage *not* to become delinquents, although some of them may become neurotics.

If, however, we take into account the *dynamic interplay of the differentiative factors from all these various levels and channels of influence, a rough causal explanation takes shape* which tends to accommodate these puzzling divergencies, at least so far as the great mass of the delinquents is concerned. As a *group*, our delinquents (residents in underprivileged urban areas) are distinguishable from the non-delinquents by the following chief traits and characteristics:

Physically, in being essentially mesomorphic in constitution (i.e. solid, closely knit, muscular); *temperamentally*, in being restlessly energetic, impulsive, extroverted, aggressive, destructive (often sadistic)—traits which may be more or less related to both their bodily structure and their erratic growth-pattern with its physiologic correlates or consequences; *in attitude*, in being hostile, defiant, resentful, suspicious, stubborn, socially assertive, adventurous, unconventional, nonsubmissive (or ambivalent) to authority; *intellectually*, in tending to direct and concrete, rather than symbolic or abstract, intellectual expression and in being less methodical than the control group in their approach to problems; *socioculturally*, in having been reared to a far greater extent than the non-delinquents in homes of little understanding, affection, stability, or moral fiber, by parents usually unfit to be effective guides and protectors or desirable symbols for emulation; and under conditions unfavorable to the building of a well-balanced and socially adequate character and conscience (superego).

It is particularly in the exciting, stimulating, but little controlled, and culturally inconsistent environment of the urban underprivileged area that such boys readily tend to give expression to their untamed impulses and their self-centered desires by 'kicking over the traces' of conventionally dictated behavior. These tendencies are apparently anchored deeply in body and mind and essentially derive from malformations of personality and character during the first few years of life.

It will be seen that virtually all the conditions enumerated are of a kind that in all probability *preceded* the evolution of delinquent careers, and in respect to *sequence of events in time* may legitimately be regarded as causally connected.

It should be borne in mind that the synthesis of causal influences derives from a *general* comparison of persistent delinquents with non-delinquents. There are doubtless small groups of offenders who would show fundamental variations from this general pattern. For example, there are instances in which the delinquents are of the thin, linear, fragile (ectomorphic) body type rather than well knit and muscular (mesomorphic). There are delinquents who are introverted and psychoneurotic rather than outgoing and energetic. There are also *non*-delinquents who have been reared in immoral and criminalistic homes. All such exceptional subtypes deserve further study, though small in number compared to the core type. Their more intensive consideration may well bring about some modifications in our basic analysis and synthesis. (We are at present engaged in such detailed analyses of atypical groups of delinquents.[176, 245])

Meanwhile, we can say with assurance that the *high probability of delinquency is dependent upon the operation of the factors noted in the above summary of all or most of the areas thus far explored.* Taken in the mass, if boys in underprivileged urban areas have in their make-up and early background a substantial number of the factors we have found markedly to differentiate delinquents from non-delinquents, they are very likely to turn out to be delinquent. In this general sense, then, a causal relationship has been established. Various subpatterns of factors, each sufficient to be causal of persistent delinquency, remain to be analysed out of this general complex of factors. We are now engaged in deriving various types.

The reader may be inclined to ask: 'Well, what do you recommend should be done about it?' I am sure you realize how tremendous is the task, how widespread the ramifications, how imperfect the tools with which society has to work. We have made some recommendations at the close of the work to which I have referred; but I should be less than candid if I were to claim that the carrying out of those recommendations is an absolute guaranty of elimination of delinquency.

I would, however, like to mention one important point. You will recall that, whereas among the delinquents various forms of school misbehavior first occurred at an average age of 9·5 years (a third of the delinquents having been but eight years old or less), it showed up that early among less than a tenth of the very few non-delinquents who had misbehaved in school, their average age at first school misconduct having been 12·5 years. When to the tender age of school misbehavior there is added the early age of first delinquent behavior (almost half the delinquents were under eight years old at their first delinquencies), it becomes crystal clear that *the signals of persistent delinquency flash their warning before puberty.* This means that the elementary schools are in a strategic position to discover *potential* delinquents before the trends of maladapted behavior become too fixed. The relationship of this to the work of the juvenile court is brought out by one of the more significant findings in *One Thousand Juvenile Delinquents*[45]; namely, that if a boy was brought to the court and examined by the clinic immediately or shortly after the onset of his misbehavior, the curbing of his anti-social tendencies was more likely of accomplishment than if the boy's misbehavior was not dealt with until it had long endured.

The schools, then, are in a strategic position to note such marked emotional deviations and difficulties of adaptation at an age when the child is first faced with the test of adapting his natural impulses to society's first code outside the home. *Character prophylaxis*—the testing of children early and periodically to discover beginnings of malformations of emotional development and habit formation at a stage when the twig can still be bent—is as necessary as are early and periodic medical or dental examinations. A crying need of the times is a *preventive medicine of personality and character*. Youngsters who, unaided, face a career of storm and stress should be discovered as early as possible and given adequate therapy long before the law's label of juvenile delinquency is affixed to them or before they develop serious mental illnesses. In an enlightened educational system the school should function as the litmus paper of personality and character maladaptation.

The intricacies of the problem of early recognition and treatment of personality and character ills, and a chief reason why so little has been accomplished towards its solution, are illuminated by the simple yet striking fact that when a child first begins to display signs of mal-adaptation it is very difficult to say whether these are true signals of persistent delinquency in the offing or merely transient evidences of the youngster's trying of his wings. Bits of maladapted and even anti-social behavior at the age of five or six are not necessarily prognostic of future persistent delinquency. It therefore becomes of prime importance to devise a method of distinguishing, very early in life, those children who, unaided, are probably headed for delinquent careers, in order that therapeutic intervention may be timely and effective.

Such a device we believe we have developed in three predictive tables presented in *Unraveling* (pp. 261–66). One of these tables is derived from the data on the parent-child relationships of the two sets of boys, the second is derived from their differences in character and personality as revealed by the Rorschach Test, and the third is derived from their differences as indicated by psychiatric interviews. The first predictive device, based on differences between delinquents and non-delinquents in discipline by the father, supervision of the boy by the mother, father's and mother's affection for the boy, and cohesiveness of the family, has already undergone three independent

29

validations by others. *These have produced strong evidence that future delinquency can be successfully foretold in some nine-tenths of the cases* even when the table is applied to boys of other ethnic origin and somewhat better economic condition than those involved in the construction of the original predictive device.[2] The New York City Youth Board, in collaboration with the New York School System, is establishing an experiment in two public schools in underprivileged areas of New York. In both of these schools this prognostic table is being applied to new pupils entering first grade. The boys predicted as headed for delinquency will in one school be given the benefit of intensive psychiatric and other relevant treatment, while those so predicted in the second school, to be used as a control, will be left to normal community action. After a few years of follow-up, the outcomes in terms of delinquency will be compared.[3]

Experiments of this type should aid considerably in a re-examination of society's methods for the early detection and effective treatment of a problem that underlies almost all other social problems—how to lessen the total amount of delinquency, crime, and other antisocial aggressions, with their attendant grief and ever mounting cost to all of us.

In coping with this tremendously important problem, school teachers and attendance officers of course have leading roles. But is their status in modern society equivalent to the importance of their roles? Far be it for me to decry any form of honest labor; but one cannot help observing that in this era of giant labor unions, society is evidently giving greater prestige and much greater compensation to miners and bricklayers than to educators of youth. Surely, teachers, attendance officers, probation officers, and others dealing with the problems of childhood deserve greater consideration. In the noble words of Epictetus, 'You will do the greatest service to the state if you shall raise, not the roofs of the houses, but the souls of the citizens; for it is better that great souls should dwell in small houses than that mean slaves shall lurk in great houses.'

[2] For example, see B. J. Black & S. J. Glick (1952), Recidivism at the Hawthorne-Cedar Knolls School: predicted vs. actual outcome for delinquent boys. *Research Monograph No. 2.* (New York· Jewish Board of Guardians); and R. E. Thompson (1952), A validation of the Glueck social prediction scale for proneness to delinquency. *J. crim. L. Criminol. & Police Sci.* 43, 451. See, also the articles in Part II hereof

[3] See R. W. Whelan (1954), An experiment in predicting delinquency. *J. crim. L. Criminol. & Police Sci.* 45, 432; and Chapter 7, note 5, below.

CHAPTER 3

Working Mothers and Delinquency

SHELDON AND ELEANOR GLUECK

AMONG the numerous causal influences to which delinquency has been attributed, that of the absence of the mother from the home in gainful employment has aroused particular interest in current discussion.[1] The proportion of mothers who spend part of their time in outside employment has been increasing rapidly since the two world wars.[2] Today there are several million mothers who go out to work; and, with the constant stimulation of high-pressure advertising to transform into urgent necessities the products of the machine and electronic age that have previously been deemed luxuries limited to high-income groups, the common desire to upgrade living standards will no doubt stimulate more and more mothers of young children to supplement the family income by seeking employment outside the home.[3]

Apart from the effect on the working mother herself, what effects will this have on family life, on the rearing of children,[4] on the

[1] According to a competent recent article, 'But going to work raises doubts—in her mind as well as in those of some moralists—as to whether she will be able to combine job and home, and be a good mother. In fact, a whole host of pathologies, from rising delinquency to increasing divorce, is being charged to working women.' *Fortune* 54 (July 1956), 172.

[2] 'In 1890 a niggling 4 per cent of the country's married women were in the work force: in 1940 there were only 15 per cent; but by April 1956, 30 per cent of married women held jobs. This development has been recent and swift. During World War II the number of married women at work had barely surpassed the number of single girls who held jobs. By 1955, working wives outnumbered the bachelor girls more than two to one.' 'The current total is 21 million women workers, or one-third of all persons employed.' ibid. 91.

[3] 'There are several elements responsible for this emerging pattern of the behavior of women, especially married women, in the labor force. There is the large number of job opportunities that an expanding economy now offers. There is the free time made available by modern household facilities (e.g. ready-cooked meals). Education, now universal, gives many women a vocational urge that home-making alone cannot satisfy. A job provides stimulus and companionship that the home in daytime does not. (Typical comment of a working wife: 'Now I have something to talk about with my husband when we both come home.') But most significant, perhaps, is the hunger for the appurtenances of a good life that multiple incomes can bring more quickly; the American standard of living has become a built-in automatic 'drive' on the part of the American wife. This asserts itself in her reasons for working.' ibid. 93.

[4] '. . . More women with small children are at work than ever before. True, the number is still small, but the rate of increase is astonishing. In 1940 only 7 per cent of mothers with children under five held jobs; by 1955 the number had jumped to 18·2 per cent. (Because of a shift in census techniques, 1955 figure includes six-year-olds.)' ibid. 91.

emotional health of youngsters and, more specifically, on juvenile delinquency?

Thus far there is little more than speculation among social workers, teachers, psychiatrists and journalists on this significant trend in American culture. Where sound and organized factual data are lacking, the winds of opinion can blow in any direction. Thus those psychiatrists who are influenced by the psychoanalytic emphasis on the crucial importance of parent-child relationships during the first three or four years of life in integrating personality and solidifying character view with alarm the growing excursions of young mothers into factory and shop. They are convinced that the loss in the emotional stability of the children is far too high a price to pay for the economic gain to the family. They point to the child's repeated traumatic experiences when again and again his mother, the major source and symbol of his security and love, goes off and leaves him yearningly unsatisfied. They emphasize that it is difficult to find a satisfactory substitute for the natural mother. They speculate that beneath the ostensible economic reason for the mother's leaving the family roof there might in many cases be the deeper motivation of a wish to escape maternal responsibility or a pathologic drive to compete with men.

On the other hand, those who justify the working of mothers claim that a woman who enjoys her activities outside the home is all the more satisfied with her maternal duties when she returns and that she can make up for her absence from home in the quality of love and care. They point to outstanding examples of career women who have reared children successfully while conducting a home of warmth and decency. Such women insist that it is possible to arrange for competent substitute care for the children at times and in areas in which it is not indispensable for the mother to be present; and that the child living under such arrangement appreciates the mother all the more during the times when she can devote herself wholly to him. In fact, they point out, there are mothers who are by nature not at all suited to motherhood; and the children of such women are better off with substitute parents.

Some persons emphasize that there is a time for mothering and a time for a career. They point out that since child guidance authorities stress the concept that the foundations of personality and character are solidly established by the first few years of life, a wise compromise is possible: ample time can be reserved for the indispensable aspects of motherhood during the crucial years of childhood but thereafter a woman can safely pursue work outside the home.

In all this speculation there is, of course, entangled the fact that among the seriously underprivileged the economics of the situation leave little free choice as to whether the mother should or should not seek outside employment.

The reader will no doubt be able to add to the pros and cons of the question; but the issue remains speculative as long as some factual foundation is not supplied.

The literature of criminology has yielded no definitive studies on this subject. In several of our prior researches we have noted the incidence of employment of mothers of male and female offenders, making comparisons with control materials where these were available. Thus, in *Five Hundred Delinquent Women*,[44] a five-year follow-up of graduates of the Women's Reformatory in Framingham, Mass., it was noted that over half the mothers of the girls involved in that research worked occasionally. About a third were factory hands, another third domestics, the remainder in various other occupations (p. 66). In a relatively comparable period (the early 1920's) only 11·6 per cent of married women in Massachusetts were gainfully employed. However, since this figure includes both married women with children and childless women it is not a perfect control statistic, although highly suggestive.

In *One Thousand Juvenile Delinquents*[45] it was pointed out that of the 937 households about which information was available the family income of 389 (41·5 per cent) was supplemented by the outside employment of the mother, this comparing with but 9·9 per cent of married women engaged in gainful occupation during the early 1920's. Since, however, this figure also includes both married women with children and childless women it too is not a perfect control statistic, although highly suggestive. Seventeen and a half per cent of the mothers included in *One Thousand Juvenile Delinquents* were factory hands, 47·5 per cent were engaged in various types of domestic work (such as washing or sewing) but stayed at home, the remainder were otherwise employed (p. 71).[5]

In these studies the element of economic status of families was not controlled. However, in a more recent research made in the 1940's, *Unraveling Juvenile Delinquency*[138], we matched, pair by pair, 500 persistent delinquents with 500 true non-delinquents, not only in respect to general intelligence, ethnico-racial derivation and age, but also with regard to residence in culturally and economically underprivileged urban areas. In considering the problem of the working mother in a matched sample of such design we are enabled to

[5] See also W. C. Kvaraceus (1945), *Juvenile delinquency and the school* (New York: World Book Co.). Of 761 cases passing through the Passaic, N.J., Children's Bureau, 25 per cent of the white mothers and 44 per cent of the Negro were gainfully employed.

hold constant the factor of low economic status (dependency or marginality), thus getting closer to the pure influence of the mother's working, in the complex of traits and forces involved in delinquency.

From the significant fact that three of the five factors most markedly differentiating the 500 delinquents from the 500 non-delinquents encompassed in the Social Prediction Table presented in *Unraveling* (p. 261) (*affection of mother for boy, supervision of boy by mother,* and *family cohesiveness*)[6] involve the maternal role in the rearing of children, one might reasonably incline to the hypothesis that absence of the mother from the home for lengthy stretches is markedly implicated in the complex of criminogenic influences. Since we had in our files the verified raw materials from *Unraveling* to test this hypothesis, we have developed the present monograph to meet a growing interest in the subject of working mothers.

METHOD OF ANALYSIS OF DATA

First, what was found in *Unraveling* regarding working mothers? We reproduce the relevant table:

USUAL OCCUPATION OF MOTHER*

| | Delinquents | | Non-delinquents | | Difference |
	No.	%	No.	%	%
Total	496	100·0	497	100·0	—
Housewife	263	53·0	333	67·0	−14·0
Regularly employed	101	20·4	91	18·3	2·1
Occasionally employed	132	26·0	73	14·7	11·9
		$\chi^2 = 25 \cdot 72 : P < \cdot 01$			

* *Unraveling*, Table X–9.

It is evident that in the lower economic ranks from which both our delinquents and the control group were drawn a considerable number of mothers, not only of delinquents but also of non-delinquents, were employed either regularly or occasionally. It is further evident that equal proportions of mothers of non-delinquents and of delinquents were regularly employed but that a greater proportion of mothers of delinquents than of non-delinquents worked irregularly.

The types of work engaged in by all the working mothers were cleaning and scrubbing, domestic service by hour or day, factory

[6] The other two factors in this predictive device, which has come to be known in the literature as the Glueck Social Prediction Table, are *discipline of boy by father* and *affection of father for boy*.

34

work, running a store or lodging house (or helping husbands do so), waiting on table, entertaining in cafés and restaurants.

From these initial findings in *Unraveling* it may be deduced (subject to more definitive information) that more of the children in the families of delinquents than in those of the controls were deprived of necessary maternal care and that this fact had a bearing on the development of their delinquency.

In what way does the working mother contribute to the destiny of the child in respect to delinquency?

To answer this crucial question we employ the same correlational and analytic technique developed in *Physique and Delinquency*[176], in which a series of tables indicates the relationship between individual psychiatric and psychologic traits and sociocultural factors, on the one hand, and physique types and delinquent or non-delinquent behavior, on the other.

TABLE I

SUPERVISION BY MOTHER UNSUITABLE*

	Delinquents		Non-delinquents		Difference	
	No.	%	No.	%	No.	%
Total	314	63·5	61	12·5	253	51·0
Housewife	126	48·1	23	7·0	103	41·1
Regularly employed	85	84·2	25	28·0	60	56·2
Occasionally employed	103	78·6	13	18·6	90	60·0

Significance of Differences

Housewife vs. regularly employed	·01	·02	—
Housewife vs. occasionally employed	·01	·10	·05
Regularly employed vs. occasionally employed	—	—	—

* *Unraveling*, Table X–10. The mother, whether in the home or absent from the home, is careless in her supervision in that she leaves the boy to his own devices without guidance or in the care of an irresponsible person.

To illustrate the method of analysis, we present a sample table, in which the factor *unsuitable supervision of boy by mother* is related to the incidence of *housewives* (non-working mothers), *regularly working mothers*, and *occasionally employed mothers* among both delinquents and non-delinquents. The factor involved in this table—*unsuitable supervision of boy by mother*—so markedly differentiates delinquents as a whole from the total control group of non-delinquents (irrespective of whether or not the mother works outside the home) that we had used it as one of five factors in the construction of the Social Prediction Table in *Unraveling*.[7]

Turning now to an analysis of the illustrative table, we find that it shows, first, that a significantly greater proportion of the mothers of the *non-delinquents* who worked (whether regularly or occasionally) than of those who were housewives neglected to give or provide suitable supervision to their children. Thus entirely apart from the problem of delinquency there is a strong hint that working mothers, at least of low-income groups, are not as conscientious about arranging for the supervision of their children as are those who remain at home. Secondly, the illustrative table shows that supervision of those children who actually became *delinquent* was far less suitable on the part of working mothers (whether they were employed regularly or occasionally) than on the part of the mothers who were housewives. Thirdly, from the column labeled *Difference*, it is learned that a boy who is carelessly supervised and who has a mother who is of the kind who works occasionally is far more likely to become a delinquent than is the poorly supervised son of a mother who does not go out to work.

From now on we shall not advert to the Difference column by name but will rather analyze each table as a whole, drawing from it what we think to be important both in the percentages and in the statistical computations of 'significance of difference'. The tables themselves are presented in the text to enable the reader to follow our reasoning in each analysis.

The use of computations of significance is familiar to many readers, but for the benefit of those not acquainted with the need of a mathematical discipline to check the reliability of conclusions suggested by inspection of percentile relationships in a correlation table we call attention to the fact that two of the comparisons in the illustrative table have been found to be significant at the ·01 'level of confidence', one at the ·02 level, one at the ·05 level, one at the ·10 level. As to the difference in the incidence of unsuitable supervision of the *delinquent* boys by non-working mothers as compared with those regularly or occasionally employed, the divergences were found to be significant at the ·01 level; this means that the probabilities are less than one in a hundred that a difference in incidence like the one found between

---

[7] For a description of the Social Prediction Table and its validations on various samples of cases, see Spotting potential delinquents: can it be done?[(182)]

non-working and working mothers of delinquents is not a true association but is due to chance. As to the difference between non-working mothers of *non-delinquents* and mothers who are regularly employed, the divergence was found to be significant at the ·02 level, indicating a less than two-in-a-hundred probability that the association found is not a reliable one but attributable to chance. As to the variations in the *Difference* column, the divergences are significant at the ·05 level, indicating a *special* etiologic impact of the already generally criminogenic influence of unsuitable maternal supervision on those youngsters whose mothers were occasional workers as compared with those whose mothers spent their full time at home as housewives.

OBSERVED DISTRIBUTION

PROBABILITY	Delinquents	Non-delinquents	Difference	EXPECTED DISTRIBUTION
< ·01	1	—	—	1·18
< ·02	4	1	1	1·18
< ·05	9	7	5	3·54
< ·10	4	8	2	5·90
< ·15	2	6	2	5·90
< ·15 and over	98	96	108	100·00
	118	118	118	118·00

The significance level is $P = < ·05$.

As pointed out in *Physique and Delinquency*[176], the line at which the level of statistical significance is drawn is partly a matter of convention and partly suggested by the nature of the materials. The statistical technique used in the present study is the same as that first applied by us to the data in *Physique and Delinquency* known as the 'multiple comparisons' method.[8] This makes it possible not only to determine that variation in the incidence of a factor among two or more categories exists, but to pinpoint and specify the locale of the variation. (The interested reader is referred to *Physique and Delinquency*, Ch. II, p. 34–35 and Appendix A, in which Prof. Jane Worcester of the Harvard School of Public Health describes the method of multiple comparisons and its implications.) Although in *Physique and Delinquency* the acceptable level of significance was determined by Dr Worcester to be ·01–·10 (with our own very

[8] Developed by Prof. John W. Tukey of Princeton University.

37

occasional advertence to a comparison at the ·15 level because it reflected trends that were consistent with other findings dealing with a related aspect of the subject under analysis), a reliable significance level for the materials included in the present analysis has been found to be ·05 (calculated by Prof. Worcester). In this study, therefore, we have adhered to the ·05 level, referring only occasionally to data at the ·10 level of significance (for the same reason that we sometimes included a ·15 level in *Physique and Delinquency*).

DEFINITION OF TERMS

A word regarding definitions: A mother designated as a *regular* worker is one who has been gainfully employed far all or most of the time since the birth of the particular child included among the cases of *Unraveling*. She need not necessarily have been on a job from 9 to 5; she may have worked on an afternoon shift or a night shift or for part of the day only. But she has been regularly away from home for several hours a day five to seven days a week, so that her absence is an accepted part of the family routine. An *occasional* worker is one who has been gainfully employed now and then. There has been no fixed pattern in her employment. She has drifted from one job to another with unpredictable frequency, laying off at will and resuming at will. Although it can be surmised that sheer necessity forces some mothers to work regularly in order to supplement an all-too-slender family income, the mother who works sporadically can hardly be looked upon as a 'provider' because her earnings cannot regularly be counted upon to prop the family budget.

Perhaps as we proceed with the analysis of the tables some clues will emerge as to the motivations, in addition to the economic, that impel such women to seek occasional jobs.

ORDER OF PRESENTATION OF SIGNIFICANT TABLES

With but one or possibly two exceptions, the factors involved in the series of tables to be analyzed are etiologically implicated in delinquency *generally* in that, as shown in *Unraveling*, they significantly differentiate delinquents from non-delinquents *en masse*; i.e. irrespective of whether or not the mothers were gainfully employed. The issue in the present monograph is whether the factors in question, though found to be already established as generally criminogenic, exert an *especially heavy impact* on the lives of children of working mothers, the aim being to determine the direct and the indirect

38

relationship between a mother's working and the delinquency of her children.

Those factors in which the statistical analysis has not revealed any difference between working mothers and housewives in relation to the delinquency of children are not adverted to in the text that follows. Such factors are listed in the appendix, however, for the benefit of any readers who may be interested and who may wish to make comparable studies of the role of the working mother in the genesis of juvenile delinquency.

EMOTIONAL DEVELOPMENT OF CHILDREN OF WORKING MOTHERS AS RELATED TO DELINQUENCY

Considering first the relationship of the mother's working to the emotional development of her children, we note that *Table II* shows that more than half of the *non-delinquents* reared by working mothers were found to be suffering from some specific form of *mental pathology* (marked instability, neuroticism, psychopathy, psychosis), as contrasted with two fifths of those whose mothers were not gainfully employed. However, the significance level ($P = <\cdot10$) suggests caution in relying too heavily on this finding.

TABLE II

BOY HAS SOME MENTAL PATHOLOGY*

	Delinquents		Non-delinquents		Difference	
	No.	%	No.	%	No.	%
Total	254	51·6	219	44·4	—	−7·2
Housewife	136	52·1	128	38·8	—	13·3
Regularly employed	51	50·5	49	53·8	—	−3·3
Occasionally employed	67	51·5	42	58·3	—	−6·8
Significance of Differences						
Housewife vs. regularly employed	—		$<\cdot10$		—	
Housewife vs. occasionally employed	—		$<\cdot10$		—	
Regularly employed vs. occasionally employed	—		—		—	

* *Unraveling*, Table XVIII–43.

We turn next to a consideration of emotional conflicts, the question being whether a relationship exists between the presence of conflicts in the boy and a mother's working outside the home. As shown by *Table III*, significant variation does not exist in the incidence of emotional conflicts among *non-delinquents* on the basis of their mothers working or not. Among the *delinquents*, however, those whose mothers worked irregularly were found, to a significantly

TABLE III

BOY HAS EMOTIONAL CONFLICTS*

	Delinquents		Non-delinquents		Difference	
	No.	%	No.	%	No.	%
Total	337	74·7	162	37·4	175	37·3
Housewife	174	74·0	115	39·8	59	34·2
Regularly employed	62	66·0	31	37·8	31	28·2
Occasionally employed	101	82·8	16	25·8	85	57·0

Significance of Differences

Housewife vs. regularly employed	—	—	—
Housewife vs. occasionally employed	—	—	<·05
Regularly employed vs. occasionally employed	<·05	—	<·05

* *Unraveling*, Table XIX–4.

greater extent than the boys of full-time working mothers, to be burdened with *emotional conflicts*. Thus it may be inferred that, granted the criminogenic influence contributed by emotional conflicts, there occurs an added pressure to delinquency on those conflict-burdened children whose mothers worked sporadically. This raises the question of whether or not these irregularly employed mothers have a different motivation from those who work steadily. Perhaps they go to work not so much to supplement the family income as to escape household routines and maternal responsibility. We leave such speculation at this point, taking note, as the analysis proceeds, of other clues to a possible fundamental difference between the mothers who worked regularly and those who worked only occasionally and irregularly, and we turn to the question of the role of deep-seated hostility among children of working and of non-working mothers.

Hostility (determined by the Rorschach test) is the presence of conscious or unconscious hatred against others without a normal reason for it, usually accompanied by a feeling of fear that others are hostile to one. *Table IV* shows that in the case of *delinquents* hostile attitudes were prevalent among some four-fifths of them regardless of whether the mother worked out or stayed at home.

TABLE IV

BOY HAS DEEP-SEATED HOSTILITY*

	Delinquents		Non-delinquents		Difference	
	No.	%	No.	%	No.	%
Total	337	79·7	202	55·8	135	23·9
Housewife	180	80·7	123	49·6	57	31·1
Regularly employed	71	80·7	36	64·3	35	16·4
Occasionally employed	86	76·8	43	74·1	43	2·7

Significance of Differences

Housewife vs. regularly employed	—	—	—
Housewife vs. occasionally employed	—	<·02	<·05
Regularly employed vs. occasionally employed	—	—	—

* *Unraveling*, Table XVIII–22, Categories: Marked and Slight.

Hence it cannot be said that the fact of the mother's working away from home is alone responsible for the development of hostile attitudes among children and thereby, indirectly, of delinquency. Of course, to the extent that a mother's absence from home in outside employment contributes to the development of hostile attitudes in a boy it is also indirectly contributing to his delinquency, even though there are other reasons for hostility in children than the fact that the mother absents herself from the home.

There is the further indication in *Table IV* that the incidence of hostility among *non-delinquents* is significantly higher in the case of mothers who worked occasionally than of mothers who presumably spent their full time in domestic and maternal duties. Here then we have another clue to the possibility that the mother who works only now and then is of a quality different from the steadily employed one, even though this difference need not be reflected exclusively in a varied effect on the delinquency of her children.

It will be seen from *Table V* that among *non-delinquents* a significantly higher proportion of boys whose mothers worked regularly outside the home were pathologically defensive than of boys whose mothers spent their full time in domestic duties. Among *delinquents*, however, there is seemingly a reverse trend, though of doubtful statistical significance.

TABLE V

BOY HAS DEFENSIVE ATTITUDE*

	Delinquents		Non-delinquents		Difference	
	No.	%	No.	%	No.	%
Total	243	56·0	187	44·5	56	11·5
Housewife	137	59·8	117	41·9	20	17·9
Regularly employed	38	43·7	41	51·9	−3	−8·2
Occasionally employed	68	57·6	29	46·8	39	10·8
Significance of Differences						
Housewife vs. regularly employed	·10		·05		> ·05	
Housewife vs. occasionally employed	—		—		—	
Regularly employed vs. occasionally employed	—		—		—	

* *Unraveling*, Table XVIII–26, Categories: Marked and Slight.

SUPERVISION OF CHILDREN BY WORKING MOTHERS AS RELATED TO DELINQUENCY

Turning now to use of leisure time of children as affected by the mother's working, we find that *Table VI* does not show a significant difference, among *non-delinquents* of working mothers as opposed to non-working mothers, in the extent to which they spent their leisure hours at home. However, a higher proportion of *delinquents* whose mothers were occasional workers occupied their spare time away from home than did the sons of either full-time housewives or of women regularly employed outside the home. Thus the impact of a factor shown in *Unraveling* to differentiate delinquents from non-delinquents generally is now revealed to exert an especially marked influence on the delinquency of sons of mothers who worked irregularly.

Perhaps we have in this finding another clue to the possibility that mothers who work now and then are more largely animated by a desire to escape household drudgery and family responsibility,

TABLE VI

BOY SPENDS LEISURE HOURS AWAY FROM HOME*

	Delinquents		Non-delinquents		Difference	
	No.	%	No.	%	No.	%
Total	289	58·3	32	6·4	—	51·9
Housewife	151	57·4	26	7·8	—	49·6
Regularly employed	50	49·5	4	4·4	—	45·1
Occasionally employed	88	66·7	2	2·7	—	64·0
Significance of Differences						
Housewife vs. regularly employed	—		—		—	
Housewife vs. occasionally employed	—		—		<·10	
Regularly employed vs. occasionally employed	<·05		—		<·05	

* Unraveling, Table XIII–14.

with a consequent excessively bad effect on the children. Such youngsters then look for security and affection in companionship among their peers outside the home. The full-time working mother, on the other hand, appears more likely to provide for the leisure hours of her children in the protected environment of the home. This is further borne out by *Table I*, which was presented at the outset by way of illustrating our method of analysis. From this it is obvious that there were significant differences in the incidence of *unsuitable supervisory practices* as between non-working and working mothers; and this is true not only of mothers of delinquents but those of non-delinquents as well. It would appear that the mothers who worked did not provide as adequately for the supervision of their children as those who were not employed. It is to be kept in mind that these were mothers from families of low-income levels. While inadequate supervision is found to be far more prevalent among the mothers of delinquents than of non-delinquents, it seems obvious that the working mother who does not provide proper oversight for her children during her absence from home thereby contributes additionally to their delinquency.

As regards *movie attendance*, it appears to be significantly more

TABLE VII

BOY ATTENDS MOVIES THREE OR MORE TIMES WEEKLY*

	Delinquents		*Non-delinquents*		*Difference*	
	No.	*%*	*No.*	*%*	*No.*	*%*
Total	217	44·7	54	10·9	163	33·8
Housewife	97	38·0	30	9·1	67	28·9
Regularly employed	54	54·0	16	17·6	38	36·4
Occasionally employed	66	50·4	8	11·0	58	39·4
Significance of Differences						
Housewife vs. regularly employed	<·05		—		—	
Housewife vs. occasionally employed	<·10		—		—	
Regularly employed vs. occasionally employed	—		—		—	

Unraveling, Table XIII–12.

excessive among boys already *delinquent* who were the sons of working mothers than among boys of mothers who were not gainfully employed. Insofar as the *non-delinquents* are concerned, they as a group attended movies far less frequently than the delinquents, regardless of whether or not their mothers went out to work. The fact that the mother is occupied outside the home is thus an independent influence which enhances whatever relationship there may exist between excessive movie attendance and delinquency.

A further effect on the delinquency of children that appears to be related to the mother's working is seen in *Table VIII*, dealing with

44

the early onset of truancy. Truancy cannot in itself necessarily be regarded as definitively causal of delinquency, for apart from the fact that to some extent it occurs among non-delinquents (*Unraveling*, Table XII–26) it often follows (or accompanies) delinquency already embarked upon. Nevertheless, as *Table VIII* shows, *early* truancy either accompanies delinquency in large measure or in some instances reinforces it after previous beginnings of antisocial behavior. It will

TABLE VIII

BOY BEGAN TO TRUANT AT TEN OR YOUNGER*

	Delinquents		Non-delinquents		Difference	
	No.	*%*	*No.*	*%*	*No.*	*%*
Total	299	60·4	14	2·9	285	57·5
Housewife	144	54·7	9	2·7	135	52·0
Regularly employed	57	56·4	3	3·3	54	53·1
Occasionally employed	98	74·8	2	2·8	96	72·0
Significance of Differences						
Housewife vs. regularly employed	—		—		—	
Housewife vs. occasionally employed	<·02		—		<·02	
Regularly employed vs. occasionally employed	<·05		—		<·05	

* *Unraveling*, Table XII–27.

be seen that avoidance of the routine of school attendance at the age of 10 or less occurred in 60 per cent of all *delinquents*, irrespective of whether or not the mother worked outside the home. However, in the case of delinquents, a higher proportion of sons of occasionally employed mothers were found to become truant in the early years than of sons of mothers who were not gainfully employed or of those who were regular workers. We can again speculate that mothers who work occasionally are primarily motivated by an urge to escape household drudgery and family responsibility and that such mothers have an adverse effect on their children. The child's sense of security is likely to be weakened and his irresponsibility enhanced by the sporadic and unpredictable absence of a mother from the home. In contrast, there is evidence of more adequate and planful arrangement for the care of the children and for keeping in touch with their school problems by mothers who had the capacity for steady employment.

In regard to the foregoing three factors just analyzed, all of which may be reflective of or associated with the delinquency of children, it can reasonably be concluded that sporadically employed mothers by their own erraticism (as reflected in irregular employment) contribute to or add to the already existing internal or external pressures that make for juvenile delinquency.

WORKING MOTHERS AND INADEQUATE FATHERS AS RELATED TO DELINQUENCY

In the following series of tables we now derive some clue as to the main reasons why the mothers of the boys whose careers were studied in *Unraveling* sought gainful employment. The reasons appear to center on economic necessity engendered by the irregular employment of their husbands; by separation, divorce, death or desertion of the principal breadwinner; by the incapacity of the husband because of mental illness.

In *Table IX* we see that, at least as far as the boys studied in

TABLE IX

WORK HABITS OF FATHER NOT GOOD*

	Delinquents		Non-delinquents		Difference	
	No.	%	No.	%	No.	%
Total	282	62·4	132	28·9	150	33·5
Housewife	139	57·0	81	25·8	58	31·2
Regularly employed	57	62·6	29	39·2	28	23·4
Occasionally employed	86	73·5	22	31·9	64	41·6
Significance of Differences						
Housewife vs. regularly employed	—		—		—	
Housewife vs. occasionally employed	<·05		—		—	
Regularly employed vs. occasionally employed	—		—		—	

* *Unraveling*, Table IX–18, Categories: Fair and Poor.

46

Unraveling are concerned, job-seeking by the mothers is related to the *irregular work habits of their husbands*. However, this is not so clearly indicated among the families of the non-delinquents as of the delinquents. Among the latter we see that the poor work habits of the father bear a significant relationship to the irregular employment of the mother, for 73·5 per cent of the delinquent boys whose mothers were sporadic workers also had fathers whose work habits were poor, in contrast with 57 per cent of the delinquents whose mothers remained at home as housewives. It is not surprising that a boy both of whose parents are industrial liabilities is more likely to become a delinquent than is one who is not the son of such inadequate parents.

Economic pressure on the mother to contribute to the family income was caused not only by the industrial incapacity of the father but also by his absence from the home by reason of death, desertion, separation or divorce. In *Table X* there is evidence that where homes were broken a higher proportion of mothers sought regular employment. This is true in the case of both the *non-delinquents* and the *delinquents*. Among the latter a significantly greater proportion of mothers were employed either regularly or occasionally. The absence of the mother in gainful employment would appear to furnish

TABLE X

BOY REARED IN BROKEN HOME*

	Delinquents		Non-delinquents		Difference	
	No.	*%*	*No.*	*%*	*No.*	*%*
Total	299	60·3	169	34·0	130	26·3
Housewife	133	50·6	102	30·6	31	20·0
Regularly employed	74	73·2	41	45·1	33	28·1
Occasionally employed	92	69·7	26	35·6	66	34·1

Significance of Differences

Housewife vs. regularly employed	<·02	<·10	—
Housewife vs. occasionally employed	<·02	—	—
Regularly employed vs. occasionally employed	—	—	—

* *Unraveling*, Table XI–8.

TABLE XI

FATHER EMOTIONALLY DISTURBED*

	Delinquents		Non-delinquents		Difference	
	No.	%	No.	%	No.	%
Total	219	44·2	90	18·1	129	26·1
Housewife	100	38·0	49	14·7	51	23·3
Regularly employed	48	47·5	25	27·5	23	20·0
Occasionally employed	71	53·8	16	21·9	55	31·9
Significance of Differences						
Housewife vs. regularly employed	—		<·10		—	
Housewife vs. occasionally employed	<·05		—		—	
Regularly employed vs. occasionally employed	—		—		—	

* *Unraveling*, Table IX–10.

added pressures to the circumstances of an already broken home, in making for delinquency in the children.

Another factor acting as an economic pressure on a mother to seek employment outside the home is the emotional illness of her spouse. The evidence that mothers work because of the need created by the emotional sickness of the husband is certainly reflected in the cases in *Unraveling*. This is now seen in the higher proportion of such mothers of both delinquents and non-delinquents engaged in gainful employment. In the case of the *non-delinquents* it is reflected in a higher percentage of mothers working regularly, and among the *delinquents* in the significantly greater proportion of mothers working occasionally. As far as the relationship to delinquency is concerned, it is evident that the combined circumstances of emotional disturbance in the father and the absence, especially the erratic absence, of the mother from home in gainful employment contributed to the delinquency of the children.

It is to be borne in mind that all the boys who were the subjects of *Unraveling* were residents of economically underprivileged areas and that by far the greater proportion of both the delinquents and their matched non-delinquents were from homes of low economic status (i.e. marginal or dependent). In such circumstances a mother may have been forced to help in the support of the family or turn to welfare agencies and relatives for assistance. From *Table XII* we get a clear reflection of the influence of economic necessity on the working of the mother and in turn on the delinquency of the children. Here we focus on those families which were very generally dependent on outside sources of support. In the homes of the *non-delinquents* there was relatively little financial dependency. However, among the families of *delinquents* who were forced to rely on sources of support

TABLE XII

FAMILY FINANCIALLY DEPENDENT*

	Delinquents		Non-delinquents		Difference	
	No.	%	No.	%	No.	%
Total	179	36·1	73	14·7	106	21·4
Housewife	92	35·0	49	14·7	43	20·3
Regularly employed	26	25·7	13	14·3	13	11·4
Occasionally employed	61	46·2	11	15·1	50	31·1

Significance of Differences

Housewife vs. regularly employed	—	—	—
Housewife vs. occasionally employed	—	—	—
Regularly employed vs. occasionally employed	<·05	—	<·10

* *Unraveling*, Table IX–14.

other than the earnings within the family a significantly higher proportion of the mothers were only occasionally rather than regularly employed women; and this fact appears to have had some bearing on the delinquency of the children. In other words, rearing in a home in which the income is so insufficient for the family as to necessitate supplementation by welfare agencies and other sources and in which the possible inadequacy of the mother as a wage-earner is reflected in her sporadic employment appeared to have a deleterious effect on the children; for a significantly higher proportion of delinquents stemmed from such homes than from those in which the mother either worked regularly or remained at home full time.

49

IRREGULAR MATERNAL EMPLOYMENT AS
RELATED TO DELINQUENCY

Additional light is thrown on the greater inadequacy of mothers who work sporadically. As the findings in *Table XIII* show, in families of delinquent boys a higher proportion of irregularly employed mothers themselves had a history of delinquency than did mothers who were either full-time housewives or worked regularly. So here again we see reflected the special influence on the delinquency of children of some characteristics of erratically employed mothers.

TABLE XIII

MOTHER HAS HISTORY OF DELINQUENCY*

	Delinquents		Non-delinquents		Difference	
	No.	%	No.	%	No.	%
Total	222	44·8	75	15·1	147	29·7
Housewife	103	39·2	47	14·1	56	25·1
Regularly employed	42	41·6	14	15·4	28	26·2
Occasionally employed	77	58·3	14	19·2	63	39·1
Significance of Differences						
Housewife vs. regularly employed	—		—		—	
Housewife vs. occasionally employed	<·02		—		—	
Regularly employed vs. occasionally employed	<·10		—		—	

* *Unraveling*, Table IX–10.

We can supply one more piece of evidence about the effect on the delinquency of children of mothers who are irregular workers. In *Table XIV* it is shown that such women (together with their husbands) were, as a group, less self-respecting than were those mothers who engaged in regular employment. This is true in families not only of delinquents but of non-delinquents as well. The significantly greater proportion of delinquents who were reared by parents who lacked self-respect and by mothers who were unstable workers as opposed to regularly employed mothers appears further to reflect a damaging effect on the children.

TABLE XIV

PARENTS LACK SELF-RESPECT*

	Delinquents		Non-delinquents		Difference	
	No.	%	No.	%	No.	%
Total	215	43·3	48	9·9	167	33·4
Housewife	113	42·9	34	10·5	79	32·4
Regularly employed	35	34·6	4	4·4	31	30·2
Occasionally employed	67	50·8	10	14·1	57	36·7

Significance of Differences

Housewife vs. regularly employed	—		—		—	
Housewife vs. occasionally employed	—		—		—	
Regularly employed vs. occasionally employed	<·10		<·05		—	

* *Unraveling*, Table X–4.

TABLE XV

MOTHER DOMINATES FAMILY AFFAIRS*

	Delinquents		Non-delinquents		Difference	
	No.	%	No.	%	No.	%
Total	237	49·9	242	50·0	−5	−0·1
Housewife	107	42·5	150	46·2	−43	−3·7
Regularly employed	57	59·4	52	59·8	5	−0·4
Occasionally employed	73	57·5	40	55·6	33	1·9

Significance of Differences

Housewife vs. regularly employed	<·05		—		—	
Housewife vs. occasionally employed	<·05		—		—	
Regularly employed vs. occasionally employed	—		—		—	

* *Unraveling*, Table X–8.

51

We already have sufficient evidence to permit of at least a guarded conclusion that the villain among working mothers is the one who seems to have some inner need to flit erratically from job to job—probably because she finds relief thereby from the burden of home-making and the rearing of children. But more of this may come to light as we proceed with an analysis of the evidence in our data of the effect on family life of the mother's working.

UNWHOLESOME INFLUENCE OF MATERNAL EMPLOYMENT ON FAMILY LIFE AS RELATED TO DELINQUENCY

We have thus far directed attention to the effect on the delinquency of the children of the mother's working outside the home and also to suggestions provided by our data as to the reasons why mothers of low-income levels work.

Now we turn to a consideration of the effects of the absence of the mother from home in gainful employment on the pattern of the family life. It was shown in *Unraveling* how crucially important a role the breakdown of the family matrix plays in the genesis of juvenile delinquency. The question now is to what extent a mother's working contributes to this breakdown.

There are four tables in our series that shed some light on this. Incomplete as the data are, they are nevertheless suggestive, for they treat of domination of the home by the mother, the effect on the father's relationship to the children when the mother is out working, the effect on the relationship between the mother and father, and finally the effect on the cohesiveness of the family group.

As all these factors except domination of the household by the mother were found in *Unraveling* to be related to delinquency, whatever special bearing the employment of mothers may have on these particular aspects of family life may in turn be regarded as contributing additionally to the delinquency of the children.

First, as regards domination of the household by the mother (frequent in the modern American family), there is some inkling even in the homes of the *non-delinquents* that a higher proportion of employed mothers play the guiding role in the household affairs than do mothers who are not gainfully employed. This is more clearly evident in the homes of the *delinquents* where a greater percentage of both the regularly employed and sporadic workers than of full-time housewives dominated the family affairs. However, since the *total* incidence of this influence is quite similar among delinquents

52

and non-delinquents, it cannot be said that this is a factor contributing to delinquency of the children.

It is clearly evident from the findings among the *non-delinquents* in *Table XVI* that lax, erratic or overstrict discipline of the children on the part of the father was far more prevalent among the families in which the wife went out to work either regularly or occasionally than in those in which the wife devoted all her time to domestic duties. Whether, in the absence of the wife, the husband usually

TABLE XVI

FATHER'S DISCIPLINE OF BOY IS NOT CONSISTENTLY FIRM
AND KINDLY*

	Delinquents		Non-delinquents		Difference	
	No.	*%*	*No.*	*%*	*No.*	*%*
Total	429	94·4	202	44·3	227	50·1
Housewife	238	94·4	120	38·2	118	56·2
Regularly employed	77	90·6	42	54·6	35	36·0
Occasionally employed	114	96·6	40	61·6	74	35·0
Significance of Differences						
Housewife vs. regularly employed	—		< ·05		< ·05	
Housewife vs. occasionally employed	—		< ·05		< ·05	
Regularly employed vs. occasionally employed	—		—		—	

* *Unraveling*, Table XI–22, Categories: Lax, Overstrict and Erratic.

tends to be more neglectful of the children or less patient with them or whether the wife seeks escape from the home because of the vagaries of her spouse is a moot question. At any rate, to the extent that a mother's absence from home in gainful employment engenders a father's inadequate discipline of the children the working mother must be charged with contributing, albeit indirectly, to the delinquency of her children. Poor discipline of the children by the father is evidently a very potent factor in delinquency as it occurred in 90 per cent to 97 per cent of all the delinquents regardless of whether or not the mother worked.

Whether or not the dissatisfaction of the father is visited upon the children because the mother is a breadwinner, it is evident from *Table XVII* that the relationship existing between him and his

TABLE XVII

PARENTS ARE INCOMPATIBLE*

	Delinquents		Non-delinquents		Difference	
	No.	%	No.	%	No.	%
Total	310	63·2	170	34·6	140	28·6
Housewife	138	52·5	93	28·3	45	24·2
Regularly employed	77	76·2	43	47·3	34	28·9
Occasionally employed	95	75·4	34	47·2	61	28·2

Significance of Differences

Housewife vs. regularly employed	< ·02	< ·05	—
Housewife vs. occasionally employed	< ·02	< ·05	—
Regularly employed vs. occasionally employed	—	—	—

* *Unraveling*, Table X–7, Categories: Fair and Poor.

TABLE XVIII

FAMILY IS NOT A COHESIVE UNIT*

	Delinquents		Non-delinquents		Difference	
	No.	%	No.	%	No.	%
Total	415	83·8	189	38·1	226	45·7
Housewife	207	78·7	111	33·4	96	45·3
Regularly employed	91	90·1	40	44·0	51	46·1
Occasionally employed	117	89·3	38	52·1	79	37·2

Significance of Differences

Housewife vs. regularly employed	< ·05	—	—
Housewife vs. occasionally employed	< ·05	< ·05	—
Regularly employed vs. occasionally employed	—	—	—

* *Unraveling*, Table X–14, Categories: Some and None.

working spouse was a deteriorating one, in some instances already reaching open breach. This holds true of the parents of the non-delinquents as well as of the delinquents. As the incompatibility of parents was found in *Unraveling* to be associated with delinquency, it can be concluded that to the extent, in turn, that a mother's working outside the home contributes to the unstable relationship between herself and her husband she contributes to the delinquency of her children. We must bear in mind, however, that in some instances she may be in gainful employment outside the home because of the inadequacy or inability of her spouse to fulfil his share of the obligations to his family.

Viewing the family situation as a whole in terms of the unity or cohesiveness of the family life ('all for one, one for all'), we see evidence in *Table XVIII* that more of the homes of working mothers than of housewives lack cohesiveness. This lack of family unity was found in *Unraveling* to be lightly associated with the delinquency of children. So, again, to the extent that the absence of the mother from home in gainful employment contributes to a weakening of the family ties, the working mother can be charged with contributing to the delinquency of her children.

DISCUSSION

The deleterious influence on the family life and on the children of the mother's working outside the home has become evident in our analysis. As regards the special impact on delinquency this too has emerged. There is evidence of a differential influence of the working mother on family life, on children, and on delinquency. There is some suggestion in our data that these influences are more potent when deriving from the mother who works sporadically than from the regularly employed mother. Actually a like proportion of mothers of both delinquents and non-delinquents were found in *Unraveling* to be regularly employed, but among the delinquents there was found a higher proportion of mothers who worked only irregularly. So even in *Unraveling* we could note that it is the working mother of this latter type who exerts the heaviest influence on the delinquency of her children.

There is some suggestion that such mothers are of a different 'breed' from women who are regularly employed. It may be that the sporadically working mother is motivated more by the enticement of getting away from household drudgery and parental responsibility than is the mother who works regularly. The latter is seemingly more interested in the need or duty of providing a steady addition to the family income.

As is true of all studies of this kind, the findings must be considered tentative. The traits and factors included in this analysis are only a sample of many other influences that may be operative. More detailed studies of the relationship of the working mother to delinquency and to family and social malaise are needed.

That wholesome family life is of crucial importance in the building of character, the inculcation of basic habits, the development of a sense of security, and the structuring of personality has been so frequently asserted in clinical case histories, statistical studies, and theoretical speculation as to have become a commonplace. There is, of course, some difference of opinion as to what 'wholesome' means. Does it, for example, have to do largely with affectional relationships of parents (especially the mother) to children, with problems of overprotection, with methods of discipline, with the effect of parental rejection or parental neuroticism, alcoholism or criminalism, and their influence on the growing child, or with some or all of these? At all events, the central significance of the family matrix for the destiny of the child, even apart from the problem of delinquency, can nowadays no longer be denied.

From a practical point of view the issue presented by our findings is not a simple one. It may be generalized that women seek employment outside the home for economic reasons. However, in many instances there are doubtless more deep-lying and subtle motivations. In some cases we are confronted with mothers who for intellectual or temperamental reasons cannot or will not adequately fulfill the role of motherhood. This would seem to suggest the need for individualization in determining how to improve the situation in the homes of working mothers. An overall governmental policy of financial grants to mothers is not enough and may even be disadvantageous in some cases where it is not true economic need but rather the desire for the latest gadgets to 'keep up with the Joneses' that may be the propulsive motive. Thus, not only economic help but educational, psychiatric and spiritual aid as well must be called into play in the constructive management of this growing social problem.

We have limited ourselves to very general suggestions. Our task essentially is to present findings growing out of the research which was the basis of the volume *Unraveling*. No doubt those who are directly concerned with seeking programmatic and legislative remedies to cope with such dangers as this all-too-inadequate study has pointed to will clothe our bare outline with many practical suggestions. For example, if the greatest danger to children derives from the mother who is a sporadic worker, such a mother appears to be in need of special counseling and her family of special attention.

There are a few more facts that we can add from the research reported on in our volume *Physique and Delinquency*[176]. In this we made a breakdown by body type of the 500 delinquents and 500 non-delinquents encompassed in *Unraveling* (mesomorphs, endomorphs, ectomorphs, balanced); and this disclosed that so far as the problem of working mothers is involved we need be most seriously concerned about *ectomorphic* children. Youngsters of this body type are predominantly linear, fragile, and sensitive. In proportion to their mass they have the greatest surface area and hence, according to Sheldon, 'the greatest sensory exposure to the outside world'.[9] Employment of the mother outside the home was found to have its most potent delinquency-inducing effect on ectomorphic youngsters, in contrast with those of the other body types (p. 174). So, also, ectomorphs tend to react more markedly than one or more of the other physique types to such unfortunate circumstances in their environment as unsuitable supervision by the mother, maternal hostility or indifference to the child, emotional disturbance of the father, broken homes, inconsistent, overstrict or lax discipline from the father, incompatibility between parents, lack of family cohesiveness and rearing by a parent substitute (pp. 167, 180, 181, 189, 193, 196, 197, 201, 203).

In all these respects, then, whatever damage to the personality and character of children may result from the fact of the mother's absenting herself from the home in gainful employment is enhanced in the case of the particularly vulnerable ectomorphic child. For we have learned in *Physique and Delinquency* that children of this body build are more sensitive and less stable emotionally than are boys of other body builds (p. 236, Exhibit 10).

Here again the evidence suggests that a mere mass program of financial subsidy to induce necessitous mothers to remain at home is not enough. Individualization is called for, both of the child and of the family; and financial aid must be supplemented by assistance in the form of educational, religious, and psychotherapeutic guidance.

Basically, the time is ripe for a reassessment of the entire situation. As more and more enticements in the way of financial gain, excitement, and independence from the husband are offered married women to lure them from their domestic duties, the problem is becoming more widespread and acute. It is a problem that should be discussed freely and frankly in all communities by mothers, fathers, clergy, psychiatrists, social workers. Only through the ventilation of the pros and cons of the problem, supported by such facts as exist, can a most vital issue of modern life be dealt with fairly and constructively.

[9] W. H. Sheldon *et al.* (1940), *The varieties of human physique*, pp. 5–7 (New York: Harper).

APPENDIX A-1

Factors in Unraveling juvenile delinquency *significantly differentiating delinquents from non-delinquents and to which mother's working is not found to bear a significant relationship**

(Table number to right of each factor is from *Unraveling*)

PHYSICAL FINDINGS

Extreme restlessness in early childhood (XIV–2a)

Enuresis in early childhood (XIV–2b)

Dermographia (XIV–13a)

QUALITIES OF INTELLIGENCE

Power of observation (XVII–4)

Common sense (XVII–6)

Tendency to phantasy (XVII–8)

Methodical approach to problems (XVII–10)

BASIC CHARACTER STRUCTURE

Social assertion (XVIII–2)

Defiance (XVIII–3)

Submissiveness to authority (XVIII–4)

Ambivalence to authority (XVIII–5)

Enhanced feeling of insecurity/ anxiety (XVIII–7)

Feeling of not being wanted or loved (XVIII–8)

Feeling of not being taken seriously (XVIII–10)

Feeling of not being recognised or appreciated (XVIII–11)

Feeling of helplessness or power-lessness (XVIII–12)

Fear of failure and defeat (XVIII–13)

Feeling of resentment (XVIII–14)

Poor surface contact with others (XVIII–17)

Suspiciousness (XVIII–23)

Destructiveness (XVIII–24)

Feeling of isolation (XVIII–25)

Dependence on others (XVIII–27)

Conventionality in ideas, feelings, behavior (XVIII–29)

Feeling of being able to manage own life (XVIII–32)

Narcissitic trends (XVIII–33)

Masochistic trends (XVIII–34)

Receptive (oral) trends (XVIII–35)

Destructive - sadistic trends (XVIII–36)

Emotional lability (XVIII–37)

Self-control (XVIII–38)

Vivacity (XVIII–39)

Compulsory trends (XVIII–40)

Extroversive trends (XVIII–41)

Psychopathy (XVIII–43c)

TRAITS OF TEMPERAMENT

Suggestibility (XIX–1b)

Inadequacy (XIX–1c)

Stubbornness (XIX–1d)

Adventurousness (XIX–1e)

Motor response to stimuli (XIX–1f)

Emotional stability (XIX–1g)

Acquisitiveness (XIX–2c)

Conventionality (XIX–3a)

Conscientiousness (XIX–3c)

Practicality (XIX–3d)

FAMILY BACKGROUND AND ATMOSPHERE

Cleanliness and neatness of home (VIII–8)

Father alcoholic (IX–10b)

Father serious physical ailment (IX–10d)

Mother alcoholic (IX–10b)

Mother emotionally disturbed (IX–10g)

Family's management of income (X–1)

* This does not necessarily mean that a relationship definitely does not exist, but only that it is not revealed in our data.

Routine of household (X–2)

Ambitiousness of family (X–5)

Family group recreations (X–11)

Attitude of parents regarding entertaining children's friends at home (X–12)

Provisions for recreation in home (X–13)

Affection of father for boy (XI–13)

Affection of mother for boy (XI–14)

Emotional ties of boy to father (XI–15)

Emotional ties of boy to mother (XI–17)

Boy's estimate of mother's concern for his welfare (XI–19d)

Mother's discipline of boy (XI–22b)

Method of control of boy by father (X–23c)

Method of control of boy by mother (XI–23d)

SCHOOL HISTORY

Retardation (XII–5)

Scholarship (XII–10)

Reading quotient (XII–11)

Attitude toward school (XII–17)

Academic ambitions (XII–19)

Adjustment to schoolmates (XII–21)

Truancy (XII–26)

USE OF LEISURE AND HABITS

Household duties (XIII–10)

Recreational preferences (XIII–11)

Stealing rides (XIII–13a)

Keeping late hours (XIII–13b)

Smoking at early age (XIII–13c)

Sneaking admissions (XIII–13d)

Destroying property (XIII–13e)

Running away from home (XIII–13f)

Bunking out (XIII–13g)

Gambling (XIII–13h)

Drinking at early age (XIII–13i)

Hanging around street corners (XIII–14a)

Seeking recreation in distant neighborhoods (XIII–14b)

Using playground (XIII–14d)

Companionships (XIII–16a)

Attitude toward supervised recreation (XIII–20)

Church attendance (XIII–21)

APPENDIX A–2

Factors in Unraveling juvenile delinquency *not differentiating delinquents from non-delinquents and to which mother's working is not found to bear a significant relationship**

(Table number to right of each factor is from *Unraveling*)

PHYSICAL FINDINGS

Irregular reflexes (XIV–6a)

Functional deviations (XIV–6b)

Sexual underdevelopment (XIV–9a)

Cyanosis (XIV–13b)

Tremors (XIV–13c)

General health (XIV–16)

QUALITIES OF INTELLIGENCE

Intuition (XVII–7)

* See note to A–1.

BASIC CHARACTER STRUCTURE

Feeling of not being taken care of (XVIII–9)

TRAITS OF TEMPERAMENT

Preponderance of introversive trends (XVIII–42)

Sensitivity (XIX–1a)

FAMILY BACKGROUND

Nativity of parents (IX–2)

CHAPTER 4

Role of the Family in the Etiology of Delinquency *

ELEANOR T. GLUECK

I

WHAT is the scientific evidence from our researches regarding the role of the family in the etiology of delinquency? It would require a series of articles to present all the available information from our research studies on the subject of the effect of family life on the delinquency of children. Those who are especially interested in this subject are referred to six of our books.[1] Here I must limit myself to a brief statement of facts from these works as they relate to the subject of the family and delinquency.

In 1951 two students in my husband's Seminar at the Harvard Law School on the Administration of Criminal Justice prepared and submitted a joint paper entitled 'Two Thousand Juvenile Delinquents',[2] in fulfillment of the course requirement, in which they combined certain factors of family background of the 500 young adult male offenders initially described in *500 Criminal Careers*, 500 young adult women offenders of *Five Hundred Delinquent Women*, and 1,000 juvenile delinquents who constituted our study entitled *One Thousand Juvenile Delinquents*.

As we had retained, with design, the same basic definitions of the factors in all three studies (and in the studies that followed) it was possible for the students to combine the three groups into a total of two thousand delinquents as regards the available factors of their family life. These included: (1) size of family, (2) birth rank of offender, (3) nativity of the parents, (4) economic status of the home, (5) education of the parents, (6) history of criminalism, mental disease, and mental defect in the family, (7) physical condition of the home, (8) conduct standards of the home, (9) extent of broken

---

* Prepared by invitation of the *Bulletin de la Société Internationale de Criminologie* for a special number (Summer 1960) on 'The Family and Delinquency', edited by Professor Jean Pinatel.

[1] *500 criminal careers*[26], *Five hundred delinquent women*[44], *One thousand juvenile delinquents*[45], *Unraveling juvenile delinquency*[138], *Physique and delinquency*[176], *Predicting delinquency and crime*[212]. (Also *Family environment and delinquency*[245] which was published since this was written.)

[2] Spark M. Matsunaga and Samuel Freed. Unpublished thesis, April 18, 1951.

homes, (10) industrial skill of the father, (11) gainful employment of the mother, (12) disciplinary practices of the parents.

Although the factors are few in number, they are important not only in themselves but as indices of numerous other influences to which they are related. Thus, they provide a useful starting point for a consideration of the relationship between family pathology and delinquency.

Briefly, most of the delinquents stemmed from *large families*, that is, appreciably larger than the average for families in the State of Massachusetts from which our cases were drawn. But the role of the size of the family in the delinquency of children is certainly not clear until we can compare delinquents with a control group of non-delinquents matched by age and ethnic origin and deriving from the same general socio-cultural background as determined by their residence in economically depressed areas.

It is to be noted that one-fourth of the 2,000 offenders were *firstborn children*. This is of interest because it is generally thought that the firstborn is the most 'spoiled' and overprotected child, and therefore the most likely to become delinquent.

Almost two-thirds of the 2,000 delinquents were the *American-born children of European-born parents*. Does this mean that American children of foreign-born parents are in a particularly vulnerable position in regard to delinquency? The answer to this will emerge later.

Over three-fourths of the families of the 2,000 delinquents were found to be of *very low economic circumstances*; that is, entirely or partially dependent for financial support on sources other than their own earnings, or barely eking out a hazardous living. Regarding the kinds of outside assistance these economically crippled families had to be given, it is to be noted that 76 per cent had received either direct financial aid or assistance with the management of problems with their children, with their marital relationships, problems of physical and mental health, obtaining employment, and similar matters. In other words, they were the kind of families who were not self-sufficient and self-managing, and for whose welfare the community had to assume a considerable amount of responsibility.

The fact that in 34 per cent of the cases the *mothers of the offenders worked outside the home* during a period when it was rare for American married women to be gainfully employed (in the early 1900s) is also reflective of the grave economic needs of these families and perhaps, also, of the possible neglect of the children. (More recently, of course, large numbers of American women work part- or full-time, some because they prefer the outside interests that such work brings to

61

them, some to supplement the husband's salary, or to provide the 'luxuries' which most American families strive for nowadays—a home of their own, at least one and even two automobiles, good clothing, television sets, opportunities for travel, and so on.)

As regards the *educational background of the families* of delinquents, it is to be noted that in 67 per cent of the 2,000 cases neither parent had had any formal schooling and that in only 4 per cent one or both parents had had more than grade schooling. Whether this reflects parental incapacity or lack of opportunity for schooling among foreign-born parents at the turn of the century cannot be determined by the facts above presented. The latter may possibly be the case, for only 28 per cent of the fathers of our 2,000 offenders were found to be engaged in skilled work.

It is to be noted that 86 per cent of these 2,000 delinquents were the offspring of *families who had delinquent members* either in the immediate family or among maternal and paternal grandparents, aunts, uncles. This suggests that children reared in such an atmosphere are exposed to examples of anti-social behavior very early in their lives; but it should be pointed out that this, like the other factors enumerated, is but one source of possible etiological influence, and can be properly evaluated only as one factor in a complex of traits and factors.

Added to the findings regarding the criminalistic backgrounds of the 2,000 offenders is the revelation that in almost two-thirds of the families (and this included close blood relatives) there was a history of either severe mental disorder or mental defect, or such marked peculiarities of personality as to have been noted in official records.

Little wonder, therefore, that an unwholesome atmosphere for the growth and development of children as reflected in low conduct standards, in lack of thrift, in the absence of sound ideals among the immediate family members, was found in the high proportion of 87 per cent of the families in which the delinquents were reared.

But this is not all. There must be added to this already grim picture of the early home background of the 2,000 delinquents the poor physical conditions by which they were surrounded in their early years, for only 16 per cent of the homes involved had even the minimal requirements of space, light, ventilation, sanitary facilities, neatness, and cleanliness. In the bulk of cases the homes were characterized by one or another combination of physical discomforts, which may well explain why so many delinquent children find their homes unpleasant and expulsive, and therefore seek their recreational activities outside the home.

It is further to be noted that almost two-thirds of the 2,000 delinquents grew up in homes that were *broken* by the death, separation or divorce of parents. Further, in almost two out of three instances in which such a breach in the normal home situation had occurred, it took place before the offender in question was nine years of age, and in only slightly less than 14 per cent did this break in the family constellation occur at the age of fifteen or more, when the offender might be considered old enough to withstand the psychological damage of such an upheaval.

Finally, it should be noted that in 95 per cent of these 2,000 offenders the disciplinary practices of one or the other parent were of a nature to be clearly assessed as inadequate, involving either extreme laxity or extreme rigidity, or inconsistency of control of the child. In only 4·5 per cent of the homes was the discipline essentially consistent and firm and entirely acceptable to the child because it was the product of sincerity and affection.

These are only a few findings concerning the family backgrounds of three groups of offenders in the United States—500 graduates of young men's reformatories, 500 former inmates of a reformatory for female offenders, and 1,000 juvenile delinquents, each investigated independently and at different periods.

The findings as to the family background of these 2,000 American delinquents, highly suggestive as they are, of course are not conclusive. It can be said, however, that other studies of delinquents and criminals in the United States (usually on smaller samples of cases and covering fewer factors and at times only one factor) generally reflect a similar family pathology. Consultation of American criminologies will in large measure confirm this statement. I have no doubt that similar findings have emerged in non-American studies.

These few findings, reflective as they are of intense family pathology, have many implications for the etiology of delinquency; but the question naturally arises whether similar conditions do not exist in the families of non-delinquents of the same general sociocultural level.

II

To answer the question (among others) of the relationship of family pathology to the etiology of delinquency, my husband and I set up a study in 1940 of 500 persistent delinquents ranging in age from eleven to seventeen years; matching every boy with a proven non-delinquent of the same age, ethnic origin, and residence in economically depressed areas. Among some 400 factors and characteristics that were examined, almost 70 dealt with various aspects of the family background, a greater number than had been included in our prior studies. I cannot advert to all of these and must ask the interested reader to consult *Unraveling Juvenile Delinquency*, from which the data for the following discussion are culled.

A comparison of the 500 confirmed delinquents and their matched non-delinquents has revealed that with few exceptions these particular factors were indeed present to a significantly greater degree in the family backgrounds of the delinquents than of the non-delinquents. However, a significant difference between delinquents and non-delinquents was not found in regard to the proportion who were native-born children of European-born parents. The potentiality for a clash of cultures inherent in this relationship can have an important bearing upon the capacity of parents not born in the United States to adapt their more rigid European standards to the conditions faced by their native-born children in the freer moral and cultural climate of America. So, also, the proportion of delinquents who were first-born children was not found to be greater than among the matched non-delinquents. Again, the educational level of the parents of the delinquents was not found in the comparative study to be any worse than that of the parents of the matched non-delinquents; nor was a lower proportion of skilled workers found among the fathers of delinquents than of non-delinquents. However, it should be mentioned that the parents of both delinquents and non-delinquents studied in *Unraveling* had more schooling than did the parents of the 2,000 offenders previously described. This is accounted for by the fact that in the later sample of cases not only was there a lower proportion of foreign-born parents, but a higher percentage of American-born parents were completing grade school and entering high school during the years of this particular study.

These factors of resemblance between delinquents and non-delinquents cannot, therefore, be looked upon as playing any significant role in the etiology of delinquency. This does not, of course, preclude the possibility that such factors in the background of *a child with a certain temperamental make-up* may act as a trigger to delinquency when they would not have that effect on another type of child. [This aspect of crime causation is the subject matter of *Family Environment and Delinquency*[245].] But, broadly speaking, the factors of resemblance between delinquents and a control group of non-delinquents do not have the potential impact on delinquency that is inherent in factors which are found more heavily to characterize the families of delinquents.

All the other factors found in the family background of the three samples comprising the 2,000 delinquents of our earlier investigations are revealed in the comparison of the 500 delinquents and the 500 matched non-delinquents of the later study to be more characteristic of the families of the delinquents.

These factors are: criminalism, mental disease, mental defect in the family; economic dependency and assistance from welfare agencies; unattractive surroundings (overcrowded, disorderly,unclean or with few sanitary facilities); broken homes; mothers sporadically employed; inadequate disciplinary practices on the part of the parents.

There is no need to present the specific findings of *Unraveling* regarding these particular aspects of the family background of delinquents, but it is well to point out that, despite the similar socio-cultural level of the families of the delinquents and non-delinquents as roughly judged by residence in economically depressed areas, a significantly higher proportion of the families of the delinquents than of the non-delinquent control group were found to be completely dependent upon sources of support other than their own earnings and a far higher proportion had to turn to community welfare agencies not only for financial assistance but for help with their multifarious problems. This would appear to reflect a lesser stability, as well as a lesser ability of the families of the delinquents to manage their own affairs.

Another finding of special interest in *Unraveling* as regards the factors already descriptive of the 2,000 delinquents has to do with the age at which the first breach in the normal home ties occurred by reason of the death, desertion, divorce or separation of the parents. Although, as might be expected, a significantly greater proportion of the delinquents than of the non-delinquents were products of early broken homes, no significant difference emerged as to the age at which the first break in the normal family constellation took place among the delinquents and the non-delinquents. As both groups of children were very young when the rift in their home life occurred, one is forced to the conclusion that the delinquent children appeared to be less able to withstand the potentially damaging effect of such a revolution in their life pattern, reared as they were (according to the findings of *Unraveling*) in a pathological atmosphere.

It is to be especially noted also that, although equal proportions of the mothers of the delinquents and of the non-delinquents worked *regularly* outside the home, a significantly greater proportion of the delinquents' mothers worked to escape the humdrum existence at home. This leads to the question whether such irregular and unpredictable wage-earning on the part of the mother has a more damaging effect on the family life than the regular absence from the home of the steadily employed mother. From our findings in a paper entitled

65

'Working Mothers and Delinquency' (Chapter 3 above) this would appear to be the case.

It is further to be noted, however, that the comparison of the 500 delinquents and 500 matched non-delinquents of *Unraveling* has revealed many factors of *resemblance* between the families of the delinquents and non-delinquents: for example, in the proportion of parents who themselves stemmed from large families; in the low economic circumstances in which both sets of parents were themselves reared; in the limited schooling of the paternal and maternal grandparents; in the age at which the parents married; in the age difference between the father and mother at marriage; in the age of the parents at the birth of the delinquents and non-delinquents in question; and (notably) in the proportion of homes in which the mother was the dominant figure, actually and psychologically the head of the household. (This is the situation in half of both sets of homes and is perhaps peculiar to the American culture of the mid-twentieth century.)

III

To the findings of difference between the families of the delinquents and non-delinquents can now be added a number of others emerging from *Unraveling* and which were not encompassed in the description of the 2,000 delinquents. For example, although equal proportions of the fathers of the delinquents and non-delinquents were skilled workers (and the two sets of fathers were of the same educational level) a much higher percentage of the delinquents' fathers were found to be liabilities to their employers and far less willing than the fathers of the non-delinquents to assume the family responsibilities. This partially explains why so much more welfare assistance was necessary to the families of the delinquents.

Apart from the more inferior physical characteristics and conditions in the homes of delinquents, there was greater inadequacy in other respects; for example, in less supervision of the children, in less planfulness in the management of the available income, in greater haphazardness in the daily life, and also in lack of ambition on the part of the parents to improve the family's condition.

As regards the *emotional relationships* of the parents to each other and to the boys in question, the findings weigh heavily to the disadvantage of the delinquents; for in a far higher proportion of instances the relationship between the parents of the delinquents was not harmonious; the parents were considerably less attached to the delinquents than was true of the parents of the non-delinquents;

in a far higher proportion of instances among the delinquents than among the non-delinquents the boys felt that their parents were not deeply concerned about their welfare (and actually, whether or not as a result of this, the delinquent boys were not nearly as much attached to their parents as the non-delinquents). It is to be noted also that as regards the attitude of the brothers and sisters to the 500 delinquents and their 500 matched non-delinquents, it was considerably less warm toward the delinquents.

Of major importance are the evidences of far less unity of purpose and spirit in the families of the 500 delinquents than of the 500 non-delinquents, as reflected in the absence of family pride, of strong ties between the members of the family, of family group recreations; and of indifference or actual inhospitality to a child's friends, in the lack of provision for leisure-time activities for the child in the home, and in the lack of planning for the boy's future.

In each of these aspects of family life the delinquents were found to be far more disadvantaged than the non-delinquents. These findings are all the more significant in the light of the fact that both groups derive from the same general sociocultural level. For, by the design of the research, the ethnic origins of the 500 delinquents and 500 non-delinquents were equally distributed and both groups of youngsters derived from neighborhoods of underprivilege, and in fact it was ascertained in *Unraveling* that like proportions of the two groups of boys lived in shabby tenement homes, that parents of the delinquents and of the non-delinquents actually were paying the same average rental per room and the furnishings of these homes were equally sparse.

IV

Substantial elements of difference between the family background of delinquents and non-delinquents emerge from this sketchy picture. One hesitates, because of the many discussions about 'etiology', 'causation', 'association', to venture the opinion that in a controlled sample of the kind studied in *Unraveling* the emergent differences do indeed have a bearing on the etiology of delinquency.[3]

Perhaps the answer to this question can be approached through another path, which should take out of the realm of speculation the true etiological impact on delinquency of at least some of the factors in the family background that have been found to be more characteristic of delinquents than of non-delinquents. This evidence derives

---

[3] But see *Delinquents in the making*[153], pp. 164–69, translated into Italian[163], French[175], and German[251].

from the result of the application to other samples of delinquents (and of non-delinquents) of a cluster of five factors markedly distinguishing the 500 delinquents from the 500 non-delinquents of *Unraveling* (Ch. XX), and which serve as the basis of what has come to be known in the literature of criminology as the Glueck Social Prediction Table. These factors are: *discipline of boy by father*, *supervision of boy by mother*, *affection of father for boy*, *affection of mother for boy*, and *family cohesiveness*. Without entering into the construction of this device, the purpose of which is to identify early in life those children who are likely to become delinquent unless suitable therapeutic intervention occurs, it need only be said that certain other factors markedly distinguishing the 500 delinquents from the 500 non-delinquents could have been substituted. Because of their possible etiological implications the choice of factors was limited to the most sharply differentiating ones in the family background. Each one of the five factors incorporated into the Prediction Table must be looked upon as an index of many other elements in the family life—a cluster against which can be rated the family pathology as it relates to the delinquency potential of a particular child.

If it be a fact that family pathology is related to delinquency in an etiological sense, the cluster of five factors, weighted in accordance with their actual occurrence in a matched sample of 500 delinquents and 500 non-delinquents, should in large measure correctly identify other groups of persistent delinquents and true non-delinquents.

To determine whether this is actually the case, several groups of experimenters in the United States and two in other countries (Japan, France) have found through a retrospective examination of the case histories of already persistent offenders that the table would have correctly identified approximately 90 per cent of the delinquents at age six, generally *before* the actual onset of antisocial behavior. Chapter 8 below provides a brief summary of such investigations.

The results have thus far indicated that, regardless of ethnic origin, color, religion, intelligence level, residence in urban or rural areas, economic status, or even sex, the predictive cluster is equally potent, not only on samples of American delinquents but in Strasbourg, France, and also in Japan (and this latter despite marked differences in the culture of a Far Eastern country).

In one of the retrospective American studies[4] as well as in the study made in Japan,[5] the prediction table was applied to non-

[4] R. E. Thompson (1952), A validation of the Glueck Social Prediction Scale for proneness to delinquency. *J. crim. L. Criminol. & Police Sci.* **43**, 451.

[5] Tokuhiro Tatezawa (1958), *A study of prediction of juvenile delinquency* (Japan: Ministry of Justice).

delinquents as well as to delinquents with equally gratifying results.

Perhaps more convincing to some than these retrospective applications of the cluster of five factors comprising the table is its application for the purpose of identifying the true potential delinquents and potential non-delinquents in a young school population, and by follow-ups to the seventeenth birthday to determine the correctness of the predictions. A brief description of the major ongoing study of this nature, which is being carried out by the New York City Youth Board, and some interim results are provided in Chapter 8. Briefly, however, application of the table to 224 boys as they entered two schools in high delinquency areas in New York City (mostly at age six) and largely including Jewish, Negro, and Puerto Rican children (the cases on which the predictive device was developed in *Unraveling* did not include any Negroes or Puerto Ricans and very few Jewish boys, thus subjecting the table to a very severe test), provides evidence of the correctness of the forecasts.[6]

The significance of these cumulative evidences from the retrospective and prospective applications of the Prediction Table is that it reflects the etiological bearing on delinquency of family pathology (of which the five factors comprising the tables are an index). Were this not the case, this factor cluster would not correctly identify the great proportion of delinquents and conversely of non-delinquents which each application of the table (retrospective or prospective) has thus far produced. The findings have been inductively arrived at and are not the result of a purely theoretical formulation regarding the etiology of delinquency.

V

I do not wish to close this brief presentation of the evidence from our researches that there is indeed an etiological relationship between family pathology and delinquency, without at least mentioning that not all children who are bred in a family atmosphere of disharmony react in the same way nor to the same degree to a similar familial pattern.

Our study of *Physique and Delinquency*[176], which deals with the distinguishing characteristics of delinquents and non-delinquents of the three dominant body builds (mesomorphic, endomorphic, ectomorphic), has clearly revealed that each body build has its distinctive traits, and tends to react differently to certain familial stresses. For example, mesomorphs (the hardy, muscular type) are far more likely than ectomorphs (the fragile, linear type) to over-react to a careless

[6] See Chapters 6-13 below.

household routine, to the lack of family group recreations, and to meagre recreational facilities in the home; while ectomorphs are far more distressed than mesomorphs by emotional disturbance in the father, by the absence of the mother from home, by a broken home, by disharmony between the parents, by a mother's lack of interest, to mention but a few such differential influences (Ch. XIII).

This does not mean however that there is no broad *common* ground of criminogenesis which affects boys of all body builds to a similar extent. But it does point up the fact that when we speak of the etiological influence of the family background we must consider the make-up of the particular individual who is exposed to it. Otherwise *all* children in the home from which a delinquent stems would be delinquent and we know this is not the case; and *all* children found to have certain clusters of factors in their background would be potential delinquents, and this also is not the case.

I do not wish to leave the impression that I am unaware of influences other than of the family life on the genesis of delinquency. But the subject of this chapter is the role of the family in the etiology of delinquency and it is to this that I have briefly addressed myself.

CHAPTER 5

Family Environment and Delinquency in the Perspective of Etiologic Research*

SHELDON AND ELEANOR GLUECK

I

CERTAIN highly suggestive findings have been made regarding statistically significant differences between a sample of 500 persistent delinquents and a matched control group of 500 true non-delinquents, both from the most underprivileged areas of Boston. These findings carried with them the implication of a complex etiologic involvement. This interplay of forces is summarized in *Unraveling Juvenile Delinquency* [138] as follows:

'The delinquents as a group are distinguishable from the non-delinquents: (1) *physically*, in being essentially mesomorphic in constitution (solid, closely knit, muscular); (2) *temperamentally*, in being restlessly energetic, impulsive, extroverted, aggressive, destructive (often sadistic) . . . ; (3) in *attitude*, by being hostile, defiant, resentful, suspicious, stubborn, socially assertive, adventurous, unconventional, non-submissive to authority; (4) *psychologically*, in tending to direct and concrete, rather than symbolic, intellectual expression, and in being less methodical in their approach to problems; (5) *socioculturally*, in having been reared to a far greater extent than the control group in homes of little understanding, affection, stability, or moral fibre, by parents usually unfit to be effective guides and protectors or, according to psychoanalytic theory, desirable sources for emulation and the construction of a consistent, well-balanced, and socially normal superego during the early stages of character development. While in individual cases the stresses contributed by any one of the . . . pressure-areas of dissocial-behaviour tendency may adequately account for persistence in delinquency, in general the high probability of delinquency is dependent upon the interplay of the conditions and forces from all these areas.

---

* Presented at XII International Course in Criminology, Hebrew University, Jerusalem, Israel, September 6 1962.

'In the exciting, stimulating, but little-controlled and culturally inconsistent environment of the underprivileged area, such boys readily give expression to their untamed impulses and their self-centred desires by means of various forms of delinquent behaviour. Their tendencies toward uninhibited energy-expression are deeply anchored in soma and psyche and in the malformations of character during the first few years of life' (pp. 281–82).

It will be observed that this statement contains no commitment either to an essentially constitutional or to an essentially environmental conclusion regarding the causation of delinquency. Yet certain sociologists insist that we have adhered to a strictly biologic (and even Lombrosian) explanation of all delinquency and have completely ignored the role of 'differential association' in delinquency and the role of the general culture of the times. Certain other critics, on the contrary, insist that we have ignored the biologic findings of *Unraveling* in favor of environmental influences, especially of the intra-family data regarding parent-child relationships which we used as the basis of a device for the early identification of potential delinquents (see Ch. 17 below).

It is necessary to emphasize, as an introduction to our latest research, *Family Environment and Delinquency*[245], that in *Unraveling Juvenile Delinquency* we made a commitment to pursue more deeply some of the clues uncovered in that work. It will be helpful to quote from *Unraveling* on this point:

'Some of the significant findings and implications of this type of research [we pointed out] can be determined only by detailed statistical intercorrelation of the specific factors of the various areas of study. Speaking generally, two types of correlation are called for: the binding together of disparate data *within any single field* or at any *single level* of the inquiry, and the *interrelation* of the pattern of most significant findings of *each area* with those of other areas. The former is necessary in order to sharpen the meaning of those factors whose ultimate significance can be seen more fully from their relative positions in an inductively patterned *cluster* of closely related elements; the latter is necessary because the order of causal sequence is more likely to be detected by intercorrelation of data from levels of varying depth or rigidity than it is by interrelation of data within any *one level*, and because *subtypes* can thereby be ascertained in terms of meaningful cross-relationships.

' . . . there are [other] facts derivable from *disparate* areas, a truer significance of which can be determined only by their

72

detailed interrelation. Indeed, the present tendency is more and more in the direction of abolishing sharp distinctions between body and mind, personality and culture—a trend reflected in the increasing employment of such concepts as "biosocial", "psychosomatic", "psychosocial", "sociocultural", and the like.' (pp. 284–85. Emphasis supplied.)

In pursuit of this general philosophy, we said that some of the more important questions which will concern us later in more detailed explorations of our materials are:

'What causal syndromes can be inductively arrived at and defined by means of correlation of the various factors within each level of the inquiry? What syndromes will emerge from a comparison of delinquents and non-delinquents on the basis of a breakdown into ethnico-racial groupings? Into somatotypes? Into age at onset of delinquency? Into kinds of home atmosphere in which the boys were reared? Into types of delinquent acts?' (p. 285.)

We went on to ask still other questions:

'What somatopsychic types will emerge from detailed cross-correlations between somatotypes and various characterial and personality traits? . . . What psychosocial types can be defined by detailed cross-correlations between character types (as determined by the Rorschach test) and fundamental social data, such as parent-child affectional relationships, different forms of disciplinary practices, and the like?' (p. 285)

We pointed out, additionally, that

'A host of subsidiary problems also awaits further exploration. For example, why is it that some of the factors often regarded by criminologists and clinicians as highly criminogenic do in fact *not* markedly differentiate our delinquents from the non-delinquents? How can we account for the numerous factors that have turned out to be neutral or "complacent"? What are the differentiating factors which account for the persistent delinquency of the boys included in this study and the non-delinquent behaviour of some of their brothers?' (p. 285. Emphasis supplied.)

Finally, we anticipated, in *Unraveling*, the need and value of introducing a *longitudinal* dimension, to improve perspective. We said:

'To round out the picture, it will also be necessary to determine the resemblances and differences between the delinquents and the non-delinquents as they reach early adulthood. Why do some of the delinquent boys abandon their antisocial behaviour while others continue in careers of crime? In what respects do those non-delinquents who later develop into delinquents differ from the rest of the non-delinquents?' (p. 285)

(In this connection, it might be mentioned that we have now completed a follow-up of the 500 delinquents and 500 non-delinquents of *Unraveling* to age 31–32.)

We think it will be generally agreed that it is far more difficult, and probably also more meaningful, to attempt answers to questions of the kind just raised than it is to indulge in the facile speculations involved in theory-building.

II

This being our point of view, how have we pursued it in studies subsequent to *Unraveling*?

First we carried out the research which led to the publication, in 1956, of the work called *Physique and Delinquency* [176]. In that inquiry we focused on one important aspect of the etiologic complex in delinquent behaviour—bodily morphology and certain of its accompanying traits. We pointed out, however, that preoccupation with the constitutional matrix in criminogenesis does not necessarily imply that we regard genetic influences as the *primary* forces making for delinquency. The relationship between body structure and delinquency-potential was merely one avenue of exploration among the many we had discovered in *Unraveling*. *Physique and Delinquency* did however show that certain physiologic, neurologic, and psychologic traits vary significantly in incidence among the somatotypes. It seemed reasonable to infer that such traits are closer to the constitutional than to the environmental border of a postulated biosocial continuum.

The isolation of the traits thus referrable to the constitutional end of the assumed biosocial continuum suggested the question of whether the remaining traits could definitely be assigned to the *sociocultural* border of the continuum; and, further, whether even among the group of traits found in *Physique and Delinquency* to vary significantly among body types, and therefore inferred to be essentially constitutional, there were some which were also markedly influenced by *environmental* factors. These and similar issues are

74

considered in our latest work, *Family Environment and Delinquency*, in which we also examine the complex problem of the *criminogenic* involvement of (*a*) the characteristics isolated as essentially constitutional (but not, of course, without some environmental involvement), (*b*) those isolated as essentially environmental, and (*c*) those characteristics in which Nature and Nurture appear to play relatively equal roles in criminogenesis.

But beyond this we looked into the influences of the social environment (dealing largely with parent-boy and sibling-boy relationships) on delinquent boys possessing certain traits. We discovered that certain traits, usually neutral in their influence on delinquency, may become delinquency-inducing when occurring in children reared in deleterious environments.

Let us now briefly summarize the major contributions of *Family Environment and Delinquency:*

(1) Certain inimical family influences during the first few years of life can affect development of delinquency in three ways: (*a*) by contributing to the formation of traits previously shown to be significantly associated with antisocial tendencies in children; (*b*) by rendering criminogenic some traits which, in the absence of such malign family influences, are usually neutral so far as delinquency is concerned; (*c*) some sociocultural factors operate to influence delinquent trends quite apart from the pressure of the physiologic, neurologic or psychologic traits previously found to be linked to delinquency.

(2) The influences of the home environment on delinquency operate *selectively* to propel toward antisocial maladjustment only those children characterized by specific traits which enhance their vulnerability. Some of these traits are essentially *constitutional* and therefore relatively rigid; and for these it is possible to reduce the hazard of delinquency by altering environmental factors. Other traits are essentially attributable to *sociocultural conditioning* and are therefore more plastic and modifiable. Those traits which result from essentially equal contributions of genetic endowment and environmental conditioning should respond in some measure to re-education of the individual, but both reconditioning and environmental manipulation would seem to be indicated where such traits are involved.

(3) Differential *contamination*, rather than 'differential association', is the generating core of the etiologic process in delinquency; and contamination depends not merely on exposure but also on *susceptibility* as opposed to *immunity*.

(4) A greater *specificity* of endeavor becomes possible on the findings of our new study. While not denying the importance of preventive and treatment programs taking account both of the total neighborhood and total person, it is also important that those engaged in the management of delinquency fix their sights on more specific targets in terms of criminogenic traits and their probable essential orientation.

In the light of these findings, we believe that *Family Environment and Delinquency* helps to illumine the hitherto unanswered question why only certain children become lawbreakers even in the most delinquent of areas, even from homes in which one or both parents are delinquent, and even from homes in which a brother or sister is delinquent.

Certainly the most important demonstration of the research is that social and cultural influences are not uniform in their impact on children, but *selective*. Two illustrations of this should suffice:

(1) It had been previously found, in *Unraveling,* that a significantly higher percentage of boys to whom the *father was unacceptable as a pattern of emulation* exists among delinquents than among non-delinquents. In *Family Environment and Delinquency* it was discovered that the impact of this emotional deprivation, on which so much of the building of character in childhood depends, is significantly greater on boys characterized by such traits as *stubbornness, uninhibited motor response to stimuli*, and *acquisitiveness*, to mention only a few traits which, in themselves, had been previously found to be significantly more common among delinquents in general than among non-delinquents. The obvious remedial approach would be to provide a substitute male adult model with whom boys with unacceptable fathers of their own might identify, such as a Boy Scout leader, an athletic director, or a man interested in various hobbies who also has a gift of understanding boys.

But such a person would be in a better position to deal effectively with a boy if he knew something of his criminogenic traits as well as their essential orientation. For instance, it would be helpful for the father-substitute to know that one of the traits linked to delinquency, *stubbornness*, does *not* vary among boys of the different body-structures; so that, as far as this particular trait is concerned, it makes little difference whether a boy is muscular and athletic (mesomorphic) or physically fragile (ectomorphic). But it would also be useful for the parent-substitute to know another fact; namely, that while a father's unacceptability as a pattern for emulation does not in itself contribute to the *formation* of the frequently criminogenic trait of stubbornness in his son, the presence of this trait does enhance the boy's *delinquency potential*.

On the other hand, the fact that a trait such as the tendency to *uninhibited motor response to stimuli is* of constitutional orientation should serve to encourage the substitute father to be concerned more with guiding his ward into socially acceptable uses of this tendency than with attempting to eradicate such a relatively fixed trait.

(2) One more illustration of the clinical as well as scientific relevancy of our newly uncovered knowledge of the *selective* impact of the environment on children having certain traits may be drawn from the influence of rearing by an *emotionally distorted* father on the delinquency of his son.

We discovered that rearing by such a father tends to develop certain characteristics in a son which were found in *Unraveling* to be much more frequent among the delinquents in general than among the non-delinquents. These traits include, to mention but a few, an excessive tendency to *flight into phantasy, marked dependency attitudes, preponderance of introversive trends*. It was, however, also established in *Family Environment and Delinquency* that the chances that a boy with an *emotionally disturbed father* would become a delinquent are *enhanced* if the boy has *feelings of inadequacy*. This last perhaps raises the exceedingly difficult problem of *temporal sequence* of trait and factor when the two are found to be significantly related. We have attempted to take this into account not only in examining the order of various traits and factors in point of time as recorded in our case-history sources, but in clinical reasoning, and have discussed this problem in some detail in *Family Environment and Delinquency*.[1]

[1] *Op. cit.*, pp. 18–20, where we say:

'. . . discovery of statistically significant associations between factors and traits does not throw light on the *nature* of the relationships. Whether the linkage is *directly* sequential, or *indirectly* so *via* another trait or factor, or whether the linked trait-factor is in turn the *product* of a prior factor-trait combination, is often very difficult to say. . . .

'One possible explanation of an association between factor and trait is that it reflects the more or less *direct influence of the factor upon the trait*; or, to put it differently, it is probable that such a trait would not exist (or would exist in a different form or degree of intensity) in the absence of the factor found associated with it. We refer to such factor-trait association as reflecting a *contribution* of the factor to the development of the trait.

'A second possible explanation of an association between factor and trait is a reversal of the above sequence; that is, the pre-existent trait in a boy serves as a stimulus to a more or less specific response of the human environment (father, mother, siblings). Here the social (environmental) factor is not necessary to the existence of the trait but is nevertheless associated with it because of the frequency with which the trait *attracts* the factor. We refer to such an association as 'reactive' (i.e. reflecting *a reaction* of the environment to a boy having the trait). (*Cont.*)

After indicating the intricacies involved in deriving meaning out of statistical intercorrelation, we say:

'All this is intended to remind the reader that association is not necessarily causation, and that much creative thought must *follow* the discovery of a statistically significant relationship between trait and factor. Readers with special professional competence in various relevant fields may not always agree with our interpretation of the meaning of one or another of the statistical patterns which are . . . analysed. Our aim is not only to answer but also to raise significant questions; we do not hesitate to "go out on a limb" when it seems, on the basis of a "feel" for and much reflection upon the raw materials, that the limb will probably bear the weight of our reasoning' (p. 20).

In concluding this brief presentation, there are two matters we should like to stress: one of these is that in *Family Environment and Delinquency* we deal with traits and factors *separately* instead of with *Gestalten* or inner-determined *patterns*; the other relates to our views of the role of theory in criminologic research. Regarding the first point, we are of course aware that the findings are incomplete because of a trait-by-trait, factor-by-factor analysis. But just as in the study of anatomy careful dissection is a first and indispensable step, so it is in the analysis of a social malady such as delinquency. But before we can arrive at *Gestalten*, we must try first to pinpoint the nexus of influence as reflected in *individual* factor-trait combinations. We are, in fact, already beginning a comprehensive inter-correlational analysis of the findings of *Family Environment and Delinquency* in order to determine (*a*) what clusters of social factors and of traits in combination most markedly distinguish true delinquents from matched non-delinquents, and (*b*) what clusters of factors and traits inductively differentiate groups of delinquents

---

'A third possible explanation of a significant association between factor and trait is that the *two are dynamically reciprocal in their influence*: given the trait, the factor is likely to follow; and given the factor, as a *response to the trait*, the trait is likely to be enhanced, crystallized, or deepened.

'As to the relationship between factors, traits and *delinquency* . . . still another dynamism may be involved: each element, standing alone, may not be sufficiently weighty to be reflected as an influence in the etiologic complex; but *together* they may be, either because the impact of the two (or more) combined is sufficient to make a telling difference in stimulating antisocial behaviour; or because the influence of one, say the trait, does not become *criminogenic* except in the presence of the other, the factor, as a sort of *catalytic agent*. Similarly, it is conceivable that the presence of a criminogenic trait can be counteracted by an *anti*-catalytic factor. In other words, an antisocial reaction can be either accelerated or retarded through the *simultaneous presence* of certain traits and factors.' (See also note 1, p. 19.)

from each other. This is the obvious next step in our search for a *typology* of delinquents.

As to the second issue—the role of *theory* in criminologic research (and this relates not only to *Family Environment and Delinquency* but to all our researches)—some critics insist that our investigations have not been guided by any unilateral theory.[2] Concern with establishing some all-unifying theory in Criminology has assumed almost obsessive dimensions among some researchers. We suspect that some of this is due to an attempt to justify the status of a particular discipline as truly 'scientific'. In *Unraveling* we made clear why we followed certain avenues of exploration—anthropologic, psychiatric, neurologic, psychologic, and social—the last with special emphasis on the *under-the-roof culture* of the home and on activities in the school. We also made it abundantly clear that we took extraordinary precautions to assemble and collate the raw materials of *Unraveling* (amounting, finally, to some 400 traits and factors), to verify the information, and to prevent contamination of a line of inquiry by one expert with the results arrived at by another expert on the same case. We regret that we are as yet not able to emerge with a single theory that will 'explain' all delinquency and crime; and there is, of course, the question whether this will ever be possible in view of the 'multitude of sins' and the varieties of acts embraced in the law's compendious concepts of 'delinquency' and 'crime'. We are searching for the relevant facts and will continue to do so, unimpeded, we hope, by the stranglehold of a vague, thin, and cloudy unilateral 'theory' of crime causation. We look upon *Family Environment and Delinquency* as only another step in the direction of our objective; in itself a difficult one to be sure, but even so only a step. And it is in this spirit that we propose to move ahead for some years to come.

[2] See Ch. 16 below, pp. 243–61.

PART II

Identification of Delinquents

CHAPTER 6

Predictive Techniques in the Prevention and Treatment of Delinquency *

SHELDON AND ELEANOR GLUECK

I. THE NATURE OF PREDICTIVE TECHNIQUES

Sheldon Glueck

IN 1955, at the Third International Congress on Criminology held in London and at the First United Nations Congress on Juvenile Delinquency in Geneva, a great deal of interest was shown in the possibilities of prognostic measures in the administration of justice. There is good reason for this. An effective predictive device would make the process of criminal justice more efficient and articulate. It would induce judges to think more in terms of the future results of the dispositions they make of the cases before them. It would furnish a helpful guide for their sentencing and paroling decisions by giving them a means of bringing objectified and organized past experience relevantly to bear on the individual case in determining which offenders might be expected to do well on probation, which are more suited to various forms of institutional control, how to deal with different types of recidivists. As Dean Roscoe Pound wrote in 1930, in an introduction to the first predictive study we published in *500 Criminal Careers*[26]:

'Study of the means of ensuring that the results of probation and kindred devices of individualized penal treatment may be made reasonably predictable is not merely in the right line of legal thought today, it is needed to save for us one of the really epoch-making discoveries of American legal history. Let it once be made clear that probation laws may be administered with a reasonable assurance of distinguishing between the sheep and the goats, let it be shown that the illusory certainty of the old system may be replaced by a regime of reasonably predictable results as compared with one of merely predictable sentence, and the paths of a modern penal treatment will be made straight' (p. 279).

* Paper presented at a joint meeting of the Family Court Probation Officers Training Institute of the Japanese Supreme Court and the Research and Training Institute of the Japanese Ministry of Justice, Tokyo, June 9, 1960. For a comprehensive discussion, see, *Predicting delinquency and crime*[212].

But predictive devices also have other values. Instead of speculating on numerous traits and factors that *might* be significant, they are built up only of those few traits and factors which have been found, in the systematic analysis of past experience, to be in fact most relevant to outcomes; they tend to focus the attention of the judge and probation officer on those facts in the make-up and background of the offender that are most necessary to cope with if his situation and behavior are to be improved. Out of the materials in a detailed case history, prediction tables provide the specific targets of therapeutic effort.

But not only do prediction devices help to structure case histories meaningfully; they also provide a rational means of narrowing the field of inquiry in the analysis of causation. Some device is necessary to render criminologic research more pointed, less sprawling, less intoxicated by the heady wine of some single favorite 'theory' which, instead of guiding research, may bias and blind it. Prediction tables are useful in this important way because they check on the results of experience with many hundreds of cases and, after a systematic relating of each trait and factor to outcomes in terms of successful or unsuccessful response to one or another form of peno-correctional treatment, they focus attention on those items that have been found to be operationally most relevant. By ameliorating conditions in respect to one or more of the predictive factors, improvement in behavior can be expected; and when this occurs we have proof that the predictive factors were significantly involved in causing the delinquency or recidivism we are trying to control.

But perhaps most important of all, prediction devices give promise of laying the foundation for a truly prophylactic and preventive approach to the problem of delinquency. Tables have been developed which are designed to identify potential delinquents at the age of five or six, when they first enter school and are first required to meet the test of coping with a code of rules of conduct laid down by an authority other than their own parents.

The idea behind them is a simple one. In the field of life insurance, the premiums are determined by a check-up on the relationship to longevity of such factors as age, various forms of disease, occupation and the like, as determined by a study of thousands of cases. Similarly, there is a significant relationship between various traits and factors of delinquents and pre-delinquents, on the one hand, and their subsequent behavior on the other. I will give you a few illustrations; others are given in Part II of this chapter.

In *Juvenile Delinquents Grown Up*[85] we presented the results of three five-year follow-ups in the history of many delinquents previously reported on in *One Thousand Juvenile Delinquents*[45]. As a result of systematic intercorrelation of numerous personal traits and environmental factors with the behavior of these delinquents during the fifteen years involved in the follow-up, it became clear that a certain group of factors bore a relatively high relationship to outcomes in terms of response to various forms of peno-correctional treatment.

For example, it was found that five factors—birthplace of father, discipline by father, discipline by mother, school retardation, and school misconduct—were so intimately tied in with success or failure on probation that they could be used in constructing a prediction table. As an illustration of one of these factors, the proportion of failures on probation in the case of boys whose paternal discipline had been *good* (that is, fair, firm, not lax or erratic, and not so strict as to arouse fear or antagonism) was only 16·7 per cent; on the other hand, the proportion of probation failures among boys whose fathers' discipline was *poor* (that is, extremely lax or extremely rigid, or erratic or leading to unrestrained freedom or antagonism to the point of rebellion) amounted to 62·9 per cent. Those in the *fair* paternal discipline group had a probation failure rate of 45·5 per cent, that is, one in between these two extremes. The other four factors also showed differences in incidence of probation failure according to the nature of the subcategory involved.

How is information of this kind useful in the construction of a prediction instrument?

By adding up the lowest 'failure score' possible on the five factors, on the one hand, and the highest on the other, the extremes of possible failure rates on probation were obtained, as based on a check-up of results in all cases. By establishing equidistant zones between these extremes, distributing the cases within these zones according to each person's status in respect to the five factors and his actual success or failure while on probation, and then converting the distributed figures into percentages, a predictive table was derived which indicates the combined impact of the influence of the five factors upon success or failure on probation. For example, by this method it was found that a boy scoring under 240 on the factors in question has more than an even chance of succeeding on probation without a suspended sentence. At the other extreme, a boy scoring 270 or over has very little chance of succeeding on probation.

A similar table was constructed showing chances of success or failure under each of the other forms of disposition: probation accompanied by suspended sentence, behavior in correctional schools, conduct in reformatories, conduct in prisons, behavior in jails and other short-term institutions, conduct on parole and, even, success or failure in the armed forces. Moreover, it was possible to introduce an age dimension.

How would a judge be aided in the proper disposal of an offender by the application of such prediction devices?

First, a probation officer would gather the necessary data on the individual case regarding each of the factors used in the construction of the tables, so that he could figure the particular offender's total scores in respect to each form of available treatment. The number of factors about which information has to be gathered for each case is not large because there is considerable overlap in the predictive factors of the various tables. A skilled investigator could assemble the necessary information and verify it in as brief a time as is at present required for an adequate probation officer's investigation and report. The scoring of each offender would require only a brief time.

Once the judge had the scores before him he could determine the particular form of treatment to which an offender of the type to which the delinquent belongs has the best likelihood of responding satisfactorily. He could also see at a glance not only what the probabilities are of the particular offender's ultimate reformation, but also within what age span he is likely to abandon his criminal career; or, if he is not likely to reform within the age span included in the follow-up study, whether he at least has a reasonable chance of becoming a minor offender.

Specifically, suppose the judge, upon consultation of the series of predictive tables, found that delinquent K, according to systematized past experience with other delinquents who in pertinent respects resembled K, has nine out of ten chances of succeeding on probation with suspended sentence, seven out of ten of acceptable behavior on probation without a suspended institutional sentence hanging over him, five out of ten of satisfactory behavior in a foster home, only four out of ten of getting along acceptably in a correctional school, only two out of ten of adjustment in a reformatory. Obviously, the judge would have very pertinent data in the light of which to individualize the case of K; that is, to discriminate scientifically among several alternatives and choose the one most promising in respect to the offender in question. Moreover, in the case of those delinquents whose traits and environmental factors forecast an equally black future irrespective of the type of existing treatment, there would be concrete data to suggest experiments with new forms of correctional therapy.

The judge's position is a very difficult one in this matter of sentencing. In the first place, he has little or no analyzed and objectified experience based on study of actual outcomes of correctional treatment as regards the *effects* of subjecting K to one or another form of sentence and treatment. Secondly, even the most sincere and able judge, devoting a good deal of time and thought to the problems of sentencing, is hampered by the paucity of methods of treatment. After all, the judge has only a few possibilities at his disposal: probation, discharge without supervision, imprisonment, and fines. Even if he gives a good deal of thought to each case, he may find his work less effective than he would like it to be, because of the few alternatives presented.

And yet judges can make vitally significant contributions to the development of a science and art of correction. The ingenious, inventive judge can encourage probation officers and peno-correctional administrators to experiment with a greater variety of treatment practices. Probation, for example, might be developed along three or four different lines in respect to intensity of supervision, prospective probationers being placed in different classes of probation dependent upon the treatment types to which they belong. So also the court might be furnished periodically with the institutional and parole histories of the offenders it has sentenced, in order to compare sentences with response to treatment.

By objectifying and organizing his experience, the judge can greatly improve his exercise of discretion in imposing sentence. By modifying these tables on the basis of further experiment, he can be doing truly scientific work beyond the daily task of imposing sentences.

For not only in the testing of existing *alternative* instruments of correctional treatment, but in developing new ones suitable to different treatment types, predictive tables might be of great value. Suppose it were found that four-fifths of delinquents with a well-defined syndrome of certain individual traits and social backgrounds fail to respond satisfactorily to *any* of the existing methods of correction. Suppose an experiment were then deliberately set up whereby an altogether new form of treatment is employed, or more intensive application made of an existing type, and it was then discovered that only half of the offenders with the designated traits and background failed to abandon their criminalistic activities during a reasonable test period. That would be a social demonstration of great value and would lead to definite improvement of treatment facilities.

I should now like to present an illustration of the importance of predictive techniques in another field; namely, as a screening device for the early discovery of *potential* delinquents, so that timely clinical

87

and social work might reduce the stream of boys flowing into the juvenile court. Let me first point out that in *Unraveling Juvenile Delinquency*[138], which is a wide-ranging research comparing a sample of 500 persistent delinquents with 500 true non-delinquents in respect to some 400 traits and factors involving body structure, health status, neurologic and psychiatric assessments, the Rorschach ('ink-blot') test, the Wechsler-Bellevue intelligence test, and intensive check-ups on the home, school, and neighborhood conditions, one of the most striking findings was that almost nine-tenths of the delinquents had already persistently misbehaved at the age of ten or younger. This shows how deeply rooted are the malformations of personality and character that have to be dealt with in courts, and usually at an average age of between thirteen and fourteen. Also it was shown in *One Thousand Juvenile Delinquents* (pp. 180, 276) that a difference in outcome was related to the length of time between the earliest onset of delinquency and court appearance plus examination in a clinic; in general, the less the time intervening between the boy's misbehavior and court-clinic intervention, the better the result. Society has too patently been neglecting the early danger signals of personality maladjustment and of criminality, in not providing adequate means of identifying children before they become overtly delinquent and in not providing adequate school-clinic facilities for the study and treatment of problem children.

That the early detection of potential delinquents is feasible has been strongly suggested by three prediction tables evolved in *Unraveling*. One is based on the five psychiatric traits that were found most markedly to distinguish delinquents from the control group of non-delinquents (adventurousness, extroversiveness, suggestibility, stubbornness, and emotional instability); a second is based on the five traits of character structure derived from the Rorschach Test—traits that were found to set off the delinquents from the non-delinquents most strikingly (social assertiveness, defiance, suspiciousness, destructiveness, emotional lability); the third, known as the Social Prediction Table, is based on five interpersonal family factors found to be of crucial potency in distinguishing delinquents from non-delinquents (discipline of boy by father, supervision of boy by mother, affection by father, affection by mother, and family cohesiveness). A high degree of interrelationship was established between these three predictive tables, the same boys forecast as delinquents or as non-delinquents in one of them being often also similarly predicted in one or both of the other two (see Chapter 7 below). However, thus far there have been opportunities to validate experimentally only the Social Prediction Table.

By validation is meant the testing of the actual efficiency of a prediction device by applying it to various samples of cases. Thus, it would have been more accurate throughout my prior remarks if, in describing the tables, I had referred to them as 'experience tables', since they reflect systematized experience with the cases on which they were constructed and do not deserve to be called prediction tables unless and until they have been applied to other samples of cases and found to work with a reasonably high degree of accuracy. The Social Prediction Table is undergoing stringent tests even in Japan. The results of such validating experiments will be briefly summarized in Part II of this chapter. I shall now describe the Social Prediction Table for the early discovery of potential delinquents.

In checking on the presence or absence of the five crucial factors (discipline of boy by father, supervision of boy by mother, affection of mother for boy, affection of father for boy, family cohesiveness) it was found that 71·8 per cent of the thousand boys included in *Unraveling* whose fathers were overstrict or erratic in their disciplinary practices turned out to be delinquent, compared with only 9·3 per cent of those whose fathers were firm but kindly. Those of lax discipline fell in between these extremes; but to simplify the exposition I shall omit the middle category. Of the boys whose supervision by the mother was unsuitable (that is, irresponsibly neglectful), 83·2 per cent were delinquents, whereas of those whose maternal supervision was suitable, only 9·9 per cent turned out to be delinquent. In respect to paternal affection, of all boys whose fathers were hostile or indifferent to them, 75·9 per cent became delinquents, whereas of those whose fathers were warm in affection, or even overprotective, only 33·8 per cent became delinquent. Similarly, as to the affection of the mother, 86·2 per cent of the boys whose mothers were hostile or indifferent became delinquent, compared to 43·1 per cent of those whose mothers were warm or overprotective. Finally, in respect to the fifth family factor included in the Social Prediction Table, *family cohesiveness*, 96·9 per cent of all boys who had been reared in unintegrated families were delinquent, and only 20·6 per cent of those brought up in cohesive families turned out to be delinquent.

By combining these conditioning factors in the early life of boys studied in *Unraveling*, it was possible to construct four-class, three-class, and two-class prediction devices, depending on the fineness of the instrument desired. In the three-class table, for example, a boy scoring under 250 on the five relevant factors has a very slight chance of becoming a delinquent; one scoring between 250 and 299 has little better than a 50–50 chance; and one whose destiny has been so loaded with adverse familial influences as to give him a score as high as 300 or more has a very great probability of becoming a delinquent.

All this is, of course, subject to the qualification that such an experience table based on our cases from the underprivileged areas of Boston, and comprising boys matched by age, global intelligence, and ethnico-racial derivation, will, when applied to other boys, prove to be a highly selective instrument. It is also subject to the qualification that although our study was made on boys of the average age of about fourteen and a half years, it will, hopefully, select potential delinquents at age five or six.

Thus far I have discussed the general idea of predictive devices and their possible usefulness in the administration of justice and in the screening of potential delinquents. Let me, in conclusion, anticipate some doubts and criticisms.

In 1955 I was general reporter on the topic of prognosis of recidivism, one of the five subjects discussed at the Third International Congress of Criminology in London. In that capacity I had to digest, organize, and comment upon numerous papers that were submitted to me by lawyers, psychiatrists, and criminologists from various parts of the world and to present a single report, which was then debated in the appropriate section meetings and at the plenary session. Among the most interesting matters found in these various papers were the objections to the use of predictive devices. I can do no better than to review those objections and to give my answers to them.

There are five main objections that have been levelled at prediction devices in the administration of justice and the prevention of delinquency:

1. Underlying predictive techniques, it is said, is the assumption of a deterministic, if not fatalistic, sequence of cause and effect in human affairs; and this supposedly does violence to the nobler conception of human action as the result of the exercise of a 'free will'.

2. It is claimed that predictive tables fail to take account of the fact of change in personal and social conditions, since they are, presumably, built on the assumption that the personal traits and environmental background factors will remain as they were when the tables were constructed.

3. Human conduct, it is pointed out, is the outcome of the dynamic interplay of numerous and complex influences of person and environment, but prediction tables can at best employ only a small number of these influences.

4. Since prediction tables deal with individuals as statistical types, they cannot, it is claimed, truly 'individualize', for, by treating the problem in the mass to start with, those who use the tables will perforce lose sight of the individual case, especially in respect to the more subtle and unmeasurable features of the personality observed in the clinical situation.

5. As to prediction tables designed to spot pre-delinquents in school before they overtly misbehave, it is urged that this could only result in an unfair labeling of innocent children.

I shall discuss these objections briefly.

1. Regarding the assumption behind predictive tables of an absence of freedom of will in human affairs, since it is impossible to measure the degree of free will which distinguishes recidivists from non-recidivists or potential delinquents from actual delinquents, this factor cannot practically be used in a prediction table. If other factors, which can be fairly well assessed, do in fact bear a high relationship to subsequent conduct, one may usefully employ them in a prognostic instrument without necessarily taking a position in respect to any particular view of human behavior. If anyone can develop a testing device to measure the extent of 'free will' in the individual case, in the sense of the degree of capacity for purposive self-direction, and if it can be demonstrated that variations in free will thus conceived bear a high relationship to behavior, such a trait can then be included in prediction tables.

2. As to the claim that prediction tables ignore fluctuations in conditions, it is true that such devices have to be modified from time to time to take account of changing situations; but this does not prevent their effective use during lengthy periods when conditions remain relatively stable. The methods of treatment by probation, commitment to industrial schools, incarceration in reformatories and prisons, and parole do not radically change in most jurisdictions over long periods. When changes do occur, the tables will, of course, have to be modified to take account of new experience.

3. Regarding the criticism that predictive methods cannot yield adequate prognoses because they take account of only a small sample of the numerous traits and factors leading to delinquency or recidivism, the fact is that they do provide a significantly high degree of predictability, as will be shown in Part II of this chapter when the workability of the tables thus far subjected to validation experiments is discussed. Indeed, as suggested at the outset, it is one of the merits of predictive devices that they narrow the field of

interest in decision making and therapy to the relatively few items most *relevant* to outcomes.

4. With regard to the point that prediction tables cannot individualize justice, this criticism springs from the misconception that judges, parole board members, and clinicians, by the use of such devices, should and will make their decisions mechanically and exclusively on the odds presented by the prediction tables. However the aim is not to substitute statistical tables for judicial or other experience in the sentencing, treatment, or release of offenders. It is rather to supply the judge and administrator with an instrument of prime importance in the work of individualizing justice. Neither a judge or a parole board member nor clinician should follow such tables blindly. They are designed to help in placing the individual offender in the perspective of organized experience with hundreds of other offenders who in certain crucial respects resemble him. As to some traits and factors, each offender, of course, remains a unique personality; but the dimensions of the special problems he presents can be much more accurately assessed by the judge or administrator if he compares the particular delinquent's crucial prognostic traits with the total picture of hundreds of other offenders than if he relies exclusively on unorganized experience or intuition. Although the opponents of parole prediction tables in Illinois, the only state I believe which thus far used them, feared that such devices would lead to mechanical parole selection, L.E. Ohlin, actuary and sociologist, has pointed out that 'the net result of the use of the tables has been to challenge the application of mechanical formulas at every point and to force more detailed examination of the unique merits of the individual case'.[1]

5. The fifth objection to prediction tables has to do with their employment as a screening device for the early spotting of delinquency-inducing influences in the case of young school children, on the ground that such identification will somehow taint and harm the children. But one may put the question whether it is better to allow delinquency-inducing influences to take their toll of youngsters until their maladjustment takes the form of overt delinquency than to detect these bad influences sufficiently early in life to do something about them that is not only constructive but timely.

One of the basic findings of our researches is the crying need for a *character prophylaxis*—the testing of children early and periodically to detect malformations of emotional and character development at

---

[1] Quoted in Prognosis of recidivism[173], p. 19.

a stage when the twig can still be bent. This is as necessary as are periodic medical examinations. The intricacies of the problem of delinquency, and a basic reason why so relatively little has been accomplished towards its solution, are demonstrated by the simple fact that when the child first begins to display aberrancies of conduct it is very difficult to say whether these are the true danger signals of future persistent delinquency or merely transient manifestations of a healthy trying of his wings. Bits of identical behavior may, at this early stage, be symptomatic of two divergent roads of future development. The deep-seated nature of the temperamental and characterial traits found to distinguish delinquents from non-delinquents, and the extremely early age at which delinquents first manifest marked difficulties in adjustment, should make us realize how absolutely essential it is for schools, particularly, to be equipped to discover potential delinquents before the trends of maladapted behavior become too fixed. For the schools are in a strategic position to note such marked deviations and difficulties of adaptation when the child enters school. With proper enlightenment of parents as to the prophylactic value of such early diagnosis, the prediction table can turn out to be of great value to parents, their children, and society as a whole.

The basic question remains: *Do predictive devices really work?* It is with this that Part II is concerned.

II. THE WORKABILITY OF PREDICTIVE TECHNIQUES
Eleanor T. Glueck

To the judge who has to make wise disposition of a particular youngster who stands before him, a predictive instrumentality is useful only if it helps in those cases in which he is uncertain about what to do in the given instance; or if it serves to reinforce the conclusion to which he has come regarding disposition of a case on the basis not only of a probation officer's investigation, but of his own mature and experienced judgment. Naturally, the only way in which judges can be really convinced of the merits of prediction tables as aids to the court (not as substitutes for them) would be to design esearch projects of their own that would involve:

1. Charting the probable behavior of an offender during various forms of peno-correctional treatment in accordance with our prediction tables.

2. Making disposition of cases without reference to the prediction tables.

3. Recording what the prediction tables point to about the merits of different forms of treatment.

4. Arranging for follow-up of the cases over several years.

5. Comparing the results of the treatment prescribed by the judge with what the prediction tables indicated as the likely outcome of the treatment given.

Judges and probation officers have the right to be skeptical about what appears to be a 'mechanical' kind of procedure, and are justified in not being content to accept the simple logic of such tables without proof that they work.

We have personally sought, and continue to seek, every opportunity to check our tables against other samples of cases. But before I discuss these efforts and the results to date, I would like to advert very briefly to the scope of the fifty-one tables we have constructed during our thirty-five years of research. Some deal with the prediction of recidivism of juvenile and adult male offenders; of adult female offenders; some with the probable behavior of juvenile and adult offenders during various forms of peno-correctional treatment; and some are designed to differentiate among very young offenders those who are likely to become persistent delinquents; and finally, to find among children not yet evidencing overt signs of antisocial behavior, preferably on entrance to the first grade in school, those who are potentially serious offenders.

Assuming (and this is a big assumption) that all or most of these tables will be successfully checked against other samples of cases, we should eventually have a network of predictive or screening instruments that, if properly applied, would increase the likelihood of more effective management of juvenile and adult offenders and reduce the danger to the public, now too often exposed to the depredations of offenders insufficiently rehabilitated and too soon released from intramural or extramural supervision. But, above all, the earnest use of such devices would stimulate experimentation with new forms of treatment, especially in those cases in which a predictive device indicates little likelihood of response to any of the available forms of peno-correctional treatment; and should serve as a special challenge in those cases in which it is shown that an offender is in the class which has just about an even chance of succeeding or of recidivating.

I have passed quickly over this series of tables because I want, in this chapter, to confine myself essentially to the ones which have a direct bearing on the problems faced daily by judges of juvenile courts and their associated peno-correctional authorities. Those who are interested will find all of our tables in *Predicting Delinquency and Crime*[212].

Among our fifty-one tables, those of special interest to officers of juvenile courts fall into two groups: 1. those which could be of aid in arriving at the most effective disposition of juvenile offenders who appear before a court, and 2. those designed to make possible early identification of children who are likely to develop into persistent delinquents unless suitable intervention occurs at a stage in life when preventive psychotherapy and community-wide preventive programs are most likely to bear fruit.

I want first to focus on a series of seven tables constructed from the cases in *Juvenile Delinquents Grown Up*[85]. In that volume we followed the boys, initially included in *One Thousand Juvenile Delinquents*[45], for fifteen years beyond the completion of the treatment prescribed by the Boston Juvenile Court. Out of these data, we were able to construct tables dealing with the probable conduct of juvenile offenders over fifteen years from the onset of their official criminal careers and covering their behavior during probation, probation under suspended sentence, in correctional schools, reformatories, prisons, and on parole.

In order to discover whether such tables really 'work', we began in the early 1940s, when taking on the 500 delinquent boys included in our study *Unraveling Juvenile Delinquency*[138], to apply to them this series of prediction tables from *Juvenile Delinquents Grown Up*, laying aside the predictive indications in each case pending follow-up of these boys, beginning with their first appearance in a juvenile court, through all their peno-correctional experiences (probation, probation with suspended sentence, correctional school, reformatory, prison, parole) until they were twenty-three years old. The results of this study are published in *Predicting Delinquency and Crime* (Ch. IV). This follow-up study covers 3,397 peno-correctional treatment periods. No effort was spared to trace the criminal careers of these 500 boys, and the predictions made for them years ago concerning their probable behavior during various forms of peno-correctional treatment have proven to be quite correct. Briefly, it has been found that of 380 *straight probation periods*, the predicted and the actual behavior was in agreement in 92·1 per cent of such periods; of 545 *periods on probation with suspended sentence*, agreement was found in 93·6 per cent; as to 1,053 *periods of parole*, the predicted and the actual result agreed in 91·9 per cent; of 1,054 *correctional school experiences*, agreement occurred in 78·8 per cent. As to *periods in*

95

reformatories and *prisons*, agreement was found in 73·1 and 75·6 per cent respectively.

In addition to determining the extent of agreement between the predicted and the actual behavior of the offenders *during* peno-correctional treatments, we have taken the opportunity which this inquiry provided to check a prediction table developed in *One Thousand Juvenile Delinquents*, designed to predict the behavior of offenders *at the end of a five-year follow-up span after treatment imposed by a juvenile court*, and presented in Appendix B of *Predicting Delinquency and Crime*. As applied to this group of offenders for the five-year period following the end of the first period of treatment in each case (and this was possible in 441 cases), it will be seen, by consulting Appendix C, Table 17 of *Predicting Delinquency and Crime*, that 435 offenders, or 98·6 per cent, were predicted as having more than an even chance of serious or persistent minor delinquency during the five-year period following the end of the first treatment period and that actually 419 of these 435 offenders, or 96·3 per cent, proved to be serious or persistent minor offenders in the five-year span.

The capacity of the seven tables to predict behavior during and following peno-correctional treatments is already clear. However, I should like now to give one illustration out of this study to demonstrate how prediction tables work:

Jimmy appeared before a juvenile court for the first time at the age of nine for evading fare, and the case was filed. At the age of twenty-six he shot and killed a man in a hold-up and is now serving a twenty-five-year prison sentence. Such a beginning and such an ending of a criminal career is an old tale.

I should like first to tell you what the prediction tables actually indicated in Jimmy's case. These were charted when Jimmy was first included in the group of 500 delinquents who are the subjects of *Unraveling* and before we had any knowledge of his criminal career. It is only subsequently that our field investigators followed Jimmy through his various correctional experiences from the onset of his criminal career (and without reference to the predictions, in the making of which they did not participate and to which they did not have access).

The prediction tables showed that:

1. The likelihood that Jimmy would continue to be a serious delinquent during a period of fifteen years following his first appearance in the juvenile court was very great.

2. The likelihood of his recidivating on probation or probation with a suspended sentence was great.

3. The likelihood of his making a reasonably good adjustment in a correctional school was small.

4. But the likelihood of his making a reasonably good adjustment in a reformatory was high.

5. The likelihood of his recidivating during parole was high.

What actually did happen to Jimmy?

1. On probation (of which he had three periods), on which he was predicted to have little likelihood of adjustment, the following happened: During his first probation, Jimmy stole, he truanted, he committed larcenies. During his second probation, this kind of behavior continued and, in addition, he became quite adept at sneaking into trains and movies. During a third probation he was no longer regular in reporting to his probation officer, his general attitude grew more and more uncooperative, his companions were almost wholly other delinquents.

2. On probation with suspended sentence (of which there were also three periods), on which he was predicted to have little likelihood of adjustment, the following happened: During his first probation with suspended sentence, he committed larcenies and subsequently truanted from school. During his second suspended sentence he was arrested for larceny. During his third suspended sentence he was frequently drunk, he truanted, he stole, he ran away from a temporary foster home, he committed burglaries.

3. During his sentence to a correctional school, where his likelihood of adaptation to the regime was predicted as slight, Jimmy ran away four times. (To suggest that he was a 'good' boy running away from a 'bad' school is to ignore the fact that Jimmy's record to date could hardly be considered that of a minor offender.)

4. During Jimmy's periods of confinement in a reformatory and one in a prison, where his adjustment had been predicted as satisfactory, actually he did behave very well. Such slight evidences of maladapted behavior as did occur were negligible. For instance, he was once found to have a dirty room, and on another occasion to be gambling with a few other inmates, but certainly there was no evidence of any serious maladaptation in either of these institutions.

5. During the one parole period he had before he was twenty-three, which was from a reformatory (and beyond which we did not follow him), he recidivated as predicted (he was often drunk, he stole cars, he ran into at least five cars, he frequently changed jobs without permission of his parole officer).

From the series of prediction tables, therefore, Jimmy's conduct had been accurately charted. The findings are particularly tragic in the light of the fact that had our Social Prediction Table (from *Unraveling*) been applied when Jimmy was six years old and before he was showing any serious signs of maladapted behavior, it would have indicated that he fell into the group of youngsters whose likelihood of becoming a serious delinquent was very high. Perhaps at that stage in his life preventive action could have been taken more readily to stem his development into a criminal.

We would not presume to tell judges and probation officers what they might have done in this case on the basis of the predictive tables. We can only suggest that the likelihood of recidivism was so great and the dangers to others from Jimmy's depredations so obvious, that to ignore the indicators seems short-sighted. Immediate commitment to an institution, with intensive treatment, would have been the only recourse justifiable in the light of what the prediction tables revealed. The fact that Jimmy ran away so often from the correctional school would appear to mean that this kind of institution, at the early age at which commitment was necessary, would not be suitable for him. This obviously indicates that treatment within the institution had to be more individualized. Eventually, in his early adulthood, the boy could (and actually did) adapt himself quite well in reformatories and prisons.

Now I turn to a prediction table already mentioned in Part I that has quite another purpose, and is directed toward the early screening of children in order to find those who are potentially serious delinquents. Those who are court officers have an interest in such a table because, if applied to an offender appearing in court, it can be of aid in determining whether, despite his commission of a relatively 'minor offense', he is potentially a serious offender, or *vice versa*.

If, as parents and as citizens, as well as court officers, you are concerned about the *prevention* of delinquency, you will be interested in the evidence that this same prediction table applied to children not yet adjudicated as delinquent, and even not yet showing outward signs of antisocial behavior, has the capacity to discover the children who are likely to become serious offenders. This clearly has great promise as a beginning for crime preventive efforts, as is evident also from the experiments which are being carried on in the United States and Japan.

It will not be amiss to repeat the factors which constitute the Social Prediction Table, although they have already been mentioned in Part I—*supervision of boy by mother, discipline of boy by father, affection of mother for boy, affection of father for boy,* and *cohesiveness of family.*

What evidence, you may well ask, do we have that such tables work?

The Social Prediction Table has been subjected to much testing, and other checks are in process. I refer you to two articles of mine for part of the story of testings of this device to identify delinquents, 'Spotting Potential Delinquents: Can It Be Done?'[182] and 'Efforts to Identify Delinquents' (Chapter 8 below). See also Chapter 7, note 5, below.

Now to the question at issue:

Would not a network of predictive devices help juvenile courts in determining what to expect of a particular child and what to do for him in order (1) to avoid peno-correctional treatments that are not promising in his case; (2) to protect society from the depredations of a particular child who does not show likelihood of responding to any of the current forms of peno-correctional treatment; (3) to develop new treatment resources for those children for whom the present treatment methods are not indicated; and (4) in general, to tighten up a much too loose and uncoordinated system of juvenile justice which still makes possible the simultaneous serving of sentences imposed by two or more different courts (as actually occurred in Jimmy's case) and the repeated imposition of sentences that are unlikely to bear the desired fruit, at least unless, and until, the quality of the peno-correctional treatment is improved?

The question is worth considering.

I would hope that what little I have been able to say at least arouses your interest in the possible usefulness of predictive techniques. The time is not far distant when juvenile court judges will be able, if they so wish, to add to their personal experience in the handling of juvenile offenders, the objectified and tested experience derived from hundreds of cases similar to the ones with which they deal.

We certainly do not wish to leave you with the impression that even if prediction tables were extensively applied the juvenile delinquency problem would be much nearer to solution; for it is one thing to have a guide to treatment and quite another to carry out *effective* treatment. It is our hope, however, that further validations of the prediction tables will spur much-needed research into the treatment process especially as it concerns preventive psychotherapy.

The major value of predictive devices is that they force us to focus on the relevant and they sharply point up the need for the strengthening of currently available treatment facilities and for the establishment of more effective ones.

And may I say, finally, that the use of an instrument or a treatment can be no more effective than the skill of the people who apply it.

CHAPTER 7

Early Detection of Future Delinquents

SHELDON AND ELEANOR GLUECK

IN *Unraveling Juvenile Delinquency*[138] we presented for consideration three tables on the basis of which we believe it should be possible to select from among young boys (at school entrance) those who will probably become persistent delinquents unless timely and effective intervention can divert their predicted course of maladapted behavior into socially acceptable channels. One is based on five social factors that sharply differentiate the delinquents from the control group of non-delinquents (supervision of boy by mother, discipline of boy by father, affection of mother for boy, affection of father for boy, and unity of the family group); a second on five traits of character structure derived from the Rorschach test (social assertion, defiance, suspiciousness, destructiveness, and emotional lability); and a third on five traits of temperament as determined by psychiatric interviews (adventurousness, extroversion in action, suggestibility, stubbornness, and emotional instability).[1] These tables show a high association between the relevant factors and the likelihood of delinquency or non-delinquency—a potentiality that (as will be indicated below) is already being converted into a high probability through the test of a series of experimental checks on other samples of cases.

As our 'weighted score' method of constructing the tables is fully reported in *Unraveling* (Ch. XX), as well as in our other works,[2] there is no need to describe it in any detail here beyond pointing out that the five predictive factors comprising a particular table were initially selected from among those showing the widest range of difference in incidence between the 500 delinquents encompassed in *Unraveling* and their 500 matched non-delinquents. The percent of delinquents existing in each subcategory of a factor provided the basis for constructing a 'total weighted score' derived from summating the individual scores on the subcategories of all five factors in which a particular boy is placed. The table itself was derived by distributing

---

[1] Titles of tables from *Unraveling* have been slightly modified.

[2] *500 criminal careers*[26], pp. 278–96; *One thousand juvenile delinquents*[46], pp. 185–90; *Five hundred delinquent women*[44], pp. 284–98; *Later criminal careers*[71], pp. 134–44; *Juvenile delinquents grown up*[85], pp. 199–234; *Criminal careers in retrospect*[102], pp. 215–83; *After-conduct of discharged offenders*[119], pp. 63–73.

all the delinquents and all the non-delinquents (for whom their status on all five factors was known) into 'weighted score classes'. Assuming validation on other series of cases, the incidence of the delinquents and non-delinquents within each 'weighted score class' expresses the likelihood of delinquency for individuals falling in that 'score class'. Whether or not such a table has applicability to samples of different composition (in respect, for example, to ethnic make-up or economic status) awaits practical demonstration.

Before presenting the tables, we set down the five social factors under consideration, the five traits of character structure, and the five traits of temperament, with their 'weighted scores':

SOCIAL FACTORS	*Weighted Score*
1. DISCIPLINE OF BOY BY FATHER	
Overstrict or erratic	72·5
Lax	59·8
Firm but kindly	9·3
2. SUPERVISION OF BOY BY MOTHER	
Unsuitable	83·2
Fair	57·5
Suitable	9·9
3. AFFECTION OF FATHER FOR BOY	
Indifferent or hostile	75·9
Warm (including over-protective)	33·8
4. AFFECTION OF MOTHER FOR BOY	
Indifferent or hostile	86·2
Warm (including over-protective)	43·1
5. COHESIVENESS OF FAMILY	
Unintegrated	96·9
Some elements of cohesion	61·3
Cohesive	20·6

TRAITS OF CHARACTER STRUCTURE

1. SOCIAL ASSERTION	
Marked	75·9
Slight or suggestive	63·8
Absent	39·7
2. DEFIANCE	
Marked	91·0
Slight or suggestive	76·7
Absent	34·9
3. SUSPICION	
Marked	67·3
Slight or suggestive	47·3
Absent	37·5 *(Cont.)*

101

	Weighted Score
4. DESTRUCTIVENESS	
Marked	77·7
Slight or suggestive	69·9
Absent	35·7
5. EMOTIONAL LABILITY	
Marked	75·2
Slight or suggestive	65·0
Absent	40·0

TRAITS OF TEMPERAMENT

1. ADVENTUROUSNESS	
Present in marked degree	75·3
Not prominent or noticeably lacking	35·4
2. EXTROVERSION IN ACTION	
Present in marked degree	66·5
Not prominent or noticeably lacking	37·8
3. SUGGESTIBILITY	
Present in marked degree	69·4
Not prominent or noticeably lacking	35·5
4. STUBBORNNESS	
Present in marked degree	83·4
Not prominent or noticeably lacking	39·0
5. EMOTIONAL INSTABILITY	
Present in marked degree	62·0
Not prominent or noticeably lacking	26·5

The 'prediction' tables derived from these three sets of data appear as *Table I*, *Table II*, and *Table III*.

TABLE I

PERCENT OF DELINQUENTS AND NON-DELINQUENTS IN EACH OF FOUR WEIGHTED SCORE CLASSES BASED ON FIVE FACTORS OF SOCIAL BACKGROUND[*][3]

Weighted Score Class	Percent of Delinquents in Each Score Class		Percent of Non-delinquents in Each Score Class		Total
	No.	%	No.	%	
Under 200	24	8·2	269	91·8	293
200–249	40	37·0	68	63·0	108
250–299	122	63·5	70	36·5	192
300 and over	265	89·2	32	10·8	297
Total cases	451		439		890

[*] *Unraveling*, Table XX–3, p. 262.
[3] Titles of tables from *Unraveling* have been slightly modified.

TABLE II

PERCENT OF DELINQUENTS AND NON-DELINQUENTS IN EACH OF FOUR WEIGHTED SCORE CLASSES BASED ON FIVE TRAITS OF CHARACTER STRUCTURE DERIVED FROM RORSCHACH TEST*

Weighted Score Class	Percent of Delinquents in Each Score Class		Percent of Non-delinquents in Each Score Class		Total
	No.	%	No.	%	
Under 205	21	14·7	122	85·3	143
205–254	79	38·9	124	61·1	203
255–279	32	64·0	18	36·0	50
280 and over	134	87·9	18	12·1	152
Total cases	266		282		548

* *Unraveling*, Table XX–7, p. 264.

TABLE III

PERCENT OF DELINQUENTS AND NON-DELINQUENTS IN EACH OF FOUR WEIGHTED SCORE CLASSES BASED ON FIVE TRAITS OF TEMPERAMENT DERIVED FROM PSYCHIATRIC EXAMINATION*

Weighted Score Class	Percent of Delinquents in Each Score Class		Percent of Non-delinquents in Each Score Class		Total
	No.	%	No.	%	
Under 220	34	10·4	294	89·6	328
220–244	74	43·0	98	57·0	172
245–269	51	63·0	30	37·0	81
270 and over	311	87·4	45	12·6	356
Total cases	470		467		937

* *Unraveling*, Table XX–11, p. 266.

Examination of the distribution of the delinquents and non-delinquents in each weighted score class in the three tables tends to indicate that their capacity to differentiate between delinquents and non-delinquents is quite similar (see note 8).

Thus far only the table based on five social factors (the Social Prediction Table, as it has come to be known) has been put to the test, largely in retrospective application on various samples of delinquents (and in one instance of non-delinquents also) of different background from those on which the table was initially constructed. As these validations are fully reported elsewhere,[4] there is no need to elaborate here beyond pointing out that the above-mentioned table could have correctly 'spotted' as potential delinquents about 90 per cent of each of the samples of delinquents, had it been applied when the boys in question were only six years old. A more definitive test is now in process, however, to determine whether the discovery of potential delinquents in a first-grade school population on the basis of the Social Prediction Table actually proves by follow-up of a substantial group of boys, not yet delinquent, that it can successfully differentiate potential delinquents from true non-delinquents at the early age of six.[5]

In order to make adequate comparison possible between the Social Prediction Table and others about to be presented that are based on various combinations of factors and traits from all three tables, it is necessary to set down a more detailed distribution by score classes than was done in *Table I*.

Now we proceed to make various combinations of factors from among the fifteen that comprise all three tables on a group of 424 boys out of the 1,000 in *Unraveling* (205 delinquents and 219 non-delinquents) in whose cases data on all the fifteen factors and traits were available.[6]

The first of these combined tables incorporates the five social factors and the five traits of temperament (derived from psychiatric examination) and results in the distribution seen in *Table V*.

Comparison of *Table V* with *Table IV* suggests that the differen-

[4] B. J. Black & Selma J. Glick (1952), *Predicted vs. actual outcome for delinquent boys* (New York: Jewish Board of Guardians); R. E. Thompson (1952), A validation of the Glueck social prediction scale for proneness to delinquency. *J. crim. L. Criminol. & Police Sci.*, 43, No. 4. *Predicting juvenile delinquency* (1955). Research Bulletin No. 124 (Trenton, N.J.: State Department of Institutions & Agencies). A summary of findings of these reports and of certain as yet unpublished studies is to be found in 'Status of Glueck prediction studies' [183]. See also Chapter 8 below.

[5] Since the above was written, a ten-year follow-up of the boys has yielded very gratifying results. See Maude Craig and Selma J. Glick (1963), Ten years' experience with the Glueck Social Prediction Table, *Crime and delinquency* (publication of the National Council on Crime and Delinquency, 44 East 23 Street, N.Y. 10), 9, 249. Another follow-up, including boys and girls referred by teachers to a school clinic in Washington, D.C., because of various maladjustments, has also established the usefulness of the Social Prediction Table. See C. D. Tait, Jr. and E. F. Hodges, Jr. (1962), *Delinquents, their families, and the community*, Springfield, Ill., Thomas. See also E. F. Hodges, Jr. & C. D. Tait, Jr. (1963), A follow-up study of potential delinquents, *The American Journal of Psychiatry*, 120, No. 5. Another definitive report on the Washington experiment, Identifying delinquency-prone children, by Nina B. Trevvett, is scheduled to appear in *Crime and Delinquency* in 1965. This confirms the earlier conclusion.

[6] All the computations were checked by William H. Angoff, Princeton, New Jersey.

TABLE IV

PERCENT OF DELINQUENTS AND NON-DELINQUENTS IN EACH OF SEVEN
WEIGHTED SCORE CLASSES BASED ON FIVE FACTORS OF SOCIAL BACKGROUND*

Weighted Score Class	Percent of Delinquents		Percent of Non-delinquents		Total
	No.	%	No.	%	
Under 150	5	2·9	167	97·1	172
150–199	19	15·7	102	84·3	121
200–249	40	37·0	68	63·0	108
250–299	122	63·5	70	36·5	192
300–349	141	86·0	23	14·0	164
350–399	73	90·1	8	9·9	81
400 and over	51	98·1	1	1·9	52
Total cases	451		439		890

* *Unraveling*, Table XX–2, p. 261.

TABLE V

PERCENT OF DELINQUENTS AND NON-DELINQUENTS IN EACH OF SIX WEIGHTED
SCORE CLASSES BASED ON FIVE SOCIAL FACTORS AND FIVE TRAITS OF
TEMPERAMENT

Weighted Score Class	Percent of Delinquents		Percent of Non-delinquents		Total
	No.	%	No.	%	
250–399	2	1·7	115	98·3	117
400–449	9	20·5	35	79·5	44
450–499	19	34·5	36	65·5	55
500–549	36	60·0	24	40·0	60
550–599	37	86·0	6	14·0	43
600–799	102	97·0	3	3·0	105
Total cases	205		219		424

tiation between the delinquents and the non-delinquents is not
heightened by the addition of the five traits of temperament to the
five social factors. The quite uniform reciprocal tendency in the
percentage of delinquents and non-delinquents within the score
classes is clearly evident.

We turn now to *Table VI* based on the five social factors and the five traits of character structure (derived from Rorschach test).

Although *Table VI* appears to reflect a slightly greater differentiative capacity than *Table IV*, it cannot be said that it is so much more discriminative that its substitution for the table based on only five social factors is warranted.

Considering next a table omitting the five social factors, and combining the five traits of temperament with the five character traits, *Table VII* shows that these ten traits are no more discriminative than the one based on the five social factors alone.

TABLE VI

PERCENT OF DELINQUENTS AND NON-DELINQUENTS IN EACH OF SIX WEIGHTED SCORE CLASSES BASED ON FIVE SOCIAL FACTORS AND FIVE CHARACTER TRAITS

Weighted Score Class	Percent of Delinquents		Percent of Non-delinquents		Total
	No.	%	No.	%	
300–399	3	2·4	125	97·6	128
400–449	10	21·3	36	78·7	46
450–499	27	40·9	39	59·1	66
500–549	31	58·5	22	41·5	53
550–649	89	89·9	10	10·1	99
650–799	58	100·0	0	0·0	58
Total cases	218		232		450

TABLE VII

PERCENT OF DELINQUENTS AND NON-DELINQUENTS IN EACH OF SIX WEIGHTED SCORE CLASSES BASED ON FIVE TRAITS OF TEMPERAMENT AND FIVE TRAITS OF CHARACTER STRUCTURE

Weighted Score Class	Percent of Delinquents		Percent of Non-delinquents		Total
	No.	%	No.	%	
350–399	2	3·6	54	96·4	56
400–449	17	16·8	84	83·2	101
450–499	35	38·0	57	62·0	92
500–549	41	70·7	17	29·3	58
550–599	52	91·2	5	8·8	57
600–749	58	96·7	2	3·3	60
Total cases	205		219		424

Next we turn to *Table VIII* in which all fifteen factors and traits are incorporated.

Comparison of *Table VIII* with *Table IV*, in which only the five social factors are utilized, shows it similarly differentiates the delinquents and non-delinquents.

Next we consider *Table IX* in which two social factors (supervision by mother and cohesiveness of family) are combined with two traits

TABLE VIII

PERCENT OF DELINQUENTS AND NON-DELINQUENTS IN EACH OF SIX WEIGHTED
SCORE CLASSES BASED ON FIVE SOCIAL FACTORS, FIVE TRAITS OF TEMPERAMENT,
AND FIVE TRAITS OF CHARACTER STRUCTURE

Weighted Score Class	*Percent of Delinquents*		*Percent of Non-delinquents*		*Total*
	No.	*%*	*No.*	*%*	
450–649	5	3·6	134	96·4	139
650–699	6	14·6	35	85·4	41
700–749	18	36·0	32	64·0	50
750–799	28	71·8	11	28·2	39
800–849	26	83·9	5	16·1	31
850–1099	122	98·4	2	1·6	124
Total cases	205		219		424

TABLE IX

PERCENT OF DELINQUENTS AND NON-DELINQUENTS IN EACH OF SIX WEIGHTED
SCORE CLASSES BASED ON TWO SOCIAL FACTORS, TWO TRAITS OF TEMPERAMENT,
AND ONE TRAIT OF CHARACTER STRUCTURE

Weighted Score Class	*Percent of Delinquents*		*Percent of Non-delinquents*		*Total*
	No.	*%*	*No.*	*%*	
100–149	3	3·8	75	96·2	78
150–199	9	11·8	67	88·2	76
200–249	20	31·2	44	68·8	64
250–299	75	65·2	40	34·8	115
300–349	66	95·7	3	4·3	69
350 and over	42	100·0	0	0·0	42
Total cases	215		229		444

of temperament (stubbornness and adventurousness) and one trait of character structure (defiance). They were selected because they distinguish delinquents from non-delinquents more markedly than do the others.

Although *Table IX* appears to be more discriminative than the one based on five social factors, there is insufficient difference between them to justify the application, in ordinary practice, of the Rorschach test and psychiatric examination to arrive at a sum total of predictive potency just as readily attained by the table made up of the five social factors only.

To experiment still further, we eliminated from the above group of factors and traits the one derived from the Rorschach test (defiance) and constructed a table based on the four remaining items.

In *Table X* the result varies so little from the discriminative capacity of *Table IX*, based on five social factors alone, that there would appear to be no need to resort to Rorschach tests and psychiatric examinations for the purpose of selecting potential delinquents.

TABLE X

PERCENT OF DELINQUENTS AND NON-DELINQUENTS IN EACH OF FOUR WEIGHTED SCORE CLASSES BASED ON TWO SOCIAL FACTORS AND TWO TRAITS OF TEMPERAMENT

Weighted Score Class	Percent of Delinquents		Percent of Non-delinquents		Total
	No.	%	No.	%	
100–149	17	6·5	244	93·5	261
150–199	67	40·4	99	59·6	166
200–249	98	66·7	49	33·3	147
250 and over	243	94·5	17	5·5	260
Total cases	425		409		834

The social factor table, already shown to be a valid instrument by several retrospective and two crucial prospective applications of it to series of cases differing in make-up from the original sample on which it was constructed, now awaits only further applications to other groups of six-year-old boys at the point of school entrance.[7] At the present writing, although the boys are as yet only in the third grade, 50 per cent of those found to be 'potential delinquents' are already manifesting obvious behavioral difficulties in school as con-

[7] See note 5 above.

trasted with 8 2 per cent of those predicted as non-delinquent. This as yet very limited 'follow-up' appears to suggest the effectiveness of the table.

In order to determine whether a statistical analysis would yield results confirming those presented above, we asked Dr William H. Angoff of Princeton, New Jersey, to compute correlation coefficients between the tables and between each table and delinquency. It will be observed that his results do tend to confirm our interpretations.[8]

[8] Statement prepared by Dr William H. Angoff: 'All figures given below are based on the group of 424 cases (205 delinquents and 219 non-delinquents) for whom all information necessary to compute these statistics was available.

'Finally, there are the correlations of the sum of the two Social plus two Psychiatric factors (I–4) and also the two Social plus two Psychiatric plus one Rorschach factor (I–5) against the criterion of delinquency. The index I–4 correlates ·681 with delinquency; I–5 correlates ·722 with delinquency. Comparison of the figures with those in Tables I and II shows these two to be intermediate in their diagnostic power; I–4 is about as valid as the Social index alone, which is the most valid of the three basic indexes. The index I–5 yields a still higher correlation, but not as high as any index-composite which contains Social. Nevertheless, it should be recalled that I–4 and I–5 consist of only four and five factors and the composites consist of ten and fifteen factors. It is noted that I–4 and I–5 even yield higher validities than the ten-factor composite of the Psychiatric plus Rorschach.

TABLE I

INTERCORRELATIONS AMONG PRIMARY DIAGNOSTIC INDEXES AND CRITERION OF DELINQUENCY

$N = 424$

	Social	Psychiatric	Rorschach	Delinquency
Social	—	·461	·410	·682
Psychiatric	·461	—	·442	·610
Rorschach	·410	·442	—	·542
Delinquency	·682	·610	·542	—

TABLE II

CORRELATIONS OF COMBINATIONS OF INDEXES WITH DELINQUENCY

$N = 424$

Sum of Indexes	Correlation of Composite with Criterion	Multiple Correlation with Criterion
Social plus Psychiatric	·755	·759
Social plus Rorschach	·740	·740
Psychiatric plus Rorschach	·675	·681
Social plus Psychiatric plus Rorschach	·781	·783

(Cont.)

Since Angoff's statistical analysis confirms our findings that combinations of factors involving social plus psychiatric data, social plus Rorschach data, or all three sets of data combined, yield only a slightly better relationship to the criterion of delinquency than that attained either by the three separate sets of data or by the Social Prediction Table alone, it does not appear that the increment in efficiency is great enough to warrant a recommendation that Rorschach tests and psychiatric skills be utilized in 'screening' or 'spotting' potential delinquents. This is especially true in view of the fact that less training is required to become adept in the gathering and classification of social factors than in the application and interpretation of Rorschach tests or the making of psychiatric examinations and assessments.

We are therefore satisfied to recommend the use of the Social Prediction Table rather than those based on Rorschach or psychiatric data; and we look forward to its development as a large-scale screening device which will not only make possible early 'case finding' but will lead the way to early preventive therapy.

'Note in *Table I* that the Social, Psychiatric, and Rorschach indexes correlate ·682, ·610, and ·542 respectively with delinquency. The Social index alone identifies delinquents better than does the Psychiatric index, and that better than the Rorschach index. Thus, if we were restricted to the use of only one index, we would choose the Social index. If we were restricted to the use of only two indexes, we would choose the Social and Psychiatric and omit the Rorschach. Note also that the three indexes are not entirely independent measures, since they correlate to some extent among themselves. Social vs. Psychiatric: ·461; Social vs. Rorschach: ·410; Psychiatric vs. Rorschach: ·442. Nevertheless, while the contribution of each index to the identification of delinquency is not independent of the contribution of the other two, each index does add something unique to the identification. For that reason, the contribution of all three together is greater than that of any one or two alone, as will be shown below.

'*Table II* gives the correlations of the indexes with the criterion when the indexes are taken in combination. The first column of figures gives the correlations with delinquency of each composite taken as a simple sum of the indexes. The second column of figures gives the correlations with delinquency of each composite taken as an optimally weighted sum of the indexes, to yield maximum (multiple) correlation with the criterion. Comparison of the two columns, row by row, reveals that the multiple correlations with the criterion are not appreciably higher than the correlations of index-composites with the criterion. By this we learn that there would be no advantage to weighting one index more heavily than another in order to achieve high correlations.

'A comparison of the first three figures in *Table II* (either of the two columns) with the last column of *Table I* shows that in every case the sum of the two indexes is a better index than either one taken alone. For example, the composite of the Social and Psychiatric indexes yields a higher correlation (·755) with the criterion than does either the Social (·682) or the Psychiatric (·610) separately. Also, the composite of the three indexes yields a higher validity (·781) than the composite of any two. It is also of interest to note that the Social index *alone* correlates higher with the criterion than the composite of Psychiatric and Rorschach.'

CHAPTER 8

Efforts to Identify Delinquents

ELEANOR T. GLUECK

IN *Federal Probation* (September 1956) appeared an article by the writer entitled 'Spotting Potential Delinquents: Can It Be Done?'[182] In this article a description was given of what is now called the *Glueck Social Prediction Table for Identifying Potential Delinquents,* and the findings of several retrospective applications of this Table were briefly summarized. As the device approaches validation, interest in it is becoming greater and, although experimentation must continue, this seems an appropriate time to summarize the efforts to check it, especially as the chapter in *Predicting Delinquency and Crime*[212] entitled 'Checkings of Table Identifying Potential Delinquents' was prepared at an earlier stage and does not, therefore, incorporate the most recent attempts to check the Table.

The purpose of the predictive instrument is to distinguish at school entrance those children who are and those *who are not* in danger of developing into persistent offenders. (It is equally important to identify the latter, especially in high-delinquency areas.) Its purpose is also to distinguish delinquents from pseudo-delinquents and non-delinquents among those already manifesting behavioral difficulties.

The Table, first published in *Unraveling*[138], derives from a comparison of 500 persistent delinquents and 500 non-delinquents matched by age, intelligence, ethnic origin, and residence in depressed areas of Boston.

The Social Prediction Table, which is one of four predictive instruments based on the findings of *Unraveling,*[1] comprises five factors in the family background (affection of mother for boy, affection of father for boy, discipline of boy by father, supervision of boy by mother, family cohesiveness), found in *Unraveling* markedly to differentiate delinquents from non-delinquents. As it was learned in *Unraveling* that half the delinquents had shown their first overt signs of antisocial behavior before age eight, and 90 per cent at ten

---

[1] A second predictive device grew out of differences in the character structure of delinquents and non-delinquents (ibid. pp. 263–64), a third from the temperamental differences between them (ibid. pp. 264–65), and a fourth from differences in their response to certain intelligence tests (published in *Predicting Delinquency and Crime*, p. 239).

111

or younger, it was necessary to limit the selection of differentiative factors to those clearly operative in a child's life prior to the time he might evidence the earliest signs of maladaptive behavior. (The interested reader is asked to refer to *Unraveling*, pp. 259–60, and to *Predicting Delinquency and Crime*, pp. 23–31, for a description of the method of constructing the Table.)

A predictive table is, strictly speaking, only an 'experience' table until it has been successfully applied to other samples of cases. For this reason, checkings on many and varied samples need to be made. During the period of the earliest efforts to check the device, attention was largely focused on determining the extent to which it would have been possible by retrospective application of the Table to already adjudicated delinquents and also to non-delinquents to have correctly identified them at age five or six as the persistent offenders or the non-offenders they actually turned out to be.

The wisdom of ascertaining to what extent the predictive cluster (derived from the comparison of 500 persistent offenders in Boston and 500 matched non-delinquents) is present in many and varied samples of cases should be self-evident. The search for 'causes' of delinquency (by which is here meant *persisting* antisocial behavior) may be narrowed, should the predictive cluster of factors be found present in great measure in other samples of already persistent offenders differing from the original sample in age, ethnic origin, intelligence level (and so on). Their far greater presence in delinquents and their far lesser presence in non-delinquents should lend confidence to their significance for a clearer understanding of certain aspects of the causation of delinquency.

RETROSPECTIVE STUDIES PREVIOUSLY REPORTED IN *Federal Probation Quarterly*

Seven retrospective studies were reported on between 1952 and 1957. The first study was made by Black and Glick of the Jewish Board of Guardians on 100 delinquent boys at the Hawthorne-Cedar Knolls School.[2] The second was by Richard E. Thompson,[3] on 100 boys originally encompassed in the well-known Cambridge-Somerville Youth Study.[4]

The third check-up on cases other than the ones on which the

[2] B. J. Black & Selma J. Glick (1952), *Predicted vs. actual outcome for delinquent boys* (New York: Jewish Board of Guardians).

[3] R. E. Thompson (1952), A validation of the Glueck social prediction scale for proneness to delinquency. *J. crim. L. Criminol. & Police Sci.* 43, No. 4.

[4] E. Powers & Helen Witmer (1951), *An experiment in the prediction of delinquency* (New York: Columbia Univ. Press).

Table was based, was made by the New Jersey State Department of Institutions and Agencies, on fifty-one parolees;[5] the fourth by clinicians of the Douglas A. Thom Clinic for Children in Boston on fifty-seven 'antisocial' young children.[6] A fifth check by Thompson comprised fifty boys who had appeared in the Boston Juvenile Court in 1950 and fifty girls committed by the Boston Juvenile Court to the care of the Massachusetts Youth Service Board during 1954–5.[7]

In the sixth study Selma J. Glick and Catherine Donnell applied the Table to 100 unmarried mothers,[8] and in still another Miss Glick applied the table to eighty-one boys from upper-income families ($7,500 a year and over).[9]

This completes the roster of *retrospective* applications of the five-factor Social Prediction Table as reported in the article 'Spotting Potential Delinquents: Can It Be Done?'

In most of these inquiries, it was found that in nine out of ten instances the offenders involved would have been correctly identified at age six as potentially persistent offenders; and in the few remaining investigations a slightly lesser result was derived. It is of particular significance that in the first of the two studies by Thompson it was ascertained that true *non-delinquents*, even though evidencing behavioral difficulties in school (thought by teachers and clinicians to be prodromal of delinquency), were correctly identified by the Table in 91·3 per cent of instances. (This is in contrast with 58·7 per cent, 53·5 per cent, and 56·9 per cent of correct predictions by three clinicians charged with selecting boys for the Cambridge-Somerville Youth Study.) It is to be noted also that in the study of unmarried mothers (the first application of the Table to girls) evidence began to suggest that the predictive instrument might be applicable to girls as well as boys.

PROSPECTIVE STUDIES PREVIOUSLY REPORTED IN
Federal Probation Quarterly

In addition to a résumé of retrospective studies, the writer made brief mention of two ongoing projects of a different nature, in which

[5] *Predicting juvenile delinquency* (1955), Research Bulletin No. 124 (Trenton, N.J.: State Department of Institutions & Agencies).

[6] E. N. Rexford, M. Schleifer & Suzanne T. Van Amerongen (1956), A follow-up of a psychiatric study of 57 antisocial young children. *Ment. Hyg.* 196.

[7] R. E. Thompson (1957), Further validation of Glueck social prediction table for identifying potential delinquents. *J. crim. L. Criminol. & Police Sci.* 48, No. 2.

[8] Selma J. Glick & Catherine Donnell (1952), Background factors in 100 cases of Jewish unmarried mothers. Presented in part (section on prediction omitted) in *Jewish soc. Serv. Quart.* 29, No. 2.

[9] Letter of 31 May 1956.

the identification of true delinquents and true non-delinquents was being attempted before clear evidence of their status was apparent—one, an investigation set up in 1953 by the New York City Youth Board in two public schools in very high delinquency areas where the Table was being applied to all first-grade boys shortly after school entrance, that is, roughly at age six; the other called the Maximum Benefits Project initiated in 1954 under the auspices of the Commissioners' Youth Council of the District of Columbia in two elementary schools in very high delinquency areas and including girls as well as boys (179 children) already manifesting severe behavioral difficulties in school.

In the New York City Youth Board inquiry the objective is to determine whether and to what extent the Social Prediction Table, if applied even before clear signs of antisocial behavior, will serve to distinguish on the basis of *subsequent* evidence the true delinquents in a high delinquency area, from the non-delinquents; while in the Maximum Benefits Project the purpose (among others) is to determine whether the Social Prediction Table, if applied to children reported by teachers as already showing evidences of severe behavioral difficulties, will correctly differentiate, as determined by subsequent follow-up, the potential delinquents from the pseudo-delinquents. Both inquiries are still in process and will, it is hoped, continue until all the subjects are seventeen. A brief résumé of the findings to date will be given below.

FURTHER RETROSPECTIVE STUDIES IN THE UNITED STATES

Subsequent to the appearance of 'Spotting Potential Delinquents: Can It Be Done?' (1956) several other retrospective checkings of the Social Prediction Table were made—one at the Thom Clinic in Boston where Dr Virginia Clower applied the Table to 100 boys 'chosen at random for a wide variety of behavior and emotional difficulties' who had been referred to the Clinic during 1953 and 1954. The results showed that of thirty-one boys in this group who had been diagnosed by the clinicians as 'antisocial characters', all 'without exception' were placed by the Prediction Table in the group having a high likelihood of persistent delinquency. Later the Clinic, continuing its experimental application of the Social Prediction Table, again reported a consistently high degree of correlation between the clinical diagnoses and the rating by the Social Prediction Table:

'Our impression is that the Scale almost invariably gives high scores to the child with aggressive, destructive behavior problems, whether these problems are seen in an individual with an anti-social character formation, neurosis or psychosis. The work we have done so far suggests a positive correlation between the ability of the child to manage aggression and his score on the Glueck scales. That is, the less tendency to act out aggressive impulses, the lower the score.'[10]

In 1957, Selma J. Glick applied the Prediction Table to a small group of boys who were independently diagnosed by the clinical staff of the Jewish Board of Guardians as true delinquents on intake into the Clinic and she found that the Table itself, 'without psychiatric and psychological studies of the children would have properly identified the same cases'.[11]

Still another retrospective study completed since the publication of 'Spotting Potential Delinquents' encompassed twenty-eight inmates of Sing Sing Prison who had been juvenile offenders. In this were involved a team of researchers at the Post-Graduate Center for Psychiatric Research headed by Bernard Glueck, Jr., and the findings presented at the Third International Congress of Criminology in London (1955) by Isa Brandon. The prisoners included rapists, men committing sexual assaults, heterosexual pedophiles, homosexual pedophiles, and nonsexual offenders. Coauthored by Bernard Glueck, Jr. and Isa Brandon, the report stated that, regardless of offense, 71 per cent of the men would have been correctly identified by the Social Prediction Table in their early years as headed for criminal careers; and that 90 per cent of the 'nonsexual' offenders would have been correctly identified.[12]

Also during 1957, the South Shore Courts Clinic of Quincy, Massachusetts, which was set up by the Massachusetts State Department of Mental Health and charged with the study and diagnosis of children referred by the local Juvenile Court, applied the Table to fifty young offenders in an effort to determine its usefulness to clinicians. The results of the pilot study were sufficiently encouraging to the research director, J. I. Hurwitz, to suggest the possibility that the Table may be of aid in differentiating between true delinquents and accidental offenders.

The above constitutes a brief résumé of American retrospective studies applying the Social Prediction Table that have come directly to the writer's attention.

[10] Letter from Dr Eveoleen N. Rexford, Director, Douglas A. Thom Clinic for Child Guidance, dated 16 May 1957.

[11] Letter of 17 May 1957.

[12] Unpublished paper presented at the Third International Congress of Criminology, London, September 1955.

In addition to the actual applications of the Table, diverse inquiries about it reflecting widespread interest have come, for example, from police departments (notably the Juvenile Aid Bureau of the New York City Police Department); from school systems in different parts of the United States, including Rochester, Denver, Los Angeles, and Tacoma; from school counselors; family service societies; youth authorities (notably the Southern Reception Center for Children of the State of California); from institutions for young children, including schools for retarded children; from child guidance clinics; from mental hospitals; from Community Chests and Councils; Governor's Committees on Children and Youth; child psychiatrists, psychologists, pediatricians, ministers; and, more recently, from a nursery school training center.

RETROSPECTIVE STUDIES IN FOREIGN COUNTRIES

Some checkings of the Social Prediction Table have been attempted also in foreign countries, notably in Japan and France. A third is in the planning stage in Belgium.

In addition have come expressions of earnest interest in a means for early differentiation between potential delinquents and true non-delinquents from England, Holland, Germany, Sweden, India, Israel, Australia, New Zealand, Uruguay and other South American countries. And world-wide interest is reflected in a resolution adopted by a vote of 260 to 10 at the Third International Congress of Criminology held in London in September 1955:

'Because of the close relationship between recidivism and early delinquency, it is advisable to encourage the development and use of prognostic devices, including predictive tables, in the prediction of early delinquency. . . . That an indispensable aspect of any improved prognostic technique is the validation of the predictive methods on samples of cases other than those on which they were developed in order to transform them as far as possible into effective instruments for prognosis.'[13]

It is noted in the Program of the Third International Penal and Penitentiary Congress of the Spanish American countries, which was held in Lisbon in the summer of 1960, that the Fifth Section was to be devoted to *'Pronostics Criminologiques'*:

[13] *Summary of proceedings*, Third International Congress of Criminology, London 1955. Published by the British Organizing Committee on behalf of the International Society for Criminology, 1957. (See pp. 222–23. Conclusion of Section IV.)

'Le choix de ce sujet dérive de la décision adoptée par le II° Congrès pénal et pénitentiaire de Sao-Paulo qui recommandait comme sujet de travail du prochain Congrès l'étude de l'examen médico-psychiatrique, psychologique et social des délinquants, spécialement en ce qui concerne les délinquants par habitude.'[14]

(a) Japan

Japanese interest in a means for the early identification of potential delinquents is especially keen, and is manifested not only by the recent organization of a Criminology Study Society within the Ministry of Justice, a major effort of which is devoted to prediction studies, but also by the publication of a 200-page book in Japanese by a public prosecutor and a psychiatrist, entitled *Introduction to the Glueck Prediction Method*.[15]

The first of the Japanese attempts to apply the Social Prediction Table was made by Tokuhiro Tatezawa, probation officer of the Yokohama Family Court, on thirty delinquents appearing before a juvenile court in Morioka, Japan, and a control group of thirty non-delinquent boys from a public school in the same neighborhood.[16]

The application of the Table appears to have been successful, because 87 per cent of the delinquents and 92 per cent of the non-delinquents were correctly identified by the Social Prediction Table. This first retrospective Japanese checking assumes particular significance in the light of the marked cultural differences between Japanese and American delinquents and non-delinquents:

'This prediction study revealed that the factors used in the Gluecks' prediction table show rather high predictive power when applied to the Japanese juvenile cases which have their own cultural and social background' (p. 30).

Subsequently, other inquiries were made in Japan, and some are still under way:

'Our Criminology Study Society has been successfully carrying out a series of studies for the validation of Glueck Social Prediction Scales. A Progress Report on one of these studies revealed that the Social Prediction Scale would have successfully detected 92 per

[14] For Program, see *Revue de science criminelle et de droit pénal comparé*, Paris, Oct/Dec. 1959, Nouvelle série, No. 4, p. 915.

[15] Haruo Abe & Kokichi Higuchi (1959), *Introduction to the Glueck prediction method* (Tokyo: Ichiryusha).

[16] Tokuhiro Tatezawa (1956), *A study of prediction of juvenile delinquency* (Mimeographed by Ministry of Justice, Japan, and distributed by the Criminology Study Society).

cent of 70 persistently delinquent juveniles, had it been applied to these cases as early as when they were nine years of age'[17]

(b) France

An ongoing study in Strasbourg, France, was initiated in 1958 by Professor Jacques Léauté of the Institut de Science Criminelle of the Faculty of Law of the University of Strasbourg, and is being carried on in cooperation with M. Didier Anzieu (Professor of Psychology and Head of the Institut Psycho-Pedagogie of the University of Strasbourg,) Dr René Oberlé (psychologist at the Centre d'Observation of the Juvenile Court in Strasbourg), and Dr Berge (Head of the Institut Psycho-Pedagogie of the Lycée Claude Bernard, Paris). They made a pilot study in 1958, applying the Social Prediction Table to forty-six delinquents at the Centre d'Observation de Délinquants Juvénile in Strasbourg and found that 91·4 per cent of these boys would have been correctly identified as potential delinquents had the prediction table been applied to them at the age of six. It is of special interest that the psychologist, M. Oberlé, who was charged with the details of the study, was initially skeptical of the ability of the Prediction Table to identify the delinquents but is now convinced of its validity.

Encouraged by the result of the pilot project, Professor Léauté and his co-workers applied the Table early in 1959 to two additional groups of offenders totalling 203 boys, one group being already adjudicated delinquents and the other, though never arrested, was brought before the juvenile court by their parents on complaint of incorrigibility. Of the 140 delinquents in the first group, 89·9 per cent would have been correctly predicted as potential delinquents at age six; while of the sixty-three boys in the second group, almost all were identified as potential delinquents.

A comparison of the findings regarding the incidence of the five predictive factors among the French delinquents and pre-delinquents with those of the 500 delinquents of *Unraveling* (on the basis of which cases the Social Prediction Table was constructed) is of interest:

In *Unraveling*, 27·9 per cent of the mothers of the delinquents were found to be indifferent or hostile to the boys as compared with 46·4 per cent of the French delinquents and 49·2 per cent of the French pre-delinquents; as regards *affection of father*, 59·8 per cent of the fathers of our delinquents of *Unraveling* were found to be indifferent or hostile to them, as compared with 75 per cent of the

---

[17] Letter from Haruo Abe, Public Prosecutor, Ministry of Justice, 21 November 1958. Additional studies have been reported (all confirmatory) since the completion of this article.

fathers of the French delinquents and 69·8 per cent of the fathers of French pre-delinquents; as regards *supervision by mother*, it was unsuitable in 93 per cent of the cases of 500 delinquents of *Unraveling*, as compared with 95·7 per cent of the French delinquents and 93·7 per cent of the French pre-delinquents; in regard to *discipline by father*, it was other than firm and kindly in 94·3 per cent of the 500 delinquents of *Unraveling* as compared with 100 per cent of the French delinquents and 98·4 per cent of the French pre-delinquents; finally, as regards *family cohesiveness*, the family was not completely cohesive in 84 per cent of instances among the 500 delinquents of *Unraveling* as compared with 95·7 per cent of the French delinquents and 98·4 per cent of the French pre-delinquents.[18]

(c) Interest in Other Foreign Countries

A study to test the usefulness of the Table is now being formulated in Brussels by Professor Aimée Racine of the University of Brussels, director of the Centre d'Etude de la Délinquance Juvénile with a subsidy from the Belgian Ministry of Justice. This study has the support of the Secretary-General of the Ministry, M. Paul Cornil, and of M. DeCant, Public Prosecutor, as well as of the Ministry of Public Health (especially of its Conseil Supérieur de la Famille, the Chairman of which was, until recently, Professor Fernand Collin of the Law Faculty of Louvain University, and who is largely responsible for initiating interest in a prediction validation project in Belgium).

'It is our intention to prepare a motion to be submitted to the Conseil Supérieur, in which we request the Government to give first priority to the study of the detection of possible delinquency among Belgian youth' (letter of 28 January 1958).

There are other significant evidences of interest in foreign countries in the early identification of potential delinquents which might be mentioned. For example, in Holland, Professor Willem Nagel of the Criminological Institute of the University of Leiden has been charged with the preparation of a report to the Dutch Ministry of Justice on the possible uses of prediction tables in Holland. This is a

[18] Findings reported to the author in July 1958 in Strasbourg, and in June 1959 in Paris by Professor Léauté and some of his co-workers and supplemented by a letter from Professor Léauté, 25 February 1960. As regards the incorrigible boys, in accordance with Article 375 of the French Civil Code (1 September 1945), a parent or guardian may, if a child is unmanageable, request the judge of the juvenile court to examine into the situation. Article 376 requests that the judge make an investigation and that he may for this purpose order that a child be held in an observation center (already adjudicated delinquents may also be held in such a center). The incorrigibles are regarded as pre-delinquents and the results of the application of the Social Prediction Table have indeed proved them to be such.

119

complete survey of predictive theories and devices, including a description of the Glueck Prediction Tables. The Dutch Ministry of Justice is now engaged in determining next steps in the application of such devices.

In Germany, Judge Wolf Middendorff of Freiburg/Breisgau has prepared a Report for the German Ministry of Justice on American and European Prediction Studies, in which considerable space is given to the Social Prediction Table. In India, D. V. Kulkarni, Chief Inspector of the Certified Schools in Bombay, and Chinnea Doraiswami, Deputy Inspector General of Prisons and Correctional Schools of India, have each expressed the hope that they might develop some experimental applications of the Social Prediction Table. From New Zealand, Henry Field, professor of educational psychology of Canterbury University College in Christchurch, wrote in February 1957:

'I am satisfied that this work of prediction is of fundamental importance and that it points the way to successful measures of prophylaxis and prevention.'

In July 1956, a report on juvenile delinquency in Australia, prepared by the Advisory Committee to the Honorable Chief Secretary of Victoria[19] indicates that 'research in this field should be undertaken in Victoria with the objective of ascertaining the extent to which, and the the manner in which, these methods may be properly used here.'

These are a few illustrations of the far-flung interest in a means for identifying delinquents and for experimenting with the Social Prediction Table.

PROJECTS DIRECTED TOWARD THE IDENTIFICATION OF POTENTIAL DELINQUENTS

I return now to two ongoing experiments in which the Social Prediction Table has been applied:

1. by the New York City Youth Board to 224 boys in the first grade of two schools in high delinquency areas of New York City, in advance of, or without knowledge of, any overt signs of antisocial behavior, in order to determine the extent of ultimate agreement between predicted and actual delinquency or non-delinquency.

---

[19] Report of Juvenile Delinquency Advisory Committee to The Honorable A. G. Rylah, M.L.A., Chief Secretary of Victoria, The Honorable Mr Justice John V. Barry of the Supreme Court of Victoria (Chairman): Printed at Melbourne, 17 July 1956. See p. 32 *et seq.*, *Prediction Studies.*

2. by the Maximum Benefits Project, to 179 boys and girls in all grades of two elementary schools in high-delinquency areas in the District of Columbia referred to the Project staff by teachers as manifesting severe behavioral difficulties. Among the questions raised in this inquiry is the extent to which the behavioral symptoms are indeed prodromal of future delinquency according to the Prediction Table when checked against the later behavior of the children.

Both inquiries are still in progess and it is hoped will continue until the youngsters are seventeen. Meanwhile, the New York City Youth Board has briefly reported in January 1960 that 'follow-up' data covering a seven-year period are available on 223 of the initial sample of 224 boys who are now $12\frac{1}{2}$ to 13 years old and scattered in 89 different schools: Of 186 boys predicted at school entrance as *non-delinquents*, 176, or 94·6 per cent, are still *non-delinquent*; of 37 boys predicted as delinquents, 13 are already adjudicated delinquents and 4 more are 'unofficial' offenders, a total of 46 per cent; of 191 boys who are still non-delinquents, regardless of how predicted, 176, or 89·7 per cent, had been correctly predicted as non-delinquents; of 27 boys already delinquents, 17, or 63 per cent, had been correctly predicted as delinquents. (The latest findings are given in Chapter 13 below.)

In considering these interim results, it should be kept in mind that the boys are only now approaching the peak years of delinquency and arrest. It is essential that the follow-up continue until they are seventeen, since it was found in *Unraveling* (App. A, p. 294) that about half of the 500 Boston delinquents did not make their first court appearance until they were between thirteen and sixteen years old.

As regards the Maximum Benefits Project, a preliminary report issued in 1958 states that 'the Glueck criteria . . . have proved in our opinion to be a very effective predictive device'.[20]

In a later interim report it is stated that of fifty-eight children already having police or court records four years after the beginning of the study, fifty-seven had been previously identified by the Social Prediction Table as potential delinquents. 'Since the average child still has 5·9 years to go before reaching 18, and since the incidence of juvenile court appearances increases in the teenage group, we are inclined to think the percentage will draw near expected levels.'[21]

And a more recent summary of the Project made in preparation

[20] E. F. Hodges, C. D. Tait, Jr., & Nina B. Trevvett (1958), *Preliminary report of the Maximum Benefits Project*, made to the Eugene & Agnes E. Meyer Foundation, p. 18.
[21] Hodges, Tait, & Trevvett (1960), *Preliminary report*.

for the 1960 White House Conference on Children and Youth now stresses that 'the Glueck scores, in conjunction with the teacher referrals, appear to be effective tools in the identification of potential delinquents'.[22]

More recent findings have been reported by the New York City Youth Board[23] and the Maximum Benefits Project. See 'Ten Years' Experience with the Glueck Social Prediction Table' by Maude M. Craig and Selma J. Glick, in *Crime and Delinquency*, July 1963; and C. D. Tait, Jr. and E. F. Hodges, Jr., *Delinquents, Their Families, and the Community* (1962).[24] See also a later report by Drs. Hodges and Tait, 'A Follow-Up Study of Potential Delinquents' in the *American Journal of Psychiatry*, November 1963. A still later report of the Maximum Benefits Project is scheduled to appear in *Crime and Delinquency* in 1965 under the title 'Identifying Delinquency-Prone Children' by Nina B. Trevvett, Executive Director of the Commissioners' Youth Council.[25] These reports establish the validity of the Social Prediction Table.

For interim steps in perfecting the Table, which now comprises three instead of five factors, see Chapters 9 and 10 below.

GENERAL TREND OF FINDINGS

The accumulated evidence thus far gathered from 'retrospective' and 'prospective' studies both in the United States and in foreign countries all seems to be tending in the same direction. A total of eighteen inquiries in which the Social Prediction Table has been applied are all suggestive of its usefulness. The studies include four samples of non-delinquents (the latter incorporated into the first of the two investigations by Thompson in 1954, in the New York City Youth Board study, in the Maximum Benefits Project, and in the first of the Japanese inquiries); three studies include girls (the second Thompson study, the study by Glick and Donnell of 100 unmarried mothers, and the Maximum Benefits Project).

The results thus far indicate that regardless of ethnic origin, color, religion, intelligence level, residence in urban or rural areas, economic level, or even sex, the predictive cluster is very potent, not only on American but on Japanese and French samplings.

[22] E. F. Hodges, C. D. Tait, Jr., & Nina B. Trevvett (1960), 'Four Years of Work with Problem Children in the Elementary Schools,' *District of Columbia Committee for the 1960 Golden Anniversary White House Conference on Children and Youth*, Part I, Reports of Project Studies (Washington, D.C.) p. 67.

[23] 79 Madison Avenue, New York 16, N.Y.

[24] Springfield, Ill., Charles C. Thomas, Publisher.

[25] 321 D Street, N.E., Washington, D.C.

The Table has to date been applied to some 1,600 young children and adolescents—preponderantly males—in three American States (Massachusetts, New Jersey, and New York) and the District of Columbia, and in two foreign countries (Japan and France), each time with highly encouraging results. This does not mean that my husband and I, who are responsible for the construction of this device based on 500 delinquents and 500 matched non-delinquents of *Unraveling*, are satisfied that it is beyond the stage of testing. We urge that checkings continue and that careful record be kept of the work done.

The instrument appears to hold promise not only for the identification of emotionally healthy potential delinquents, but also for the identification of neurotic, psychotic, or psychopathic children who are likely to give overt expression to their conflicts in aggressive behavior. Some gleanings of the capacity of the Table to identify this latter group of potential delinquents come from the experiments with it in the Thom Clinic by Rexford, Van Amerongen, and Schleifer[26]; by Glick at the Jewish Board of Guardians; and in the study of twenty-eight cases at Sing Sing Prison.

The Table also holds promise of distinguishing among children already manifesting behavior difficulties those who are and who are not likely to develop into persistent offenders.

RESOLUTION OF DIFFICULTIES IN APPLYING TABLES

A pioneer venture must to some extent proceed by trial and error, and the one of checking even a carefully constructed predictive device is no exception. Difficulties have emerged in the course of the experimental use of the Social Prediction Table that could not have been fully anticipated, and this has provided an invaluable opportunity to find ways of coping with them.

A device of this kind, the use of which is in part at least based on observational skills and the capacity to make judgments on data gathered from home interviews as well as from already recorded data in the files of social agencies, police, probation departments, and other repositories of information about children and their families, is naturally subject to pitfalls. It has become abundantly clear that the difficulties stem from variations in the training and experience of those applying the Tables (psychiatrists, social workers, psychologists, and others) as well as from occasional inadequacies in

[26] See Eveoleen N. Rexford (1959), Antisocial young children and their families. Reprinted from *Dynamic psychopathology in childhood*, edited by Lucie Jessner & Eleanor Pavenstedt, pp. 186–220, especially 197–200 (New York: Grune & Stratton).

data. Questions have arisen, for example, as to the particular sub-category of one or another of the five factors into which to place a case. Likewise, there have at times emerged disagreements among different investigators in the same inquiry about the rating of some factors, especially *affection of parents for a child* which psychoanalytically oriented observers interpret in accordance with Freudian depth psychology and others on the basis of *surface* manifestations of parental affection. In addition to the difficulties encountered in the rating of parental affection, is the rating of *discipline by father* (as well as *affection of father*) in instances in which the father or a father-substitute had never been a part of the family group, or left the home before the child was three years of age. Still another difficulty relates to the assessment of *family cohesiveness* in instances in which chilldren were reared solely by the mother or mother substitute.

These and similar considerations led us to investigate the possibility that the rating of one or another of the five factors could be dispensed with in instances in which the data appeared insufficient for purposes of making an accurate judgment, or was altogether lacking. This was accomplished with the aid of the Research Bureau of the Harvard Business School (which had on punch cards for each of the thousand cases of *Unraveling* the five factors comprising the original Table). Correlations were systematically pursued between the total scores for the five factors (affection of mother for boy, affection of father for boy, supervision by mother, discipline by father, and family cohesiveness) and every possible combination of 4, 3, and 2 factors, eliminating those combinations in which the coefficient of correlation was less than ·90. Actually, the coefficients were found to range from ·932 in a Table made up of two factors to ·987 in a Table made up of four factors. (The interested reader is invited to examine *Predicting Delinquency and Crime*, Appendix B, Tables IX–1 to IX–1e, pp. 233 to 235, for all possible combinations of four and fewer factors that nevertheless retain a very high predictive potential.)

In instances in which the five-factor Table cannot be used, one or another of the shorter Tables should meet any problem reflected in the course of the validation efforts, except those arising from lack of sufficient training in gathering and interpreting the needed data. Some illustrations of how the shortened prediction Table would meet the problems that have been revealed in the course of attempts to check the Social Prediction Table against various samples of cases might be helpful. For example, the inconsistency of ratings of *affection of mother* or *affection of father* by workers of differing 'persuasions' has been eliminated by confining the scoring in certain instances to

124

the three remaining factors (supervision by mother, discipline by father, and family cohesiveness). The coefficient of correlation between the three-factor total scores and the total scores for the five factors is ·961. To those who may conclude that the elimination of these factors implies that they are not potent in the etiology of delinquency, the writer wishes to emphasize that this is not the case; for these two factors were found in *Unraveling* markedly to differentiate delinquents from non-delinquents. It is rather to be stressed that the remaining three factors reflect parental affection and it is for this reason that the fewer number of factors have been found in the original sample to be as potent as the greater number in differentiating between persistent delinquents and true non-delinquents.

The problem of rating *discipline by father* in a situation in which he has not been part of the family group since a child was three years old is met in turn by the use of a two-factor Table (supervision by mother, family cohesiveness), the coefficient of correlation between the total scores and those for the two factors being ·932 in the cases included in *Unraveling*. And the rating of *family cohesiveness* in instances in which one of the parents, usually the father or a father-substitute, has not been an integral part of the family group since the child in question was three years of age is met by considering the relationship between mother and children as 'cohesive' if the ties between them are close and warm, rather than rating such a situation as having only some elements of cohesiveness by reason of a father's absence. Our attention was particularly directed to this clarification because in both the Youth Board and the Maximum Benefits Projects this kind of family pattern, rarely present in the cases of *Unraveling*, emerged in a particular ethnic group that had not been there included.

By reducing the burden of data-gathering and increasing the accuracy of the rating of cases, the Social Prediction Table becomes more usable and more efficient. Certainly, nonpsychiatric workers should not encounter difficulties in the rating of *supervision by mother*, *discipline by father*, and *family cohesiveness*.[27]

The New York City Youth Board has already corrected errors of rating resulting from the first two difficulties, but must yet give consideration to the third; and the Maximum Benefits Project is now in process of re-rating cases to take account of all three of the above-mentioned difficulties.[28]

It is clear that the accuracy of the predictive device is being

---

[27] Definitions of terms appear in Appendix B of *Predicting delinquency and crime*.

[28] For further resolution of rating problems and other difficulties in connection with the Social Prediction Table, see Chapters 9 and 10 below.

sharpened and it is to be hoped that experimentation by the Youth Board and the Maximum Benefits Project will continue to the advantage of those who may ultimately wish to apply the Social Prediction Table. There is still much to learn, however, and many difficulties to be resolved in connection with any large-scale use of this or any other device for the identification of potential delinquents.

There are additional problems that would follow the general acceptance of this device as a means for differentiating soon after school entrance among those children who are not and those who are likely to develop into persistent offenders unless suitable measures of intervention are applied. Among them might be mentioned the wisdom of using such devices at all. In this connection, the interested reader should consult pages 91–93 above, as a means of orientation in the pros and cons.

Still another basic issue has to do with meeting the challenge of 'doing something' following the identification of potential delinquents. The way points to the early treatment of families and children by the constituted agencies of society when the interpersonal relations between the parents and a particular child make him vulnerable to delinquency. The rationale for such intervention is embraced in the already accepted philosophy of 'reaching out' casework and poses only the problem of the *stage at which* this 'reaching out' is to be initiated, i.e. *after* signs of delinquent behavior have become clearly evident or *in advance* of them.

Beyond this is the need for a new profession of 'family educators' drawn from among psychiatrists, social workers, psychologists, ministers, pediatricians, public health nurses, teachers, and others, whose first task it would be to explore *methods* of re-educating the families of children found to be vulnerable to delinquency. Despite the many forms that delinquency may take and the many 'types' of delinquents, the common denominator is persistent, aggressive antisocial behavior and it is to the prevention and control of this that family educators must direct themselves.

CHAPTER 9

Toward Improving the Identification of Delinquents *

ELEANOR T. GLUECK

THE SOCIAL PREDICTION TABLE

THE purpose of this chapter is to report upon certain steps which have been taken to improve the Glueck Social Prediction Table developed from the data in *Unraveling Juvenile Delinquency*[(138)]. This Table is based on five social factors reflecting parent-child relationships found sharply to discriminate the 500 'true' juvenile delinquents studied[1] from the 500 non-delinquents with whom the delinquents had been matched case by case, age for age, ethnic derivation, general intelligence (I.Q.), and residence in urban underprivileged areas. These social factors are *discipline of boy by father, supervision of boy by mother, affection of father for boy, affection of mother for boy*, and *family cohesiveness*. (See *Table I-A*.)

Although there were discriminating factors other than the five included in the Social Prediction Table, the aforementioned five were selected because they were clearly operative in the lives of children *before* school entrance. Since *Unraveling* was a retrospective study, many of the factors embraced in it (such as gang membership, school retardation, and truancy from school) obviously did not become operative until later in the life span of the boys.[2]

---

* Revised from an address delivered at the Annual Meeting of the American Society of Criminology in Denver, Colorado, 30 December 1961.

[1] We label as 'true' delinquents those who commit acts of a kind which, had they been committed by persons beyond the statutory juvenile court age, would have been recognized as felonies (larceny, burglary, sex offenses, robbery, arson, firesetting, etc.) and/or who have a history of repeated minor offenses (such as malicious injury to property, destruction of property, trespassing, evading fare, stealing rides, ringing false alarms, throwing missiles, stoning trains, breaking windows, running away from home, assault and battery). In *Unraveling*, we did not label as 'true' delinquents boys who up to the time of their inclusion in that study had committed only one or two minor acts (such as violating a city ordinance or town by-law) or boys who very occasionally in the face of exciting temptations stole a toy in a ten-cent store, sneaked into a subway or motion picture theatre, played hookey, and the like. See *Unraveling* Table XIII–13. Whether any of these pseudo-delinquents actually develop into serious or persistent minor offenders later in their lives (they ranged in age from 11–17 when we first selected them for investigation) is another question and can be answered only by intensive follow-up of the non-delinquents of *Unraveling*. The follow-up on both the delinquents and the non-delinquents has continued to age thirty-two.

[2] The Social Prediction Table was constructed by summing the delinquency scores

127

TABLE I–A

IDENTIFICATION OF POTENTIAL JUVENILE DELINQUENTS
BASED ON FIVE FACTORS OF SOCIAL BACKGROUND*

Score Class	Delinquency Rate	Non-delinquency Rate	Total Number of Cases
	%	%	
Less than 200	8·2	91·8	293
200–250	37·0	63·0	108
250–300	63·5	36·5	192
300 and over	89·2	10·8	297

Predictive Factors†	Delinquency Scores
DISCIPLINE OF BOY BY FATHER	
Firm but kindly	9·3
Lax	59·8
Erratic or overstrict	71·8
SUPERVISION OF BOY BY MOTHER	
Suitable	9·9
Fair	57·5
Unsuitable	83·2
AFFECTION OF FATHER FOR BOY	
Warm (including overprotective)	33·8
Indifferent or hostile	75·9
AFFECTION OF MOTHER FOR BOY	
Warm (including overprotective)	43·1
Indifferent or hostile	86·2
COHESIVENESS OF FAMILY	
Marked	20·6
Some	61·3
None	96·9

* *Unraveling*, Table XX–3.
† For definitions, see id. p. 261; *Predicting Delinquency and Crime* [212] pp. 245–55.

for the particular subcategory of each of the five factors which characterized the individual boy. For example, if a boy was overstrictly disciplined by his father he was scored 71·8, because 71·8 per cent of all the boys of *Unraveling* who had been over-strictly disciplined by the father were in the persistent delinquent group. If the same boy was found to have been unsuitably supervised by his mother, he was assigned the score 83·2; if his father was indifferent to him, the assigned score was 75·9; if his mother did not love him, he rated a score of 86·2; and, finally, if he had been reared in an uncohesive family, he was scored 96·9. The sum of these scores resulted in a total score of 414·0. Table I–A was derived by distributing the total scores of all the delinquents and all the non-delinquents into graduated score classes. For further details concerning the method of constructing the Social Prediction Table, see *Unraveling* 259–64.

Our aim is to heighten the capacity of the Social Prediction Table in order to differentiate: (*a*) at school entrance, the children likely to develop into *persistent* delinquents from those not headed for delinquent careers; and (*b*) among youngsters already evidencing symptoms of delinquent-like behavior, those who are *true* delinquents from those who are not.

One of the major questions that has to be answered in determining the applicability of the Social Prediction Table is whether a screening device, constructed *retrospectively* on one group of persistent juvenile offenders and their matched non-offenders, will select among $5\frac{1}{2}$ to 6-year-old boys of similar (and, hopefully, of dissimilar) socio-economic, ethnic, and intellectual status those who *are likely to develop* into serious or persistent juvenile offenders as contrasted with those who *are not*. Testing on a variety of samples is necessary before the Table can be regarded as more than an 'experience table', describing the presence of the weighted cluster of five factors among the delinquents and non-delinquents of *Unraveling*. The progress of such testing on groups already manifesting delinquent-like symptoms, as applied *retrospectively* to other samples of confirmed offenders, as well as on groups of young children before the manifestation of overt symptoms of delinquent-like behavior (with follow-up to compare their predicted and their actual behavior) is reported in 'Spotting Potential Delinquents: Can It Be Done?'[182] and in Chapter 8 above.

IMPROVEMENTS AND SAFEGUARDS FOR USE OF PREDICTION TABLE

The value of experimental applications of the Social Prediction Table lies not only in determining the range of its usefulness but also in resolving any difficulties that may emerge in the course of applying it. Although none of the checkings of the Table has been carried on by us, the experimenters have at times turned to us for assistance in clarifying definitions of terms and resolving problems associated with the rating of cases. From this we have learned much that has alerted us to the need of placing additional safeguards around the use of the Table. Some of the difficulties that developed are mentioned in Chapter 8.

Unanticipated difficulties have arisen because of variations in the training and experience of those applying the Table, and from occasional inadequacies in the collection of the necessary data. In one inquiry, for example, questions arose as to the particular subcategory of a factor into which to place a boy, and disagreements emerged among the investigators as to the rating of some of the factors. One problem concerned the factor of *affection of parents for boy*, which psychoanalytically-oriented observers interpret in accordance with Freudian depth psychology and others on the basis of surface manifestations of parental affection. Other problems arose in regard to the rating of *discipline of boy by father* (as well as *affection of father for boy*) in instances in which the father or a father-substitute had never been a part of the family group or had left home while the boy was still very young. Questions were also raised regarding the assessment of *family cohesiveness* in instances in which a boy was reared solely by the mother or a mother-substitute.

These and other difficulties led to the consideration that one or another of the five factors could be dispensed with if data or skills were insufficient to make an accurate assessment of all of them. Correlations were systematically pursued between the total five-factor scores for each boy in *Unraveling* and every possible combination of four, three, and two factors. Only the combinations with coefficients of correlation of ·90 and over were considered. These factor combinations had correlation coefficients ranging from ·932 for a two-factor Table to ·987 for a four-factor Table.[3] Therefore, in instances in which the five-factor Table could not be used, an appropriate abbreviated Table could be substituted. For example, the inconsistent ratings of *affection of mother for boy* or *affection of father for boy* by workers of differing psychological persuasions were eliminated by confining the scoring to the three remaining factors: *supervision of boy by mother*, *discipline of boy by father*, and *family cohesiveness*. The difficulty of rating *discipline of boy by father* in a situation in which the father had not been an integral part of the family group was met by use of a two-factor Table (*supervision of boy by mother, family cohesiveness*).

BETTER IDENTIFICATION OF BOYS IN 'EVEN CHANCE OF DELINQUENCY' GROUP

What I have thus far said briefly summarizes our efforts to improve the Social Prediction Table and to place additional safeguards around it. But the most important step toward reducing errors in the classification of children as true delinquents or non-delinquents has only recently been undertaken. This is directed toward the problem of more specific identification as delinquents or non-delinquents of youngsters classified as having about an even chance of becoming

---

[3] See *Predicting delinquency and crime* [(212)] Tables IX–1 to IX–1e, for all possible combinations with high predictive potential.

delinquent or remaining non-delinquent. This problem has rightly given concern to other predictionists and to some critics of predictive devices. To determine whether this might be accomplished, a redistribution of the cases of *Unraveling* was undertaken to identify the particular score class in which approximately half the boys were delinquents and half were non-delinquents. This proved to be the category 200–300.[4] (See *Table I–B*.)

In order to be able in future applications of the Social Prediction Table more specifically to identify as probable delinquents or non-delinquents those now found to have an even chance of delinquency and non-delinquency, we have recently prepared a subsidiary screening device from among the factors of social background that most sharply differentiate the delinquents from the non-delinquents in the 200–300 score class.[5]

Although six factors met the necessary criteria,[6] we selected two—*discipline of boy by mother* and *rearing by parent substitute*—omitting from present consideration *unsuitable supervision of boy by mother*, because this factor is already included among the five comprising the original Social Prediction Table.

Following our usual procedures for constructing a screening device, *Table I–C* was derived. (Note that information for one factor was not available for one boy.) Examination of the Table reveals that 58 of the 299 boys previously placed in a group that showed an even chance of delinquency and non-delinquency could now be placed in one in which 87·9 per cent are classifiable as *non-offenders*;

---

[4] The comparable score class in one of the three-factor Tables is 100–200, and in the two-factor Table, 75–125.

[5] The statistical work was executed at United Research Inc., Cambridge, Mass., under the supervision of Rose W. Kneznek.

[6]

Factors	%s of Respective Factor Totals		Difference Between Dels. and Non-dels.	P
	Dels.	Non-dels.		
	%	%	%	
Unsuitable Discipline of Boy by Mother	95·1	56·9	38·2	·01
Unsuitable Supervision of Boy by Mother	43·8	22·5	21·3	·01
Rearing by Parent Substitute	33·3	14·5	18·8	·02
Physical Punishment of Boy by Father	63·6	45·1	18·5	·02
Indifference or Hostility of Mother to Boy	32·9	14·5	18·4	·02
Emotional Disturbance in Mother	40·7	24·6	16·1	·02

TABLE I–B

REDISTRIBUTION OF SCORE CLASSES IN *Table 1–A* TO DETERMINE SCORE CLASS WITH EVEN CHANCE OF DELINQUENCY OR NON-DELINQUENCY

Chance of Delinquency (Score Class)	Delinquency Rate	Non-delinquency Rate	Total Number of Cases
	%	%	
LOW CHANCE (Less than 200)	8·2	91·8	293
ABOUT EVEN CHANCE (200–300)	54·0	46·0	300
HIGH CHANCE (300 and over)	89·2	10·8	297

TABLE I–C

MORE SPECIFIC IDENTIFICATION ON BASIS OF NEW CLUSTER OF SOCIAL FACTORS OF POTENTIAL JUVENILE DELINQUENTS AMONG 299 BOYS (IN *Table I–B*) HAVING AN EVEN CHANCE OF DELINQUENCY OR NON-DELINQUENCY

Chance of Delinquency (Score Class)	Delinquency Rate	Non-delinquency Rate	Total Number of Cases
	%	%	
LOW CHANCE (Less than 75)	12·1	87·9	58
ABOUT EVEN CHANCE (75–125)	58·2	41·8	177
HIGH CHANCE (125 and over)	81·3	18·7	64

Predictive Factors*	Delinquency Scores
DISCIPLINE OF BOY BY MOTHER	
Firm but kindly	6·1
Lax, overstrict, or erratic	73·7
REARING BY PARENT SUBSTITUTE	
No	38·0
Yes	79·3

* For definitions, see *Table III–A*.

132

while 64 boys could now be placed in a group in which 81·3 per cent are classifiable as potential *delinquents*.

The question remaining is whether a means can be found to screen the 177 boys *still having an even chance of delinquency and non-delinquency* in order to designate them as 'true' delinquents or probable non-offenders. To arrive at this much-desired result, we first

TABLE I–D

MORE SPECIFIC IDENTIFICATION ON BASIS OF FIVE PERSONALITY TRAITS OF 169 OF THE 177 BOYS (IN *Table I–C*) HAVING AN EVEN CHANCE OF DELINQUENCY OR NON-DELINQUENCY*

Chance of Delinquency (*Score Class*)	Delinquency Rate	Non-delinquency Rate	Total Number of Cases
	%	%	
LOW CHANCE (Less than 220)	14·6	85·4	48
ABOUT EVEN CHANCE (220–270)	52·3	47·7	44
HIGH CHANCE (270 and over)	88·3	11·7	77

Predictive Traits†	Delinquency Scores
ADVENTUROUSNESS	
Absent	35·4
Present	75·3
EXTROVERSION IN ACTION	
Absent	37·8
Present	66·5
SUGGESTIBILITY	
Absent	35·5
Present	69·4
STUBBORNNESS	
Absent	39·0
Present	83·4
EMOTIONAL INSTABILITY	
Absent	26·5
Present	62·0

* See *Predicting Delinquency and Crime* Table IX–3.
† For definitions, see id. pp. 245–55.

undertook a series of correlations between the remaining social background factors and the delinquents and non-delinquents in this group, but did not uncover any factors sufficiently discriminative to warrant their use in a subsidiary screening device.

In determining the next steps to be taken in order to ascertain which boys of the remaining 177 could be designated as potential delinquents, we gave consideration to the possibility of applying two discriminatory devices that we had previously published. One is based on five traits of basic character structure (as derived from Rorschach tests) and the other on five temperamental traits (as determined by a skilled psychiatrist). We abandoned application of the first one because the Rorschach data were not available for a sufficient number of the 177 boys; but we were able to utilize the screening Table based on the five temperamental traits (*adventurousness, extroversion in action, suggestibility, stubbornness,* and *emotional instability*),[7] data for which were available for 169 of the 177 boys.

The application of this Table to the 169 boys resulted in placing 48 into a group in which the chances of delinquency are about $1\frac{1}{2}$ in 10, and 77 into a group in which the chances of delinquency are 9 in 10—thereby leaving as not yet clearly identifiable only 44 of the original 890 on whom the Social Prediction Table had been constructed. (See *Tables I–A, I–B,* and *I–D.*)

I have no doubt that further refinement of the Table, if supplemented by intensive clinical examination focused on locating brain damage, pre-psychoticism, feeblemindedness, and other pathologic conditions that might aid in prognosis, and by inquiries concerning the impact of neighborhood influences upon youngsters, would make possible the more specific identification even of this small group of boys as probable delinquents or non-delinquents.

SCREENING DEVICE FOR CHILDREN ALREADY MANIFESTING DELINQUENT-LIKE CONDUCT

Thus far, attention has been directed toward the more specific identification of potential delinquents at about $5\frac{1}{2}$ to 6 years of age. There is understandably much discussion about the wisdom of efforts to identify children as delinquents in advance of clear signs of delinquent-like behavior (i.e. fighting, sneaking into movies, 'acting up' in school, truanting, firesetting, joining gangs). However, the idea of trying to determine *after* a youngster begins to show some evidences of such antisocial behavior what his chances actually are of developing into a serious or persistent minor offender is more

[7] *Unraveling* Table XX–10; *Predicting delinquency and crime* p. 238.

acceptable to many than is the proposition that societal intervention should begin *before* the onset of overt evidences of an antisocial development.

Regardless of the pros and cons of identifying children *in advance* of clear symptomatology, it does seem desirable to develop a screening device to be applied to children *already manifesting evidences* of delinquent-like conduct. Re-examination of the findings of *Unraveling*

TABLE II–A

IDENTIFICATION OF TRUE DELINQUENTS AMONG THOSE ALREADY MANIFESTING EVIDENCES OF DELINQUENT-LIKE BEHAVIOR*

Chance of Delinquency (Score Class)	Delinquency Rate	Non-delinquency Rate	Total Number of Cases
	%	%	
LOW CHANCE (Less than 200)	3·2	96·8	373
ABOUT EVEN CHANCE (200–300)	58·3	41·7	168
HIGH CHANCE (300 and over)	95·6	4·4	316

Predictive Factors†	Delinquency Scores
RECREATIONAL PREFERENCES	
Nonadventurous	35·3
Adventurous	82·9
AGE OF COMPANIONS	
Younger, same age, varied ages	38·1
Predominantly older	81·2
ACADEMIC AMBITIONS	
Continue schooling	28·5
Stop school as soon as possible	76·0
ATTITUDE TOWARD SCHOOL	
Indifference or ready acceptance	30·2
Marked dislike	85·7
TRUANCY	
None	5·5
Persistent or occasional	89·8

* Based on five factors in social background of adolescents. See *Unraveling* 135–68. This table has not been previously published.
† For definitions, see *Unraveling* 135–68.

to see what data of a clearly *symptomatic* nature might be incorporated into a screening device has resulted in a Table based on differences between the true delinquents and the non-offenders in their *recreational preferences and companionships, academic ambitions, attitudes toward further schooling,* and *truancy.* (See *Table II–A.*)

Examination of *Table II–A,* which was constructed on 857 boys of *Unraveling,* indicates that it is indeed a good discriminatory device; 373 boys could be placed in a group with less than 1 chance in 10 of being true delinquents, while, at the opposite pole, 316 boys

TABLE II–B

MORE SPECIFIC IDENTIFICATION ON BASIS OF CLUSTER OF THREE SOCIAL FACTORS (SEE *Table III–A*) OF 165 OF THE 168 BOYS (IN *Table II–A*) HAVING AN EVEN CHANCE OF BEING OR BECOMING TRUE DELINQUENTS*

Chance of Delinquency (Score Class)	Delinquency Rate	Non-delinquency Rate	Total Number of Cases
	%	%	
LOW CHANCE (Less than 75)	6·7	93·3	30
ABOUT EVEN CHANCE (75–125)	53·3	46·7	45
HIGH CHANCE (125 and over)	78·9	21·1	90

Predictive Factors†	Delinquency Scores
SUPERVISION OF BOY BY MOTHER	
Fair or suitable	29·7
Unsuitable	83·2
DISCIPLINE OF BOY BY MOTHER	
Firm but kindly	6·1
Lax, overstrict, or erratic	73·7
REARING BY PARENT SUBSTITUTE	
No	38·0
Yes	79·3

* It is possible to get as good a result by applying *Table I–D* to the 168 boys, but this is not recommended except for use by psychiatrists who may wish to explore the personality traits of certain boys.
† For definitions, see *Table III–A.*

136

could be placed in a group having better than 9 in 10 chances of being true delinquents. However, 168 boys (score class 200–300) cannot as yet be clearly defined as delinquent, pseudo-delinquent or

TABLE III–A

IDENTIFICATION OF POTENTIAL JUVENILE DELINQUENTS ON THE BASIS OF A NEW CLUSTER OF THREE FACTORS OF SOCIAL BACKGROUND*

Chance of Delinquency (Score Class)	Delinquency Rate	Non-delinquency Rate	Total Number of Cases
	%	%	
LOW CHANCE (Less than 125)	4·7	95·3	316
ABOUT EVEN CHANCE (125–175)	47·9	52·1	236
HIGH CHANCE (175 and over)	85·9	14·1	429

Predictive Factors†	Delinquency Scores
SUPERVISION OF BOY BY MOTHER	
Fair or suitable	29·7
Unsuitable	83·2
DISCIPLINE OF BOY BY MOTHER	
Firm but kindly	6·1
Lax, overstrict, or erratic	73·7
REARING BY PARENT SUBSTITUTE	
No	38·0
Yes	79·3

* Note that data for the cluster of three factors were available for a larger number of boys (981 cases) than for the cluster of five factors (890 cases).
† Definitions:
SUPERVISION OF BOY BY MOTHER: *suitable*, if she personally keeps close watch over boy's activities at home or in the neighbourhood, or provides for his lesiure hours in clubs or playgrounds (if for good reason she is unable to supervise boy's activities, she makes provision for a responsible adult to do so); *fair*, if mother (although not working and not incapacitated) gives or provides only limited supervision to boy; *unsuitable*, if mother leaves boy to his own devices, without guidance, or in the care of an irresponsible person.
DISCIPLINE OF BOY BY MOTHER: (refers to usual or typical discipline of the boy on the part of mother or surrogate): *lax*, if mother is negligent, indifferent, allows boy to do as he likes, *overstrict*, if mother is harsh, unreasoning, demanding obedience through fear; *erratic*, if mother vacillates between strictness and laxity, is not consistent in control; *firm but kindly*, if her discipline is based on sound reason which the child understands and accepts as fair.
REARING BY PARENT SUBSTITUTE: may include step-parent, foster parent, or relative (grandparent, aunt, older sibling) but not person with whom boy spends only brief periods away from his own parents (or parent) in foster homes or with relatives, or in an institution. See *Unraveling* 124–25 for further explanation of this factor.

non-delinquent. No doubt one or two subsidiary screening devices focused on the 168 boys would result in greatly reducing the proportion not yet clearly identifiable. Meanwhile it should be noted that the coefficient of correlation between the total scores of the original five-factor Table (*Table I–A*) and of this (*Table II–B*) is ·949. (Since the initial presentation of this paper, the author has found that by applying *Table III–A* to the 168 boys, the number still not identifiable as potential delinquents or non-delinquents is reduced to forty-five. See *Table II–B*.)

TABLE III–B

MORE SPECIFIC IDENTIFICATION ON BASIS OF FIVE PERSONALITY TRAITS OF 223 OF THE 236 BOYS (IN *Table III–A*) HAVING AN EVEN CHANCE OF DELINQUENCY OR NON-DELINQUENCY*

Chance of Delinquency (*Score Class*)	Delinquency Rate	Non-delinquency Rate	Total Number of Cases
	%	%	
LOW CHANCE (Less than 220)	8·1	91·9	74
ABOUT EVEN CHANCE (220–270)	43·8	56·2	64
HIGH CHANCE (270 and over)	85·9	14·1	85

* See *Table I–D* for predictive traits and delinquency scores.

TABLE III–C

MORE SPECIFIC IDENTIFICATION ON BASIS OF FIVE BEHAVIORAL FACTORS OF 51 OF THE 64 BOYS (IN *Table III–B*) HAVING AN EVEN CHANCE OF DELINQUENCY OR NON-DELINQUENCY*

Chance of Delinquency (*Score Class*)	Delinquency Rate	Non-delinquency Rate	Total Number of Cases
	%	%	
LOW CHANCE (Less than 200)	0·0	100·0	19
ABOUT EVEN CHANCE (200–300)	50·0	50·0	12
HIGH CHANCE (300 and over)	90·0	10·0	20

* See *Table II–A* for predictive factors and delinquency scores.

THREE-FACTOR SOCIAL PREDICTION TABLE

In the course of seeking ways of improving the Social Prediction Table, a new cluster of social factors has been found that might be substituted for the original Social Prediction Table. It comprises *supervision of boy by mother* (already in the original Table), *discipline of boy by mother*, and *rearing by parent substitute*. The latter two factors are already incorporated in the first of the two subsidiary tables (*Table I–C*) designed to identify more clearly the true delinquents in the group having an even chance of delinquency and non-delinquency. The coefficient of correlation between the total scores for the original five-factor Table (*I–A*) and those for the new three-factor Table (*III–A*) is ·972.

The obvious advantage of using the latter Table (and its subsidiary Tables *III–B* and *III–C*) instead of the original five-factor Table is the greater ease of gathering and classifying the data. An experiment in applying this new Table, as related to the subsequent behavior of youngsters predicted as delinquents or as non-delinquents, is necessary in order to contrast the results with those derived by the original Social Prediction Table.

CONCLUSION

The sum and substance of this brief presentation is that there are indeed ways of improving and sharpening screening devices for the early identification of delinquents both before and after the onset of evidences of delinquent-like behavior. This brings us closer to the time when individual children can be identified with a small margin of error either as serious or persistent minor offenders, or as pseudo-offenders or non-offenders. We must, of course, test these newly developed devices on other samples of similar and differing ethnic origins, socioeconomic levels, intelligence levels, and age groups; on children from rural as well as urban areas; and on girls as well as on boys.

In general, the results of our efforts to make the Social Prediction Table more effective suggest that delinquency is not always associated with the 'under-the-roof' environment, but is in some instances more closely related to personality make-up; and in the very small group of still unidentifiable boys, other primary associations must now be looked for.

Such findings provide a realistic frame of reference for the study of etiologic types (and also of treatment types) among delinquents. But before proceeding further, it would be well to consolidate the gains already made.

It is important not only to test and refine the screening tables but also to sharpen the definitions of the factors,[8] improve the methods of data-gathering, and objectify the factors utilized in the construction of the Tables. It would be advantageous also to devise short, carefully-structured interviews with parents, and one validation project has been experimenting along these lines.[9] It might even be advisable to develop group tests to replace the personal interviews. Above all, it is important to remain open-minded about the uses of these and similar devices and to look upon predictive devices as research tools in a search for the etiology of delinquency, even though questions exist about the wisdom of attempts to identify delinquents in advance of the presence of overt evidences of delinquent-like behavior.

[8] Definitions have already been slightly modified as a result of the New York City Youth Board's inquiry. Experimenters wishing to apply this table are invited to communicate either with the author or with Mrs Maude Craig, Director of Research, New York City Youth Board, 79 Madison Avenue, New York 16, N.Y.

[9] The Maximum Benefits Project of the Commissioners' Youth Council of Washington, D.C. For a brief description of the Project, see Chapter 8 above.

CHAPTER 10

Toward Further Improving
the Identification of Delinquents

ELEANOR T. GLUECK

In Chapter 9 a method was described of reducing 'false-positive' identifications of potential delinquents and non-delinquents screened by the Glueck Social Prediction Table initially published in *Unraveling Juvenile Delinquency* [138] (p. 262). The original table was composed of five factors: *affection of mother for boy*, *affection of father for boy*, *supervision of boy by mother*, *discipline of boy by father*, and *family cohesiveness*. Subsequent abbreviations of the table resulted in four-, three- and two-factor tables.[1] These shortened tables were necessitated by difficulties experienced by various scorers in rating certain of the original five factors, notably *affection of mother for boy*, *affection of father for boy*, and *discipline of boy by father*. in situations in which the father had not been an integral part of the family group. As the coefficients of correlation between the original and the abbreviated tables on the same cases ranged from ·932 for a two-factor table to ·987 for a four-factor table, there was virtually no loss in rating efficiency:

'Therefore, in instances in which the five-factor table could not be used, an appropriate abbreviated table could be substituted. For example, the inconsistent ratings of *affection of mother for boy* or *affection of father for boy* by workers of differing psychological persuasions were eliminated by confining the scoring to the three remaining factors: *supervision of boy by mother*, *discipline of boy by father*, and *family cohesiveness*. The difficulty of rating *discipline of boy by father* in a situation in which the father had not been an integral part of the family group was met by use of a two-factor table (*supervision of boy by mother, family cohesiveness*)' (p. 130 above).

It is unnecessary at this point to detail the further steps taken to reduce false identifications of delinquents and non-delinquents beyond pointing out that these steps consisted essentially of isolating

---

[1] See *Predicting delinquency and crime* [212] App. B, Tables IX–1a, 1b, 1c, 1d, and 1e.

that group of boys having about an even chance of becoming delinquents or remaining non-delinquents. (These steps are described on pp. 130–34 above.) Subsidiary screening devices were then constructed to be applied to this as yet ambiguous group of boys. These subsidiary tables were based on discriminatory social factors other than the ones already utilized in the initial five-factor table.

Although the boys of *Unraveling* having an even chance of delinquency were thereby reduced from 300 to 177, the problem remained of further reducing this unclear group. As no additional discriminatory social factors could be found, five personality traits comprising a prediction table published in *Unraveling* (*Table XX–12*, p. 266) were applied to the still ambiguous group of cases. The five traits are *adventurousness, extroversion in action, suggestibility, stubbornness,* and *emotional instability.*[2]

Application of this table reduced the ambiguous category to 44 cases, or 5 per cent of the 890 cases on which the original prediction table was constructed. No attempt was made to reduce the number still further, but the writer suggested that this could no doubt be accomplished:

'I have no doubt that further refinement of the table, if supplemented by intensive clinical examination focused on locating brain damage, prepsychoticism, feeblemindedness, and other pathologic conditions that might aid in prognosis, and by inquiries concerning the impact of neighborhood influences upon youngsters, would make possible the more specific identification even of this small group of boys as probable delinquents or non-delinquents' (p. 134 above).

In the course of this experimentation with possible subsidiary tables, it was discovered that a three-factor table consisting of *supervision of boy by mother, discipline of boy by mother,* and *rearing by parent substitute* (*Table III–A,* p. 137 above) immediately placed 236 boys out of 981 for whom all the data were available into the group having about an even chance of delinquency, and that the application to them in turn of the prediction table comprised of five personality traits further reduced this group of uncertain cases to 64 or 6 per cent of cases. In other words, the desired result was

[2] Definitions: *Adventurousness*—has impulse for change, excitement, or risk. *Extroversion in action*—gives free expression to feelings in activity. *Suggestibility*—swayed by appeal to feelings even though against better judgment. *Stubbornness*—resistive or persistent, but not in a freely expressed drive; probably the result of thwarted dynamic qualities. *Emotional instability*—unharmonious and inappropriate feeling reaction, conflict of feeling tendencies; not to be confused with lability of emotion.

accomplished in *one step beyond the initial prediction table* rather than the two stages described in Tables I–C and I–D (pp. 132, 133 above). The writer therefore suggested that

'An experiment in applying this new table, as related to the subsequent behavior of youngsters predicted as delinquents or as non-delinquents, is necessary in order to contrast the results with those derived by the original Social Prediction Table' (p. 139 above).

The New York City Youth Board, which since 1952 has been conducting a study applying the Social Prediction Table and its modifications to 5½–6 year old boys, undertook to experiment with the new three-factor table. The Board has recently reported to the writer, concerning this table, that the factor *rearing by parent substitute*, although theoretically discriminative of delinquents and non-delinquents, does not in reality play a significant role in the predictive cluster, because relatively few children fall into this category. The writer therefore has experimented with replacing the factor *rearing by parent substitute* by *family cohesiveness*, which had been included not only in the original five-factor table but in all the abbreviated versions of that table.[3] This has resulted in the construction of *Table IV–A* (numbered in this way as it follows the last series of tables in 'Toward Improving the Identification of Delinquents').

It is to be noted that this table immediately reduces the number of ambiguous cases (that is, those having about an even chance of delinquency) to 194, or 19 per cent of the 979 cases involved. At this stage a reduction of this small proportion was further accomplished by applying to this group (actually to 185 of the 194 cases) the five personality traits comprising the predictive device already described above. This step reduced the number of unplaced cases to 56, or 5 per cent of the total number of cases.

Both the New York City Youth Board and the Commissioners' Youth Council of Washington, D.C., in its Maximum Benefits Project,[4] have made experimental use of this latest discriminatory device for the identification of delinquents—the Board, with a population of 5½–6 year olds just entering school, and the Maximum Benefits Project, with older children already evidencing signs of delinquent-like conduct in school. Both groups have prepared interim reports of their projects; that of the New York City Youth Board has appeared in the July 1963 issue of *Crime and Delinquency*, under the authorship of Maude Craig and Selma J. Glick, and that

[3] See Tables cited *supra* note 1.
[4] For a brief description of these projects, see Chapter 8 above.

TABLE IV–A

IDENTIFICATION OF JUVENILE DELINQUENTS ON THE BASIS OF THE
NEWEST CLUSTER OF THREE FACTORS OF SOCIAL BACKGROUND*

(Coefficient of correlation between the total five factor scores for
each boy and the three-factor table is ·903)

Chance of Delinquency (Score Class)	Delinquency Rate	Non-delinquency Rate	Total Number of Cases
	%	%	
LOW CHANCE (Less than 140)	8·6	91·4	395
ABOUT EVEN CHANCE (140–200)	58·2	41·8	194
HIGH CHANCE (200 and over)	89·0	11·0	390

Predictive Factors†	Delinquency Scores
SUPERVISION OF BOY BY MOTHER	
Suitable	9·9
Fair	57·5
Unsuitable	83·2
DISCIPLINE OF BOY BY MOTHER	
Firm but kindly	6·1
Erratic	62·3
Overstrict	73·3
Lax	82·9
COHESIVENESS OF FAMILY	
Marked	20·6
Some	61·3
None	96·9

The statistical work has been handled by Rose W. Kneznek, formerly Director of Research
Services, United Research Inc., Cambridge, Mass.
    * Data for the cluster of three factors were available for 979 cases of *Unraveling*.
    † Definitions:
SUPERVISION OF BOY BY MOTHER: *suitable*, if she personally keeps close watch over boy's activities
at home or in the neighborhood, or provides for his leisure hours in clubs or playgrounds (if for
good reason she is unable to supervise boy's activities, she makes provision for a responsible adult
to do so); *fair*, if mother (although not working and not incapacitated) gives or provides only
limited supervision to boy; *unsuitable*, if mother leaves boy to his own devices, without guidance,
or in the care of an irresponsible person.
DISCIPLINE OF BOY BY MOTHER: (refers to usual or typical discipline of the boy on the part of mother
or surrogate); *lax*, if mother is negligent, indifferent, allows boy to do as he likes; *overstrict*, if
mother is harsh, unreasoning, demanding obedience through fear; *erratic*, if mother vacillates
between strictness and laxity, is not consistent in control; *firm but kindly*, if her discipline is based
on sound reason which the child understands and accepts as fair.
COHESIVENESS OF FAMILY: *Marked:* There is a strong 'we' feeling among members of the immediate
family as evidenced by cooperativeness, group interests, pride in the home, affection for each other.
Marked cohesiveness can exist even though the father or father substitute is not a part of the family
group. *Some:* Even if the family group may not be entirely intact (because of absence of one or
more members), the remaining group has at least some of the characteristics of the cohesive family.
None: Home is just a place to 'hang your hat'; self-interest of the members exceeds group interest.

of the Maximum Benefits Project has been published in the November 1963 issue of the *American Journal of Psychiatry*, under the authorship of Emory F. Hodges, Jr., M.D., and C. Downing Tait, Jr., M.D. *The results in both instances are more than promising, and it looks very much as if the newest three-factor table can now be recommended for general use.* See Chapter 7, note 5, above.

The Youth Board experimenters are preparing a small manual of instructions for those wishing to utilize the prediction device. This is bound to stimulate employment of the newest and most effective of our prediction tables for the early identification of delinquents. We will appreciate reports of any applications of this table.

CHAPTER 11

Body Build in the Prediction of Delinquency

ELEANOR T. GLUECK

INTRODUCTORY

THE need for screening devices to identify potential delinquents before they have embarked on criminal careers is being more and more recognized as fundamental. A pioneer effort in the construction of three such instruments[1] and several checkings of one of them encourages further experimentation with such devices as the cornerstone of a wide and comprehensive prophylactic attack on juvenile delinquency. A description of these three predictive instruments, and validations of one of them, are presented in 'Early detection of future delinquents' (Chapter 7 above) and 'Spotting potential delinquents: can it be done?' [182]. One of these devices is based on five traits of temperament, another on five traits of underlying character structure, and a third on five interpersonal factors of family life.

Because of findings made subsequent to the construction of these predictive devices concerning the role of body build in delinquency, it now becomes pertinent to re-examine them to see if they can be strengthened; for in *Physique and Delinquency*[176] it was found that because of basic differences in certain aspects of temperament and character structure, some body types have a greater delinquency potential than do others, and that there are significant differences in the response of youngsters of different body builds to environmental stresses.

How, if at all, does the newly established dimension of body build in the patterning of delinquency modify the construction, and enhance the usefulness, of screening devices for identifying potential delinquents?

BODY BUILD AND THE PREDICTION TABLES IN
Unraveling Juvenile Delinquency

To answer this query it is necessary to review the findings in *Unraveling* that pertain to differences in the body build (physique) of delinquents and non-delinquents. It will be recalled that for the purposes of that

---

[1] *Unraveling juvenile delinquency* [138] Ch. XX.

inquiry 500 persistent male juvenile offenders and 500 non-offenders were matched case for case, by age, intelligence, residence in under-privileged areas, and ethnic origin. The ethnic matching of the delinquents and non-delinquents (Italian with Italian, Irish with Irish, Polish with Polish, and so on) enhances the significance of the differences in body build that were found in *Unraveling*, namely, that twice the proportion of delinquents as of non-delinquents were of predominantly mesomorphic physique[2] (60·1 per cent : 30·7 per cent); while one-third the proportion of predominantly ectomorphic physiques were found among the delinquents as among the non-delinquents (14·4 per cent : 39·6 per cent). About equal but small proportions of predominantly endomorphic boys (11·8 per cent : 15 per cent) and of the balanced type (13·5 per cent : 14·7 per cent) were found among the delinquents and non-delinquents (*Unraveling, Table XV–I*).

TABLE I

INCIDENCE OF CLUSTERS OF PREDICTIVE TRAITS AND FACTORS IN *Unraveling Juvenile Delinquency* BY BODY TYPE

	Meso-morphs	Endo-morphs	Ecto-morphs	Balanced	Total Cases
	%	%	%	%	
Five character traits	47·8	48·4	51·4	48·1	123
Five traits of temperament	68·5	69·2	54·4	64·4	307
Five sociocul-tural factors	57·7	60·0	80·3	60·6	275

[2] As derived from W. H. Sheldon *et al.* (1940), *The varieties of human physique* (New York: Harper), pp. 5–6: 'Mesomorphy means relative predominance of muscle, bone, and connective tissue. The mesomorphic physique is normally heavy, hard, and rectangular in outline. Bone and muscle are prominent and the skin is made thick by a heavy underlying connective tissue. The entire bodily economy is dominated, relatively, by tissues derived from the mesodermal embryonic layer.

'Ectomorphy means relative predominance of linearity and fragility. In proportion to his mass, the ectomorph has the greatest surface area and hence relatively the greatest sensory exposure to the outside world. Relative to his mass he also has the largest brain and central nervous system. In a sense, therefore, his bodily economy is relatively dominated by tissues derived from the ectodermal embryonic layer.

'Endomorphy means relative predominance of soft roundness throughout the various regions of the body. When endomorphy is dominant the digestive viscera are massive and tend relatively to dominate the bodily economy. The digestive viscera are derived principally from the endodermal embryonic layer.'

There is still a fourth body type—one in which endomorphy, mesomorphy, and ectomorphy occur in about equal proportion. This is called the balanced type.

Any reader who is interested in a more detailed breakdown of body types (thirteen in all), is referred to *Unraveling* (Ch. XV) especially Table XV-1.

Analysis of the five traits of character structure comprising one of the three prediction tables in *Unraveling* (social assertiveness, defiance, suspiciousness, emotional lability, and destructiveness) shows that only destructiveness is found to exert a significantly different impact on the delinquency of the physique types, being much more characteristic of delinquent mesomorphs than of ectomorphs. Of the five traits of temperament based on psychiatric findings (adventurousness, extroversiveness, suggestibility, stubbornness, and emotional instability), only emotional instability was found to vary in its influence on the delinquency of the physique types, being more highly associated with the delinquency of mesomorphs as compared with its role in the delinquency of boys of predominantly ectomorphic physique.

In contrast to these findings, four of the five sociocultural factors comprising a predictive device generally called the Social Prediction Table (discipline of boy by father, supervision of boy by mother, affection of mother for boy, and family cohesiveness) were found to play a selective role in the delinquency of the body types, having more to do with impelling *ectomorphs* to delinquency than mesomorphs and/or endomorphs.[3] (The fifth factor is affection of father for boy.)

Thus it will be seen that the efficacy of the first two of the three predictive tables developed in connection with *Unraveling* is largely independent of body build, but that the third table (encompassing interpersonal family factors) would appear to have an even greater prognostic power in the case of ectomorphic boys than when applied to boys irrespective of body build.

The actual incidence among the delinquents of the four physique types of the clusters of (*a*) the five character traits, (*b*) the five traits of temperament, and (*c*) the five sociocultural factors which were found in *Unraveling* most markedly to distinguish delinquents from non-delinquents, is shown in *Table 1*.

There is clearly a *greater* concentration of the cluster of five predictive sociocultural factors among ectomorphic delinquents (80·3 per cent) than among juvenile delinquents of other body types. It is evident also that there is a lesser concentration among delinquent ectomorphs of the cluster of the five predictive traits of temperament. But the combination of five traits of character structure does not vary significantly in incidence among the delinquents of the four body types.

The contrast revealed between the ectomorphs and the other physique types would suggest that the exogenous factors of unharmonious family life are even more highly associated with the delin-

---

[3] *Physique and delinquency*, Tables 95, 98, 103, 104.

quency of ectomorphs than with that of the other physiques; and that the endogenous traits of temperament have less of a bearing on the delinquency of ectomorphs than of the other body types.

The query is now partly answered, 'How, if at all, does the newly established dimension of physique type in the patterning of delinquency modify the construction of and enhance the usefulness of the screening devices for identifying potential delinquents, especially of the Social Prediction Table?' Certainly, if further validations of this Table continue to show its usefulness as a means of identifying children who are likely to become persistent delinquents unless suitable therapeutic intervention occurs, there would appear to be no special need to incorporate into this already existing prediction device the knowledge gained in *Physique and Delinquency* of the clusters of the sociocultural factors that have an even more pronounced influence on the delinquency of ectomorphs than on youngsters of other body builds. However, this additional knowledge should help to diversify prophylactic and therapeutic efforts in accordance with the special vulnerabilities of this physique type.

NEW PREDICTIVE CLUSTERS IN *Physique and Delinquency*

Although there are difficulties inherent in somatotyping children at a stage sufficiently early in their lives to make preventive efforts most meaningful, it may still be desirable to construct prediction tables for each body type, using as a basis those clusters of traits and sociocultural factors that have been found in *Physique and Delinquency* most sharply to differentiate delinquents from non-delinquents within each predominant physique type. For example, in the case of mesomorphs, we have isolated three traits (feeling of inadequacy, emotional instability, emotional conflicts) that in combination most sharply distinguish delinquent from non-delinquent mesomorphs. In addition to this are two aspects of the home environment— haphazard household routine and lack of family group recreations (op. cit. pp. 258–59)—which together most sharply distinguish delinquent from non-delinquent mesomorphs. On the basis of these five factors, a prediction table designed to find potential delinquents among boys of predominantly mesomorphic physique could be constructed.

As regards ectomorphs, we have isolated two traits that in combination most sharply differentiate delinquent from non-delinquent ectomorphs—extreme restlessness in early childhood and receptive trends; and a cluster of four sociocultural factors—rearing in homes of low conduct standards, in homes lacking in cultural refinement, and in families lacking cohesiveness, and by fathers whose discipline of the boy is other than firm and kindly (op. cit. p. 259). These six traits and factors could be used in a predictive device for predominantly ectomorphic boys.

As regards endomorphs and boys of balanced type, there are no home and family factors that differentiate the delinquents from the non-delinquents. Therefore, the prediction tables already constructed would be most useful for them.

BODY BUILD AND THE PREVENTION OF DELINQUENCY

Although it does not appear necessary as yet to refine the already existing prediction tables to include body build, or to construct new tables for each body type, the findings of *Physique and Delinquency* should be suggestive to those who are concerned with the more effective management of juvenile offenders and with the prevention of juvenile delinquency. As it is not the purpose here to discuss the implications of the findings of *Physique and Delinquency* for preventive programs, the interested reader is referred to the volume itself, especially to Chapters XI, XV, and XVI. Chapter XI, 'Mesomorphs and Delinquency', contrasts boys of this body build, who represent the great majority of persistent offenders, with boys of other body builds, and indicates which traits and sociocultural factors contribute most significantly to their delinquency in contrast with other body types. Chapter XV deals with the more effective management of juvenile delinquency as a result of the knowledge gained about the differences in characteristics and environmental responses of youngsters of different body builds. In Chapter XVI are presented some hypotheses regarding physique and the etiology of delinquency, which bear further exploration regarding the role of body build in delinquency.

CHAPTER 12

Identifying Juvenile Delinquents and Neurotics

ELEANOR T. GLUECK

INTRODUCTION

SINCE the publication of *Unraveling Juvenile Delinquency*[138] there has been much speculation concerning the capacity of the Social Prediction Table based on five factors in the intra-family relationships of the juvenile offenders and their matched non-delinquents (supervision of boy by mother, discipline by father, affection of mother for boy, affection of father for boy, cohesiveness of family) to distinguish at the the age of six (i.e. roughly at the point of school entrance) those boys who, even though not yet necessarily showing indisputable signs of delinquency, are likely to become delinquents unless appropriate therapeutic intervention occurs. There has been concern in some quarters that data initially gathered about children between the ages of seven and seventeen years may not necessarily reflect conditions that existed when they were six; and there have been questions concerning the 'typicality' of the sample of cases studied in *Unraveling*, leading quite naturally to an uncertainty as to whether we have really developed 'predictive' instruments or merely a syndromization of factors that markedly distinguish the 500 juvenile delinquents studied in *Unraveling* from their matched non-delinquents.[1]

It seemed to us that there is only one meaningful answer to such speculation and that is, in the words of the eminent biometrician Edwin Bidwell Wilson, who has followed our attempts to construct 'prediction' tables since the preparation of the first one (published in *500 Criminal Careers*[26]) through 48 such tables:[2]

[1] E. W. Burgess (1951), book review in Symposium on the Gluecks' latest research. (*Federal Probation* 15, 2); E. D. Monachesi (1951), book review in Symposium on the Gluecks' latest research (*Federal Probation* 15, 6); J. W. Polier (1951), book review in Symposium on *Unraveling juvenile delinquency* (*Harv. L. Rev.* 64, 1036); A. J. Reiss, Jr. (1951), *Unraveling juvenile delinquency*, II: an appraisal of the research methods (*Amer. J. Sociol.* 57, 115); S. Rubin (1951), *Unraveling juvenile delinquency*, I: illusions in a research project using matched pairs (*Amer. J. Sociol.* 57, 107); J. T. Shaplin & D. V. Tiedeman (1951), Comment on the juvenile delinquency prediction tables in the Gluecks' *Unraveling juvenile delinquency* (*Amer. sociol. Rev.* 16, 544); P. W. Tappan (1951), book review in Symposium on *Unraveling juvenile delinquency* (*Harv. L. Rev.* 64, 1027).

[2] A history of this development and lists of all the tables are to be found in 'Status of Glueck prediction studies'[183]. (See also *Predicting delinquency and crime*[212].)

'A tool for distinguishing confirmed delinquents from non-delinquents may or may not be serviceable in distinguishing within a group of non-delinquents those who are potential delinquents from those who are not.

One may argue about the probable serviceability of the tables for this suggested use. If one holds that the personality of an individual in respect to liability to delinquency is largely determined genetically or at any rate almost wholly determined genetically and environmentally prior to entrance to school, and that the syndrome of delinquency attributes can be observed as determinately in the earlier predelinquent age as later when delinquency has become confirmed, then one might also hold that the prediction tables would work pretty well—and one might fear that the preventive treatment might not easily be successful. If, however, one holds that personality or behavior is extremely labile and that delinquency arises not from genetic constitution nor even from pre-school conditioning but from associations and conditions surrounding the individual during his school years, then one might hold that the prediction tables would work badly, but he could entertain the hope for good success with preventive treatment if only he knew to whom to apply it.

A priori argument will not get far, howsoever it be extended. What one needs is trial and observation. . . . That the Gluecks realize all these difficulties is manifest throughout their writings; but they have not been deterred thereby from setting up prediction tables. And in respect to a table in an earlier book, namely, one which predicted behavior of civilian delinquents in the armed forces, they had a noteworthy success *a posteriori* in showing that of 200 military offenders who had been civilian offenders about 85 per cent would have been so predicted to be.[3] The proof of this pudding came in the eating'.[4]

Since the publication of *Unraveling* we have sought and encouraged opportunities first to test the Social Prediction Table by retrospective application to groups of delinquents (and in one instance it was possible to include non-delinquents), and then to subject it to the far more severe test of application in a first grade public school population.

Several validations applying this table retrospectively to boys already delinquent have been made to date and others are in process.

---

[3] A. J. N. Schneider, C. W. LaGrone, Jr., E. T. Glueck & S. Glueck (1944), Prediction of behavior of civilian delinquents in the armed forces (*Ment. Hyg.* 28, No. 3).
[4] E. B. Wilson (1951), in Symposium on *Unraveling juvenile delinquency* (*Harv. L. Rev.* 64, 1041).

(See Chapter 8 above.) While the findings cannot be regarded as absolutely definitive, they do afford persuasive evidence that the table is soundly based and markedly discriminative of delinquents versus non-delinquents.

OPPORTUNITY TO CONSTRUCT DIAGNOSTIC TABLES DISTINGUISHING JUVENILE DELINQUENTS FROM NEUROTICS

Encouraged by the evidence thus far at hand, we determined to pursue our quest from data available in *Unraveling* to construct by the weighted score method[5] three tables designed:

1. To distinguish neurotic delinquents from emotionally healthy delinquents.
2. To distinguish neurotic delinquents from neurotic non-delinquents.
3. To distinguish neurotic non-delinquents from emotionally healthy non-delinquents.

Because there were relatively few delinquent or non-delinquent boys in *Unraveling* who were either pre-psychotic or frankly psychotic, we excluded them from consideration entirely.[6] For present purposes we also excluded those who were diagnosed as psychopathic or 'asocial' because—although there was a considerable group of these among the delinquents (in a category combining the two)—there were relatively few among the non-delinquents. It should be possible at a later time, however, to construct a table that would discriminate emotionally healthy youngsters not only from neurotics but also from those who are psychopathic or asocial.

It is to be hoped that similar devices for the 'spotting' or 'screening'

[5] As our weighted score method of constructing prediction tables is fully described in *Unraveling* (Ch. XX), as well as in our other works, there is no need to do more here than to point out that the five factors comprising the Social Prediction Table, for example, were initially selected from among those showing the widest range of difference in incidence between the 500 delinquents and their matched 500 non-delinquents. The percent of delinquents existing in each subcategory of a factor provides the basis for a total weighted score derived from summating the individual scores on the subcategories of all five factors in which a particular boy is placed. The table itself was derived from separately distributing all the delinquents and all the non-delinquents (for whom their status on all five factors was known) into 'score classes'. The incidence of the delinquents and of the non-delinquents within each 'score class' expresses the likelihood that a distribution essentially like the one actually obtained in such an 'experience table' will be found to exist in other similar samples of cases. Whether or not such a table has applicability to samples of different composition (in respect, for example. to ethnic make-up or economic status) had to await practical demonstration.

[6] *Unraveling*, Table XVIII–43, Mental Pathology, p. 239.

or early 'identification' or early 'diagnosis' not only of delinquent but of emotionally disturbed non-delinquent children will be developed by others, notably by psychiatrists and psychologists, who have access to extensive and intensive case materials.

The reader is invited to consult *Unraveling* (Chs. XVIII and XIX) regarding the diagnostic procedures that led to a determination of neuroticism (including marked and mild neurotics and those with neurotic trends). Briefly, a comparison of diagnostic findings made by the Rorschach experts[7] and the psychiatrist who examined the boys[8] was made and differences in diagnostic classification were resolved in those few instances in which the diagnoses were conflicting.[9]

Before proceeding to the construction of a table distinguishing neurotic from non-neurotic (emotionally healthy) delinquents, I should like to point out that we did not design the research which eventuated in *Unraveling* to encompass the development of the tables which form the subject of this paper. Had this been among our primary objectives, we would in the initial selection of delinquents and matched non-delinquents have deliberately included a greater number of neurotics as well as youngsters with other forms of mental pathology. The use of the data for the present purpose is purely a by-product of the larger work and must be accepted only as illustrative of the kind of instruments that mental hygienists might well develop to aid (by large-scale early identification) in the prophylaxis of emotional disturbance, in the hope of preventing or intercepting the development of personality distortions.

For the present purpose analysis was made of forty-seven social factors, forty-two traits of character structure (derived from the Rorschach test), and eighteen traits of temperament (derived through psychiatric examination). Although in *Unraveling* we found when comparing delinquents as a group with their non-delinquent controls that they differed markedly in the factors reflecting what we have chosen to call the 'under-the-roof culture', this did not prove to be significantly so in differentiating neurotic from non-neurotic (emotionally healthy) delinquents, neurotic delinquents from neurotic non-delinquents, and neurotic non-delinquents from emotionally healthy non-delinquents. It may well be that there were more subtle aspects in the early rearing of these children which would have reflected marked differences between the two groups, but in this inquiry, at least, they were not revealed.

[7] Ernest G. Schachtel and the late Anna Hartoch Schachtel.

[8] Dr Bryant E. Moulton, who was for twelve years associated with the Judge Baker Guidance Center.

[9] *Unraveling*, p. 242, note 8.

Examination of the factors studied disclosed the most significant differences to be in traits of basic character structure (derived from the Rorschach test), i.e. in the deposits in the personality of intrapsychic tension or conflict.[10]

DISTINGUISHING NEUROTIC FROM NON-NEUROTIC (EMOTIONALLY HEALTHY) JUVENILE DELINQUENTS

The first 'screening' table that we have developed (which, of course, requires testing against other samples of cases) has to do with differentiating in a group of true delinquents (excluding for the present those who are pre-psychotic, psychotic, psychopathic, or asocial) between those who are neurotics and those who are emotionally healthy. Sufficient differences were not disclosed in the social background of neurotic and non-neurotic delinquents to make possible the construction of a diagnostic table utilizing social factors. But among the traits of basic character structure (derived from the Rorschach test) there are eighteen (out of a total of forty-two) from among which we could make a choice of five as a basis for the 'screening' or 'diagnostic' table.[11] (*For footnote*[11] *see p. 156.*)

In selecting five traits[12] from among the eighteen, we were guided

[10] In order to develop suitable diagnostic instruments it was necessary to limit the initial selection of basic character traits (from among which five were to be chosen) to those not only significantly differentiating the neurotic delinquents from the neurotic non-delinquents, but at the same time also differentiating the neurotic non-delinquents from the non-delinquents who were non-neurotic (i.e. emotionally healthy). Otherwise, we would, in effect, be making a comparison of delinquents as a group with non-delinquents as a group (already accomplished in *Unraveling*—see Table XX–7).

[12] *Common Sense:* 'The faculty of thinking and acting in the ways of the community; it may be present even if some acts of the individual run counter to accepted mores; there may be, for instance, a conflict between common sense and a fantastic thirst for adventure.' *Enhanced Feeling of Insecurity and/or Anxiety:* 'While insecurity and anxiety play a considerable role not only in pathological cases but also in many normal persons, enhanced insecurity and/or anxiety designates a state in which these feelings play a decidedly stronger role in the personality, either quantitatively or qualitatively, than is usual in the average person. They may, however, remain largely unconscious.' *Feeling of Helplessness and Powerlessness:* 'Particularly frequent and important, and very often unconscious kind of insecurity feeling, in which the individual feels he cannot do or change or influence anything, especially with regard to the course of his own life.' *Fear of Failure and Defeat:* 'A frequent consequence of anxiety, especially in persons with an overcompetitive attitude. Fear of failure may concern every sphere of life, not only work or play, but all human relations. It may lead either to greater effort or to inhibitions, aloofness, and to recoiling from competition.' *Defensive Attitude:* 'Unwarranted defensiveness, either exaggerated in proportion to the attack, or the attack is entirely imagined. The means of defending oneself are varied: they consist sometimes of a "shell-like" attitude of warding off every approach and erecting a wall around oneself; they sometimes take a more aggressive form, as, for instance, in persons who are very sensitive to any criticism and are provoked by it to defiant or obstinate or opinionated behavior; and so on.' (All terms defined by Ernest and the late Anna Hartoch Schachtel for *Unraveling*.)

by considerations largely related to (*a*) the number of known cases, and (*b*) the size of the differences between the incidence of a trait among the emotionally healthy delinquents, on the one hand, and the neurotic delinquents, on the other. The five traits chosen, with their subcategories and their weighted scores, are as given on page 157.

[11] (*To preceding page.*)

Trait*	Non-neurotic Delinquents	Neurotic Delinquents	Difference
	%	%	%
Common Sense—XVII–6			
(354 delinquents)	92·8	64·7	28·1
Social Assertiveness			
XVIII–2 (288 delinquents)	52·7	17·9	34·8
Defiance—XVIII–3			
(326 delinquents)	35·5	56·0	−20·5
Enhanced Feeling of Insecurity and/or Anxiety			
XVIII–7 (338 delinquents)	6·4	52·9	−46·5
Feeling of Not Being Taken Care Of—XVIII–9			
(235 delinquents)	19·6	46·3	−26·7
Feeling of Not Being Taken Seriously—XVIII–10			
(274 delinquents)	28·9	87·2	−58·3
Feeling of Not Being Recognized—XVIII–11			
(298 delinquents)	29·0	54·9	−25·9
Feeling of Helplessness			
XVIII–12 (317 delinquents)	30·7	75·5	−44·8
Fear of Failure and Defeat			
XVIII–13 (306 delinquents)	36·4	78·4	−42·0
Feeling of Resentment			
XVIII–14 (295 delinquents)	66·7	87·7	−21·0
Marked Suspiciousness—XVIII–23			
(314 delinquents)	43·5	73·7	−30·2
Feeling of Isolation—XVIII–25			
(262 delinquents)	31·8	72·1	−40·3
Defensive Attitude—XVIII–26			
(321 delinquents)	43·5	82·2	−38·7
Conventionality—XVIII–29			
(260 delinquents)	36·8	14·6	22·2
Feeling of Ability to Manage Own Life—XVIII–32			
(242 delinquents)	87·9	44·9	37·0
Vivacity—XVIII–39			
(145 delinquents)	50·0	31·1	18·9
Compulsory Trends—XVIII–40			
(347 delinquents)	14·1	33·6	−19·5
Introversive Trends—XVIII–42			
(260 delinquents)	23·7	42·5	−18·8

* The chapter and table numbers following each trait are from *Unraveling*, to facilitate cross-reference. The figures in parentheses represent the number of known cases.

Trait	Weighted Score
COMMON SENSE	
Present*	73·9
Absent	28·8
ENHANCED FEELING OF INSECURITY AND/OR ANXIETY	
Absent	81·7
Present	21·4
FEELING OF HELPLESSNESS AND POWERLESSNESS	
Absent	85·6
Present	46·1
FEAR OF FAILURE AND DEFEAT	
Absent	86·4
Present	50·0
DEFENSIVE ATTITUDE	
Absent	86·4
Present	51·4

* In *Unraveling*, the Rorschach traits were divided into three categories: If a trait was present in large degree in the character structure or dynamics, it was designated as *marked*; if the presence of a trait was only suggestive or indicated to a low degree, it was designated as *slight* or *suggestive;* if a trait did not play a relevant or significant role in the character structure, it was designated as *absent*. Ernest Schachtel has said of this categorization: 'I suppose that one can find almost every trait at some time and to some degree in most persons; . . . but by the use of these classifications we want to indicate whether or not the traits in question play a considerable role in the structure of the personality.' (p. 209)

Examination of the findings resulted in combining in four of five of the traits the category *marked* and *slight or suggestive*; and in one trait the category *slight or absent*.

The highest possible weighted score that any one boy can be assigned is 414, the lowest 197·7.

The resulting table provides for four score classes.

TABLE 1

EMOTIONALLY HEALTHY AND NEUROTIC JUVENILE DELINQUENTS IN EACH OF FOUR WEIGHTED SCORE CLASSES BASED ON FIVE CHARACTER TRAITS DERIVED FROM RORSCHACH TEST

Weighted Score Class	Emotionally Healthy Delinquents		Neurotic Delinquents		Total
	No.	%	No.	%	No.
Under 200	0	0·0	15	100·0	15
200–299	8	21·1	30	78·9	38
300–399	92	76·7	28	23·3	120
400 and over	69	100·0	0	0·0	69
Total cases	169		73		242

Coefficient of Correlation 0·872.

Assuming its validation, the table indicates that if a boy scores under 299 on the five traits the likelihood that he is neurotic is very great. It would appear to be a certainty that he is if he scores under 200. If he scores 300 and over there is a strong likelihood that he is emotionally healthy; this becomes practically a certainty if he scores 400 or over.

DISTINGUISHING NEUROTIC DELINQUENTS FROM NEUROTIC NON-DELINQUENTS

The second screening device made possible by our materials is designed to distinguish neurotics who are likely to act out their aggressive impulses from those who turn their aggressiveness against themselves. Such a differentiation ought to be of assistance to clinicians who are charged with the psychotherapy of neurotics.

Of the total of forty-two traits, there were twelve which sufficiently differentiated the two groups to be utilizable in a screening table.[13]

[13]

Trait*	Neurotic Delinquents	Neurotic Non-Delinquents	Difference
Enhanced Feeling of Insecurity and/or Anxiety—XVIII–7	%	%	%
(104 dels., 148 non-dels.)	52·9	72·3	−19·4
Feeling of Not Being Recognized or Appreciated—XVIII–11			
(91 dels., 96 non-dels.)	54·9	38·5	16·4
Suspiciousness—XVIII–23			
(114 dels., 146 non-dels.)	73·7	54·8	18·9
Destructiveness—XVIII–24			
(85 dels., 134 non-dels.)	47·1	22·4	24·7
Conventionality—XVIII–29			
(89 dels., 117 non-dels.)	14·6	38·5	−23·9
Manage Own Life—XVIII–32			
(69 dels., 119 non-dels.)	44·9	26·9	18·0
Masochistic—XVIII–34			
(108 dels., 124 non-dels.)	27·8	61·3	−33·5
Destructive-Sadistic—XVIII–36			
(85 dels., 134 non-dels.)	48·2	23·1	25·1
Self-Control—XVIII–38			
(116 dels., 166 non-dels.)	37·9	55·4	−17·5
Vivacity—XVIII–39			
(61 dels., 94 non-dels.)	31·1	6·4	24·7
Compulsory Trends—XVIII–40			
(113 dels., 155 non-dels.)	33·6	56·8	−23·2
Preponderance of Extroversive Trends—XVIII–41			
(90 dels., 129 non-dels.)	38·9	22·5	16·4

* The chapter and table numbers following each trait are from *Unraveling*, to facilitate cross-reference. The figures in parentheses are the number of known cases.

158

In the final selection of five traits, we were again guided essentially by considerations relating to (*a*) the number of known cases, and (*b*) the widest percentage differences between the incidence of a trait among the neurotic delinquents and the neurotic non-delinquents. These considerations resulted in utilizing the following five traits,[14] which are presented with their subcategories and weighted scores:

Trait	Weighted Score
ENHANCED FEELING OF INSECURITY AND/OR ANXIETY	
Absent	54·4
Present	34·0
SUSPICIOUSNESS	
Present	51·2
Slight or absent	31·3
MASOCHISTIC TRENDS	
Absent	61·9
Present	28·3
SELF-CONTROL	
Absent	49·3
Present	32·4
COMPULSORY TRENDS	
Absent	52·8
Present	30·2

Summations of the highest and of the lowest possible total weighted score that can be achieved by an individual in order to establish his status on the five traits are 269·6 and 156·2 respectively. Within these limits, the neurotic delinquents and the neurotic non-delinquents were distributed within 'score classes' in each of the two groups separately.

This resulted in *Table* 2 from which it is determined (assuming its validation on other samples of cases) that among a group of neurotics a boy scoring under 200 is not likely to act out his aggressive impulses; one scoring 250 and over very probably will do so.

[14] *Enhanced Feeling of Insecurity and/or Anxiety:* (See note 12 for definition.) *Suspiciousness:* 'Indiscriminate or exaggerated suspicion toward others, not warranted by the objective situation. The person is usually not aware that he is unduly suspicious. He thinks rather that he is merely cautious or realistic, or that he is really being persecuted, and so on.' *Masochistic Trends:* 'A tendency to suffer and to be dependent.' *Self-Control:* 'The faculty of controlling the discharge and expression of affectivity (in no way identical with the faculty of the healthy and mature person of determining the direction and way of his life and what he wants to get out of his life within the given circumstances).' *Compulsory Trends:* Includes 'both the classical neurotic compulsions as well as the less dramatic and less manifest cases of a rigidity that does not permit of flexible adaptation to changing situations, and usually originates from anxiety. It is an attempt to overcome anxiety and to defend oneself against it. The anxiety may be conscious or, more often, unconscious.'

TABLE 2

NEUROTIC DELINQUENTS AND NEUROTIC NON-DELINQUENTS IN EACH OF THREE
WEIGHTED SCORE CLASSES BASED ON FIVE TRAITS OF CHARACTER STRUCTURE
DERIVED FROM RORSCHACH TEST

Weighted Score Class	Neurotic Delinquents		Neurotic Non-delinquents		Total
	No.	%	No.	%	No.
Under 200	16	20·7	61	79·3	77
200–249	56	70·9	23	29·1	79
250 and over	12	92·3	1	7·7	13
Total cases	84		85		169

Coefficient of Correlation ·613.

DISTINGUISHING NEUROTIC NON-DELINQUENTS FROM NON-NEUROTIC (EMOTIONALLY HEALTHY) NON-DELINQUENTS

Although our primary focus of interest is in the development of instruments for the early detection of delinquents, the control group of non-delinquents in *Unraveling* makes it possible for us to step out of the area of distinguishing between those among delinquents or potential delinquents who are neurotic and non-neurotic to consider the screening of non-delinquents as neurotics or non-neurotics. Although we are hesitant to go beyond the limits of our special field of inquiry, we permit ourselves to do so because there is significance, as will be seen below, in the fact that three of the five traits that markedly distinguish neurotic delinquents from non-neurotic delinquents also distinguish neurotic non-delinquents from *non-neurotic* non-delinquents. As two of the traits are different, however, there would appear to be evidence that delinquency is an entity always different in some respect from other forms of emotional disturbance. Apart from this, those who are concerned with the early recognition and treatment of emotional illness may find this third table suggestive and worthy of testing against other samples of cases.

Unlike the other two tables, in which an insufficient number of social background factors was found to differentiate the two groups involved, there are six social factors that distinguish neurotics from emotionally healthy boys among the non-delinquents in *Unraveling*.

The factors are: working mother (40·2% among neurotics vs. 26·3% among the non-neurotics), inadequate supervision by mother

(40·8% vs. 28·7%), unsuitable (lax, erratic, overstrict) discipline by mother (44·3% vs. 28%), unfriendliness of parents to children's friends (66·9% vs. 57·7%), meager home recreational facilities (41·2% vs. 30·9%), lack of attachment of boy to father (40·1% vs. 32·4%). However, the differences are not as great as those found in the incidence of certain character traits.[15] (Even were the differences more marked than they are, we would prefer to utilize traits of basic

15

Trait*	Neurotic Non-Dels.	Non-Neurotic Non-Dels.	Difference
	%	%	%
Common Sense—XVII–6			
(441 non-delinquents)	66·9	94·9	−28·0
Methodical Approach to Problems—XVII–10			
(428 non-delinquents)	25·3	44·0	−18·7
Social Assertiveness—XVIII–2			
(381 non-delinquents)	3·7	31·7	−28·0
Enhanced Feeling of Insecurity and/or Anxiety—XVIII–7			
(414 non-delinquents)	72·3	4·9	67·4
Feeling of Not Being Taken Care of—XVIII–9			
(295 non-delinquents)	58·7	8·4	50·3
Marked Feeling of Not Being Taken Seriously—XVIII–10			
(335 non-delinquents)	83·0	32·0	51·0
Feeling of Helplessness and Powerlessness—XVIII–12			
(370 non-delinquents)	88·7	33·3	55·4
Fear of Failure and Defeat—XVIII–13			
(395 non-delinquents)	89·1	47·7	41·4
Feeling of Resentment—XVIII–14			
(296 non-delinquents)	81·7	33·2	48·5
Hostility—XVIII–22			
(333 non-delinquents)	76·7	40·2	36·5
Marked Suspiciousness—XVIII–23			
(377 non-delinquents)	54·8	8·7	46·1
Feeling of Isolation—XVIII–25			
(321 non-delinquents)	70·5	17·2	53·3
Defensive Attitude—XVIII–26			
(389 non-delinquents)	77·5	24·4	53·1
Feeling of Being Able to Manage Own Life—XVIII–32			
(303 non-delinquents)	26·9	89·7	−62·8
Masochistic Trends—XVIII–34			
(358 non-delinquents)	61·3	26·1	35·2
Self-Control—XVIII–38			
(424 non-delinquents)	55·4	77·1	−21·7
Vivacity—XVIII–39			
(166 non-delinquents)	6·4	38·9	−32·5
Compulsory Trends—XVIII–40			
(417 non-delinquents)	56·8	15·6	41·2

* The table number following each trait is from *Unraveling*, to facilitate cross-reference. The figures in parentheses are the number of known cases.

character structure in order to keep to a uniform method of screening large populations of children.)

Applying the same considerations as in the two prior tables to the selection of five traits on which to construct a screening table, we have utilized the following five traits[16] presented here with their subcategories and weighted scores:

Trait	Weighted Score
ENHANCED FEELING OF INSECURITY AND/OR ANXIETY	
Present	89·2
Absent	14·0
FEAR OF FAILURE AND DEFEAT	
Present	54·9
Absent	12·0
FEELING OF RESENTMENT	
Present	58·9
Absent	13·8
DEFENSIVE ATTITUDE	
Present	66·9
Absent	15·9
COMPULSORY TRENDS	
Present	68·2
Absent	23·3

TABLE 3

NEUROTIC AND NON-NEUROTIC (EMOTIONALLY HEALTHY) NON-DELINQUENTS IN EACH OF FOUR WEIGHTED SCORE CLASSES BASED ON FIVE CHARACTER TRAITS DERIVED FROM RORSCHACH TEST

Weighted Score Class	Neurotic Non-delinquents		Non-neurotic Non-delinquents		Total
	No.	%	No.	%	No.
Under 200	13	10·8	112	89·2	125
200–249	10	41·7	15	58·3	25
250–299	20	76·9	9	23·1	29
300 and over	33	94·1	2	5·9	35
Total cases	76		138		214

Coefficient of Correlation ·923.

[16] *Feeling of Resentment:* 'The feeling of frustration, envy, or dissatisfaction, with particular emphasis not on the positive attempt or hope to better one's own situation, but on the negative wish that others should be denied the satisfaction or enjoyment that one feels is lacking or withheld from oneself.' For definitions of the other traits, see notes 12 and 14.

The highest possible score in an individual case is found to be 338·1, the lowest 79·0.

Table 3 has been constructed from these five traits and (assuming its validation) is designed to distinguish neurotics from non-neurotics in a general school population (without reference, however, to pre-psychotic, frankly psychotic, or psychopathic or asocial children).

From this table it is determined (assuming its validation on other samples of cases) that if a boy scores under 200, there is little probability that he is a neurotic; if he scores 300 and over, he can be described as a neurotic.

The value of such discriminative instruments will be determined only by experimental application. The problem of skillful administration and interpretation of Rorschach test findings may limit the usefulness of such instruments. It may be, however, that simpler projective tests can be developed which would elicit the data needed.

Perhaps a group Rorschach test (or other projective tests) could be devised which would focus on the particular traits of basic character structure that appear to be significant in differentiating between neurotic delinquents and neurotic non-delinquents, between neurotic delinquents and non-neurotic (emotionally healthy) delinquents, and between neurotic and emotionally healthy non-delinquents.

A beginning must be made in utilizing tables such as the three presented here in order to determine how well they apply in other samples. Some such syndromization of traits or 'symptoms' makes possible the arrival at 'diagnoses' by methods other than purely psychiatric, and by persons other than psychiatrists. From the trend of evidence in the checks that have thus far been made of the Social Prediction Table developed in *Unraveling*, we are encouraged to think that we have in these three new diagnostic instrumentalities additional means for early recognition of neuroticism in delinquents and non-delinquents. We envisage the use of these three discriminatory tables as a supplement to the Social Prediction Table in order that following the 'spotting' of potential delinquents a further step can be taken in distinguishing the emotionally healthy delinquents and non-delinquents from the neurotics, and also in sorting out from among neurotics those who are likely to act out their aggressive impulses and those who are not. If, in addition, we can develop a table designed to identify those who are psychopathic or asocial, the mass screening of children (through group projective tests) at the point of school entrance would be closer to realization, making possible a concerted attack on delinquency and emotional disturbance in their incipient stages.

CHAPTER 13

Potential Juvenile Delinquents can be Identified: What Next?*

I. POTENTIAL JUVENILE DELINQUENTS CAN BE IDENTIFIED

Eleanor T. Glueck

In 1952 the New York City Youth Board, a municipal agency, undertook to check the usefulness of the Glueck Social Prediction Table designed to identify potential delinquents on school entrance at the age of about five and a half to six and a half years. The definition of delinquency used for this investigation is the one we adopted for *Unraveling Juvenile Delinquency*[138]:

'. . . delinquency refers to repeated acts of a kind which when committed by persons beyond the statutory juvenile court age of sixteen are punishable as crimes (either felonies or misdemeanors) —except for a few instances of persistent stubbornness, truancy, running away, associating with immoral persons, and the like. Children who once or twice during the period of growing up in an excitingly attractive *milieu* steal a toy in a ten-cent store, sneak into a subway or motion picture theatre, play hooky, and the like, and soon outgrow such peccadilloes, are not true delinquents even though they have violated the law' (p. 13).

The New York City Youth Board sample comprised 303 boys, on 244 of whom the findings are now definitive. Follow-up will continue for another two years on the remaining fifty-nine boys, as they are not yet seventeen. Those who are familiar with *Unraveling*, from the data of which the Social Prediction Table was constructed, know that we made an intensive study of 500 true delinquents and a control group of 500 non-delinquents, matched by age, ethnic origin, intelligence level, and residence in underprivileged areas of Greater Boston. The delinquents and non-delinquents were subjected to numerous tests and examinations, including a determination of their body build; physical and neurological condition; psychological

* Address delivered at the Sixteenth Annual Meeting of the World Federation for Mental Health, Amsterdam, The Netherlands, July 22, 1963.

make-up (as derived from Wechsler-Bellevue tests and Group Tests in Reading and Arithmetic); temperament (as determined by psychiatric examination); character structure (as determined by the Rorschach test); and an intensive study of the criminal history, family history, school history, recreational interests, and employment history.

A total of 402 traits and factors were studied for each boy, and eventually a comparison was made between the incidence of these traits and factors among the delinquents and their matched nondelinquents; and those traits and factors were identified which very markedly distinguished the delinquents from the non-delinquents. From these statistically significant differentiations a selection was made on the basis of which three predictive devices were constructed: one incorporating five traits of character structure (social assertiveness, defiance, suspiciousness, destructiveness, emotional lability); another utilizing five traits of temperament (adventurousness, extroversion in action, suggestibility, stubbornness, emotional instability); a third utilizing five factors of the 'under the roof culture' (affection of mother for boy, affection of father for boy, supervision of boy by mother, discipline of boy by father, and family cohesiveness).

As a beginning of experimentation with our method of screening potential delinquents, we recommended the use of the table based on the five social factors. It is this device which has come to be known in the literature of criminology as the Glueck Social Prediction Table.

Our hope in constructing the tables was that if there is indeed a very marked difference between delinquents and non-delinquents as determined in a study of true delinquents in comparison with matched non-delinquents who ranged in age between ten and seventeen, perhaps these differences would identify *potential* delinquents and non-delinquents at a point in their lives before the onset of antisocial behavior. This was of course a hope, and whether or not the application of the Social Prediction Table to samples of children in the general population would give the desired results, naturally had to await application and follow-up in order to determine whether the predicted results were borne out by what happened to the children in later years. In this connection, an eminent biostatistician, Edwin Bidwell Wilson,[1] had this to say:

'What one would like to do if he has to predict the occurrence or nonoccurrence of some specified phenomenon is to find some attribute or practicably small group of attributes which can be observed before the phenomenon and whose presence has been

[1] Professor Emeritus of Vital Statistics, Harvard School of Public Health.

invariably associated with its occurrence and whose absence has been invariably associated with its nonoccurrence in a large group of instances in the past. Then, if the future unrolls in these respects on the pattern of the past, prediction would be sure. The conditions for this assurance are hard to meet. . . .'

And, further, he commented:

'. . . A tool for distinguishing confirmed delinquents from non-delinquents may or may not be serviceable in distinguishing within a group of non-delinquents those who are potential delinquents from those who are not.

'One may argue about the probable serviceability of the tables for this suggested use. . . . *A priori* argument will not get far, howsoever it be extended. What one needs is trial and observation. . . .'[2]

The New York City Youth Board, which in 1952 undertook to test the Social Prediction Table, selected two schools in very high delinquency areas in New York City and applied the Table to all the boys in the entering grades. The initial group encompassed 244 boys who were five and a half to six and a half years old. As it was soon discovered that the ethnic derivation of these boys differed greatly from the boys of *Unraveling* on whom the original Table was constructed, questions arose as to the wisdom of continuing the study. The initial Youth Board sample was made up of a few white children, a large group of negroes, and some Puerto Ricans; the *Unraveling* sample comprised boys largely of Italian, Irish, Lithuanian, English, and Old American derivation.

We agreed with our Youth Board colleagues that if the screening device was to be of general use, it should be applicable to children of all ethnic origins, but we urged that at least the white and negro groups be numerically equalized. The total New York sample eventually reached 303, of whom 130 were whites, 131 negroes, and 42 Puerto Ricans.

Those especially interested in the prediction-validation project are referred to the article, 'Spotting Potential Delinquents: Can It Be Done?' [182] and to Chapters 8, 9, and 10 of this volume, which describe the problems encountered and the changes that were made during the course of the experiment in the direction of improving the predictive instrument.

Briefly, the original table comprising five factors has gone through

[2] Wilson (1951), A Symposium on *Unraveling Juvenile Delinquency. Harvard Law Review*, **64**, 1039.

a considerable evolution, being subsequently reduced to three factors, omitting *affection of mother for boy* and *affection of father for boy* because agreement among raters on these factors was found to be very low. However, correlation between the status of the boys of *Unraveling* on the original five-factor table with their status on the three-factor table resulted in a coefficient of 0·96. Later the factor *discipline by mother* was substituted for *discipline of boy by father*, to provide more effectively for a considerable number of situations in which the father is not a member of the family group. (The three factors now being utilized are *family cohesiveness, supervision by mother, discipline by mother*.) I should point out that *discipline by mother* could have been incorporated in the initial prediction table because it distinguished just as markedly between the delinquents and the control group of non-delinquents as did *discipline by father*.[3]

The changes made in the original five-factor table are all in the direction of reducing the danger of false-positive and false-negative identifications and making easier the gathering and the rating of factors.

An examination of the boys who were being falsely identified as delinquents or as non-delinquents had pointed to the need of refining the Social Prediction Table in the direction, first, of determining the score-class in which about an equal proportion of the boys were predicted as delinquents and as non-delinquents, and developing a method of pinpointing in this score-class the boys who are likely to become delinquent and those who are not. Those interested in knowing how this was accomplished are invited to consult Chapters 9 and 10 above.

But of greatest interest is how the follow-up turned out.

The New York City Youth Board has recently reported its findings on 244 boys in a paper, 'Ten Years' Experience with the Glueck Social Prediction Table for the Identification of Potential Delinquents'.[4] I can give only the briefest presentation of the results:

Of 193 boys identified as having a very low chance of delinquency, 186, or 96·4 per cent, have remained non-delinquent to the age of seventeen when the follow-up ceased.

At the other extreme, of 27 boys identified by the three-factor table as having a very high chance of delinquency, 23 or 85·1 per cent have become serious, or persistent minor, offenders. (It should be said that in two of the three ethnic groups the results are far better than the average percentage indicates.)

In the middle category, that is those predicted as having about an even

---

[3] See *Unraveling*, p. 131, Table XI–22, *Parents' discipline of boy.*
[4] Prepared by Maude M. Craig & Selma J. Glick, *Crime and Delinquency*, July 1963.

chance of delinquency or non-delinquency, there are 19 boys. Of these,
9 are now clearly serious, or persistent minor, offenders and 10 remain
non-delinquent.

If the New York City Youth Board had had the information
necessary to further define the middle group of cases (I might say
that this requires knowledge of certain traits of temperament) it
would have been possible to distribute most of the 19 boys into those
clearly having a low chance, as opposed to those having a fairly high
chance of delinquency, as is the case in another study carried
on by the Commissioners' Youth Council in Washington, D.C.,
known as the Maximum Benefits Project; *there* only *4 out of 179*
boys and girls were *not clearly identified* as potential delinquents or
non-delinquents.

As regards this latter investigation on 132 boys and 47 girls who
were drawn from a group of schools in one of the highest delinquency
areas in Washington, D.C., because teachers thought these children
might be on the road to delinquent careers, preliminary findings have
recently been reported by Emory F. Hodges, Jr. and C. Downing Tait,
Jr., both child psychiatrists, in their paper, 'A Follow-up Study of
Potential Delinquents':[5]

Of the boys and girls initially identified as non-delinquents, all but
one remained non-delinquent at the end of 8 years of follow-up.

Of the boys and girls identified as potential delinquents, 81 per cent
are already delinquent.

As some of these boys and girls are still only 14 years of age,
follow-up must continue at least until they reach 17.

Drs Hodges and Tait have concluded:

'. . . Although the follow-up study of the prediction program
is still incomplete, results so far certainly suggest that the Gluecks'
method of assessing the child's family life is a useful instrument
for identifying potential delinquents. We believe it logical that
any comprehensive delinquency prevention program should include such a system of early detection of delinquency. . . .' (p. 452).

As regards the conclusions of the New York City Youth Board
the following quotations are relevant:

'The Glueck Prediction Table has undergone many changes
since its original construction, all aimed at refining it and making
it a better method of examining the family backgrounds of boys,
and for sensitizing us to the specific factors in family life which, if
allowed to persist, tend to produce delinquency.'

'The revised three-factor table appears to be an important guide

[5] *The American Journal of Psychiatry*, November 1963.

in highlighting those factors. We do not regard it as a substitute for sound clinical judgment but as an additional tool to aid in the diagnostic process.' (p. 261. See also note 5, Chapter 7 above.)

Since the New York study was concerned with identifying true delinquents and non-delinquents at school entrance at the approximate ages of five and a half to six and a half years, and in *advance* of overt evidences of delinquent or pseudo-delinquent behavior, and the Washington Project focused upon distinguishing true delinquents from pseudo-delinquents among school children *already* showing signs of difficult behavior, the latter study may be said to complement the findings of the former.

In both experiments the predictive device emerges as a good operational tool.

What is to be done now that a device has been successfully tested for the early identification of delinquents? There follows a brief examination of some implications of this important question.

II. IMPLICATIONS OF THE FACT THAT POTENTIAL DELINQUENTS ARE IDENTIFIABLE EARLY IN LIFE*

Sheldon Glueck

WITH all due caution, we think it can now be said that a method has been developed for identifying potentially delinquent children. A great problem remains, however: How can this be built into a community-wide program of prophylaxis and therapy designed to supply timely intervention at an early age in order to deflect from their predicted course children identified as probable pre-delinquents?

To state the issue is to alert the public to the seriousness and immediacy of a vast and growing social problem with which courts, correctional and punitive facilities, that take hold of the problem when persons are already persistently delinquent, have not been able to cope adequately.[6]

* Address delivered at the Sixteenth Annual Meeting of the World Federation for Mental Health, Amsterdam, July 22 1963.

[6] The appallingly high statistics of recidivism are too well known to require specific citation, but the interested reader might bear in mind that of 1,000 delinquent boys who appeared in the Boston Juvenile Court between 1917 and 1922, 88 per cent continued their delinquencies during a five-year period following their court appearance. See *One thousand juvenile delinquents; their treatment by court and clinic* [45]. There have doubtless been improvements since the study was made; but the figures of recidivism continue high, as is shown by the substantial proportion of adult offenders who have a juvenile delinquency record. One might summarize traditional efforts to deal with delinquency as a case of too little and too late.

It is clear, beyond any reasonable doubt, that the greatest promise lies in early detection and timely preventive intervention; for we have long been convinced from the materials in our numerous researches that *in delinquency one is dealing not with destiny but with destination*; and destination can (hopefully) be altered.

In the United States, in recent years, a number of criminologists have been urging—and to a considerable extent the federal Government has responded—that broad, all-embracing programs of general economic and social welfare are the answer to the delinquency and crime problems. This ignores the fact that, whether one looks at neighborhoods, or classes, or cultures or subcultures, only certain individuals are chosen or choose themselves for careers of crime. It ignores the fact that most social pressures are selective and not universal, and that individuals vary in their responses to quite similar social influences. In other words, the mass-attack on delinquency overlooks the fact that, in maladjustment, one is dealing with differential contamination; and contamination involves not merely subjection to unwholesome environmental influences—which affect everybody—but also individual immunity or lack of immunity. This basic truth, so frequently overlooked by sociologic criminologists, means that the individual clinical approach cannot be ignored.

We are all in favor of general programs to abolish poverty, to provide decent housing, to 'improve the status of the working class', to control the 'population explosion', and so on. But such reforms are only remotely and indirectly involved in the etiology of delinquency in the individual case.

The famous European criminologists—Lombroso, Ferri, Garofalo, Aschaffenburg, Bonger, and others—tended to couch their preventive programs in terms so general as to amount to little more than baffling *clichés*. Thus, Aschaffenburg concluded that 'every measure that helps to make the people physically, mentally and economically healthier is a weapon in the struggle against the world of crime'. Ferri, though somewhat more specific, still emphasized broad-ranging reforms, suggesting what he called 'penal substitutes', such as free trade, reduction in hours of labor and in the consumption of alcohol, and the like. Socialistic criminologists, convinced that all crime is due to the capitalistic private-profit system, argue that crime will disappear under a Socialist economy. At the other end, certain eugenists contend that delinquency would be eliminated at the source, or at least greatly reduced, through birth-control measures. There may be some truth in all such general approaches.

However, it seems to us that where some precision has been obtained in a segment of the vast and complex sociocultural web, which gives promise of guiding action *specifically*, it ought to be made use of. That is why we say that, granting there are widespread and deep-stirring socioeconomic currents arising out of population movements from agricultural to industrial occupations and from rural to urban residence, and that these problems rightly command the attention of researchers and planners, there are also more specific and immediate areas in modern urban life that challenge to action.

Pre-delinquency is one of the most significant and vital of such specific problems. It can no longer be left exclusively to the untutored and frequently planless efforts of parents. In that connection, let me quote from something we said in *Unraveling Juvenile Delinquency*:

> 'Although misconduct either prior to or after school entrance may cause real concern to parents and teachers, their recognition of true danger signals of delinquency for the purpose of applying preventive and early corrective measures is not to be expected; and it certainly cannot be determined in advance of the onset of external signs of maladjustment whether a particular child is a potential delinquent or merely evidencing emotional growing pains. Even an experienced clinician generally cannot ascertain, until the beginning of puberty, whether certain kinds of aberrant behavior mark the beginning of a delinquent career' (p. 258).

Before making specific suggestions, let me point out that of course we do not limit desirable effort to early discovery of potential delinquents, vitally important as this is. In a work called *Delinquents in the Making* [153], which is a less technical version of the data of *Unraveling*, we defined several areas of preventive effort:

1. Those designed to cope, through reconditioning, education and psychotherapy, with the traits and characteristics of the delinquent himself.
2. Those involving parent-child relationships and other aspects of family life.
3. Those dealing with school curricula and teacher training.
4. Those concerned with the wholesome and constructive use of leisure time.

However, one can begin with the application of screening devices in the schools, designed not merely to discover which children are being distorted emotionally and characterially, but to aid parents and teachers with practical advice on the relationship of affectional and disciplinary practices to the formation of personality and character.

I suggest that a pilot project be set up in several cities, designed

171

(*a*) to use prediction devices to determine at an early age which school children are in substantial danger of developing into persistent delinquents because of faulty parental attitudes and behavior; (*b*) to develop techniques for informing parents, tactfully and helpfully, of necessary modifications in their child-rearing practices; (*c*) to give practical aid, through clinics attached to school systems, in bringing about such modifications.

The fears expressed in some quarters that the use of our Social Prediction Table would unjustly 'stigmatize' innocent children as delinquents are, in our opinion, unfounded. One aspect of the proposed pilot project is the development of school counselors both to assess home conditions and to carry out clinical instructions with tact and sympathy. The prediction device is not some gadget to be applied by anybody untrained in the assessment of parent-child relationships. It is an instrument to be used only by those who have had sufficient training in its employment.[7]

The pilot project should of course include competent clinicians in a position to devote time and thought to furnishing necessary prophylactic advice in the case of those children shown to be in substantial danger of developing into delinquents.

In brief, the question which challenges us and should challenge all concerned with preventing delinquency is, simply: Is it better to let children and parents drift into attitudes and practices that have been shown to have a marked tendency to produce delinquency; or is it preferable, both for the family and for society, to detect early signs of impending trouble and furnish skilful and timely therapy and instruction to children and parents in situations found to be critical?

We are convinced that persons sincerely concerned with human welfare and with advancing the resources of mental hygiene will not find it difficult to know how to answer this question. As Hippocrates, the Classical prophet and leader of medicine, long ago said, 'Healing is a matter of time, but it is sometimes also a matter of opportunity.'

[7] While we do not ourselves have the time or facilities for training personnel for the pilot projects, it is believed that such a service might well be performed by the New York City Youth Board and the Washington (D.C.) Commissioners' Youth Council, which have pioneered in the experiments concerned with the validation of the Social Prediction Table.

PART III

Progressive Penology

CHAPTER 14

Predictive Devices and the Individualization of Justice
SHELDON GLUECK

I

IT is becoming belatedly evident to scholars and practitioners in the administration of criminal justice that the most pervasive and complex issue is not so much the definition of crimes and the manner of their proof, but rather how to obtain a more efficient and just system of sentencing. The familiar cliché about the need to 'individualize justice' had worn thin before it was quite clear exactly what individualization involves.

How can a court individualize the sentence? This fundamental question has been all too lightly treated in the literature, the statutes, and penologic congresses. It has just been assumed that, given a probation officer's investigation report on the particular offender before him for sentence, the judge will, by his learning and experience, be able to decide the exact penal or correctional measure suited to the particular person undergoing sentence, as well as the limits of the time the offender needs to be subjected to such treatment in order to reform or be rendered non-dangerous.

But truly to 'individualize' the sentence in the case of any specific offender means, first, to differentiate him from other offenders in personality, character, sociocultural background, the motivations of his crime, and his particular potentialities for reform or recidivism; and, secondly, to determine which, among a range of punitive, corrective, psychiatric, and social measures, is best adapted to solve the special set of problems presented by that offender in such a way as materially to reduce the probability of his committing crimes in the future. When one pauses to reflect on all that this implies, it becomes evident that to speak glibly about 'individualization' is one thing; to be able to accomplish it is quite another.

It is time, therefore, that reformers of the criminal law faced the fact that the feasibility of a reliable technique of individualization is crucial to the entire program of scientific and humane criminal justice. If, in fact, a reasonably sound individualization cannot be accomplished by the means at hand, then, despite the lofty aims of

175

modern correctional philosophy, and regardless of the most elaborate investigations and case histories, the system will not work.

II

It is no wonder that, considering that individualization is a very difficult art, the product of judicial discretion in the sentencing process has not been good. It reflects a certain guesswork and even arbitrariness. Outstanding administrators have been disturbed by the haphazard product of criminal justice as seen in the sentencing results. Thus, in his 1940 *Annual Report*, Attorney General Robert H. Jackson complained:

'Inequality and disparity between sentences imposed in different districts for similar offenses involving like circumstances is a troublesome and vexatious problem. . . . It is obviously repugnant to one's sense of justice that the judgment meted out to an offender should be dependent in large part on a purely fortuitous circumstance; namely, the personality of the particular judge before whom the case happens to come for disposition. While absolute equality is neither desirable nor attainable, a greater approach to similarity of treatment than now prevails appears to be desirable, if not essential' (pp. 5–6).[1]

Although sentencing practices in the federal courts have improved in recent years, there are still evidences of erraticism. Thus, in the 1955 report of the Federal Bureau of Prisons, the average sentence for all offenses to federal institutions during the fiscal year ended 30 June 1955 was 25 months. While in the Third Circuit as a whole the mean was 24·4 months, looking at the picture by districts, the average sentence in Delaware was 13·7 months; in New Jersey, 20·8 months; in the Eastern District of Pennsylvania, 21·6 months; in the Middle District of Pennsylvania, 53 months; and in the Western District of Pennsylvania, 25·7 months. The sentences for individual crimes also varied with the different districts. There were similar divergencies in other circuits.[2]

In the important choice between imprisonment and probation, there was also considerable disparity. True, in the Third Circuit the proportion of persons placed on probation in the different districts

---

[1] See also *Annual Reports* 1941, pp. 11–12, 36, and 1942, p. 17 (Washington: U.S. Government Printing Office).

[2] U.S. Bureau of Prisons, Dept. of Justice (1956) *Federal Prisons* 1955, Table 22, pp. 74–7. At the time the above was written, neither the 1956 nor the 1957 reports was available.

was remarkably uniform, ranging from 48 per cent in the Western District of Pennsylvania to 54·6 per cent in the Middle District of Pennsylvania; but such consistency did not exist in a number of the other circuits. For example, in the First Circuit the total perecntage of probation was 61·8 per cent, or almost twice that of the 34·5 per cent norm throughout the federal system; in Maine it was 39·6 per cent, while in New Hampshire it rose to 84·2 per cent. So, also, in the Second Circuit, the total proportion of probationers was 41 per cent; but in Connecticut it was 53·3 per cent, while in the Northern District of New York it was only 29·1 per cent, and in the Eastern District of New York it was 37 per cent. Similarly, the percentages of probationers received from the courts by the federal probation system ranged in the Fourth Circuit from 25·5 per cent in Maryland to 62 per cent in the Eastern District of North Carolina; in the Fifth Circuit from 8·4 per cent in the Western District of Texas to 67 per cent in the Southern District of Mississippi; in the Sixth Circuit from 8·5 per cent in the Western District of Tennessee to 39·5 per cent in the Eastern District of Michigan; in the Seventh Circuit from 19·9 per cent in the Southern District of Indiana to 46 per cent in the Eastern District of Wisconsin; in the Eighth Circuit from 28·1 per cent in the Eastern District of Missouri to 52·3 per cent in the Eastern District of Arkansas; in the Ninth Circuit from 5·5 per cent in Arizona to 51·2 per cent in Oregon; and in the Tenth Circuit, omitting territories, from 29·9 per cent in Wyoming to 67·9 per cent in Utah (ibid., Table 32, p. 92).

To be sure, the indicated differences in the length of sentences and in the proportion of persons placed on probation are partly affected by variations in the size of the samples of cases involved in the comparisons; so that the results are to some extent a statistical artifact of comparing small numbers with large numbers. Nevertheless, a residue of considerable disparity remains; and the percentages and proportions still pose the question of the extent to which subjective influences enter into the process of individualization.

That the sentencing product in state courts is also very hard to explain or justify has been shown by several significant studies. Some time ago, for example, an analysis was made of over 7,000 sentences imposed by six judges over a nine-year period in a county in New Jersey. Each of these judges dealt with such crimes as larceny, robbery, burglary, embezzlement, assault and battery, rape. Since there was no special assignment of cases to any particular judge, each judge received cases in which, considering them as a whole and over a long period of time, the felonies were committed under similar circumstances and the offenders, as groups, did not vary in general personal make-up and social background. Yet, the study disclosed that while Judge A imposed sentences of imprisonment in 36 per cent of his cases and Judge B in 34 per cent of his, Judges C, D, E, and F imposed such sentences in 53, 58, 45, and 50 per cent, respectively, of their cases. Thus, an offender convicted of a serious crime had but three chances out of ten of going to prison under Judges A and B, and five chances out of ten if sentenced by Judges C, D, E, or F. Allowing the defendant to remain free in the community on probation, instead of sending him to prison, ranged, among the various judges, from 20 to 32 per cent; suspension of sentence, from 16 to 34 per cent. Other American studies have shown similar discrepancies in courts of different states.[3]

The writer once analyzed the sentences by judges in Massachusetts over a period of years, and he found a refinement in the exercise of judicial discretion that it would be difficult to justify. In 194 successive admissions to prison in one year, no fewer than fifty-three separate types of sentence were imposed. The sentences varied so much that there was great difficulty in reducing them to a few categories. A complex of motives is involved, including an attempt to influence the action of the parole board; but whatever the motives, how can one justify sentences that range from between $2\frac{1}{2}$ years and 3 years at one extreme to between $42\frac{1}{2}$ and 45 years at the other? Even if the best available information regarding the characteristics and background of each offender was laid before the judges as a basis for the exercise of their discretion—and this is not uniformly the case—they could not possibly tell, in advance, that it would take X from $2\frac{1}{2}$ to 3 years to reform, Y from $2\frac{1}{2}$ to $3\frac{1}{2}$ years, A from 40 to 45 years, and B from 42 to 45 years; or, if deterrence be stressed, that X's punishment should be half a year shorter or longer than Y's because they respectively need these different sentences to frighten them into not repeating their crimes, or the public requires this fine distinction to deter it from violating the various laws. Such ultra-precision is, on its face, irrational. It satisfies neither the prisoner's nor the public's conception of justice; nor does it meet the demands of a realistic individualization of sentence.

Sentencing erraticism is, of course, not limited to courts dealing with felonies; there is ample proof that it exists as well in the disposition of misdemeanants. Thus, as far back as 1912, a Commission on the Inferior Courts of the County of Suffolk (Massachusetts) prepared a report (No. 7) showing wide differences in dispositions, by total

[3] See F. J. Gaudet (1949), The sentencing behavior of the judge, in Branham & Kutash (Eds.), *Encyclopedia of criminology*, pp. 449–61 (New York: Philosophical Library).

and by individual offenses, in the various courts involved. The investigation concluded that

> '. . . these courts . . . exercise within their several districts the same criminal jurisdiction, . . . and although the social and economic conditions of the various districts do not differ essentially, there exists a radical and multiform variation and antagonism of practice in matters essential to the enforcement of law.'

A study of the New York City magistrates' courts showed like variations in sentence. In the report for 1914, the chief justice of those tribunals seems to have condoned this practice:

> 'I have never attempted, although the power of assignment of magistrates to this court is vested in me, to lay down any iron-clad rules as to punishment, because individual cases exceptional in nature so often arise.'

He overlooked the fact, however, that, given a large enough number of cases, the 'individual cases exceptional in nature' would turn up about as frequently before one judge as another.

Bearing in mind the reflex effect of any process of justice on every other, it must, in fairness, be pointed out that not all the responsibility for the sentencing situation is the judges'; prosecuting attorneys must take their share, for their recommendations as to sentence are involved. But, essentially, judges are the officials entrusted with the determination of sentence; and this decision has a significant effect on everything that follows: the place and length of possible or actual peno-correctional treatment. Commenting on the above-mentioned New Jersey study, the investigators fixed the judges' responsibility in the following reasonable manner.

> '. . . given a sufficient number of cases, one could expect that two judges would give sentences whose average severity would be about equal (providing that the judges were influenced only by the circumstances of the crime and those of the prisoner). Conversely, given a sufficiently large number of cases, if one finds that the average severity of the sentences of two judges is appreciably different, one is justified in saying that the factors which determine this difference in the sentencing tendencies are to be found outside the circumstances of the crime and those of the prisoner and hence probably in the judge, since he is the other factor which is always present.'[4]

[4] F. J. Gaudet, G. S. Harris, & C. W. St. John (1933), Individual differences in the sentencing tendencies of judges. *J. crim. L. & Criminol.* **23**, 813.

The New Jersey study concluded that

'the sentencing tendency of the judge seems to be fairly well
determined before he sits on the bench. In other words, what
determines whether a judge will be severe or lenient is to be found
in the environment to which the judge has been subjected previous
to his becoming an administrator of sentences' (ibid. p. 814).

This is not a novel problem in the administration of justice. In
England, at the turn of the century, Sir Henry Hawkins, an experienced magistrate, criticized sentencing practices in these words.

'The want of even an approach to uniformity in criminal sentences is no doubt a very serious matter, and is due, not to any
defect in the criminal law (much as I think that might be improved
in many respects), but . . . to the great diversity of opinion, and
therefore of action, which not unnaturally exists among criminal
Judges. . . .
'. . . The result of this state of things is extremely unsatisfactory,
and the most glaring irregularities, diversity and variety of sentences, are daily brought to our notice, the same offence committed
under similar circumstances being visited by one Judge with a long
term of penal servitude, by another with simple imprisonment,
with nothing appreciable to account for the difference.
'In one or the other of these sentences discretion must have been
erroneously exercised. . . . Experience, however, has told us that
the profoundest lawyers are not always the best administrators of
the criminal law.'[5]

Some legal philosophers have gone so far as to make a sort of
virtue of erratic judicial practices. Thus, Ehrlich, discussing 'freedom
of decision' on the Continent, cheerfully regards the personality
of the judge as the desirable crux of the problem. The administration
of justice, he says,

'has always contained a personal element. In all ages, social,

[5] Harris (Ed.) (1904), *The reminiscences of Sir Henry Hawkins Baron Brampton*,
pp. 285–7. See also S. Romilly (1810), *Observations on the criminal law in England as
it relates to capital punishment, and on the mode in which it is administered*, in which
the author says, 'It has often happened, it necessarily must have happened, that the
very same circumstance which is considered by one judge as matter of extenuation,
is deemed by another a high aggravation of the crime. The former good character of
the delinquent, his having come into a country in which he was a stranger to commit
the offence, the frequency or the novelty of the crime, are all circumstances which
have been upon some occasions considered by different judges in those opposite lights;
and it is not merely the particular circumstances attending the crime, it is the crime
itself, which different judges sometimes consider in quite different points of view.'
(p. 17).

political and cultural movements have necessarily exerted an influence upon it; but whether any individual jurist yields more or less to such influences . . . depends of course less on any theory of legal method than on his own personal temperament. The point is that this fact should not be tolerated as something unavoidable, but should be gladly welcomed. For the one important desideratum is that his personality must be great enough to be properly entrusted with such functions. The principle of free decision is really not concerned with the substance of the law, but with the proper selection of judges; in other words, it is the problem of how to organize the judiciary so as to give plenty of scope to strong personalities. Everything depends upon that.'[6]

This is all very well. But how these 'strong personalities', once they are brought into judicial service, are to function efficiently without being erratic or prejudiced in their sentencing judgments is a basic issue that cannot be avoided. Discretion there should certainly be; but the problem is to provide a technique whereby discretion shall be allowed ample creative scope and yet be subjected to rational external discipline or self-discipline.

III

There are several ways of doing this. The familiar one is to permit sentence revision by some appellate body.[7] But such a twice-removed tribunal could not greatly improve on the original sentencing practices, or at best could only bring about a superficial uniformity of sentence.[8] The basic problem—the proper exercise of creative discretion at the sentencing and releasing stages—cannot be met in this way.

Another device is detailed legislative prescription of criteria to be applied by the judge in assessing the length and nature of the sentence. The difficulty here is that the legislature may surround the judge with so clumsy an apparatus of control as to permit of but a poor counterfeit of scientific individualization. An illustration of a legislative attempt to cabin and confine judicial discretion is the

[6] E. Ehrlich (1921), Judicial freedom of decision: its principles and objects, transl. by E. Bruncken from Freie Rechtsfindung und freie rechtswissenschaft (1903), in *Science of legal method* pp. 47, 74.

[7] See Soboloff (1955), The sentence of the court: should there be appellate review? *A.B.A.J.* **41**, 13.

[8] This is the distinct impression obtained by the author from an analysis of a large sample of the decisions of the English Court of Criminal Appeals. See also Hall (1937), Reduction of criminal sentences on appeal. *Colum. L. Rev.* **37**, 521, 762.

Italian penal code project of the late Professor Enrico Ferri.[9] In accordance with his policy of emphasizing the dangerousness of the offender and, at the same time, providing for 'necessary guarantees' of the individual's right to uniformity of consideration at the sentencing stage, Ferri furnished an elaborate schedule of 'conditions of dangerousness' and 'conditions of less dangerousness' to be prescribed by the penal code in advance and to be applied by the judge as a basis for computation of the type and length of the individual convict's penal treatment. At the same time, he emphasized the need of providing for 'segregation for a period relatively or absolutely unlimited'.

He listed no fewer than seventeen 'circumstances which indicate a greater dangerousness in the offender' and eight circumstances of 'less dangerousness'. Among the former, he included such items as 'dissoluteness or dishonesty of prior personal, family, or social life'; 'precocity in committing a grave offense'; 'having acted through ignoble or trivial motives'; 'time, place, instruments, manner of execution of the offense, when these have rendered more difficult the defence by the injured party or indicate a greater moral insensibility in the offender'; 'execution of the offense by means of ambush or stratagem or through the commission of other offenses or by abusing the aid of minors, the deficient, the unsound of mind, the alcholic'; and other such considerations. Among the circumstances presumed to indicate 'less dangerousness in the offender', Ferri's code lists, for example, 'honesty of prior personal, family, and social life'; 'having acted from excusable motives or motives of public interest'; 'having yielded to a special and transitory opportunity or to exceptional and excusable personal or family conditions'; 'having in repentance confessed the offense' not yet discovered or before being interrogated by the judge; and other such considerations.

Doubtless these are all useful and relevant hints; and similar data are, of course, often taken into judicial account, whether prescribed in a statute or not. But the Ferri code contains numerous directives regarding the application of these criteria to measure off the dimensions of the judge's discretion. For example, it is provided that 'if there occurs only one circumstance of greater dangerousness, the judge shall apply the sanction in a measure not less than half between the minimum and the maximum set forth for the offense committed by the accused'; and 'if there occurs only one circumstance of less dangerousness, the judge shall apply the sanction in a measure less

---

[9] For a more extended and detailed exposition and analysis of this work than is here indicated, see 'Principles of a rational penal code'[19], reprinted in *Crime and correction*[152].

than half between the minimum and the maximum'. Similarly, other fractions of the total indeterminate sentence are to be measured off, depending on the presence of two or more circumstances of dangerousness or of less dangerousness.

The Ferri code also provides an elaborate system of punishments ('sanctions') which must be taken into account by judges in connection with the conditions of dangerousness and of less dangerousness, thus further complicating the process of individualization. For example, for ordinary offenses by persons over eighteen, it provides the 'mulct' (a species of fine); 'local relegation' (prohibition of residence in the place of the offense for from three months to three years); 'confinement' (compulsion to reside in the commune named in the sentence, which must be 'distant not less than 100 kilometres' from that where the offense occurred, where the injured party resides, and where the offender resides); obligatory day labor (in workhouse or agricultural colony, without night detention, for from one month to two years); simple segregation in workhouse or agricultural colony (with compulsory industrial or agricultural day labor and night isolation for from three months to fifteen years, the type of labor to conform to 'the previous life and aptitudes for labor' of the convict); and rigorous segregation in 'an establishment of seclusion' (with compulsory day labor and night isolation for from three to twenty years, or for an indeterminate period of not less than ten years). There are similarly elaborate provisions to be juggled by the judge in the case of social-political offenders, juvenile offenders, and adults in a state of 'mental infirmity'; and there are 'complementary sanctions' to be taken into account, such as special publication of the sentence, suspension from exercise of trade or profession, interdiction from public office, expulsion of a foreign convict, binding over for good behavior, etc.

The foregoing analysis provides a vivid conception of what can happen when the code drafter or legislature concocts a clumsy admixture of the oil of discretion and the water of rule. The Ferri system is so mechanical and complicated in conception and design that one has a picture of a judge checking up on whether, say, 'circumstances of greater dangerousness' numbered 1, 3, 7, 10, 12, and 17 and 'circumstances of less dangerousness' numbered 2, 4, 6, and 8 are applicable to a defendant before him; ascertaining which of the numerous sanctions or combinations thereof are pertinent; then, using a computing machine to figure out just how much incarceration is called for in the application of the individual's sentence and where. In making such detailed provisions to be automatically applied at the time of sentence by means of a judicial arithmetic, the purpose of realistic individualized treatment is largely defeated. Is it not possible to have a less mechanical system which will still guide judges in the process of individualization?

This is attempted in the sentencing provisions of the Model Penal Code, which the American Law Institute is in process of drafting.[10] Section 7.01, for example, provides 'Criteria for Withholding Sentence of Imprisonment and for Placing Defendant on Probation':

'1 The Court may deal with a person who has been convicted of a crime without imposing sentence of imprisonment if, having regard to the nature and circumstances of the crime and to the history and character of the defendant, it deems that his imprisonment is unnecessary for protection of the public, on one or more of the following grounds:

(*a*) The defendant does not have a history of prior delinquency or criminal activity, or having such a history, has led a law abiding life for a substantial period of time before the commission of the present crime;

(*b*) The defendant's criminal conduct neither caused nor threatened serious harm;

(*c*) The defendant did not contemplate that his criminal conduct would cause or threaten serious harm;

(*d*) The defendant's criminal conduct was the result of circumstances unlikely to recur;

(*e*) The defendant acted under the stress of a strong provocation;

(*f*) The victim of the defendant's criminal conduct consented to its commission or was largely instrumental in its perpetration;

(*g*) The imprisonment of the defendant would entail excessive hardship because of his advanced age or physical condition;

(*h*) The character and attitudes of the defendant indicate that he is unlikely to commit another crime.

'2 When a person who has been convicted of a crime is not sentenced to imprisonment, the Court shall place him on probation if he is in need of supervision, guidance or direction that it is feasible for the probation service to provide.'

The Model Penal Code provides other criteria to be taken into account in the imposition of fine and for sentence of imprisonment.

[10] Model Penal Code 47–52 (Tent. Draft. No. 4, 1955). The Chief Reporter is Professor Herbert Wechsler; the sentencing provisions are largely the product of Professor Paul W. Tappan, Associate Reporter. Since this was written, the Code has been completed.

For example, among the criteria for a sentence of 'extended term' of imprisonment which the court may impose on a person convicted of a felony, section 7·03 specifies:

'1 The defendant is a persistent offender whose commitment for an extended term is necessary for protection of the public. . . .

'2 The defendant is a professional criminal whose commitment for an extended term is necessary for protection of the public. . . .

'3 The defendant is a dangerous, mentally abnormal person whose commitment for an extended term is necessary for protection of the public. . . .

'4 The defendant is a multiple offender whose criminality was so excessive that a sentence of imprisonment for an extended term is warranted. . . . '

True, many judges tend, at present, to take into account the type of criteria included in the Model Penal Code; but the spelling of them out should be helpful in reminding judges to consider, systematically, various matters deemed relevant by the code drafter. Unlike the situation in the Ferri code, freedom of judicial discretion remains unhampered; but the listing of the considerations to be taken into account should, in the long run, bring about greater sentencing consistency. Still, as will be indicated shortly, even such a device is inadequate.

An approach similar to that of the American Law Institute was taken in 1957 by a distinguished Advisory Council of Judges, of the National Probation and Parole Association, in *Guides for Sentencing*. After soundly advising the judge that 'moderation and objectivity should be his goals', this publication provides some useful hints as to the kind of factors the judge should take into account. Some of these are similar to and may have been suggested by the factors which have emerged in follow-up and predictive research as relevant to expectable subsequent behavior. This is true, for example, of the following:

'The defendant whose first involvement in crime came late in life is more likely to succeed on probation than one who began at an early age and has continued in criminal behavior since then' (p. 38).[11]

Again,

'The defendant whose parents, brothers, and sisters have respected society's demands of law and order, whose family life

[11] This age factor has been proved to be of great significance in numerous follow-up studies.

demonstrates mutual love and consideration, whose parents have given him reasonable and consistent discipline, and whose family members are eager to help him, is a better probation risk than one who does not have these advantages.'[12]

As in the case of the Model Penal Code's criteria, such suggestions are helpful; but they are insufficient. For the judge has no way of knowing how closely related such suggested factors are to various types of postsentence behavior. The criteria have not been evaluated regarding the relative weight to be assigned to them in the total size-up of the offender. This can only be done through systematic follow-up investigations which have related numerous traits and factors in the make-up and background of various types of offenders to their actual postcorrectional conduct.

The question thus presented is whether there is available, for the purposes of scientific differentiation of treatment, an instrument that can aid the judge in determining which factors have been demonstrated, by systematic analysis of objectified past experience, to be truly relevant to the expectable behavior of various offenders, and how much relative weight to give such factors in the particular case before the judge for sentence.

IV

This brings one to a striking, yet usually overlooked, aspect of the history of penology and code drafting; namely, that all the reform devices of the present century—the juvenile court, probation, the indeterminate sentence, classification within institutions, parole—depend for their efficiency on the reasonable predictability of human behavior under given circumstances. Yet, all these forward-looking additions to the apparatus of criminal justice were adopted long before this indispensable basis for their success—predictability—was available, and they still ignore or minimize the crucial element of predictability.

Since scientific individualization of justice promises to reduce recidivism, it is desirable. But can it not be more efficiently brought about than by merely supplying the judge with a set of criteria which he should, more or less, take into account, without knowing their relative weights in terms of expectable behavior, and which many

---

[12] This statement is reminiscent of the Social Prediction Table derived from *Unraveling juvenile delinquency*[138]. But it should be noted that, unlike that Table, it does not indicate the relative weight to be accorded good discipline as opposed to poor, family cohesiveness as opposed to family disintegration, parental affection as opposed to various types of parental neglect.

dedicated and intelligent judges nowadays actually do take into account anyhow?

Some American and a few foreign criminologists believe that the answer lies in the prognostic instrument known as the prediction table. In several follow-up researches which have checked on the posttreatment careers of various classes of ex-prisoners, my wife and I have constructed a series of prognostic instruments which we believe give reasonable promise of ultimately bringing about better sentencing practices and treatment results than are achieved at present. It would require too extensive a discussion to describe and illustrate in detail the predictive devices developed for sentencing to various types of imprisonment, for placement on probation, for release on parole, and for predicting the postparole conduct of former prisoners over a considerable span of time. Our various publications, moreover, render full account of the techniques of prediction.[13] A brief exposition of the method, however, is justified by way of illustration.

In our first study, *500 Criminal Careers*, we thoroughly investigated the preinstitutional life histories of 500 former inmates of the Massachusetts Reformatory for young adult felons during a five-year postparole 'test period' following their discharge from that institution. Some fifty factors in the constitution, social background, and behavior of these offenders, from childhood through the parole and postparole periods, were explored and analyzed. By means of correlation tables, the degree of relationship between each of these biologic and social factors and the postparole behavior of the men was determined. To give one example, in respect to their prereformatory industrial habits, the men were subclassified into 'good worker', 'fair worker', and 'poor worker'.[14] By correlating each of these indus-

---

[13] 500 *criminal careers*[(26)], *One thousand juvenile delinquents*[(45)], *Five hundred delinquent women*[(44)], *Later criminal careers*[(71)], *Juvenile delinquents grown up*[(85)], *Criminal careers in restrospect*[(102)], *After-conduct of discharged offenders*[(119)], *Unraveling juvenile delinquency*[(138)], *Predicting delinquency and crime*[(212)]. See also 'Spotting potential delinquents; can it be done?'[(182)] For a scholarly survey of many prediction studies in the United States (not including, however, the prognostic devices developed in *Unraveling*), see Monachesi (1949), Prediction of criminal behavior, in Branham & Kutash (Eds.), *Encyclopedia of criminology*, p. 324 (New York · Philosophical Library), and Monachesi (1950), American studies in the prediction of recidivism, *J. crim. L.* 41, 269.

[14] *Good worker:* One who is reliable, steady, industrious, shows promise of continuing in regular employment, and is commended by his employers.

Fair worker: One who has the qualifications of the regular worker, but who permits his work to be interrupted by periodic drinking, the drug habit, occasional vagabondage, stealing, or the deliberate choice of irregular occupations, such as longshoring, for the chief purpose of having leisure time.

Poor worker: One who is unreliable, a loafer, lazy, dishonest, unstable, a vagabond, and wayward.

These factors were considered independently of the nature of the employment

trial categories with the criminal behavior of the men during the five-year test period, it was found that of the good workers, 43 per cent continued to commit crimes during the postparole test period; among the fair workers, 59 per cent recidivated; and of the poor workers, 68 per cent were criminalistic. These percentages we call 'failure-scores', because they indicate the proportion of the different subclasses of men who failed to reform, considered from the point of view of their status in respect to such a factor as prereformatory industrial habits.

Similar correlations were established between each of the fifty biologic and sociologic factors, on the one hand, and the actual postparole behavior, on the other, with the result that many factors were found to bear very little relation to recidivism, while some showed a very high association therewith.[15] In addition to industrial habits preceding entrance to reformatory, the following five factors, among those of greatest relationship to postparole conduct, were then employed in the construction of a table which judges could use in the sentencing of offenders: (1) seriousness and frequency of prereformatory crime; (2) arrest for crimes preceding the offense for which sentence to the reformatory had been imposed; (3) penal experience preceding reformatory incarceration; (4) economic responsibility preceding sentence to the reformatory, and (5) mental abnormality.[16]

(except where support was derived through proceeds of prostitution or other illegitimate occupations) or seasonal or other fluctuations in industry, and they express the man's general disposition toward work. The judgments were based upon the combined opinions of employers, police, and relatives, the last being given the least weight. Thus, a poor worker is one who, in the long run, constitutes a liability to the employer.

[15] Thus, the coefficients expressing the relationship between the failure-score on the factors used in the prognostic instrument were high, ranging from ·44 to ·68, the greatest possible value of the Pearsonian 'mean square contingency coefficient' in a threefold table being ·82. But the coefficient expressing the relationship between the type of offense committed—that is, whether it was a burglary, larceny, robbery, or sexually-motivated crime—and postparole recidivism or reform was only ·12; and the coefficient of contingency measuring the relationship of the seriousness of the offense for which the men were sentenced to the reformatory and their postcriminal record was only ·05, or practically nil. Yet, the disposition of cases is fundamentally based on these latter factors!

[16] The percentages of 'total failures' for the subcategories of the above factors are:
(1) serious offender, 67%; frequent minor offender, 53%; occasional minor offender, 35%; non-offender, 21%;
(2) offenders with prior arrests, 69%; those without prior arrests, 32%;
(3) offenders with prior penal experience, 74%; those without prior penal experience, 47%;
(4) economically-responsible offenders, 41%; economically-irresponsible offenders, 64%; and
(5) offenders showing no marked mental abnormality at time of entrance to reformatory, 60%; psychopathic personalities, 75%; psychotics, 87%.

By adding all the lowest percentages of failure (recidivism) associated with the various subcategories of these six factors, on the one hand, and all the highest, on the other, the two possible limits of 'total failure-scores' were determined. These turned out to be 244 as the lowest and 396 (or more) as the highest. Within this range of lowest and highest total failure-scores, the following subclasses of total failure-scores were then established: 244–295, 296–345, 346–395, and 396 and over. Finally, all 500 cases were distributed in a table according, on the one hand, to each offender's total failure-score on all six predictive factors and, on the other, to whether, so far as postparole behavior is concerned, he turned out to be a success, partial failure, or total failure.[17]

Total Score on Six Factors	Status Regarding Postparole Criminality (Percentage)		
	Success	Partial Failure	Total Failure
244–295	75·0	20·0	5·0
296–345	34·6	11·5	53·9
346–395	26·2	19·1	54·7
396 and over	5·7	13·7	80·6
All cases	20·0	15·6	64·4

From such a table, a judge who is considering whether or not to sentence any particular offender to a reformatory can, with reasonable accuracy, determine the advisability of such disposition of the case before him, provided he has reliable information as to that offender's status in respect to the six simple predictive factors upon

[17] *Success:* No police or court record, except occasional technical automobile law violations; no dishonorable discharge or desertion from armed forces; and no actual commission of individual criminal acts, whether or not arrest or prosecution resulted.

Partial Failure: Conviction on two minor offenses; or arrest for not more than three minor offenses, or five technical automobile or drunkenness offenses, not followed by conviction; or arrest for not more than two serious offenses not followed by conviction; or arrest for one serious offense not followed by conviction, and not over two minor offenses not followed by conviction or occasional minor offenses for which the violator of the law was neither arrested nor prosecuted (i.e. cases of sporadic, rather than continuous, misconduct definitely known to have occurred, but as to which no official action was, for various reasons, taken).

Total Failure: Arrest for three or more serious offenses not followed by conviction; or arrest for more than three minor offenses, except technical automobile or drunkenness offenses not followed by conviction; or convictions for one or more serious offenses; or convictions for more than five technical automobile or drunkenness offenses; or desertion or dishonorable discharge from the armed forces; or flight or escape from justice; or known commission of one or more serious offenses or a continuous course of minor offenses for which the violator of the law somehow was neither arrested nor prosecuted.

189

which this prognostic instrument is based. A prisoner scoring as low as 244 to 295 on these six factors—which have been found, by comparison of factors with outcomes in hundreds of cases, to be relevant to the question of reform or recidivism—belongs to a class that has about $7\frac{1}{2}$ out of ten chances (75 : 100) of turning out a success—i.e. of not committing crimes during the postparole period. On the other hand, one with as high a failure-score as 396 or over has but half a chance out of ten (5·7 : 100) of succeeding under this type of peno-correctional treatment. The first man also has two out of ten chances (20 : 100) of failing only partially and only half a chance out of ten (5 : 100) of turning out a total failure. The second has only $1\frac{1}{2}$ chances out of ten (13·7 : 100) of partial failure and the high probability of eight out of ten chances (80·6 : 100) of turning out to be a complete failure.

Since this first table was published, we have improved and refined many predictive instruments and have prepared them for each of the existing types of correction—e.g. probation with and without suspended sentence, jail, industrial school, reformatory, prison, and parole—for predicting varied response when offenders reach different ages, and for success or failure during a fifteen-year follow-up span. (See *Predicting Delinquency and Crime* [212].) By consulting a battery of tables covering all available forms of peno-correctional treatment, a judge could bring to bear on the instant case the added light of systematized and objectified experience, gleaned from hundreds of prior cases, regarding the behavioral potentialities of the individual before him for sentence.

V

But do such tables really work? Although many check-ups on various samples of cases are desirable, the probable effectiveness of such tables is today beyond mere speculation. Validation of the prognostic instruments by applying them to other large samples of offenders is most encouraging. For example, one of the tables we presented in *Criminal Careers in Retrospect* in 1943 deals with the conduct of the former prisoners of the Massachusetts Reformatory as soldiers in the armed forces during the first World War. By applying that table to a random sample of 200 soldiers who had committed crimes while in the army in the second World War, it was demonstrated that in 84·5 per cent of the 200 cases the prediction table would have foretold that the young men in question would commit military offenses; while in an additional 10 per cent of the

190

cases the table would have shown that the chances of the young men not committing offenses while in the army were only 50–50.[18]

But much more important is a validation experiment involving many cases and various types of sentence. We have recently completed a detailed check-up of the predictions based on our tables in *Juvenile Delinquents Grown Up* (1940), which had been systematically applied, case by case, as each boy was studied, to the 500 delinquents in *Unraveling Juvenile Delinquency* (1950). After a sixteen-year intensive follow-up, convincing evidence has been obtained that the tables in question actually did predict the behavior of these 500 youths while on straight probation, on probation with suspended sentence, in industrial schools, in reformatories, in prisons, on parole, and during a substantial follow-up period thereafter, and they did so with a total of 86 per cent accuracy. The detailed results will be found in *Predicting Delinquency and Crime*, Chapter IV.

While other validations are desirable, there is sufficient promise in the method to justify its cautious experimental use at the sentencing and paroling stages (see Part II of this volume, especially Chapter 8); and, indeed, prediction devices have for some years been employed by the Illinois Parole Board.[19]

In recommending the use of prognostic devices, the aim is, of course, not to substitute statistical tables for judicial experience in the sentencing of offenders. It is rather to supply the judge with an instrument of high promise in his work of individualizing justice. A judge should not follow these tables blindly; indeed, proof of a mechanical use of the tables might even raise an issue of denial of due process. The tables are, rather, designed to help the judge to see the individual offender in the perspective of organized experience with hundreds of other offenders who, in many crucial respects, resemble the person before him for sentence. The dimensions of the special problem each offender presents can be much more accurately assessed by the judge if he compares the crucial prognostic traits in the individual case with the total picture of hundreds of other offenders than if he relies exclusively on his unorganized experience or on a check-through of statutory criteria which, although listed, must still be weighed and assessed in each case and which have not been

[18] A. J. N. Schneider, C. W. LaGrone, E. T. Glueck & S. Glueck (1944), Prediction of behavior of civilian delinquents in the armed forces. *Ment. Hyg.* **28**, 456. For a detailed analysis of validations of the Glueck Social Prediction Table for early discovery of potential delinquents and for a device for distinguishing juvenile delinquents from youthful neurotics, see 'Identifying juvenile delinquents and neurotics', pp. 151–63, *above*.

[19] See Lloyd E. Ohlin (1951), *Selection for parole*.

evaluated in regard to their relevancy in terms of their relationship to recidivism or reform.[20]

But the use of prediction tables should not be lightly embarked upon. During the immediate future, it is preferable for a judge to continue to make his sentencing decision in each case as he does at present; then, to consult prediction tables and set down the predictive indications. After a few years, a thorough follow-up investigation can be made to compare outcomes on the basis of the existing *ad hoc* method with outcomes as predicted by the tables.

The prediction table, like the probation officer's presentence report, is but one instrument in aid of the individualizer of justice. A basic integration of the judge's sentencing role with the work of classification, treatment, and parole should improve the entire picture. If a clinical reception and classification center were established in the federal system for each circuit or in the state system for some appropriate administrative and jurisdictional area, if convicted persons were sent to such a regional center for a few weeks' observation and study, and if the judges were then furnished a comprehensive report on each offender, in which the relevant predictive factors were included, they would be in a better position than they are today to tailor the sentence to the individual case.[21]

Indeed, even greater integration seems desirable. The writer would favor a procedure which would permit of judges taking turns, on assignment by the chief judge, in serving as chairman of a regional classification and parole board for a year's period. Under such a scheme, the sentencing judge would fix the minimum sentence to take account of community reaction and the claims of general deterrence; and the judicial arm— not necessarily the particular judge involved in the case—would participate in determining the place of incarceration, the corrective-therapeutic treatment program, and the time and conditions of parole. The suggested arrangement would have several values: it would, first and foremost, have a tendency to correlate sentencing practices with treatment and releasing policies; it would also give the legally-trained judge a realistic education in the rele-

---

[20] The argument that since the judge 'saw the prisoner in court' and sometimes heard him testify, he is enabled to assess him expertly is obviously erroneous. In the first place, the crime and the brief contact with the prisoner in court are not only insufficient for a sound size-up, but may even be deceptive; in the second place, a considerable proportion of accused persons plead guilty and the judge can get very little idea about them. For these reasons, the probation officer's presentence report has assumed great importance.

[21] Under the provisions of the Federal Youth Corrections Act, the youth offender may be sent by the district court to the classification center at Ashland, Kentucky, for a period of observation and study prior to sentence, and a report of the findings is submitted to the sentencing court.

vancy of the behavioral disciplines to the carrying out of the mandates of justice; and, finally, it would furnish the necessary trained legal discipline and concern with a climate of due process at the treating, releasing, and supervisory stages. In brief, it would give both practical and symbolic reality to the policy that in the administration of justice the nonlegal expert—psychiatric, psychologic, sociologic, educational, religious, or other—should be 'on tap and not on top'.

In this way, the judge can be aided in assuming the noble role of social physician that Aristotle, over two thousand years ago, had in mind when he said:

' . . . the knowing what is Just and what Unjust men think no great instance of wisdom because it is not hard to comprehend those things of which the laws speak. They forget that these are not Just actions, except accidentally: to be Just they must be done and distributed in a certain manner: and this is a more difficult task than knowing what things are wholesome; for in this branch of knowledge it is an easy matter to know honey, wine, hellebore, cautery, or the use of the knife, but the knowing how one should administer these with a view to health, and to whom and at what time, amounts in fact to being a physician.'[22]

[22] *The Nicomachean Ethics of Aristotle*, Book V, 1137a (Chase transl.).

CHAPTER 15

Two International Criminologic Congresses :
A Panorama

SHELDON GLUECK

I

Two international gatherings of importance to the study of crime and the improvement of the administration of criminal justice convened in Europe during the summer of 1955. One was the First United Nations Congress on the Prevention of Crime and the Treatment of Offenders, held in Geneva 22 August to 3 September; the other was the Third International Congress on Criminology, held in London 12 to 18 September. The United Nations Congress is a successor to the quinquennial congresses of the International Penal and Penitentiary Commission beginning in 1872; the criminologic gathering is a periodic feature of the International Society for Criminology, a non-governmental organization.

The United Nations assemblage was made up of official delegations appointed by the various governments, observers from invited specialized agencies, representatives of non-governmental organizations, and several relevant categories of persons 'participating in an individual capacity', including members of the bar and judiciary and university professors. The criminologic congress was made up of private participants interested in various aspects of the delinquency and crime problems.

Both meetings were prepared for with much care, and the documentation for both was of an exceptionally high order. If any criticisms on this score are to be made they are, first, that the participants were overwhelmed with an embarrassment of riches in the numerous documents involved and, second, that much of the material to be discussed did not reach the members in sufficient time to be thoroughly studied before the meetings. One of the most useful documents, which digested and discussed the relevant reports prepared or assembled by the secretariat, was compiled by the Federal Bureau of Prisons for use by the American delegation to the Geneva congress.[1]

---

[1] *Information for U.S. Delegates to the First United Nations Congress on the Prevention of Crime and the Treatment of Offenders* (mimeographed).

194

Over fifty of the eighty-five governments invited to participate in the United Nations Congress sent some 300 official delegates, each delegation having one vote. Hundreds of other interested persons attended on invitation. Preparations for the Congress took considerable time and were carried on not only in New York but in consultative groups in South America, Europe, the Middle East, and Asia. Recommendations digesting the conclusions of the regional conferences were deliberated on by the appropriate sections of the Congress, modified to meet the views of the discussants, and transmitted to the plenary sessions for debate and adoption.

Resolutions and recommendations of the Congress do not, of course, have the force of law; but they can have a powerful influence because of the governmental status of the participants as well as the wealth of learning and experience represented at such internation technical assemblages. The resolutions should strengthen the hands of leaders in the correctional field in countries which are still far behind the procession of correctional enlightenment.

The United Nations Congress considered the following topics:

1 Standard minimum rules for the treatment of prisoners.
2 Selection and training of personnel for penal and correctional institutions.
3 Open penal and correctional institutions.
4 Prison labor.
5 Prevention of juvenile delinquency.

It is obvious that the first four topics form a theoretical and functional whole; the fifth appears to have been brought in as an afterthought. Perhaps the reason for the inclusion of juvenile delinquency in an agenda so heavily loaded with penologic issues involving adults is the tremendous recent interest in children's problems and the belated recognition that the study, treatment, and prevention of child delinquency is the really crucial issue; that while there is considerable room for improvement in the area to which the first four items of the Congress were devoted, the problems there involved have previously received a great deal of discussion in both national and international gatherings;[2] and that even with marked improvements in the incarceration and correction of adult offenders the total influx of crime will not be greatly affected unless the wholesale supplier of adult criminalism—juvenile delinquency—is effectively coped with at the source.

[2] See, for example, The international prison congress of 1930[31] and Pre-sentence examination of offenders to aid in choosing a method of treatment[149].

Mimeographed versions of the resolutions and recommendations adopted by the Congress, as well as an edited compilation of these, have been issued by the United Nations General Assembly.[3] Each set of proposals serves as an annex to a resolution adopted in plenary session at the Congress, which requests the secretary-general to submit the recommendations to the Social Commission of the Economic and Social Council for approval; expresses the hope that they will be approved by the Council; provides that they be transmitted to the various governments with the recommendation that favorable consideration be given to their adoption; and that they be given the widest publicity by the secretary-general.[4]

It would require too much space to detail the numerous conclusions of what was a very busy Congress. The following are among the points of major interest.

I

The first section adopted a series of humane rules for the treatment of prisoners in institutions.[5] While general standards and recommendations for improvement of peno-correctional practices have been set forth in the conclusions of past international congresses,[6] the Geneva assembly spelled out the standards in detail, modernizing them and converting the platitudinous into the realistic and practical. Only a sampling of the ninety-four items involved can here be given. At the outset the framers took into account the 'great variety of legal, social, economic, and geographical conditions of the world' as making it 'evident that not all the Rules are capable of application

[3] U.N. Doc. A/Conf. 6/L. 17, Dec. 1, 1955. Credit is due the general rapporteur, Professor Thorsten Sellin, for the skill with which he wove together the numerous suggestions for recommendations and resolutions.

[4] The resolutions also express the wish that the governments send information on progress, for publication. There are certain variations among the resolutions, especially the one pertaining to juvenile delinquency which requests the General Assembly to transmit the 'Report to the Social Commission of the Economic and Social Council, calling its attention to the necessity of maintaining the priority already given to the question of juvenile delinquency in the program of work of the Social Commission', and recommending that the suggestions be included in the 'social defense work program'.

[5] *Standard Minimum Rules for the Treatment of Prisoners*, report by the secretariat, United Nations, A/Conf. 6/C. 1/L. 1; Amendments A/Conf. 6/L. 4.

[6] See note 2. The draft of rules considered by the Congress was prepared by the secretariat on the basis of regional conferences on the draft of standard minimum rules adopted in 1951 by the International Penal and Penitentiary Commission, A/Conf. 6/C. 1/L. 1, pp. 4–5, and *Information for Participants*, United Nations General Assembly, A/Conf. 6/Inf. 2, pp. 1–2. The rules 'are not meant to be purely optional, but on the contrary to be in the nature of a pledge on the part of prison administrations'. *Information for Participants*, op. cit., p. 2.

in all places and at all times', but that they are intended to 'stimulate a constant endeavor to overcome practical difficulties in the way of their application, in the knowledge that they represent, as a whole, the minimum conditions which are accepted as suitable by the United Nations'.

A basic principle is that the rules should be applied impartially; that 'there shall be no discrimination on grounds of race, color, sex, language, religion, political, or other opinion, national or social origin, property, birth, or other status'. At the same time it is provided that 'it is necessary to respect the religious beliefs and moral precepts of the group to which the prisoner belongs'.

Among the outstanding features of the rules is the requirement that no person shall be received in an institution 'without a valid commitment order', the details of which are to be entered in a bound registration book covering matters of identity, reasons and authority for the commitment, time of admission and release. There shall be segregation of inmates by sex, age, criminal record, legal reasons for detention, and treatment needs. Accommodations should meet detailed health requirements in respect to sleeping, working, and bathing quarters and general sanitation. Wholesome food 'of nutritional value adequate for health and strength' should be furnished. Open-air exercise and physical and recreational training should be provided. The services of at least one medical officer with 'some knowledge of psychiatry' should be made available at every institution, and there should be prenatal and postnatal care and treatment in women's institutions. A detailed program is set forth for the work of institutional medical officers.

Provisions for discipline and punishment are carefully enunciated, and 'inhuman or degrading punishments and use of instruments of restraint' are completely prohibited. Prisoners are entitled to make requests or complaints to the prison administration or judicial authority, and such petitions are to be promptly dealt with. Communication with family, friends, and religious and legal representatives is permitted.

High standards are required for prison personnel (a topic also separately dealt with in another section of the Congress); and it is provided that 'so far as possible, the personnel shall include a sufficient number of specialists such as psychiatrists, psychologists, social workers, teachers, and trade instructors'.

Excellent correctional philosophy is reflected in a number of guiding principles. The aim of imprisonment being 'ultimately, to protect society against crime', it is stated that 'this end can only be achieved if the period of imprisonment is used to insure, so far as possible, that upon his return to society the offender is not only willing but able to lead a law-abiding and self-supporting life. . . . To this end, the institution should utilize all the remedial, educational, moral, spiritual, and other forces and forms of assistance which are appropriate and available, and should seek to apply them according to the individual treatment needs of the prisoners', and 'should seek to minimize any differences between prison life and life at liberty which tend to lessen the responsibility of the prisoners or the respect due to their dignity as human beings'. The always difficult transition from prison to freedom is recognized in the provision that 'before the completion of the sentence, it is desirable that the necessary steps be taken to insure for the prisoner a gradual return to life in society . . . the treatment of prisoners should emphasize not their exclusion from the community, but their continuing part in it. Community agencies should, therefore, be enlisted wherever possible to assist the staff of the institution in the task of social rehabilitation of prisoners.'

Advanced practices of classification and of individualization of treatment are recommended. Post-institutional aftercare is set forth in detail.

There are special provisions for the mentally ill prisoners, for those awaiting trial, and for open correctional establishments.

Discussion. All in all, the rules comprise a chart and compass oriented toward the most advanced thinking in the correctional field. Not a few jurisdictions, both in the United States and abroad, have a considerable distance to travel if they would thoroughly implement their correctional attitudes and systems with provisions of which the foregoing are but samples. Some countries will have to change, fundamentally, their penal philosophy, to minimize the retributive and deterrent aspects and maximate the therapeutic and rehabilitative. The draft rules are intended to be not optional but 'in the nature of a pledge on the part of prison administrations'. But there is of course neither inspective nor coercive power on the part of any international agency to check on their adoption and on the nature of their implementation in practice. However, the wise provision for the furnishing of technical assistance in the correctional field to governments requesting it may in the long run prove much more efficacious than coercion would be. Even if many of these rules are not soon adopted, their publication should have the desirable indirect effect of causing a re-examination of fundamental conceptions and misconceptions in penal law from the realistic point of view of judging regimes by practical results in terms of reform versus recidivism.

II

An important *leitmotif* of the recommendations of the section dealing with the *selection and training of personnel*[7] is the statement in a heading that 'prison service [is] in the nature of a social service'. This is said to be a 'new conception . . . reflected in the tendency to add to the staff an increasing number of specialists, such as doctors, psychiatrists, psychologists, social workers, teachers, technical instructors', working together as a team. It is recommended that the full-time institutional staff have the status of non-political civil servants with high qualifications, professional training, and attractive salaries and living conditions. Training prior to final appointment, in-service training, discussion groups, and staff conferences are provided for.

Discussion. It is obvious that when a state shifts its practices from an essentially retributive-repressive program to one emphasizing human dignity and reformability it must place its correctional apparatus in skilled hands and emotionally well-balanced personnel. Surely, the perplexing task of salvaging human personality and character in cases where parents, teachers, and clergy have apparently failed is one that requires the highest talents and the marshaling of the deepest wisdom that the biosocial disciplines can contribute.

A familiar source of failure of reform movements in the correctional field is reliance on a new statute or code or prison structure to solve problems which only human dedication and ingenuity can hope to deal with successfully. This is not to say that the 'behaviorai scientists' can be expected to 'cure' crime through magic nostrums. The chief justification for staffing the correctional agencies with professional personnel is that they represent a deliberate effort to be *thoughtful* in coping with human maladjustments, instead of prejudiced or emotionally biased in angry resentment or superficial sentimentality.

In calling attention to the need for professional staffs in the correctional process the standards adopted by the Congress should strengthen the hand of the pioneers in the improvement of correctional practices in countries where it is still believed that repression is the prime remedy for crime and that professional personnel are not needed because it requires no special psychiatric, sociologic, or anthropologic training to use force. But even in certain American states where some effort is made to modernize the peno-correctional

[7] *The Recruitment, Training, and Status of Personnel for Adult Penal and Correctional Institutions*, report by the secretariat, United Nations, A/Conf. 6/C. 1/L. 2; Amendments A/Conf. 6/C. 1/L. 2.

régime, the recommendations, if brought to public attention, should raise questions about whether political affiliation should continue to be a chief qualification for appointments in the correctional field and whether a state can afford the wasteful luxury of untrained and unenlightened prison personnel. For here, as in so many of the affairs of life, it is not so much statutes, systems, or 'set-ups' as human beings who make or break the situation; and Pope's famous couplet holds true, particularly in the government of peno-correctional institutions:

> For forms of government let fools contest;
> What'er is best administer'd is best.

III

The recommendations pertaining to open institutions,[8] that is, those 'characterized by the absence of material or physical precautions against escape (such as walls, locks, bars, and armed or other special security guards) and by a system based on self-discipline and the inmate's sense of responsibility toward the group in which he lives', provide that the selection of persons for admission to such semi-free establishments should 'be made on the basis of a medico-psychological examination and a social investigation', since 'the criterion governing the selection of prisoners for admission to an open institution should be, not the particular penal or correctional category to which the offender belongs, nor the length of his sentence, but his suitability for admission to an open institution and the fact that his social readjustment is more likely to be achieved by such a system than by treatment under other forms of detention'. The advantages of the open institution are set forth. It is considered that it 'represents one of the most successful applications of the principle of the individualization of penalties with a view to social readjustment'; and, since it also has the merit of counteracting many of the disadvantages of short-term imprisonment, it is recommended that the open system be extended 'to the largest possible number of prisoners', subject to the necessary conditions of careful selection of the prisoners and proper management of the institution. Detailed measures are set forth intended to facilitate success under open-institution treatment.

A difficulty frequently encountered in connection with open establishments is presented by the understandably apprehensive attitude of residents nearby. The recommendation includes the necessity of obtaining 'the effective cooperation of the public in

---

[8] *Open Institutions*, report by the secretariat, United Nations, A/Conf. 6/C. 2/L. 1; *Open Institutions*, recommendations adopted by Section II, A/Conf. 6/L. 2.

general and of the surrounding community in particular for the operation of open institutions'. Emphasis is placed on the need of limiting the inmate body to a group small enough to permit of the officers' thorough acquaintance with the character and needs of the individual prisoner.

In addition to the series of pamphlet reports prepared by various national contributors to the symposium on open institutions and to the general report by the secretariat, two are of particular value in supporting the conclusions of the section regarding the value of open institutions as a major facility of the apparatus of correction and in assessing the conditions as to personnel and regime which are necessary for successful operation of the open institution.[9]

Discussion. The considerable interest of the section and Congress in the value of correctional establishments in which both the mental climate and the physical facilities are symbolic of a belief in the possibilities of therapy and rehabilitation of many offenders is a good antidote to the frequent American emphasis upon fortresses of 'maximum security'. It is becoming recognized that only a relatively small proportion of prisoners require the steel bars and high wall treatment to which the vast majority of prisoners are unnecessarily subjected. The occasional escapes are not too great a price to pay for the favorable opportunities afforded to many by an open institution for which residents are carefully chosen. Only in this way can the bedeviling internal contradiction in imprisonment be resolved: the incarceration of persons who have demonstrated that they are not sufficiently 'socialized' in an artificial, restricted, repressive environment which can only further prevent them from becoming socialized. In an open institution the inmate receives constant practice in balancing his selfish motive to decamp against the responsibility he owes the group to which he belongs and the officers who have expressed their confidence by transferring him to a relatively free environment. He has the opportunity of wholesome identification with desirable parent-figures. He gets practice in the art of 'live and let live' and in the satisfactions that come with group approval.

Both as a fundamental institution for the majority of those imprisoned, and as a proving ground for those en route to freedom via parole, there are great potentialities in various types of professionally staffed open institutions. In many countries and in most of the United States, however, the generous adoption of the philosophy,

[9] *Open Institutions: Selection of offenders suitable for treatment in open institutions,* by Jose A. Mendez, United Nations, A/Conf. 6/C. 2/L. 3; *Open Institutions: The place of the open institution in the penal system and in the community,* by Sir Lionel Fox, United Nations, A/Conf. 6/C. 2/L. 2.

techniques, and personnel of the open establishment will involve fundamental changes in the punishment provisions of criminal codes, the minimizing of the retributive and deterrent impulsions in the criminal law and the maximating of the therapeutic and rehabilitative, the increasing of flexibility of sentences as to both time and place, the enhancing of the role of the administrator of the correctional system, and the employment of therapists of various kinds.

IV

The recommendations on the perennial topic of *prison labor* are also essentially in harmony with the most advanced thought in the field.[10] For example, one of the general principles attacks a major evil in existing prison labor systems, in insisting that 'the interests of the prisoners and of their vocational training must not be subordinated to the purpose of making a financial profit from an industry in the institution'. Some penal institutions are still more concerned with the making of money for the state's treasury than the making of men for the state's welfare. The recommendations hold that 'work is not to be conceived as additional punishment but as a means of furthering the rehabilitation of the prisoner, his training for work, the forming of better work habits, and of preventing idleness and disorder'.

The state-use system, with compulsory governmental purchase of prison-made goods, is evidently preferred to the private-profit contractual system;[11] however, a compromise provision states that 'recourse may be had to private industry when sound reasons exist, provided adequate safeguards are established to insure that there is no exploitation of prison labor and that the interests of private industry and free labor are protected'. Vocational training is stressed.

[10] *Prison Labour*, published by the Department of Economic and Social Affairs, United Nations, ST/SOA/SD/5. (A questionnaire study involving thirty-eight countries.) *Prison Labour: Note on Various Aspects of Prison Labour*, memorandum prepared by the secretariat, A/Conf. 6/C. 2/L. 28. *Prison Labour*, draft resolution submitted by the general rapporteur, A/Conf. 6/L. 9. *Prison Labour*, recommendations adopted by Section II, A/Conf. 6/L. 8.

[11] The position on this matter is somewhat ambiguous. The recommendations as adopted by Section II (31 August 1955), dealing with prison labor (A/Conf. 6/L. 8), state that when adequate and suitable employment 'cannot be organized by private industries or by other means, the state-use system with compulsory government markets may offer a satisfactory solution'. The later (1 December 1955) compilation by the general rapporteur of *Resolutions and Recommendations Adopted by the Congress* (A/Conf. 6/L. 17) states that 'it is preferable that this be done under the state-use system with compulsory government markets'. In connection with this problem an interesting debate was held at the plenary session when Edward R. Cass, of the American delegation, offered an amendment to the section's resolution. He urged that the state-use system be given preference. On the vote, fifteen countries favored the amendment, fourteen opposed it, and there was one abstention.

Trade training is to be adapted to the demands of the free labor market, and trades should be sufficiently varied to permit of fitting occupational instruction to the different qualifications of inmates. Equitable remuneration for prison labor is recommended. 'It is desirable that it should be sufficient to enable prisoners, at least in part, to help their families, to indemnify their victims, to further their own interests within the prescribed limits, and to set aside a part as savings to be returned to them on discharge.'

Certain fundamental issues were left open, and it was recommended that regional consultative groups study such problems as the integration of prison labor with the national economy, remuneration for prison work, 'with particular reference to the principle that prisoners should be paid for their work on the basis of normal wages paid in the free labor market', appropriate labor programs for such special prisoners as the mentally abnormal, the 'work-shy', and professional classes; work opportunities for prisoners awaiting trial; aid to ex-prisoners in finding work on release.

A very promising resolution was adopted expressing the hope that as a means of facilitating the implementation of the Rules and Recommendations the United Nations will provide technical assistance 'to those governments requesting it', through sending needed experts, establishing institutions for training personnel, organizing seminars, and publishing guides or handbooks 'to facilitate the application of the standard minimum rules and the training of personnel'.

Discussion. It is doubtful whether certain of the countries represented at the Congress are in a position to carry out most of the recommendations. Even in the United States of today, the special interests of labor unions and manufacturers tend to clash with what would be a desirable inmate-centered program. It is difficult to see why prison labor is held to compete seriously with free labor if the industries are sufficiently varied.[12] The amount of prison goods produced is very small compared to the total free labor product of the country,

[12] 'Although the issue of competition is not currently an active one in general, the data presented above, when considered in conjunction with information contained elsewhere in the report, indicate that most of the states of Europe, North America, and Oceania have either capitulated to those raising complaints of competition by extensive modification of their prison labor programs, or have achieved an uneasy truce with the complainants, the existence of which is contingent upon continuation of high levels of employment and of economic stability. It would be rash to claim that the problem of the relationships between free labor and industry and prison labor has, in any realistic sense, been solved within the more highly developed countries. The issue may be latent rather than settled.' *Prison Labour*, ST/SOA/SD/5, United Nations Department of Economic and Social Affairs, New York, 1955, p. 47.

and since most prisoners were already at work at the time they committed their crimes it is hard to justify an attitude that by continuing to work in prison they will seriously compete with free labor.

Gradually, there should evolve in many countries a rational and fair solution of the prison labor problem in which (as in the federal and California systems) representatives of organized labor, industry, agriculture, and the public will pool their points of view, bearing in mind that the vast majority of inmates must at all events be freed some time, that members of organized labor and manufacturers' groups form part of that 'society' to which ex-prisoners will return for better or for worse, and that it remains true that 'Satan finds some mischief still for idle hands to do'. In the meantime, the setting of good standards for the prison labor problem should aid prison administrators in persuading legislators of the need of healing a major sore spot in the correctional field by bringing about constructive use of the inmates' working time.

V

It will be noted even from the partial samples presented above that the recommendations, suggestions, and provisions in respect to the adult offender are commendable, both in reflecting the most seasoned thought and experience in the field of penology and in setting standards which the different governments and correctional agencies within the various countries can measure up to at various stages of progress. It is interesting to note, however, that many of these 'advanced ideas' were embodied almost a century ago in the famous 'Declaration of Principles' of the American Correctional Association in 1870![13]

The most important aspect of the work of the Congress, however, was one which is truly fundamental—juvenile delinquency and predelinquency—on which an important basic report was prepared in advance by the secretariat.[14] Much time of the section involved was used in getting this aspect of the agenda on the right track, there being at the outset considerable fruitless discussion of the definitions of delinquency. But the resolution and recommendations that

[13] Formerly the National Congress on Penitentiary and Reformatory Discipline, organized in 1870. For an analysis of the Declaration of Principles, see Significant transformations in the administration of criminal justice[28] or *Crime and correction*: *selected papers*[152], pp. 27–53.

[14] *The Prevention of Juvenile Delinquency*, report by the secretariat, United Nations, ST/SOA/Ser. M/7–8 (Provisional uncorrected edition); *General Principles with Regard to the Prevention of Juvenile Delinquency*, note by the secretariat, United Nations, A/Conf. 6/C. 3/L. 3.

finally emerged from the work of the section are important.[15]

In its basic resolution, the Congress recognized that much fundamental investigation would have to be done. It was recommended that with the aid of expert non-governmental organizations certain researches be included in the social defense work program of the Social Commission of the Economic and Social Council, among them a detailed study of the methods for prevention of juvenile delinquency, 'in two stages': the first to be devoted to the 'possibility of organizing a social and health care or guidance system co-operating closely with the diagnostic services, and assistance to parents, particularly in the task of guidance'; the second to be an assessment of the 'practical value of certain direct and indirect measures for the prevention of juvenile delinquency', by means of regional projects in both developed and underdeveloped lands.

Another recommended study was an evaluation of the methods of 'special police services dealing with juveniles'.

The United Nations Regional Consultative Groups and Seminars were urged to continue to devote attention to juvenile delinquency. Organizations planning future congresses and seminars were asked so to select topics as to permit of 'useful comparison of the experience acquired in the various countries'. This theme of comparative study was emphasized by a number of speakers. The writer, for example, pointed out that through systematic cooperation between researchers in different lands it may be possible to develop a new science of comparative criminology involving investigations which employ standard definitions and methods; that thereby those influences found to be uniform in different countries could be detected, with the way open for a solid science of criminology. This idea was embodied in the list of recommendations comprising the annex to part 5F of the resolutions and recommendations of the Congress, which deals with research.

The deliberations on delinquency became fruitful after the barren search for definitions was replaced by a proposal that 'the discussion and study of the Congress should include not only those juveniles who have committed an act regarded as a criminal offense by the law of their country, but also those whose social situation or whose character places them in danger of committing such an act, or who are in need of care and protection'; and it was emphasized that 'preventive work should cover all three categories'. Without such a comprehensive point of view the discussions, like the usual activities of juvenile courts, would have been confined to situations in which

---

[15] 'Prevention of Juvenile Delinquency', recommendations adopted by Section III, A/Conf. 6/L. 11.

delinquency is already a *fait accompli*, when even at an early age it is extremely difficult to curb. Once the more realistic point of view was adopted by the section on delinquency, it became evident that the most promising approach was to emphasize *pre-delinquency*. To have a manageable method of discussion it was decided to deal with preventive work with pre-delinquents in the community, the family, the school, and the social services and other agencies, despite the obvious overlap in the classification.

After emphasizing the importance of the community[16] and neighborhood and their influence on behavior 'through the family, the school, religious and other social institutions', the conclusions and recommendations point out that community action to prevent delinquency is largely a matter of organizing the numerous local resources (through coordinating councils or similar devices) to provide a *milieu* 'in which children may develop without abnormalities of character' and in which 'those who are in danger of becoming delinquent may be discovered and guided toward conformity to normal standards'. The recommendations that follow include the integration of official and unofficial services for youth to meet the basic needs of early childhood, not only through wholesome and constructive activities of the family, school, and other social institutions, but also by means of child guidance clinics, parental counseling services, constructive leisure time outlets, and special schools.

Selection and adaptation of preventive activities from other countries are recommended, taking account of cultural differences. Special attention to 'delinquency areas' is urged. While it is pointed out that programs of 'general social welfare are not sufficient by themselves' to dispense with specific policies directed toward the prevention of delinquency, general improvement in urban housing conditions is called for, to 'be so organized as to provide for full community living'.

In introducing the recommendations regarding the family,[17] it is emphasized as axiomatic that the family is fundamentally important in development of personality, attitudes, and behavior, and that the impact of industrialization and urbanization has brought about considerable 'social, family, and personal disorganization. According to current opinion, delinquency appears to be intimately connected with the social and cultural changes that have operated through the family.'

Profiting from experience, it is recommended 'that in those societies that are recently becoming industrialized and where the family is

---

[16] See *Unraveling juvenile delinquency*[(138)], Chs. XIII, XXII.
[17] See *Unraveling*, Chs. VIII, IX, X, XI, XXII.

still a well-integrated and effective unit of control, serious effort should be directed to maintaining its cohesiveness in order to mitigate so far as possible the disorganizing consequences of industrialization'. It is of major importance that 'preventive efforts be designed to produce closer family ties, thus achieving greater affection, emotional security, and control through the family'. Recognising the family as the cradle of personality and character, the recommendations embrace provision of material needs to underprivileged households, including children's allowances where required 'to keep the family intact', to avoid the necessity of mothers working outside the home and to protect children of broken homes.

Counseling aids for parents and children are recommended. Conciliation devices for estranged parents, as well as psychologic aid to parents, should be provided. Children should, as far as possible, be kept in the family and there be given treatment for emotional and social needs, due process of law being observed when it is necessary to remove children compulsorily. Where the family situation is seriously inadequate, use should be made of foster homes. Placement in special institutions for delinquents should not be resorted to unless children have actually violated the law and supervision in their own homes has failed. Similarly, placement in caretaking institutions should occur only when care in the child's own home or in some foster home is impossible.

In discussing the role of education,[18] it is pointed out that, next to the home, the school is in the most intimate contact with the child up to adolescence, and that it plays an important role, not merely in his intellectual growth but also in his emotional and social development. Among the recommendations for the preventive work of the school is the provision of flexible curricula, to take account of individual differences; the school's playing of a 'constructive role in the development of character and attitudes among children, with the object of counteracting unhealthy influences in the community'; provision in the educational program of cooperation between school and family, in order to minimize children's difficulties of adjustment; and the placing of greater emphasis upon vocational guidance and other measures designed to aid adolescents in the transition from school to working life.

In connection with such school activities, it is recommended that the training of teachers should include preparation for understanding the problems of childhood and for discovery of children with emotional or behavioral difficulties, and that teachers should be of the type 'with which children can properly identify themselves in the

[18] See *Unraveling*, Chs. XII, XXII.

development of their character and goals of living'.[19] It is recommended that psychologic and social services attached to the school should be developed to advise both parents and teachers and that guidance clinics and testing and treatment facilities for children be established.

In the part of the recommendations dealing with social services (including health agencies) it is pointed out that 'as a consequence of the development of conditions of life in the modern community, the ordinary social institutions, such as the family, school, and religious institutions, have encountered increasing difficulty in the effective performance of their functions. In particular, they have had limited success in maintaining stability, integrity, a sense of independence and responsibility of the individual'. It is claimed that the 'corollary of such a situation is that more and more juveniles are becoming delinquent and it is also responsible for other forms of emotional and social disorders such as psychoneuroses, psychoses, alcoholism, suicide, family breakdown, unemployment'.

For the solution of such problems special social agencies are being increasingly called upon. A 'full network of social and health services' by both official and unofficial agencies is called for where 'necessary and feasible', including welfare agencies, psychiatric clinics, family agencies, children's guidance centers, and the like.

Integration and coordination of the various community services are necessary to avoid duplication and discover gaps. The coordinating agency can determine which type of aid a maladjusted child needs, and serve both as a clearing house for cases referred to it by different agencies in close contact with children that require therapy, guidance, or control, and as a central referral device.

Specialized training is required for psychiatrists, psychologists, social workers, probation officers, special school teachers, and others entrusted with children's problems.

Provision should be made for the evaluation of new forms of social action.

There are recommendations also for the development of placement centers for children, legislation for encouraging vocational training, homes and hostels for juvenile workers and better control of the working conditions of children.

Recommendations were also made regarding the role of various general agencies in the community which are in a favorable position to discover 'children who display social or emotional problems'. In this connection reference was made to religious bodies, police organi-

---

[19] 'We must properly recognize . . . the role of teachers as parent-substitutes and "ego-ideals" in the structuring of character.' *Unraveling*, p. 288.

zations, and different services concerned with constructive use of leisure. As to these general agencies, it was recommended that their activities be integrated more closely into the services and objectives of the other social institutions concerned with the prevention of delinquency.

On the much-debated issue of the influence of cinema, radio, television, and comic books, it was concluded that 'more may be gained by a positive emphasis upon the development of constructive and diversified activities . . . than rigid and negative measures of control and censorship'.

The final recommendation has to do with the need to advance research, not only to study 'causation, prediction, and prevention', but to evaluate the effectiveness of existing preventive measures. 'Comparative, co-ordinated, and interdisciplinary research should be carried out to determine the relative effects of programs in different countries' and 'through co-operation between researchers from different countries . . . to develop a highly promising new field of comparative criminology', in order to determine 'uniformities and differences in causal influences, in predictive factors, and in results of preventive and treatment programs' and to develop 'a true science of criminology'. To these ends 'the United Nations is urged to continue its support of significant research in these fields'.

Discussion. In all these provisions regarding juvenile delinquency there is nothing startlingly new and nothing that informed students of the problems of delinquency and predelinquency would not subscribe to. But one cannot help wondering whether the call for more and more social welfare agencies to put fingers in the holes of the societal dike is enough to hold back the cultural waters that are said to bring on the evils not merely of delinquency but of neurosis, psychosis, alcoholism, and the like. One is reminded of the statement in *Unraveling*:

'To the extent that general cultural pressures and disharmonies make for antisocial behavior on the part of those who find it difficult, or are unwilling, to conform, we are confronted with a tremendous problem which can be managed only by society and an overall social policy. Basic modifications in the general culture are bound to be slow and are usually unplanned. However, we can take advantage of the fact that parents are to a great extent not only the bearers, but also the selective filters, of the general culture, and thus take steps to mold the under-the-roof culture of the homes of young children around socially desirable goals' (p. 287).

A major difficulty with the type of recommendations for the treatment of children's problems adopted by the United Nations Congress derives from the fact that the array of countries represented included on the one hand relatively simple, economically primitive agricultural lands, and on the other the most highly industrialized and urbanized countries the world has ever seen. One can subscribe to the conviction that unwholesome socioeconomic conditions which present to the ordinary family in backward lands a desperate elementary struggle for bread and bed are there very relevant to family disintegration, to parental neglect of children, to delinquency. In more developed countries, with a very high standard of living, such factors take second place to more subtle and perhaps more serious disturbances of the individual personality and of the family as the matrix of character. In the light of the ease with which colorless, abstract generalizations might have resulted from the wide variety of cultures represented at the Congress it is gratifying that the recommendations which emerged are as specific as they turned out to be. Certainly, they should serve as a warning to those lands now eagerly exploring the glittering El Dorado of an industrialized, mechanized, atompowered, urbanized way of life, to set up social Geiger counters to warn of the necessity of preserving the time-tested values of cohesive family life and affectionate parent-child relationships in the face of the onrushing transformations of the general culture.

A noteworthy omission in the recommendations is the absence of any adequate discussion and suggestions in respect to the early prediction of delinquency. The preparatory document on juvenile delinquency,[20] a statement of general principles drafted by an *ad hoc* advisory committee of experts called together to advise the secretariat, states that 'specific preventive measures fall into three categories, of which the first two are:

(i) Prevention by early detection and treatment of potential delinquents before they present a manifest problem.
(ii) Prevention at the stage of pre-delinquency, i.e. by diagnosis and treatment of the 'problem personality'.

It would seem that predictive devices for the early screening of potential delinquents should therefore have been hailed as the most valuable techniques of a preventive program. Yet in the document prepared by the secretariat, which in certain respects is a very competent piece of work, the part devoted to prediction (dealt with in

---

[20] *The Prevention of Juvenile Delinquency*, report by the secretariat, United Nations, ST/SOA/Ser.M/7–8, p. 8; reprinted in *International Review of Criminal Policy*, Nos. 7–8, 1955.

connection with discussing causation) is as disappointing as it is non-persuasive. A typical sample of the kind of argument presented in opposition to the prediction technique is the following:

'Even if those juveniles who were predicted to be pre-delinquents or potential delinquents do become delinquents after X number of years reckoned from the original prediction, such results do not necessarily imply a validation of the prediction tables. The reason is that during the intervening years factors other than those originally taken into consideration in preparing the tables may have played a more decisive role.'

Thus one is asked to ignore specific, clearly defined factors which have been demonstrated to be predictively effective in distinguishing potential delinquents from non-delinquents at a very early age (when timely intervention promises really successful preventive effort) in favor of some mysterious, unidentified factors which *may*, through the long arm of coincidence, account for the results in the case of the delinquents only! It is unfortunate that so patently untenable a discussion of a device which is the most promising approach to effective prophylaxis should receive wide circulation. It can only serve to discourage some workers in foreign countries who might be inclined to accept it at its face value. At one session of the Congress, I took occasion to answer the criticisms of predictive methods as screening devices for the early detection of potential delinquents, and my wife reported on the validations of the Glueck Social Prediction Table; it was evident that considerable interest was aroused in the great promise of such instrumentalities in a realistic program of delinquency prevention. But, the following sentence of item F of part V of the *Resolutions and Recommendations Adopted by the Congress* illustrates the limited formal discussion of prediction: 'More important, perhaps, than any of the specific conclusions and recommendations submitted above is the obvious need for the development of more research relating to the definition of the term "juvenile", to delinquency causation, prediction, and prevention' (p. 47).

A real opportunity was missed, in discussing the role of the school in a crime-prevention program, to encourage the development of what promises to be a crucially important device. Since the school is the first testing ground of the child's ability to cope with the systems of prohibitions laid down by society, it is an excellent vehicle for the early identification of symptoms of maladjustment. As was said in *Unraveling*, 'In an enlightened educational system, the school could function as the litmus paper of personality maladaptation, reflecting the acid test of the child's success or failure in his first attempts to cope with the problems of life posed by a restrictive, impersonal society and code' (p. 269). A highly promising Social Prediction Table, which was developed in connection with a careful comparative study of delinquents and non-delinquents and published in *Unraveling* together with two other tables designed to predict delinquency, has already undergone several successful validations on samples of cases other than the ones on which the table was built and is at present being applied, experimentally, by the Youth Service Board of New York City to several schools in underprivileged sections, with a view to testing its efficiency and to determining the value of timely therapeutic intervention in preventing delinquency.[21] The school seems to be the most logical agency for the use of such screening devices as part of a widespread prophylactic program designed to nip delinquency in the bud.

It is evident from the recommendations involving juvenile delinquency that the Congress ranged over a wide field of discussion and that, apart from its inadequate treatment of pre-delinquency predictive devices, it took ample account of various approaches to the pressing problem of delinquency prevention. It is hoped that the next United Nations Congress will be devoted fully to the problem of child delinquency, since this is the crucial prologue to the tragedy of adult criminalism.

II

THE LONDON CONGRESS ON CRIMINOLOGY

The Third International Congress on Criminology in London dealt with a more unified topic than did the United Nations assemblage at Geneva; namely, *recidivism*. It was characterized also by a greater representation of researchers, scholars, and practitioners and a

[21] R. E. Thompson (1952), A validation of the Glueck Social Prediction Scale for proneness to delinquency. *J. crim. L. Criminol. & Police Sci.* **43**, 451; S. Axelrad & S. J. Glick (1953), Application of the Glueck Social Prediction Table to 100 Jewish delinquent boys. *Jewish soc. Serv. Quart.* **30**, 127; R. W. Whelan (1954), An experiment in predicting delinquency. *J. crim. L. Criminol. & Police Sci.* **45**, 432; *Predicting juvenile delinquency* (1955), Research Bulletin No. 124 (Trenton, N.J.: State Department of Institutions & Agencies). Two other validations were presented in papers at the London Congress; one, by Dr Augusta Bonnard, involving a follow-up of children examined at the clinic of the London County Council; the second, by Isa Brandon, a study of adult sex offenders at Sing Sing Prison. Both indicated high predictive power on the part of the Social Prediction Table. Another Glueck validation is to be found in R. E. Thompson (1957), Further validation of the Glueck Social Prediction Table for identifying potential delinquents. *J. crim. L. Criminol. & Police Sci.* **48**, 175. (A study of fifty boys from Boston Juvenile Court and fifty girls committed as delinquents to the Massachusetts Youth Service Board.) (See Chapter 8 above.)

lesser emphasis on political and governmental representatives than was the Geneva meeting. Some 400 members, drawn from 52 countries, attended.

Five sections, each under two General Reporters, dealt with the topics of *Definitions of Recidivism and Their Statistical Aspects, Descriptive Study of Forms of Recidivism and Their Evolution, Causes of Recidivism, Prognosis of Recidivism*, and *Treatment of Recidivism.* Numerous individual reports prepared by invited scholars representing different countries were submitted to the ten General Reporters, who condensed these contributions, commented on them and arrived at conclusions, recommendations, or resolutions. The general reports were discussed at the section meetings and the outcomes of these discussions were laid before the entire body at the plenary sessions, not so much for voting and adoption as for presenting, as it were, 'the sense of the meeting'. In addition, certain individual papers and lectures were delivered both in section meetings and at plenary sessions before the assemblage as a whole.[22]

Since the constituent papers of the sections other than Section IV (of which the writer was one of the General Reporters) are not available, discussion must be confined to the general reports.

[22] The papers and lectures included the presidential and closing addresses by Dr Denis Carroll, The individualization of after-care by Dr Vladimir Hadzi, Case history of a recidivist thief by Dr L. Rubenstein, Correlation between recidivism and functional or anatomical changes in the brain by Dr Brousseau, Status of Glueck prediction studies by Dr Eleanor T. Glueck, The treatment of recidivism by Dr Marcel Frym; a symposium on homicide presented at a plenary session and consisting of Psychosociological study of murderers in Sweden by Prof. G. Rylander, Emotional reaction of arrested murderers to their crime, their trial and their sentence by Dr J. A. Hobson, Murderers and their victims by Prof. M. Wolfgang; a plenary session preview of Physique and delinquency[176] by Sheldon & Eleanor Glueck, 'specialist meetings' consisting of papers on Sex offenders and recidivism by Dr G. B. Smith and Sex offenders—a team study by Dr Bernard Glueck, Jr. (read by Isa Brandon, a member of the research team involved), International aspects of forgery of works of art by Prof. T. Würtemburger, and Recidivism and banknote forgery by Prof. F. Castejon; lectures on An anthropometric study of young and adult offenders by Profs. M. Verdun & G. Heuyer, Masked schizophrenic reactions and persistent criminal behavior by Dr R. Banay, The criminality of unpunishables by Prof. V. V. Stanciu, Specialized methods and techniques in the psychotherapy of delinquents by Dr M. Schmideberg, Ductless glands and recidivism by Prof. C. V. Ferreira; Maconochie—an early pioneer of penal treatment, presented at a plenary session by Justice J. V. Barry of the Supreme Court of Victoria, Australia; Frontiers of research in criminology by Prof. Marshall B. Clinard, and The psychological and penological aspects of various types of recidivism by Dr Gregory Zilboorg, both presented at a plenary session; lectures on The psychological background of recidivism by Dr H. Ritey, Clinical standards of prognosis in juvenile delinquency—an after-history study by Dr A. Bonnard, Public attitudes towards stealing by Prof. E. Smigel, The legislator and the problem of recidivism by G. Koskoff, The treatment of recidivism and the attitude of the public by Dr Leon Stern, Recidivism in narcotic addiction by Dr H. Berger. In addition there were the usual welcoming and closing speeches by various dignitaries. Because of the great interest in the Glueck prediction techniques, Mrs Glueck, on invitation, held two special sessions explaining the techniques.

VI

Section I dealt with the *Definitions of Recidivism and Their Statistical Aspects*, for which the General Reporters were Professor Roland Grassberger (Austria) and Professor Norval Morris (Australia). Dr Grassberger[23] devoted his paper largely to statistical problems and presented a series of charts and graphs illustrating such matters as the criminality of recidivists in the total body of criminalism, the role of 'accidental criminals', the 'dynamic' of recidivism, punishment and recidivism, the success of the sentence administered, study of the criminal career. He noted the impossibility of any single or uniform definition of recidivism, the term being used according to its context and the point of view of the person (doctor, lawyer, statistician) concerned. He adverted to legal differentiations according to such criteria as the time elapsing between the prior and subsequent offense, the similarity in types of offense or variations in offense indicative of the same underlying tendency; the fact that definitions in recent legislation take into account the original offense and its 'inner connection' with the subsequent offense as indicating an 'asocial penchant' and prescribe severer sanctions therefor. Through adequate statistics 'the legislator can be informed about the degree of recidivism in various types of offenses, the penal administrator can check the success of his measures, and the policeman can get information regarding the likelihood of offenders who specialize in one type of crime switching to a different offense' (*Summary*, p. 3). Current official statistics cannot, however, furnish adequate data for special, intensive research, involving the detailed study of case histories. The condition *sine qua non* for all statistics on recidivism is a '*casier judiciare*' which operates according to a plan that deals with problems not merely retrospectively, centering upon the past of the offender, but prospectively, following the offender during his career after conviction (*Les Definitions*, pp. 19–20).

During the discussion of Grassberger's report, it was brought out that an important development in official statistical material in the different countries is 'a trend from descriptive statistics to operational research, i.e. to statistics related to action' (*Memorandum of Conclusions*). The following resolution was unanimously adopted by the Congress:

'*Be it Resolved*: That the Congress recommend that a committee

[23] R. Grassberger, *Les définitions de la récidive et leur importance pour les statistiques*, Rapport Général, Section I. Some of the material mentioned in the text was derived from the English digest of the general reports, *Summary of General Reports*, Sections I–V. It is not known whether the summary of his paper was prepared by Prof. Grassberger himself.

be appointed to examine the data on recidivism in the official criminal statistics of various countries and to prepare a report suggesting minimum objectives and standards for the collection and publication of such data' (ibid. p. 2).

It was further agreed that 'such a committee could be formed by the International Society of Criminology and that detailed suggestions of individual members should be made to the Society'.

Professor Morris confined his paper to the always baffling task of definition. He noted a 'surprising similarity of approach' on the part of the thirteen contributors to his symposium. He presented the following 'somewhat contentious propositions':

'that it is both impossible to achieve and unwise to seek a single definition of recidivism;
'that we must define recidivism differently for the purposes of at least three different aspects of the application of the criminal law;
'that recidivism has a different connotation to the lawyer, the penal administrator, and the criminologist, when considered from the viewpoint of their own disciplines; and
'that though there are elements in common in these three types of definition of recidivism they are too few to form the foundation of any useful single definition.'[24]

Following the propositions noted, Professor Morris analyzed the penal, the legal, and the criminologic definitions of recidivism, noting their individual relevancy to these respective areas and citing examples from a wide variety of countries. His conclusion follows:

'The essential unifying concept behind recidivism is the repetition of crime after conviction. The penal administrator tends to test this by reappearance in prison; the lawyer by reappearance as a convicted person in court; while the criminologist desires to test it by the subsequent commission of crime. The penal, legal, and criminological definitions will all be narrowed by the interpolation of many other factors qualifying the personality of the offender and the type and number of his crimes and sentences; these will vary according to the particular proposition or inquiry concerning recidivism being made and will vary considerably from one legal system to another and from one criminological, legal, and penal inquiry to another' (ibid. p. 16).

In the deliberations of the section it was brought out that definitions vary with aim; that 'every definition, either legal or criminological, can be regarded as a tool, as a means to apply legal sanctions

[24] N. Morris, *Definitions of recidivism*, General Report, Section 1, pp. 2–3.

or to organize research material. For that reason there must be a variety of definitions according to different laws, legal systems, and research requirements' (*Conclusions*, p. 1). The following statement was unanimously accepted at the plenary session:

'For different purposes the criminologists need different definitions of recidivism. Recidivism in the criminological sense, therefore, includes the following main forms. It means:

(1) that a person after having committed a first crime which was legally established, and having been convicted of it or in any other way dealt with officially by society, then commits another crime (recidivist *stricto sensu*),

(2) that a person having committed a first crime legally established and dealt with as before resumes his criminal activity because of his "dangerous state" (recidivist *lato sensu*)' (ibid.).

Discussion. Dr Grassberger's charts and graphs deserve study by all those interested in a system of administrative statistics that can keep its pulse on the processes of justice. Regarding the investigation into the subsequent careers of offenders, it is doubtful whether this can be effectively accomplished under governmental auspices. Reliance must be had on researchers in universities and institutes, since the techniques involved are complex and subtle and the researchers in follow-up studies must above all be neutral,[25] and not influenced by a propagandistic desire to prove the high effectiveness of certain penal régimes, or probation or parole.

Properly implemented by an active committee, the resolution of the Congress on statistics of recidivism can lead to fruitful results, especially in encouraging the development of operational statistics as an instrument of administrative control and for the guidance of policy in the light of measured results.

The adopted statement on the definitions of recidivism is hardly an improvement over Morris's down-to-earth approach which seems to the writer to be the only way of avoiding wasteful entanglements in a variety of differing concepts sailing, confusedly, under a single flag. It is the approach which those conducting the deliberations on the definitions of juvenile delinquency at the Geneva Congress should have taken to save time and ruffled spirits; for while working definitions are usually necessary to the focusing of an investigation, the nature of a definition depends on the aim and context of an intellec-

---

[25] Intensive and unbiased field investigations usually prove that the officially published failure rate is materially lower than the actual one. See, for example, the follow-up studies: *500 criminal careers*[26], *One thousand juvenile delinquents*[45], *Five hundred delinquent women*[44], *Later criminal careers*[71], *Juvenile delinquents grown up*[85], *Criminal careers in retrospect*[102], *After-conduct of discharged offenders*[119].

tual exploration, and it is familiar wisdom that meaningful definitions develop toward the end of an inquiry rather than at its beginning.

VII

In Section II, which dealt with *Forms and Evolution of Recidivism*, Dr C. H. Andersen (Belgium) and Professor Walter Reckless (U.S.A.) presented thought-provoking general reports. At the outset, Dr Andersen[26] sketched the sources of motivation in instinctual equipment and early conditioning. He pointed out that an etiologic classification is possible according to the origin of the habits of an individual —instinctual, those derived largely through education, through example, through emotional conflicts, through frustrations, through integration in a group. 'The study of instinctual motives reveals two possible anomalies. Recidivism can be a habit of [original] impulse (*habitude pulsionnelle*), assuring an instinctual satisfaction not inhibited by the brake of socialization; it can be also a secondary habit, born of a poorly resolved conflict of impulse, that is, a neurosis' Andersen distinguishes no fewer than six types of classification of recidivists; *legal* (which is weak in that it ignores psychologic motivation); *descriptive* (which treats of a variety of repeaters under a single stereotype, ignoring the important fact that while like offenses reveal a similarity of criminal intent they may have a wide variety of motivations); *classification by criminal career* (contrasting those who recidivate because of bad social conditions, such as ostracism of the ex-prisoner, with the professional recidivist of antisocial character); classification according to *psychologic type* (based on a character typology derived from temperamental or affective make-up, Andersen including here the comparative study of Rorschach test and psychiatric traits in *Unraveling*, which he regards as useful for both prognosis and therapy but which he claims is inapplicable to adults since their 'character and the reactive potentialities have been modified by experience, by incident and by examples');[27] classification by *criminologic type* (Andersen pointing out that the method of psychologic analysis in the Gluecks' work permits of determining types of probable recidivists through the isolation of certain constellations of factors among the numerous combinations of person-*milieu*, and listing various patterns); *psychiatric* classification (based not only on cognitive and affective anomalies but also on anatomic or physiologic determinants, including the findings of constitutional

---

[26] C. H. Andersen, *Formes et évolution du récidivisme*, Rapport Général, pp. 1–2.
[27] See *Discussion* of materials on *Prognosis*.

217

psychology, and involving the view that the tendency to recidivate despite punishment is essentially a congenital weakness).

This analysis of types of classification of recidivists is followed by a detailed consideration of different patterns of non-recidivists and recidivists from the point of view of practical correctional administration, somewhat along the lines of the typology suggested by Reckless (below), but with greater emphasis on psychiatric and psychoanalytic concepts, especially in discussing the role of the superego and ego. This practical classification of recidivists is first broken down into four types who are neither rendered more wise nor intimidated by the punishment they have undergone and four types who are influenced thereby.

He ends with a stirring plea for the study of personality in both its mental and physical aspects and under the impact of the environment.

Professor Reckless[28] emphasized the great need of case history preparation and analysis as a complement to mass statistical studies. He posed the questions whether a standard outline should be developed and used for the systematic collection of case histories of recidivists; whether this should be done by research teams, 'representing several methods and approaches'; what comprises 'an adequate sample of case histories which can give authority and validity to the findings of criminologists' and 'what are the case history criteria of a recidivist?' He suggested as basic criteria 'the meaning or function of the recidivistic behavior in the individual case-history' and the 'dominant etiological factor in the individual case-history'. He said that there are patterns of recidivism reflecting a criminal career or vocation and those 'representing the uncontrollable repetition of criminal acts, which . . . are merely the behavior of . . . habitual and abnormal delinquents and criminals'. Like Andersen, Reckless submitted a thought-provoking breakdown of the general area into principal patterns of recidivism, but his system takes more account of sociologic concepts:

(a) *Criminal careers, vocations, or trades,* divided into (1) ordinary criminal career ('a mixture of gainful property crimes', which emerge out of bad environments, social and economic inadequacies, criminal associates, etc.); (2) criminal trades of a 'special group tradition', such as 'moonshiners', gypsies, etc., the recidivist here acquiring the criminalistic pattern 'as a perfectly normal member of his special social group'; (3) organized criminals (gangsters, racketeers, traffickers in women and drugs, criminal receivers, etc.), these following

[28] W. C. Reckless, *The forms of recidivism*, General Report, Section II.

'the route of those in pattern 1 until they make connection with definitely organized criminal enterprise'; (4) professional criminals (confidence men, forgers, counterfeiters, etc.), who have not 'emerged out of pattern 1 but rather have middle class origin', have developed an antisocial expression of their skills 'as a result of contact with other professionals', stay aloof from ordinary criminals, and often manage to keep out of prison; (5) the middle and upper class white-collar criminals, or violators of positions of trust and governmental controls, who also usually manage to escape imprisonment and who recidivate because of the 'lure of great gains at little risk, the example set by dishonest and unscrupulous colleagues, the failure to get caught'. (The extent of patterns 3 and 5 depends greatly on the 'particular development of business, the professions, and government service in various countries'.) (6) The physically handicapped, driven into crime by inferiority feelings or difficulty in making an honest living.

(b) *Habitual and abnormal offenders* comprise (7) the antisocial characters (of 'weak ego structure and weak internal controls', and of 'very little superego (conscience)' and capacity to identify with others, who 'renege on their social and economic obligations, often gravitate to alcoholism, drug addiction, vagabondage, and frequently become sexual deviates'. This group includes the 'psychopaths'. (8) Psychoneurotic delinquents and criminals, 'usually acting from compulsion . . . but sometimes acting from anxiety tensions. . . . The psychoneurotic offender does not want to be criminal. Criminal break-through increases the neurotic's anxiety but at the same time discharges his more basic tensions.' (9) Habitual delinquents and criminals deriving from such pathologic conditions as epilepsy, post-encephalitis, brain injury, etc., who are often confused with persons falling in pattern 7. (10) Abnormal recidivists due to psychosis or mental defect.

Recognizing that there is some overlap in this typology and that such a list might not apply as much in one country as another, Reckless asked whether the Congress should 'accept the principle of identifying and distinguishing the principal forms of recidivism according to function (meaning) of the behavior and dominant etiological factor as shown in the case-history of each recidivist. If not, should some other criteria for identifying forms of recidivism be used?'

Finally, Reckless proposed 'a central theme of study which gives perspective, meaning, and significance to all contributions'; namely, the assessment of the individual along a continuum of socially

acceptable conduct, according to the extent of his 'capacity or incapacity to play acceptable roles in life'. Thus 'due to the components
which have contributed to his socialization or asocialization . . . an
individual may be a saint upon earth, a very conventional person, a
good citizen, a wayward person, a delinquent, a recidivist, or an
uncontrollable deviate. He might have expectancy to maintain his
position on the continuum of socially acceptable behavior or he
might have expectancy to improve or retrogress, according to the
interaction of the components of his personality with the demands
of his immediate social environment.'

The *Conclusions* unanimously adopted by the Congress divide
recidivists into professional, sophisticated offenders and those whose
repeated criminalism is essentially due to their social and psychologic
maladaptation. The *Conclusions* aver that criminology is as yet unable
to give a 'valid explanation' of the etiology of recidivism, limiting
itself essentially to a symptomatic description. Nevertheless, such a
typology has considerable importance for prevention and treatment.
'The scientific study of recidivism must involve simultaneous
research in different countries of the world with different groups of
recidivists.' It is requested that the Scientific Commission of the
International Society of Criminology establish a subcommittee to
'study the scientific and practical conditions under which criminological research can proceed with teams of competent workers,
using uniform lists of data in the collection of case-history information', in a way to permit of comparisons among the various countries
and of 'statistical graphing and analysis' (*Conclusions*, p. 2).

Discussion. It would require too much space to go into detailed
consideration of the typologies presented by the two General
Reporters. Suffice it to say that their scope is both wide and deep,
and that the psycho-social patterns underlying the classifications
'ring true'. They should serve as a source of fruitful hypotheses for
the purposes of both treatment and research. Andersen's belief that
predictive factors useful in forecasting delinquency on the part of
children will not work with adults is something that only the passage
of time can determine.

Conceived of as working hypotheses, Reckless's tentative patternings of the major types of criminalism suggest promising lines of
research. Reliable case histories can throw light on the extent to which
the divergent paths of the various types of offender he describes have
a common origin in the family matrix of the first few years of life
and permit of tracing the intervening influences that operate in adolescence and later to incline the original, commonly maladjusted children

toward one or another of several adult antisocial patterns. In this way much of the basic research tending to show a crucial influence of parent-child relationships in the *origins* of antisocial maladjustment[29] might be reconciled with the basic researches emphasizing group, community, or class influences and specialization in antisocial conduct.[30]

As to Reckless's proposed 'central theme of study' for all criminologists, the writer is less certain. He cannot see that the emphasis on 'role playing' in assessing the individual along a continuum of socially acceptable conduct greatly advances understanding of the phenomenon of antisocial behavior. Does it not merely substitute words for words? If the objective behavior be in issue, how does it improve matters to speak of the subject's 'role' as father, parent, worker, worshiper, recreational companion? If the subjective attitude of the self toward the various activities involved in these objective behavioral outlets be in issue, how is the reference to 'role playing' an improvement over ordinary clinical description and interpretation?

The *Conclusions* of Section II adopted by the Congress are valuable. However, in the writer's opinion they over-emphasize the alleged absolute difference between 'symptomatic description' and 'valid explanation'. Explanation is, after all, refined description; and if symptomatic patterns are important to understanding and efficiency in prevention and treatment of recidivism (as the *Conclusions* admit them to be), that is good enough even though 'ultimate answers' (if there be such) are not as yet forthcoming. The distinction between 'mere empiricism' and 'scientific explanation' which some social scientists love to emphasize to prove they are really 'scientists' is not as profound as it appears.

The establishment of a subcommittee to bring some standardization into the gathering of case-history data should help to develop a comparative criminology.

---

[29] For example, S. Hartwell (1931), *Fifty-five bad boys* (New York: Knopf); *One thousand juvenile delinquents*[(45)]; W. Healy & A. Bronner (1936), *New light on delinquency* (New Haven: Yale U.P.; London: Oxford U.P.); C. Burt (1925), *The young delinquent* (9th ed. 1961. London: University of London Press); J. Bowlby (1947), *Forty-four thieves* (London: Baillière, Tindall & Cox); *Unraveling juvenile delinquency*[(138)].

[30] Such as F. M. Thrasher (1927), *The gang* (2nd rev. ed. 1936. Chicago: University of Chicago Press); C. Shaw (1929), *Delinquency areas* (Chicago: University of Chicago Press); E. H. Sutherland (1955), *Principles of criminology* (5th ed. Chicago: Lippincott); M. Clinard (1949), Secondary community influences & juvenile delinquency. *The Annals*, p. 42.

VIII

In Section III, on the *Causes of Recidivism*, Professor P. A. H. Baan (Netherlands) was the General Reporter.[31] Baan begins his report by asking whether recidivists are (*a*) those who have repeatedly fallen afoul of the law, or (*b*) those who, whether they fall 'into the arms of the law or not', repeat actions which render them liable to punishment, or (*c*) those who have 'more than once offended against the general standards on which a well-organized community is based'.[32] He points out that group (*a*), which is the one usually studied, represents but a very small fraction of humanity; that '95 per cent of all human beings have never come into contact with the law as the result of any crime', an astonishing yet too little noticed fact; and that since 'nearly everyone whose social life is governed by regulations and standards' (such as those in the Ten Commandments) 'has a constant tendency to infringe these standards', it is 'unjust' to exclude them from the discussions of the Congress even though they remain out of the reach of the law and largely out of the scope of our knowledge. He raises the question whether there is a fundamental difference or only one of degree between the (*a*) recidivists and the (*b*) and (*c*), especially the last.

Baan claims that since 'the essence of every "*einmalige*" conduct or misconduct (i.e. performed once only), its underlying normal or abnormal mental state, is still . . . only seldom considered and elucidated', a prognosis or prediction on the material in the researches is impossible.

Referring to a six-year intensive psychiatric study of a thousand recidivists in the Netherlands, during which each was 'very closely observed daily for a period of six weeks to two or three months, by a staff of male and female nurses, while psychiatrists, psychologists, a physician, and social workers were able to carry out their very precise examinations against the background of a carefully prepared anamnesis . . . and an accurate description of the hereditary and environmental circumstances', Baan says that the results thus far justify his taking a stand 'against the too-crude stating of superficial diagnoses and the all-too-easy assumption of the existence of endogeny, psychopathy, and other incurable conditions' (a modern research position 'steeped in the blackest pessimism'); and he gives some illustrations, based on the proposition that 'going back as far as birth, psychogeny and sociogeny cannot be separated from any

---

[31] Although the program also lists Prof. J. J. Panakal (India) as a General Reporter, the *Summary of General Reports* does not include any digest of a paper by Panakal.
[32] P. A. H. Baan, *Causes of recidivism*, General Report, Section III.

possible components of predispostion'. Thus, of 100 persons ad-mitted to his hospital as psychopathic 'only ten at most were psycho-pathic in a strict sense; ninety or more of those who were termed psychopaths owing to disturbances of conduct turned out not be so, though the disturbances in adaptation from which these delinquents suffered showed strong resemblance to the symptoms of the original conceptions of psychopathy.' He raises the question 'whether it will ever be possible to separate endogeny on the one hand and psycho-geny and sociogeny on the other. Further scientific research, which will be costly both in time and trouble, will shed more light on this question' (ibid. p. 6). As with psychopaths so with mental defectives, *insanis moralis*, and 'the fairy tale, the myth of the professional criminal'. In all these, the nature-nurture puzzle prevails.

Neglect (including pampering) 'proved indeed to be an important factor' in the research; and a basic discovery is that the criminal records are not homogeneous, so that in a 'series of economic offenses one may find an aggressive or a sexual offense, or both, and when a criminal record does happen to be homogeneous, thorough psychi-atric, psychological, and social investigation nevertheless indicates that there are also deep-lying disturbances in the other spheres of the personality' (ibid, pp. 8–9). Dr Baan's striking descriptions of person-ality and of the influence of childhood *neglect* on antisocial behavioral tendencies deserve quotation:

'In general one could say that for the optimal functioning of man in society, an integration and a fine regulation of a great variety of biological, somatic, and psychical components are necessary . . . if the individual is to hold his own in the world in his interactions with other people, and to take part in it in a posi-tive sense as well. Owing to the normal and adequate development of factors which at present we clumsily explain in concepts of intellect, feeling, intuition, instinct, emotionality, etc.—though it is only through contact with others that these become facets of the entire personality of the individual in his interaction with the world—an infinitely fine combination of factors is created, a regulative system and organism, capable of realizing intangible concepts such as love of one's neighbor, fidelity, responsibility, feeling of guilt, etc. . . . It may be . . . that the one who did wrong did not happen to possess such a highly integrated regulative mechanism that the development of responsibility and therefore of accountability was possible. And here . . . the factor of neglect comes into play. In the same way as organic neglect—lack of vitamins, albumen, carbohydrates, fats, calories, iron, nitrogen,

223

and innumerable other constituents—can have the most serious and disastrous results for normal development, the shortage of constituents indispensable for the normal development of the psychical personality, such as love, affection, warmth, cherishing, safety, etc., can have the most marked and disastrous results. In the same way as the body, the psychical personality can remain defective or can become distorted and acquire all kinds of other symptoms which make it impossible for him to accept responsibility like the average person, to love his neighbor, to be faithful, etc. All these things can be seen in an endless number of so-called normal beings, who never come into contact with the psychiatrist or the judge. They can be seen, however, most frequently in criminals in general, and in recidivists in particular. Is this disease, is this disturbance? I do not know' (ibid. p. 10).

Drawing on several contributory papers and on his own psychiatric experience, Dr Baan also has wise things to say about the administration of criminal justice:

'In prison, as well as during judicial proceedings, methods of treatment that are inadequate, inexpert, loveless, too severe or too mild, can create all sorts of possibilities, which the delinquent adopts to project his unassimilated feelings of guilt on others. An over-severe regime, the exclusion from the outer world, the senseless daily round, the bad treatment, insufficient, inadequate work and the abnormal situation of prison communities, all give insufficient opportunity for the feelings of guilt to ripen and to be assimilated, or for the offender to live through the crime committed, and to reach a catharsis. . . . Unsolved feelings of guilt tend on the one hand towards the repetition of forbidden actions within the framework of a guilt-punishment complex, on the other hand, to that crust formation that brings about a mask of sanity and turns the delinquent into a quasi-hardened criminal. . . . The suitable punishment or treatment must satisfy two criteria. On the one hand it must take into account the very personal idiosyncratic nature of the rather exceptional individual who, presumably owing to his emotional disturbances, fails in his respect for the legal order. On the other hand, after satisfactory examination and diagnosis, it must above all things provide an opportunity for the feelings of guilt of the delinquent to ripen and be dissolved, and give him the chance to make up for his crimes by adequate adaptation to society. There he can make amends, whilst society also needs to make amends for so much to him. . . . If . . . we approach the offender from an unprejudiced, accepting attitude as a fellowman, our recognition of his individuality will not fail to draw out his individuality, though perhaps only after much patience and repeated efforts. Our confidence will finally reveal, slowly but surely, the still unimpaired responsibility under the ruined personality, and make him susceptible to a therapeutic approach which ought to be applicable in prisons as well as in therapeutic institutions. No threats, no enmity, but an approach which accepts him as a fellow-creature, both during the judicial stage and during the execution of the punishment or treatment. In this procedure, based on a sense of common humanity, the lawyer, psychiatrist, psychologist, sociologist, and social worker must be combined in a team, at a level where all of them have outgrown narrow professionalism, moved as they are by their compassion for their fellowman who has sinned against this legal order, which, too, is in need of their compassion' (ibid. pp. 12–13).

Dr Baan naturally regards it as 'unjust to make recidivism a reason for increasing the length of punishment'. He is convinced that recidivism will be materially reduced 'if careful observation, accurate selection before relegation to differentiated prisons and institutions, and careful, very expert treatment by large staffs of psychiatrists, psychologists, sociologists, ministers of religion, social workers, together with good nursing and penitentiary personnel, are all linked closely with a well-thought-out and expert aftercare' (ibid. pp. 13–14).

Research, says Dr Baan, should not be limited to recidivists. 'Particularly juvenile and first offenders urgently need our attention and care, because they may, unfortunately, be potential recidivists.'

The lengthy *Conclusions* of Section III may be summarized in the following propositions: Recidivism 'covers a variety of forms of conduct, and the individual cases . . . grow out of a complicated interplay between hereditary, personal, and environmental factors in ever-changing constellations' (*Conclusions*, p. 3). The concept of 'cause' should be examined thoroughly, and it may prove helpful to use 'the tools of modern analytic philosophy and semantics' in the process. Although the section sought to determine which traits of personality or social conditions distinguish the recidivist from both the first offender and the law-abiding citizen, it has been impossible to discuss the causes of recidivism apart from the causes of criminal conduct in general. The issue really is, 'In what cases, and for what reasons, are the sanctions which society applies unable to counteract effectively the criminogenic factors involved?' Although a 'common thesis' among criminologists has been that social factors play the dominant part in etiology of the casual offender while personality factors predominate among recidivists, this broad generalization is subject to numerous exceptions; evidently, mental disease and abnormal personality are more involved in grave and persistent recidivism than in casual offense; but there is little evidence that innate low-grade intelligence is important. Nor is the neurotic conscious or unconscious seeking out of punishment (associated with a pre-existing guilt feeling) frequently involved. There was an unresolved difference of opinion in the section as to whether professional criminals (e.g. pick-pockets, car thieves, etc.) are essentially the product of the deliberate choice of a professional criminal career involving high gain with little risk, 'together with a certain lack of moral standards', or (a view held by Professor Baan) they are rather the result of 'emotional factors, such as hurt pride, disappointment, frustration, resentment, etc.', nobody deliberately choosing a criminal career 'out of normal and rational considerations'. A multidisciplinary attack on the problem of recidivism is necessary, in which psychologists, psychiatrists, sociologists, social anthropologists, lawyers, police officers, prison administrators, clergymen, and social workers need to cooperate.

Discussion. Dr Baan's thoughtful paper rightly warns against the intellectual blight of too hasty labeling and classification of personality. Yet his typical attitude of the 'individual case' clinician appears to the writer as itself rather stultifying. One can only commend the call for more intensive and penetrating study of the individual case; but if each case is to be regarded as absolutely unique it is difficult to see how a science of Man can ever be developed. The scientist seeks uniformities and differences in masses of cases; but before he can use a thousand cases he must, like the clinician, be sure that each single case contains reliable and relevant data. Relevancy of course changes with ever-deeper penetration of scientific exploration; but the pragmatic test of relevancy is *manageability*. If, for example, the predictive factors in a table in fact separate the sheep from the goats, then, crude as these factors may be, they serve a useful purpose, useful not merely for immediate administrative control but as a means of narrowing and defining areas for more intensive exploration.

Dr Baan's views on penology are not only in the best humanitarian tradition but throw psychoanalytic light on the role of guilt feeling in the correctional and reformative processes. 'Treatment' does not necessarily exclude the *therapeutic* need of emotional suffering. It is not the absence of all pain that is called for in the correctional regime (if, indeed, it were possible to achieve that), but rather the proper guidance of unavoidable suffering to bring about its constructive contribution to self-understanding and to personality growth. While not ignoring the most frequently cited causes of recidivism, such as the robotizing influences of penal institutions, the inadequate official aid to the ex-prisoner during the crucial early stages of his return to free life, and the unfriendly attitude of the public toward the 'jail bird', Dr Baan gives glimpses of the deeper influences.

The *Conclusions* of Section III are certainly not earthshaking. Typically, a feeling of inferiority on the part of criminologists is evident in their shying away from the idea of 'cause' and in the call for aid from philosophy and semantics. The section seems to have overlooked the probability that the best approach to ideas of etiology in criminologic problems is the experimental one which checks on results in terms of treatment given in the light of operational assumptions that certain factors are causally implicated. In this connection, predictive instrumentalities are of value in narrowing the field of intensive effort and in defining specific targets for correctional activity.

That cooperation between representatives of numerous relevant disciplines is necessary in reducing recidivism is so obvious as to require no reiteration.

IX

It is fair to say that Section IV, on the *Prognosis (and Prediction) of Recidivism*, of which Dr Israel Drapkin (Chile) and the writer were the two General Reporters, aroused the greatest interest at the Congress. The importance of prediction methods was emphasized in the persuasive presidential address and closing remarks by Dr Denis Carroll; Section I, which dealt with the *Definitions of Recidivism and Their Statistical Aspects*, included in its findings unanimously adopted by the Congress the statement, 'In particular prediction techniques were advocated as the best method in order to decide on the type of treatment which would suit the individual offender' (*Conclusions*, p. 1); the great interest in prediction devices called for extra sessions to discuss techniques. A special issue of the *British Journal of Delinquency* (Vol. VI, No. 2) was published; a book dealing with prediction was brought out[33] though not in time to be the subject of discussion. It is obvious that the rather cavalier treatment of prediction devices in the United Nations Congress at Geneva was not followed by the International Congress on Criminology in London.

[33] H. Mannheim & L. T. Wilkins (1955), *Prediction methods in relation to Borstal training*. London: HMSO.

Dr Drapkin[34] left the discussion of prediction tables in prognosis to his fellow reporter and devoted himself to the clinical approach. Even with the clinical approach, he suggested accuracy in prognosis can be aided by a scheme employing three sets of prognostic factors: (a) the life experience of the offender, including hereditary, familial, and personal background and criminal record; (b) the offender's personality as determined by clinical examination, particularly morphological, physiological, and neuropsychiatric findings; (c) intra- and extra-institutional therapeutic possibilities and the personal and social conditions to which the ex-prisoner returns. Taking into account the perpetual fluctuations in the two basic sets of variables—the individual and the *milieu*—Dr Drapkin discussed the limitations of prognosis and emphasized the 'unique experience' that is produced by the interaction of person and environment.

Only through teamwork can the most difficult task of criminology —prognosis—be accomplished. He would not rule out prediction tables as one of the techniques to be employed, recognizing that they are statistical refinements of a process that the experienced clinician goes through more impressionistically in prognosticating on the individual case.

Exceptionally fine papers[35] were submitted to the writer for his general report on the *Prognosis of Recidivism.*[36] The General Reporter discussed the subject under the topics of the Nature and Extent of Recidivism, 'Prognosis' and 'Prediction', The Uses of Prediction Tables, Objections to the Use of Prediction Tables as Instruments of Prognosis, Improvement of Predictive Devices, and Resolutions on prognosis of recidivism to be presented to the Congress.

[34] I. Drapkin, *Pronostico del recidivisimo,* Informe General, Seccion IV. The textual statement of Dr Drapkin's position is derived largely from the *Summary of General Reports,* pp. 19–20, and from the writer's recollection of Dr Drapkin's statements at the section meetings.

[35] In alphabetical order, the individual reports were submitted by the following contributors: Dr Eleanor T. Glueck, research associate, Harvard Law School, Cambridge, Mass. (U.S.A.); Dr Auguste Ley, honorary professor of psychiatry at the University of Brussels (Belgium); Dr Elio D. Monachesi, professor of sociology, University of Minnesota, Minneapolis, Minn. (U.S.A.); Dr Lloyd E. Ohlin, director, Center for Education and Research in Corrections, University of Chicago, Chicago, Ill. (U.S.A.); Mr W. H. Overbeek, avocat-général près de la Cour d'Appel à Amsterdam (Netherlands); M. Jean Pinatel, secretary-general, International Society of Criminology, Paris (France); Dr Peter Scott, physician, Maudsley Hospital, and psychiatrist, London Remand Home, London (England); Dr R. S. Taylor, senior psychologist, H.M. Prison, Wandsworth (England); Dr Estaban Valdes-Castillo y Moreira, professor of legal medicine, University of Havana (Cuba), and Dr Eduardo Valdes Santo Tomas, president of the Council for the Direction of the Prison of Havana and professor of the National Penitentiary School (Cuba); Prof. J. M. Van Bemmelen, Leiden (Netherlands); Mr L. P. Wilkins, London (England).

[36] S. Glueck, *Prognosis of recidivism,* General Report, Section IV[(173)].

The first topic needs no discussion, since it formed the subject-matter of other sections. As to the second, the writer pointed out that while prediction has come to denote the use of tables or charts in which the recidivism or non-recidivism of a large sample of offenders has been systematically correlated with the presence or absence of certain traits and factors in the make-up and background of those who have behaved satisfactorily as compared with those who have not, prognosis refers to the more impressionistic approach to the individual case by the clinician. Nevertheless, the two concepts have in common the fact that the clinician, too, relies on his past experience with numerous other cases in prognosticating on the case before him and the fact that both require a check-up, or validation, to see if their forecasts have been borne out by subsequent events. The European and Latin American contributors to the symposium on *Prognosis of Recidivism* tended to deal with prognosis in the clinical sense; the American, with prediction, involving the use of tables which summarize and objectify experience with hundreds of past cases.

Under the topic the Uses of Prediction Tables, the General Reporter described the two basic methods employed in America—that of Burgess and that of the Gluecks—and adverted to various modifications. He then discussed the value of predictive devices (*a*) in forecasting recidivism, (*b*) in determining, at the outset, which children will probably become delinquent unless timely intervention diverts the predicted course, and (*c*) in suggesting fruitful lines of research into the causes of recidivism.

He answered (to the satisfaction, he believes, of most participants in Section IV) the main objections to the use of prediction tables: (*a*) that they assume a deterministic, even fatalistic, sequence of cause and effect in human affairs and leave no room for 'free will'; (*b*) that they allegedly fail to take account of changing personal and social conditions because built on the assumption that the traits and background factors as they entered into the table originally will remain constant; (*c*) that they employ only a small fraction of the numerous and complex influences involved in human conduct and do so as separate items rather than by way of a unitary dynamic syndrome; (*d*) that they cannot truly 'individualize', since they deal with a person as a statistical type.[37]

Under the topic of Improvement of Predictive Devices, the General Reporter discussed (*a*) improvement of the raw materials entering into predictive tables and of check-ups on the relationship of the predictive factors to outcomes; (*b*) improvement of

[37] For the answers to these criticisms, see pp. 90–97 and *Prognosis of recidivism*, pp. 16–17.

statistical techniques; and (c) validation of experience tables.

(a) The General Reporter pointed out that many of the contributors to the symposium emphasized the need of building prediction devices on sound raw materials. 'All the neat tables and sophisticated mathematical statistics in the world cannot transform unverified raw data regarding temperament, character, and sociocultural conditions into trustworthy information. This applies also to the reliability of the check-up on recidivism' (ibid. p. 19). In the experience of the writer and his co-worker, Dr Eleanor T. Glueck, official records are commonly not sufficiently comprehensive and reliable to be the basis of predictive techniques.

(b) After pointing out that control groups are necessary, the General Reporter adverted to the sophisticated mathematical techniques which in recent years have characterized work in the prediction field (especially the work of Ohlin and Wilkins), in respect to such problems as the relative accuracy of different syndromes of factors as indices of the total set of forces affecting behavior on parole; degree of 'predictive efficiency' (i.e. the extent to which a predictive device improves forecasts over choices based simply on knowledge of an overall actual rate of recidivism); improvement of the prognoses of the behavior of the 'unpredictable' (i.e. cases with an equal chance of success or failure under the factors first used); maintenance of 'predictive stability' of tables when they are applied at successive periods; 'overlap' of factors; and guidance of the selection of predictive factors in accordance with some pre-existing theory of criminal causation or recidivism. The Reporter expressed the view that while all these mathematical refinements are not to be discouraged and are indeed indications that prediction technique is entering the hallowed halls of Science, they are not as important as is the basic work and may not be necessary in constructing a useful prediction device. 'In this matter what will determine the issue is not so much mathematical theorizing as the pragmatic test expressed in the proverb that "the proof of the pudding is in the eating"' (ibid. p. 22).

(c) Validation of 'experience tables' was emphasized as the last step in determining their usefulness and reliability. Several validations of the Glueck Social Prediction Table were mentioned.

Unlike the other General Reports, the one by the writer ended with certain Resolutions to be presented to the Congress. After lively discussion, the section adopted these Resolutions, with minor modifications; and upon their presentation to the Congress at the plenary session they were adopted by a vote of 260 to 10:

'1. That fundamental attention should be paid by legislators, judges, correctional officials, clinicians, and researchers in criminology to the problem of recidivism as a major issue in the prevention of crime and the treatment of offenders. In order to achieve these purposes it is recommended that adequate prognostic services should be established in the various countries.

'2. That the prognosis of recidivism can be improved, among other methods, with the aid of prediction tables based on a demonstrated high relationship between certain personality, character, biological, and sociocultural factors on the one hand, and varieties of conduct on the other.

'3. That the use of systematic methods of prognosis, including validated predictive devices, should be encouraged; provided that such methods are not applied automatically, but used as instruments in the hands of teams composed of professional skilled workers serving agencies charged with the administration of justice involving juvenile and adult offenders.

'4. That, because of the close relationship between recidivism and early delinquency (*Frühkriminalität*), it is advisable to encourage the development and use of prognostic devices, including predictive tables, in the prediction of early delinquency.

'5. That the utmost care needs to be taken in the definition, assembling, and verification of the factors which form the basic data on which prognostic methods, including prediction tables, are built, and in checking up on the actual extent of recidivism as related to such factors.

'6. That an indispensable aspect of any improved prognostic technique is the validation of the predictive methods on samples of cases other than those on which they were developed, in order to transform them as far as possible into effective instruments for prognosis' (*Conclusions*, pp. 5–6).

Discussion. While, at the opening of the section meetings, it appeared that the views of Dr Drapkin and the other General Reporter (the writer) were at opposite extremes, frank discussion, in which many participated, disclosed that Drapkin was not opposed to the employment of predictive devices provided they were soundly constructed, not used by amateurs, and employed not exclusively but as adjuncts to clinical and judicial practices. Such prerequisites were envisioned by the writer in his General Report.

All the General Reports and most of the individual reports were of high calibre; and it is doubtful whether the topic of recidivism has previously received such a thoroughgoing examination from various points of view. But the idea that there are methods of predicting

231

recidivism which hold high promise seemed most to intrigue the members of the Congress. And well it might; for the approach to criminologic and penologic problems through the avenue of the prediction table has value not merely as an aid to improved administration of justice but also as a rational means of narrowing the field of inquiry in analysis of causation and in the structuring of case-histories. Some device is necessary to render criminologic research more pointed, less sprawling, less intoxicated by the heady wine of some single 'theory' which, instead of guiding research, may bias and blind it; and the writer is convinced that the most direct road to these desiderata is the prediction table, which checks systematically on the results of organized and objectified experience and focuses attention on the operationally relevant.

X

Mr Charles Germain (France) and Dr George K. Stürup (Denmark) were the reporters in Section V, on the *Treatment of Recidivism*. After considering the legislative and administrative problems involved, Mr Germain[38] underscores the proposition previously emphasized in several sections that the control of recidivism, like the prevention of original misconduct, entails the utilization of exact knowledge of causes. Yet, he claims, even the best researches have thus far not produced a formula to express, with scientific rigor, the combination of elements which bring about the criminalistic reaction, since many factors found in the careers of delinquents exist also in those of the law-abiding.

Like other Reporters, Mr Germain points out that the aims and methods for preventing recidivism do not differ essentially from those applicable to control of first offenders, since, apart from chance delinquents who are not likely to recidivate anyhow, the factors leading to recidivism are in large measure the ones involved in the original delinquency. Nevertheless, a basic cause of recidivism is the ineffectiveness of treatment, either at the origin of delinquency or during the first peno-correctional efforts. Germain deplores the sharp differentiation between the treatment of juvenile delinquents and the treatment of adult offenders, since there is a continuity in the evolution of criminal tendency in a person. Inadequate employment of probation, and especially improper execution of the first sentence of imprisonment, far from failing to counteract a criminalistic tendency, may even enhance it. Imprisonment should be avoided

---

[38] C. Germain, *Le Traitement du récidivisme*, Rapport Général, Section V.

where other measures are more promising. The giving of short-term sentences should be limited. Longer sentences should be designed, on the one hand, to omit useless rigors (which can only aggravate an antisocial sentiment on the part of the prisoner) as well as influences which lead to social maladaptation and render rehabilitation more difficult, and, on the other hand, to provide re-educative influences adapted to the needs of the individual and planned to bring about his progressive readaptation to society. It is also indispensable to provide post-penal assistance and gradually to restore the ex-prisoner's civil rights. In the case of habitual offenders, a period of relatively indeterminate duration is required, to be applied by judicial authority after a thorough criminologic study which should continue both during incarceration and thereafter.

Dr Stürup[39] reserves the term 'professional treatment' for that of a specialized character 'with stronger emphasis in some cases on psychological structure; in other cases on the more directly educational procedure'. But for all cases an 'emotional contact' with one or more persons is basic, 'in order to normalize the recidivist's group membership and in order to give him a true picture of his status in relation to the norms of the society'.

Preliminary evaluation of the total situation is needed as a basis of diagnosis, which must be kept fluid. Both analysis and synthesis of personal and background data involve, admittedly, 'a more or less intuitive' act. Since factors are not stable, the therapist must be elastic, 'and not once but over and over again must attempt to place the criminal in situations affording possibilities for better adjustment and giving better opportunities for avoidance of later maladjustments'.

'Planned treatment' should realistically take into account the fact that the measures adopted must usually be carried out not only by the professionals but also by the security and workshop staffs, and that some members of these groups have no full view of the consequences of their actions and may even vent their aggressions on inmates with intent to destroy rehabilitative efforts. Stürup points out that 'a therapeutic climate may in itself act as a general strengthening of personal resources and thus be an important aid in the healing power of nature' in reducing the ill consequences of personal conflicts, including aggressiveness.

Discussing environmental maladjustments, Stürup makes a telling distinction between the sociologist's general environmental influences, which are only potentials to certain individuals, and the actual environmental experiences.

[39] G. K. Stürup, *Treatment of recidivism*, General Report, Section V.

'It is a fact that a man is rewarded and punished by the sort of reputation he has, and especially by the reputation he thinks he has. This means that serving a sentence—forcing upon the man a 'bad reputation'—can mean a greater risk for new crimes as well as greater risk for detection. We may add that the psychology of learning reveals that punishment is no effective remedy for unlearning a type of behavior. On the other hand, we see the opposite effect of the reputation as it is experienced by the criminal himself when after some years it is proved to him that it was possible to come through several of the difficulties that in earlier life were followed by criminal reactions. After such a period, he feels relieved of a very heavy burden, and it is much easier for him to continue a life as a normal citizen' (ibid. p. 5).

On the problem of classification, Stürup warns against the possible ill effects of too homogeneous a grouping of prisoners (e.g. as 'untreatables', which may result in 'identification with the other "hopeless" and stimulate the devaluation of the personality and outward aggressiveness'). To minimize the risk of antisocial contamination, groups should be small enough to permit the officer in charge to maintain personal contact with each inmate, thereby counteracting 'unsuitable group-building'. Before parole, prisoners should be permitted to work or to attend an apprentice school outside the institution, returning at night. 'It helps the prisoner to obtain a feeling of security to know that he really is able to manage normal work, together with free people, and helps to prepare free people to see that "prisoners are also people".'

The psychiatrist is indispensable to the treatment task, but he must work with a team. For the more seriously maladjusted, a more psychiatrically oriented treatment is necessary, the same staff operating both during the offender's institutional stay and during parole Collaboration with the prisoner's family in the treatment program is of the utmost necessity. Stürup emphasizes the prime importance of means to counteract the ex-prisoner's 'emotional loneliness' on parole and to contrive ways of giving the satisfaction that comes from 'belonging'. To prepare the prisoner to meet the economic, social, and personal problems facing him on release, he reommends 'group-work of a more advisory character, directed by a senior staff-member in collaboration with the social worker who is going to take charge in the parole period'.

Diagnosis, Dr Stürup pointed out, should provide a plan of action, taking into account not only the individual's endowment, needs, and wants but 'what part of these things that are going to be of

234

importance to behavior can be expected in a given environment'. In a valuable analysis of the general and special problems of treatment, Stürup emphasizes that:

'The initial examination should define the possible therapeutic situation. Does the new inmate already realize a need for another solution to his problems? Has he an obvious satisfaction through his criminal deeds (special sexual needs, special forms of aggression, etc.)? Will he be willing to accept difficulties during the period of treatment? What is needed in order to make him accept such troubles? How can his own collaboration be secured?' (ibid. p. 8).

Stürup points out that the prisoner conceives even the examination by professionals as directed against him, since it is part of the prison régime; and he speaks penetratingly of the psychology of treatment:

'When in spite of this a positive rapport is established, and the employee is identified with a friendly person, it will help to give the inmate a matter-of-fact attitude toward authorities. He will see that some authorities are able to smile, to understand a joke, and perhaps what is most important, be able to accept the possibility of making mistakes themselves. The process then taking place can in many cases be described as some sort of neurotization. Insecurity and sometimes a conscious anxiety can be found behind the expressed need for help. When a transference is established, it is important to carry it over to someone else. At the time of parole, such transference should include the social worker in charge of the case. . . .

'The value of the treatment for the individual himself should be especially considered. The neurotic may eventually feel relieved, the criminal will often, when treatment succeeds, be more neurotic than before and consequently more insecure. Sometimes after parole, he says that he does not like the new way of life, and it will often take a long time for him to be able to obtain personal gains out of this change. If the outward aggression is changed to an inward aggression, perhaps with suicidal problems, the personal value of such a result may be difficult to accept. If without this change, the public danger had been great, it may still, from a social point of view, be wanted. In such cases, the prisoner himself may think this new state better than the former with its risk of new crimes, new despair, and new imprisonment' (ibid. pp. 8–9, 13–14).

The therapeutic process should help the prisoner to render more

235

realistic the level of his aspirations; he must be aided to obtain self-knowledge and a better 'emotional balance'.

As to ordinary medical treatment, Stürup makes, among other interesting suggestions, the observation that 'some of the more explosive prisoners may, through periodic hormonal treatment, be helped to endure forced celibacy. When carefully controlled, this treatment seems a very safe procedure and can give such a prisoner sufficient self-reliance so that he can more easily accept his special problems.' Stürup is also in favor of castration in cases 'where indicated', and 'after intensive psychiatric preparation, and together with ordinary rehabilitative efforts'. He believes it gives a 'man a fair possibility to resist abnormal impulses which he, before the operation, could not resist'. He recommends follow-up clinics to aid ex-prisoners in need of psychiatric or general medical advice.

He suggests that prediction tables could be an aid in the development of the individual treatment program. 'At the time for parole and the time for final discharge, new tables could help to demonstrate the alterations obtained.'

The *Conclusions* of Section V may be summarized as follows: The subjects of prevention, legal aspects and penal aspects were discussed (p. 6). As to prevention, recidivism has many causes. Social conditions should be improved, particularly the 'less glamorization of the criminal in the press'. As to legal aspects, such devices as the indeterminate sentence or measures of security are 'essential on a sufficient basis of law to insure adequate treatment of the recidivist'. Mechanical increase of length or severity of sentence upon recidivists is not recommended; the judge's choice in sentencing should not be too limited. As to treatment, while work, vocational training, and general education are useful, they are not sufficient and should be viewed as only part of a 'general plan directed towards the reclamation of the individual' to be achieved through greater staff collaboration. Gaps in knowledge of treatment are (a) absence of long-term study of the offender, for the remedy of which it was proposed that 'an international group should be formed to exchange case-histories', and (b) the need to create 'suitable classifications in view of the nature of institutional treatment'.

As to the role of professional treatment, (a) it is more necessary for treatment purposes to know 'the prisoner's personality pattern, his estimation of himself, his educational background and social possibilities and type of criminal behavior, than his formal conviction' (p. 7); (b) all members of the treatment team, including custodial officers, must be trained to understand the general plan of treatment and the importance of accurate, detailed observation;

236

(*c*) for continuity of treatment, the prison staff must have a clear idea of the conditions under which the offender will live and the aftercare officer should be part of the team; (*d*) to counteract the prisoner's feeling of loneliness and sense that nobody respects him as a human being, the offender should be included 'in groups with professional and security staff', after careful preparation for such treatment; (*e*) the section discussed 'the value and application of specialized medical and surgical methods of treatment, in particular lobotomy, castration and, especially for paranoids, the use of new drugs'.[40]

Discussion. Germain's recommendations on treatment are in line with an increasingly widespread recognition that society is only cutting off its nose to spite its face by using imprisonment to vent its anger on an offending member; and that the wise policy, from the point of view of the soundest social protection, is to employ its institutions as human repair stations, where personality and character damage can be determined and remedied if possible.

Germain's familiar argument that little is known about causation of delinquency because many factors found among delinquents are also found among non-delinquents is a theme which, as some of the prior comments have suggested, has recently been greatly overplayed. There are likewise numerous factors among seriously ill persons that are also found among the well; yet it is possible to make a successful diagnosis and prognosis of many illnesses even with imperfect knowledge. There has been altogether too much seemingly profound but essentially superficial writing on the theme (derived from the physical sciences) that one must never use the term 'cause', but only such evasive terms as 'associated factor' or 'decision theory'. But the issue is a pragmatic, not a semantic, one. Where a considerable number of factors that make sense from the point of view of common and clinical experience are found to characterize delinquents far more than non-delinquents (the difference not being due to chance), it is highly probable that what is involved is a causal *connection* between such factors and misconduct (or recidivism) rather than an accidental *coincidence* between them; that, in other words, the delinquency (or recidivism) not only follows the traits and conditions that precede it but follows *from* them. That such a conception of causation is sound from a practical point of view is provable by (*a*) the fact that the concatenation of differentiative traits and factors yields high predictive power when applied to a

[40] See, for example, R. H. Dinerstein, & B. C. Glueck, Jr. (1955), Sub-coma insulin therapy in the treatment of homosexual panic states; and W. Bromberg (1955), Sex deviation and therapy. *J. Soc. Therapy* **1**, 182–6, 203–10.

variety of samples of cases; and (b) that when such patterns of differentiative traits and factors are eliminated from a situation, delinquency (or recidivism) usually does not result. The fact that some day variations in people's behavior may be explainable in the more ultimate terms of differences in, say, endocrine gland function or of microscopic physico-chemical reactions does not in the meantime prevent effective action on the basis of the existing cruder assessments of reality, any more than the recent development of nuclear science prevented effective coping with many problems of nature through employment of pre-nuclear chemistry and physics.[41] In the meantime, it can serve no useful purpose for workers in criminology and penology to keep wringing their hands about the inadequacies of the etiologic researches thus far produced. Medicine made therapeutic strides in several fields long before the specific causal agents in certain diseases were discovered.[42] It behooves us to work with the findings we possess until further development of the biosocial disciplines can produce better ones.

The importance of Dr Stürup's contribution lies in his penetrating definition of the role of therapy in both institutional and post-institutional settings. The prison psychiatrist is shown to be much more than an affixer of labels, such as 'not insane', 'psychopathic personality', etc. Unless the psychiatrist is ready and willing to undertake various forms of therapy he serves no really useful purpose in the correctional institution but only creates an exaggerated impression of the impotency of his profession in coping with complex problems of personality, character, and conduct. Dr Stürup's report is also valuable in stressing the need of a mental hygiene point of view on the part of all who deal with the prisoner; not merely the psychiatrist and social worker but also the guards, shop foremen, and others. Finally, he is on solid ground also when he conceives of the therapeutic process as involving thorough diagnosis and re-assessments, on the one hand, and an extension of the supportive and interpretive assistance to the ex-prisoner in the community, on the other. It is probable, however, that most American criminologists would not accede to his views regarding the desirability of castration.

The *Conclusions* of Section V are not new or startling. It is good that they emphasize the need of recognizing that the entire staff—custodial as well as professional—are involved in both the institutional and post-institutional therapeutic process; and that they all need training in analyzing treatment plans and making, as it were,

[41] For a commonsense analysis of causation in criminology, see *Delinquents in the making*[(153)], pp. 164–71.
[42] See *Preventing crime*[(66)], p. 4.

238

proper 'bedside notes'. That more attention should be paid to therapy in a truly fundamental sense is a conclusion that deserves more attention in the observance than in the breach. The use of psychiatrically indicated drugs, if not the more drastic surgical methods of lobotomy and castration, is something that, under proper guidance, might perhaps improve the life and labor of prisoners. As to gaps in knowledge, that there is need for the long-term study of offenders cannot be denied; but reliable American follow-up studies have taught us much about the operation of Father Time and Mother Nature in the correctional process and about the great promise of prediction methods in both the sentencing and paroling procedures.[43]

The foregoing panorama of ideas, suggestions, and recommendations presented at the two Congresses, long as it is, is of course not as comprehensive as it might be; and because its construction involves the subjective process of selection of a sample of data from each of the numerous reports and other documents involved, it is unavoidably tainted with certain biases. Conceding these blemishes, the foregoing pages nevertheless show a lively awareness on the part of scholars, researchers, and administrators of the most complex issues involved in coping effectively with crime and recidivism. The views expressed by the various contributors afford food for thought to correctional workers in both the more simply organized societies and in those most thoroughly entangled in industrial, economic, and cultural complexity.

There emerges from it all a feeling that the free world is moving away from the old reliance on force and repression and pain-infliction as 'cures' for crime to an attitude compounded of humanitarianism and a reliance on scientific method. It is being recognized far and wide that to prevent children from failures of adaptation that lead to delinquency, to prevent juvenile delinquents from becoming adult offenders, to prevent adult criminals from becoming chronic recidivists will take more than the ancient incantations of legal formulas and the multiplication of ever harsher punishments and more maximal 'maximum security' fortresses. It will take patience, understanding, and dedication—commodities all too scarce in the management of human affairs. In the meantime, the friendly exchange of ideas by representatives of many nations is all to the good.

[43] See *500 criminal careers*[26], *One thousand juvenile delinquents*[45], *Five hundred delinquent women*[44], *Preventing crime*[66], *Later criminal careers*[71], *Juvenile delinquents grown up*[85], *Criminal careers in retrospect*[102], *After-conduct of discharged offenders*[119], *Unraveling juvenile delinquency*[138], *Delinquents in the making*[153], *Physique and delinquency*[176], *Predicting delinquency and crime.*[212]

PART IV

Philosophy of Criminologic Research

CHAPTER 16

Theory and Fact in Criminology

SHELDON GLUECK

I

BEFORE and after Lombroso published his theory of the 'born criminal' in 1897, there have been attempts to attribute crime to some unilateral cause. Intellectual defect as an exclusive or major explanation followed atavism, degeneracy and epilepsy; mental disease followed intellectual defect; the psycho-analytic concept of criminalism 'from a sense of guilt' followed traditional psychiatric explanations. The older unilateral sociological explanations in terms of poverty, movements of the business cycle and the like, were succeeded by the over-emphasis of residence in economically underprivileged and culturally conflicting 'interstitial' urban areas.

In more recent years, the theory of 'differential association' has been put forward by the late Professor E. H. Sutherland and elaborated in Professor D. R. Cressey's new edition of Sutherland's popular text-book on criminology.[1] This theory plays a prominent part in American criminological circles.[2] The proponents of this view disclaim that they, like their forerunners, are resorting to a unilateral explanation of crime; they do not call differential association a 'cause' but rather a 'theory'. The theory is alleged to explain crime not in terms of a single etiological influence but rather in terms of many variables which it supposedly 'organizes and relates'.

It is the thesis of this paper that the theory of differential association, supported by its related concept of 'definitions of the situation', fails to organize and integrate the findings of respectable research and is, at best, so general and puerile as to add little or nothing to the explanation, treatment and prevention of delinquency.

Simply stated, the theory explains criminality as the result of an excess of 'definitions favorable to violation of the law over definitions unfavorable to violation of the law',[3] learned by the prospective

---

[1] E. H. Sutherland (1955), *Principles of criminology*, 5th ed. revised by D. R. Cressey (Philadelphia: Lippincott).
[2] Virtually all criminological text-books published in the United States during the past three decades are by dedicated sociologists.
[3] Op. cit., p. 78.

offender in social interaction with existing criminals. However, as stated in the text-books the theory is not too clear. One form of explanation (in the quotation that follows) seems to emphasize the individual rather than the *milieu*, and to include, thereby, early childhood experiences and perhaps even original natural endowment of the offender in the bringing about of delinquent behavior; but, if this be so, the theory adds nothing but the excess baggage of confusing terminology to what is already well known and explainable without the benefit of the theory:

'In another sense, a psychological or sociological sense, the situation is not exclusive of the person, for the situation which is important is the situation as defined by the person who is involved. That is, some persons define a situation in which a fruitstand owner is out of sight as a "crime-committing" situation, while others do not so define it. Furthermore, the events in the person-situation complex at the time a crime occurs cannot be separated from the prior life experiences of the criminal. This means that the situation is defined by the person in terms of the inclinations and abilities which the person has acquired up to date. For example, while a person could define a situation in such a manner that criminal behavior would be the inevitable result, his past experiences would for the most part determine the way in which he defined the situation. . . . The following paragraphs state such a genetic theory of criminal behavior on the assumption that a criminal act occurs when a situation appropriate for it, as defined by the person, is present' (ibid. p. 77).

While it is true that a person's 'inclinations and abilities' and his prior experiences influence his latest experience, it is difficult to see what is added to understanding by all this talk about 'definitions of the situation'. It comes down to saying that if a person's make-up and experiences are such as to incline him to criminalism he will consciously become a criminal—something with which nobody can quarrel except for the unwarranted exclusion of the subconscious and unconscious influences in behavior. Why place major emphasis on a 'definition of the situation' which the prospective offender supposedly goes through? The important question is what makes him a delinquent, or, if we must pay tribute to the sociological formula, what makes him define a situation as conducive to criminalism?

But another form of exposition of the differential association theory emphasizes the influence of the *milieu*. We are informed, first, of the discovery that 'criminal behavior is *learned*' and that 'Negatively, this means that criminal behavior is not inherited, as such; also, the person who is not already trained in crime does not invent criminal behavior, just as a person does not make mechanical inventions unless he has had training in mechanics'.[4]

Consider the first part of this statement. Does anybody nowadays believe that criminal behavior 'as such' is inherited? Did even Lombroso believe so? Those criminologists who call attention to variations in the strength of different hereditary drives and controlling mechanisms do not claim that criminalism *per se* is inherited, but merely point to the too-often sociologically underemphasized if not ignored biological fact that, in the eyes of nature, all men are not created equal and that some, because of certain traits useful to the kind of activities involved in criminal behavior, probably have a higher delinquency *potential* than others.[5]

Consider, now, the second part of the quotation, to the effect that a person cannot invent criminal behavior or commit crime without training. This is so contrary to obvious fact that it is surprising to see it seriously advanced. It attributes all criminal conduct to indoctrination by other criminals or contagion by criminalistic 'patterns' and utterly ignores such primitive impulses of aggression, sexual desire, acquisitiveness, and the like, which lead children to various forms of antisocial conduct before they have learned it from others. What is there to be learned about simple lying, taking things that belong to another, fighting, and sex play? Do children have to be taught such natural acts? If one takes account of the psychiatric and criminological evidence that involves research into the early childhood manifestations of antisocial behavior, one must conclude that it is not delinquent behavior that is learned; that comes naturally. It is rather *non*-delinquent behavior that is learned. Unsocialized, untamed, and uninstructed, the child resorts to lying, slyness, subterfuge, anger, hatred, theft, aggression, attack, and other forms of asocial behavior in its early attempts at self-expression and ego formation. What he is normally forced to learn in his earliest struggles with the adult environment, in order to develop a personality and win the affection and sense of security and approval he craves, is not the non-conforming behavior of egoism and delinquency but the conventional behaviour of altruism and non-delinquency; not the expression of natural asocial, dissocial or antisocial

---

[4] 'The differential association theory, which is considered by most sociologists as the best formulation to date of a general theory of criminality, holds, in essence, that criminality is learned in interaction with others in a process of communication.' D. R. Cressey (1954), The differential association theory and compulsive crimes. *J. crim. L., Criminol. & Police Sci.* **45**, 29.

[5] See *Physique and delinquency*[176].

impulses and desires, but how to tame these primitive tendencies sufficiently to win parental love and approval. Law-abiding character formation is a hard-won process.

If, as the proponents of the 'differential association' theory insist, 'the person who is not already trained in crime does not invent criminal behavior just as a person does not make mechanical inventions unless he has had training in mechanics', how account for a basic finding in *Unraveling Juvenile Delinquency*[138] that the onset of delinquent behavior occurred at the tender age of seven years or less in 44·4 per cent of the delinquents and at ten years or less in 87·6 per cent? (p. 28). These are not theoretical speculations but carefully verified facts.[6] Just where and when did these very young children 'differentially associate' with delinquents or criminals in order to learn how to commit their delinquencies? True, another finding of *Unraveling* was that 56 per cent of the delinquents, compared to only three individuals among the non-delinquents, became members of boy gangs (p. 163); but since nine-tenths of the delinquents were, as has been indicated, committing offenses at under eleven years of age, and since the gang is an adolescent phenomenon,[7] it cannot be said that the delinquents learned their antisocial behavior from the gang.

If what is meant by the proponents of the 'crime is learned' school is that most criminals consolidate their antisocial attitudes in contact with others, or learn *techniques* of various crimes from others, there is less objection (although this does not account for the *origins* of misconduct); but even this is exaggerated. We found little evidence in our numerous solidly grounded follow-up studies involving (in addition to the 500 delinquents reported on in *Unraveling*) 1,000 juvenile delinquents and 500 adult reformatory offenders studied over a period of fifteen years, as well as 500 female offenders, that the great majority of these criminals would have failed to pass from juvenile delinquency to adult criminalism had it not been for 'differential association', or that they learned their techniques from each other.[8]

[6] For a detailed account of method, see *Unraveling*, Chs. II–VII.

[7] See F. M. Thrasher (1936), *The gang*, 2nd rev. ed. (Chicago: University of Chicago Press). 'The lure of the gang is undoubtedly due in part to the fact that the gang boy is in the adolescent stage which is definitely correlated with gang phenomena. Although this period has no exact limits for any individual, it includes broadly for the boy the years from twelve to twenty-six' (p. 36). Of some 1,200 cases of gang membership studied in Chicago, only 1·5 per cent of the boys were six to twelve years old, while 63 per cent were classified as adolescents (p. 74).

[8] *500 Criminal careers*[26], *One thousand juvenile delinquents*[45], *Five hundred delinquent women*[44], *Later criminal careers*[71], *Criminal careers in retrospect*[102], *After-conduct of discharged offenders*[119].

By way of further elucidation of the differential association concept, the crux of this theory is presented in the following words:

'The specific direction of motives and drives is learned from definitions of the legal codes as favorable or unfavorable. In some societies an individual is surrounded by persons who invariably define the legal codes as rules to be observed, while in others he is surrounded by persons whose definitions are favorable to the violation of the legal codes. In our American society these definitions are almost always mixed, with the consequence that we have culture conflict in relation to the legal codes. A person becomes delinquent because of an excess of definitions favorable to violation of law over definitions unfavorable to violation of law. This is the principle of differential association.[9]

'The ratio between such definitions and others unfavorable to law violation determines whether or not a person becomes criminal.'[10]

Consider these statements. In the first place, has anybody actually counted the number of definitions favorable to violation of law and definitions unfavorable to violation of law, and demonstrated that in the pre-delinquency experience of the vast majority of delinquents and criminals the former exceed the latter?[11] Indeed, it is highly probable that, by the very extent, frequency and intensity of conventional home and school and church influences, and the very early

[9] Sutherland–Cressey, op. cit., p. 78.
[10] D. R. Cressey (1952), Application and verification of the differential association theory. *J. crim. L., Criminol. & Police Sci.* **43**, 43.
[11] The only systematic check-up I know of, by Cressey himself (and that not involving a count of 'definitions'), resulted in the conclusion that the theory will hardly stand up. Reporting on sixty-five prisoners in the Illinois State Penitentiary at Joliet, twenty in the California Institution for Men at Chino, and forty in the United States Penitentiary at Terre Haute, Indiana, who were 'questioned in detail about the acquisition of the techniques and rationalizations' pertaining to their common offence of criminal trust violation, Cressey says: 'On the basis of evidence found in interview materials gathered from these men, the first hypothesis, that the techniques are learned in association with identifiable criminal behavior patterns, was rejected.' A second hypothesis was supposedly established (partially) on the following reasoning: 'Since a rationalization that one is "borrowing" rather than "stealing" or "embezzling" the entrusted funds, for example, must be learned, it is inconceivable that it could be present unless the individual using it had been in contact with persons who presented it to him or had been in contact with some other cultural source which gave him a general acquaintance with it. . . . It is not possible for trust violators to use rationalizations in the manner indicated without first having come into contact with definitions of situations which to a greater or less degree sanction the criminal violation of financial trust.' . . . However, 'rather than naming a specific source, the subjects referred directly or indirectly to rather general cultural ideologies with which they had informal contact at some vague period in their lives. For this reason, that portion of the second hypothesis which pertains to the identification of the specific sources of the rationalizations was rejected, and a calculation of the differential association ratio could not be attempted.' Cressey, op. cit., pp. 45, 47, 48, 49. It is submitted that the proponents of the differential association theory can derive little comfort from this experiment.

stage of the development of character at which these influences operate, there is an excess of 'definitions *un*favorable to violation of law' even in the case of most of those who become delinquent and criminal.

In the second place, the theory in question, by emphasizing a quantitive excess of 'definitions', ignores the patent fact that the individual influences of the human and physical environment to which persons are subjected vary in their impact. But more seriously, it fails to take account of obvious differences in the somatic, temperamental, and characterological make-up of individuals subjected to a superficially similar environment.

Those sociological criminologists who have taken up the ideas of W. I. Thomas are not as discerning as was the master. For right at the threshold of Thomas's significant *Primitive Behavior*,[12] he points out that conditioning is only half the process, the other half being the varied nature of those conditioned; and that these involve both experience and original endowment:

> 'The reaction of different individuals in the same culture to identical cultural influences will depend partly on their different trains of experience and partly on their biochemical constitutions and unlearned psychological endowments. Local, regional, nationalistic and racial groups are in turn conditioned, in the formation of their behavior patterns and habits, by their several trains of experience and conceivably by their particular biochemical and psychological constitutions' (p.1).

He includes, among the problems of individual and group adjustment, the 'capacity and opportunity of the individual to be adjusted (*constitutional* factors, incentives, social position)' (p. 2. My italics.).

But by emphasizing the *number* or *ratio* of 'definitions' as controlling, the differential association theory treats all persons as *equally* influenced by stimuli of one kind or another—something patently contrary to elementary biology and psychology. If the quantitative emphasis of the theory is sound, then, to press it to its logical conclusion, the biggest criminals of all would be professors of criminology, prison guards, and prison chaplains! They certainly spend a great deal of time and effort in numerous instances of 'differential association' with criminals. These persons are not criminal but essentially law-abiding, because of their original endowment and early home influences and training; and to say they 'define the situation' differently from criminals is to add no insight whatsoever

[12] W. I. Thomas (1937), *Primitive behavior, An introduction to the social sciences* (New York: McGraw-Hill).

to the understanding of delinquency and non-delinquency, but to state, in pseudo-scientific language, the fact that they are not criminally inclined or do not wish to be criminals.

However, the proponents of this theory want to have it both ways. They also tell us that 'differential associations vary in frequency, duration, priority, and intensity'. If these influences vary in these different ways, how can one say that it is a mere numerical excess of definitions favorable to criminality that determines the issue? In discussing 'intensity', Professor Cressey says that ' "intensity" is not precisely defined but it has to do with such things as the prestige of the source of a criminal or anti-criminal pattern and with *emotional reactions related to the associations*'.[13] But if this be so, it is not the *stimulus* of the 'differential association' that is crucial but rather the *response* in terms of the emotional reaction of the individual to such stimulus; and this response obviously must vary with differences in the biopsychologic structure of those who make it. What is added to this by the *deus ex machina* of 'definitions of the situation'? How much more illuminating is Dr Bernard Glueck's formulation: 'A factor is not a cause unless and until it becomes a motive.'

There remains the mention of a significant phenomenon which the 'differential association' and 'definition of the situation' theory fails to explain, and which is rationally explainable on other grounds; namely, the phenomenon of fluctuations in criminality and recidivism with age. Cressey states, among other features, that 'the age of maximum general criminality is probably during or shortly before adolescence', that it varies with type of crime, that 'in general . . . criminal behavior varies widely with age and sex', that 'the age of concentration of the more violent types of crimes, such as burglary and robbery, has remained relatively constant for several centuries', that 'the crime rate decreases regularly and steadily from the age of maximum criminality until the end of life' (ibid., pp. 108–109).

By way of explanation of such phenomena, Cressey considers certain biological views, as follows:

'One of the theories presented as an explanation of the age ratios in crime is that they are due directly to biological traits such as physical strength and vigour: crimes are committed frequently by persons who are strong and active and infrequently by persons who are weak and passive. Another biological theory is that crimes are concentrated in three periods, ages three to six, fourteen to sixteen, and forty-two to forty-five, and that these periods are products of libidinal tides due to changes in the instincts of sex

[13] Sutherland–Cressey, op. cit., pp. 78–79. (My italics.)

and aggression and to changes in the ego strength. A third biological theory is that inheritance is the direct cause' (pp. 110–11).

He does not discuss these views. He disposes of them by this simple *ipse dixit*: 'These biological theories *obviously* [*sic*] provide no explanation of many of the variations in the age ratios in crime; indeed, it may be said that they do not explain even one of the facts outlined above when that fact is considered in its ramifications. On the other hand, all of these facts are consistent with the general theory that crime is a product of social experiences and social inter-action' (p. 111. My italics.). But where is the evidence that the number and/or 'duration, priority, and intensity' of 'definitions favorable to crime' fluctuates with age, so as to explain the ebb and flow of crime at various biological stages? Cressey claims that 'the general conclusion from this survey of the facts regarding physical and physiological conditions is that these conditions have not in any case been demonstrated to be a direct force in the production of crime or delinquency. On the contrary, it is *apparent* [*sic*] that these conditions are related to crime only as they are socially defined and interpreted' (p. 115. My italics.). How apparent? To whom apparent?

Nobody claims any direct or exclusive relationship between physical characteristics and crime. The difference between the eclectic criminologist and the type of sociological criminologist whose reasoning is reflected above is that the latter evidently argues that original nature means nothing, that all is sociocultural conditioning, that you can make a silk purse out of a sow's ear; while the former, basing his views on carefully validated data from biological as well as sociocultural sources, attributes the end-product of criminality to an interplay of various more or less well-defined increments of nature and nurture.

Even well-recognized social processes are dogmatically shaped to fit into the prejudices of the pre-existing theory of 'differential association'. For example, in discussing culture conflict between foreign-born parents and native-born children, Cressey adverts to the following facts:

'Psychiatrists and social workers find these conflicts within the home to be highly significant in emotional disturbances of children, and they feel that the emotional disturbances are conducive to delinquency. Levy has reported that differences in language, manners, methods of discipline, and ideals presented by the parents are important factors in the maladjustment of children' (ibid., p. 92).

Is this satisfactory? No. These clear findings which reasonably explain certain behavior must be forced into the theory of differential association. The quoted passage is followed by this: 'However, it is likely that culture conflict is significant to delinquency principally as it determines differential associations with behavior patterns sanctioning violation of American laws pertaining to delinquency' (pp. 92–93). Proof?

We are told that 'a test of the theory is how well it accounts for all the variations in the values of the variables' (p. 61) involved in the etiology of delinquency. Only by assuming the basic fact which the proponents of the differential association theory have not proved —namely, that in the life of all or the vast majority of delinquents and criminals there is an excess of 'definitions of the situation' favorable to criminality—and by assuming that all people react uniformly to the same sociocultural stimuli—something that is patently not true—can this theory be upheld.

Cressey repeats Sutherland's not very persuasive dogma that 'It is not necessary, at this level of explanation, to explain why a person has the associations which he has; this certainly is a complex of many things...' (p. 79)[14]. It most assuredly is necessary to explain it, if 'this level of explanation' is to descend from the clouds; for the 'complex of many things', disposed of in such cavalier fashion, is the very essence of the issue. Without ventilation of this fundamental matter, the theory of differential association as the basic explanation of delinquency is a roof without a house. Here are a few items in this 'complex of many things': We have shown, in *Unraveling*, that 98·4 per cent of the delinquents sought out other delinquents as companions, while only 7·4 per cent of the non-delinquents, who lived in similar neighborhoods, often in the same block and sometimes in the very same house as the delinquents, had companions among delinquents (p. 163). We found that the delinquents had many temperamental and personality traits and early childhood home experiences in common, as well as similar interests distinguishing them clearly from the control group. It is this combination

---

[14] A similar avoidance of the basic issue is found in another exponent of this theory, Clinard: 'Many here might say, why does one and why not another person engage in delinquent or criminal behavior when most all persons have been exposed to some contact with deviant norms. At this stage all we can say is something like Sutherland's answer that criminal behavior varies according to the frequency, intensity, priority, and continuousness of such associations. In the balance of contacts of pushes and pulls one individual may be drawn toward crime and another away from it.' M. B. Clinard, (1949), Criminal behaviour is human behaviour. *Federal Probation* 13, 24. If all that can be said in explanation of criminalistic behaviour 'at this stage' is the foregoing, one cannot avoid the conclusion that the differential association-definition of the situation theory is 'at this stage' in a half-baked stage. It rests on unproven assumptions; and even if they were proven they would deal with but a single minor influence in a complex totality of biocultural influences.

of influences that led them to chum with other delinquents. To say that they were non-delinquents before and only became delinquents because of differential association with other delinquents and because they had 'an excess of definitions favorable to delinquency' is, factually, to put the cart before the horse and to ignore proved relevant differences between the delinquents and controls, in favor of guesses that the former became delinquent because of differential association and an excess of unfavorable 'definitions'.

Incidentally, elsewhere in his text-book, Cressey states that 'practically all juveniles commit delinquencies' (p. 110), an assumption requiring the conclusion that virtually *all* children 'differentially associate' with delinquents and are subjected to an excess of 'definitions' favorable to misconduct.[15] If he means that they are delinquent *before* they 'differentially associate' he is contradicting the Sutherland–Cressey theory.

II

In order to contrast the superficiality of the 'differential association' theory with the facts of life among delinquents as determined by intensive, verified and relevant biological and sociocultural research data, let me indicate those traits and factors (among many others) in *Unraveling* which were so highly differentiative of delinquents from non-delinquents as to be usefully embodied in three prediction tables, one of which, that dealing with factors of family life, has thus far been subjected to validation through its application to several other and varied samples of cases, and found to have remarkably high discriminative power.[16] The predictive traits derived from the

[15] In response to the obvious fact that the 'ecologic characteristics of the interstitial area' could not be the major influence in the etiology of delinquency because even in the worst possible 'delinquency area' of the urban slums the great majority of boys somehow manage *not* to become delinquents, the answering tactic of the extreme environmentalists seems to be to throw all ballast overboard and claim that the great majority, if not *all*, boys are in fact delinquents—a *reductio ad absurdum* clearly without proof to support it and contrary to the published findings of Clifford Shaw and his associates. In *Unraveling*, hundreds of *truly non-delinquent* boys were found residing in the same underprivileged 'interstitial' areas in which the delinquents resided. This is fact, verified by intensive check and re-check from many sources, and not guesswork.

[16] R. E. Thompson (1952), A validation of the Glueck Social Prediction Scale for proneness to delinquency. *J. crim. L. Criminol. & Police Sci.* **43**, 451; S. Axelrad & S. J. Glick (1953), Application of the Glueck Social Prediction Table to 100 Jewish delinquent boys. *Jewish soc. Serv. Quart.* **30**, 127; R. W. Whelan (1954), An experiment in predicting delinquency. *J. crim. L. Criminol. & Police Sci.* **45**, 432; *Predicting juvenile delinquency* (1955), Research Bulletin No. 124 (Trenton, N.J.: State Department of Institutions & Agencies). Two other validations were presented in papers at the Third International Congress of Criminology in London, 1955; one, on *adult* sex offenders studied in Sing Sing Prison, presented by Isa Brandon, the other, by Dr Augusta Bonnard, involving a follow-up of children treated at the clinic of the London County Council. See also Chapters 8 and 13 above.

Rorschach ('ink-blot') test, applied to delinquents and non-delinquents, are the following: *social assertiveness, defiance, suspiciousness, destructiveness,* and *emotional lability.* The traits derived from psychiatric examination of the delinquents and non-delinquents are the following: *adventurousness, extroversiveness, suggestibility, stubbornness,* and *emotional instability.* The factors derived from the social investigation of the homes of both the delinquents and non-delinquents are: *discipline of the boy by the father, supervison of the boy by the mother, affection of the father for the boy, affection of the mother for the boy, family cohesiveness.*

In order to show how strikingly these traits and factors distinguish delinquents from non-delinquents and are therefore (at least indirectly) causally involved in antisocial behavior, a few illustrations may be given. Ninety-one per cent of all the boys whom the Rorschach test showed to have in their make-up a *marked degree of defiance* were delinquents, while of those in whom this trait was absent only 35 per cent were delinquents;[17] 83 per cent of those who were shown by psychiatric examination to be *markedly stubborn* were delinquents, compared to only 39 per cent in whom this trait was absent; 72 per cent of the boys whose paternal discipline of them was *overstrict or erratic* were delinquents, compared to only 9 per cent of those who were guided by *firm but kindly discipline*; 97 per cent of the boys who came from *unintegrated families* were delinquents as compared to only 21 per cent of those who came from *cohesive families.* These are only a few illustrations. Wide distinctions in the incidence of traits and factors were also found in respect to a great many other influences in the make-up and background of the boys in this research.

Can the differential association theory make such meaningful discriminations between delinquents and non-delinquents? Can it be used as a predictive factor?

And just how does the differential association theory account for, integrate and reconcile such established biological differences between delinquents and non-delinquents in the Glueck researches as the statistically significant predominance of mesomorphs among the delinquents? Or such temperamental-characterical variations between delinquents and non-delinquents as the predominance in the former of aggressiveness, defiance, emotional lability, impulsivity, to name but a few; or the vital differences in the emotional parent-child relationships of the first few years, such as the lack of parental affection, hostile or erratic disciplinary practices, lack of supervision,

---

[17] The tests were given by a group of psychologists in Boston and interpreted by two Rorschach experts in New York, without the latter knowing which test protocols came from delinquents and which from non-delinquents.

family disunity, and other faulty parent-child relationships which were found to be much more numerous in the families of our delinquents than in those of the control group?

The only integration and reconciliation that the theory under discussion can make of these diverse influences which highly differentiate delinquents and criminals from control groups and some of which vary in their relative weights in different circumstances, times, and places is to ascribe everything to differential association and an excess of crime-inducing definitions over law-abiding ones. Just what does such a formula add to understanding? Does it say more than that, if conditions and desires are favorable to crime, persons will resort to crime?

In the Preface to his book, Cressey says: 'The differential association theory and alternative theories of crime causation are evaluated in the light of their comparative capacity to "make sense" of the facts' (p. v). Applying this test, is it not more in accordance with facts, clinical experience, and common sense to attribute delinquency to a patterned concatenation of various combinations of the above-listed traits and factors which markedly distinguish delinquents from non-delinquents than to advance as an overall explanation the view that among the boys included in the research in question only those who just happened to have learned the ways of crime from association with other delinquents, or who somehow or other acquired or were subjected to an excess of antisocial 'definitions of the situation', became offenders while the others did not?

The multiple factor method of assigning causal power to a combination of traits and factors which in fact demonstrably distinguishes the vast majority of delinquents from non-delinquents is criticized by the proponents of the differential association theory as not involving a 'theoretical framework'. But, as successful validations of the statistical prediction tables based on combinations of relevant factors demonstrate, this approach is unquestionably more realistic and revealing of etiologic involvements than is the cloudy adumbration of a 'theory' the proponents of which are so eager to establish the pre-eminence of nurture in the causal complex as to leave out of account fundamental variations in nature.[18] In attacking the multiple factor theory, it is claimed that researchers who have followed that method presume that each factor is 'independent of all other factors'.[19] In the Gluecks' researches in delinquency, this is not true. Not only their synthesis of the most discriminative factors

---

[18] One notable exception is Donald Taft. See his intelligent appraisal of Sutherland's theory, D. R. Taft (1942), *Criminology* (New York: Macmillan), pp. 284–86.
[19] Sutherland–Cressey, op. cit., p. 62.

into prediction tables but the following summary of *Unraveling* proves that the authors in question fully recognize the *interdependence* of the factors involved:

'It will be observed that in drawing together the more significant threads of each area explored, we have not resorted to a theoretical explanation from the standpoint, exclusively, of any one discipline. It has seemed to us, at least at the present stage of our reflections upon the materials, that it is premature and misleading to give exclusive or even primary significance to any one of the avenues of interpretation. On the contrary, the evidence seems to point to the participation of forces from several areas and levels in channeling the persistent tendency to socially unacceptable behaviour . . .

'We are impelled to such a multidimensional interpretation because, without it, serious gaps appear. If we resort to an explanation exclusively in terms of somatic constitution, we leave unexplained why most persons of mesomorphic tendency do *not* commit crimes; and we further leave unexplained how bodily structure affects behavior. If we limit ourselves to a sociocultural explanation, we cannot ignore the fact that sociocultural forces are selective; even in underprivileged areas most boys do *not* become delinquent and many boys from such areas do not develop into persistent offenders. And, finally, if we limit our explanation to psychoanalytic theory, we fail to account for the fact that the great majority of non-delinquents, as well as of delinquents, show traits usually deemed unfavorable to sound character development, such as vague feelings of insecurity and feelings of not being wanted; the fact that many boys who live under conditions unfavorable to the development of a wholesome superego do not become delinquents, but do become neurotics.

'If, however, we take into account the dynamic interplay of these various levels and channels of influence, a tentative causal formula or law emerges, which tends to accommodate these puzzling divergencies so far as the great mass of delinquents is concerned:

'The delinquents as a group are distinguishable from the non-delinquents: (1) physically, in being essentially mesomorphic in constitution (solid, closely knit, muscular); (2) temperamentally, in being restlessly energetic, impulsive, extroverted, aggressive, destructive (often sadistic)—traits which may be related more or less to the erratic growth pattern and its physiologic correlates or consequences; (3) in attitude, by being hostile, defiant, resentful, suspicious, stubborn, socially assertive, adventurous, unconventional, non-submissive to authority; (4) psychologically, in tending to direct and concrete, rather than symbolic, intellectual expression, and in being less methodical in their approach to problems; (5) socioculturally, in having been reared to a far greater extent than the control group in homes of little understanding, affection, stability, or moral fibre by parents usually unfit to be effective guides and protectors or, according to psychoanalytic theory, desirable sources of emulation and the construction of a consistent, well-balanced, and socially normal superego during the early stages of character development . . .

'In the exciting, stimulating, but little-controlled and culturally inconsistent environment of the underprivileged area, such boys readily give expression to their untamed impulses and their self-centered desires by means of various forms of delinquent behavior. Their tendencies toward uninhibited energy-expression are deeply anchored in soma and psyche and in the malformations of character during the first few years of life.

'This "law" may have to be modified after more intensive, microscopic study of the atypical cases. . . . "A scientific law must always be considered as a temporary statement of relationships. As knowledge increases this law may require modification. Even the natural sciences state all generalizations in terms of probability" ' (pp. 281–82).

Thus the enigmatic question of whether one factor or another 'causes' delinquency is shown to be an unsound one; for, given certain surrounding conditions, internal or external, various combinations of biologic or social factors referred to by criminologists in the past can precipitate antisocial behavior. A *variety* of causal syndromes can bring about the very same criminalistic behavior. In one case certain biological ones predominate, in another certain sociocultural ones, in the sense that they apparently contribute the most *weight* in the combination of internal and external forces that culminates in antisocial expression.

Hence, there should be substituted for the notion of specificity or unity of causation (or of cause thinly disguised as 'theory') the concept of internal and external pressures and inhibitions. If the total weight of pressures to antisocial behavior exceeds the total strength of inhibitory forces, the person commits crime. Theoretically, say, twenty factors of minor pressure (weight) are just as likely to conduce to criminal behavior as four or five factors of heavy pressure. By substituting this concept of varied forces or energy reaching a point of antisocial discharge, for the insistence upon a certain specific theory or factor, or even syndrome, as inevitably and always conducing to delinquency, we arrive at a conception of *interchangeability* of etiologic traits and factors and thus at a realistic and relatively accurate doctrine of causation. At any time, the person is poised between a natural tendency to egoistic antisocial behavior and a habit-disciplined tendency to conform to the socio-legal taboos. Biosocial pressures of one sort or another tend to turn the scales in one direction or another. (Of course, the relationship between energy pressure and inhibitory tendency is not usually simple or direct; there are, as a rule, complex intermediary processes.) Consequently, it is not mesomorphic constitution, or strong instinctual impulse, or an hereditary aggressive tendency, or weak inhibitory mechanism, or low intelligence, or excessive emotional lability, or marked suggestibility, or an unresolved Oedipus situation, or residence in a poverty-stricken 'delinquency area' or in a region with a tradition of delinquency, or 'differential association' with those already criminal, or an excess of antisocial 'definitions of the situation' or any other biological, social, or cultural factor that *inevitably* conduces to delinquent behavior. Any of these factors alone or in various combinations may or may not bring about delinquency, depending on the balance of energy tendencies at a particular time, in the particular individual involved. In times of great crisis, emergency, poverty, unemployment, and the like, many persons will commit crimes who, under normal conditions, would not.

However, as was shown in *Unraveling*, certain factors in combination are found to occur so frequently in the constitution and developmental history of delinquents and so seldom among non-delinquents, that we may legitimately conclude that the *weight* they contribute to the causal scales is very excessive, and usually so, in comparison to that of other influences. This is a realistic conception of causation; for, by isolating the biosocial syndromes most *usually* operative in the lives of delinquents and most usually absent in the lives of non-delinquents, it not only adds to understanding of cause and effect but it highlights the traits, factors, and areas *most relevant* to prediction, to therapeutic effort in the individual case, and to prophylactic effort in general.

It may be that some day variations in the way people conduct themselves will be explainable in the more ultimate terms of differences in endocrine gland structure and function, or of microscopic physico-chemical reactions. However, we can in the meantime reasonably speak of cause-and-effect when we disentangle even the cruder forces at play in inclining persons to one course of behavior or another, just as chemistry and physics opened the doors to the solution of many problems of nature even before the dawn of nuclear science. The question is, whether such an explanation in the field of our concern brings us closer to an understanding of delinquency and therefore to its control. If it does, then, even though we are dealing with forces which may some day be reduced to more subtle constituents, we have made a stride forward in the understanding and possible management of delinquent behavior.

III

So much for the contrast between the differential association–definition of the situation theory and our eclectic approach to causation.

What now of the recommendations for the prevention of delinquency that flow from the 'differential association–definition of the situation' theory? They consist essentially of a call for 'local community organization' to cope with the problem! We are told, preliminarily, that 'the policy implied in the earlier chapters . . . is that control of delinquency lies principally in the personal groups within the local community.'[20] We are told that 'it was *shown* [sic] that delinquency is explained principally by an excess of delinquent associations over anti-delinquent associations'[21]. (Where is the proof that this has been shown?) We are told that 'moreover it was *shown* [sic] that the factor in these local and personal groups which had the greatest significance was the definition of behavior as desirable or undesirable.'[22] (Where is the proof of this showing?) We are then solemnly assured that 'the closest approximation to a formula for the control of delinquency that can be made at present is that delinquency must be defined as undesirable by the personal groups in which a person participates.'[23] Surely a minuscule mouse, brought forth after all the mountainous labors of 'differential association' and 'definitions of the situation'!

How are these 'definitions' of delinquency as 'undesirable' to be brought about? Will not this process require a probing into original endowment and parent-child relationships in early childhood, and the moral re-education of adults? Just how helpful in all this are the formulæ of 'differential association' and 'definitions of the situation'? Do they say anything except the obvious fact that people must somehow be made to desire to be good?

The sum and substance of advice regarding crime prevention is stated by Cressey in these words:

'Policies for prevention of delinquency and crime, therefore,

[20] Sutherland–Cressey, op. cit., p. 609.
[21], [22], [23] ibid. My italics.

should be directed primarily at these personal groups [the family, school and neighborhood groups, work or recreational groups, religious groups, or others]. In this sense, control of delinquency and crime lies within the local community. This means, first, that the local community must be the active agency in reducing its own delinquency. The personal groups can be modified through the efforts of local organizations such as the school, the church, the police, welfare agencies, and civic groups; they also can be modified through the efforts of laymen' (pp. 609–10).

There is nothing in these well-worn generalizations about crime prevention that is attributable, as a novel discovery, to the theory of differential association-definitions of the situation. By contrast, reliable researches, with their solidly verified factual foundations, indicate much more pointedly and specifically the how and why of participation of community institutions in delinquency prevention programmes[24] and in addition indicate the role of various forms of psychotherapy and group therapy in a preventive program, as well as other approaches *relevant to the facts* revealed in the intensive study of several samples of delinquents and criminals and non-delinquents.

All the agencies and methods of crime prevention discussed in the work by Sutherland-Cressey have been suggested by other writers, without benefit of the illumination of the theory of differential association and definitions of the situation. The theory has not enhanced, in the slightest, understanding of the methods of delinquency prevention. It has the demerit, in comparison with views derived from the researches which meticulously compare the incidence of biopsychological traits and sociocultural factors in the make-up and background of delinquents and non-delinquent matched controls, of *not* integrating and *not* reconciling the variety of delinquency-etiologic elements and at the same time of being so abstract and cloudy as not to be useful either in explaining or in controlling delinquent behavior.

There can be no doubt that science advances most rapidly through the discovery of theories or systems which account for a variety of facts already known and lead in turn to the discovery of new ones. But how does the theory under consideration compare in these crucial respects with Einstein's theory of relativity, or with the Copernican system, or the Newtonian generalization, or the Darwinian insight into the processes of natural selection? One has only to put the question to see how absurdly deficient is the elaborately

[24] See, for example, *Delinquents in the making*[153], Ch. XVI; *Unraveling*[138], pp. 285–89; *Preventing crime*[66], *One thousand juvenile delinquents*[46], pp. 272–84; *500 criminal careers*[26], pp. 335–39, and others.

adumbrated theory of differential association and its accompanying definitions of the situation.

There are evidently criminologists who find such a 'theory' helpful in their thinking. To me it is a superficial and superfluous generalization. The multiple factor approach is much more illuminating and much more in accord with the variety of original natures involved in crime, the variety in kind and intensity of human and physical environmental influences involved in crime, the variety in the behavior patterns of the acts and mental states and mechanisms embraced in the single legal concept of 'crime'. For this not only recognizes the evident fact of a wide variation in influences, weights, and combinations of traits and factors in crime causation; it recognizes, too, that while there is a 'core type' of offender, there is also a variety of subtypes or fringe types. It recognizes that just as the fact of death, although always the same terminal event, may nonetheless be the result of various preceding sequences of conditions, so the terminal event of persistent delinquency may have in its etiologic background a variety of different sequences leading to the same ultimate result. It recognizes that all behavior is conditioned by both biological and sociocultural influences.

The foregoing analysis leads to the conclusion that a *wise eclecticism*, guiding research in which investigations, examinations, and tests are thorough, and sociocultural data are carefully verified and collated, is still the only promising and sensible credo for the modern criminologist. At all events, neither 'differential association' nor an inadequate conception of human psychology and motivation reflected in the mechanical totting up of the number of 'definitions of the situation favorable to delinquency' as opposed to the number unfavorable to delinquency can satisfy the researcher who has observed again and again that it is the dynamic interplay of certain discernible, and more or less measurable, elements of nature and nurture that best accounts for the phenomena of delinquency and crime. Penetrating theories, which summarize and integrate existing reliable findings and which lead in turn to further discoveries, are highly desirable. But premature theorizings can only act as blinders, excluding or grossly underemphasizing facts that do not fit into preconceptions and ending up with a thin abstraction that neither integrates nor explains.[25]

[25] Compare Albert Morris's critique of the theory that the crime rate is a function of the differential between frustration and expectancy of punishment: 'This, and other all-encompassing theories, seem to me of modest value and analogous to trying to develop a theory of ill-health in terms of a high incidence of germs and a low expectancy of sanitary engineering.' A. Morris (1955), *Homicide: An approach to the problem of crime*, University Lecture, 14 April 1955 (Boston: Boston Univ. Press), p. 4.

260

POSTSCRIPT

After the above piece was written, Glaser's recent paper, 'Criminality Theories and Behavioral Images',[26] appeared. This attempts to save the differential association theory through assuming that 'association' includes 'identification'. It sets forth a 'differential identification' theory as a 'reconceptualization' of Sutherland's theory. Although more sophisticated, this theory has all the weaknesses of the differential association theory. Like differential association, it is a roof without a house, with little furniture and that little barren. It does not account for the early delinquency of children nor for the criminalism of those adults who steal, commit assaults, rapes or murders on the spur of the moment or 'in the heat of passion'. It does not explain the participation of the numerous biological and sociocultural influences involved in delinquency and criminalism nor account for the variety of causal syndromes which multidisciplinary research shows to be involved in the various types of antisocial behavior.

The theory of 'differential identification' can be of little practical help in predicting delinquency or recidivism because, standing alone, it does not adequately differentiate between offenders and non-offenders; because there is no proof that most criminals begin their careers by deliberate identification with criminal patterns; and because, in the case of a criminal career, by the time such a person has completely identified with the criminal culture he is already a criminal. Thus the theory is at best tautological.

The theory is inadequate for treatment and preventive purposes, since where identification does play a role it is not so much the fact of identification as the reasons and conditions of identification that are relevant.

[26] D. Glaser (1956), Criminality theories and behavioral images. *Amer. J. Sociol.* **61**, 433.

CHAPTER 17

Ten Years of 'Unraveling Juvenile Delinquency': an Examination of Criticisms*

SHELDON GLUECK

TEN years have elapsed since the publication of *Unraveling Juvenile Delinquency*[138]. The work on that book spread over eight years, and to accomplish the project we had to call upon the aid of a staff of social investigators, a psychiatrist-physician, two physical anthropologists, six psychologists, two Rorschach test analysts, a statistical consultant, two statisticians, and several secretaries.

The book attracted a great deal of attention both here and abroad. Shortly after publication of *Unraveling*, the Supreme Court of Japan ordered its translation into Japanese; therafter, a distinguished board of representatives of the several disciplines involved completed the translation, 3,000 copies of which were distributed to judges, prosecutors, probation officers, and others in Japan. Parts of the book have also been translated into Hebrew, and a Spanish translation is almost completed. The more popular work, founded on *Unraveling, Delinquents in the Making*[153], has been rendered into French, German, Italian, and Urdu.

The book has greatly influenced research here and abroad and is well known to students of criminology, psychiatrists, anthropologists, juvenile court judges, and others.

We are grateful to all who wrote reviews and articles about *Unraveling*. It should be realized that it was a pioneering effort. We, as well as our critics, can profit from its shortcomings—a happy consequence in the tradition of the history of science.

Unraveling has been honored by three symposia of reviews: one in the Harvard Law Review,[1] a second in the Journal of Criminal Law, Criminology, and Police Science,[2] a third in Federal Probation.[3] It has been very widely reviewed in other journals both here and

---

* Prepared at the special request of the Board of Editors of the *Journal of Criminal Law, Criminology, and Police Science* in commemoration of the Journal's fifty years of publication.

[1] A symposium on *Unraveling juvenile delinquency* (1951), *Harv. L. Rev.* **64**, 1022.

[2] *Unraveling juvenile delinquency*—a symposium of reviews (1951), *J. crim. L., Criminol. & Police Sci.* **41**, 732.

[3] *Unraveling juvenile delinquency*—a symposium of reviews (1951), *Fed. Prob.* **15**, 52.

abroad. It was the subject of two extremely critical articles in the American Journal of Sociology.[4] On the other hand, most of the reviews have been favorable.

The most confident and severest critics have been a group whose writings have the tone of fire-breathing chevaliers eager to do battle for that purest queen of the exact sciences, Sociology, to which the authors of *Unraveling* allegedly did not pay adequate tribute.[5]

We have waited for most of the reviews to appear before attempting a reply to the principal points raised. These may be summarized under the heads of (I) The Sample, (II) The Techniques of Investigation, (III) Causative Analysis, (IV) The Role of Culture, and (V) The Prediction Method.

I. THE SAMPLE

A. Areas from which the sample of delinquents and that of non-delinquents were drawn. The simplest way to attack any piece of research involving a complex biosocial problem is of course to deny at once the 'typicality of the sample'. Now it is elementary that *any* sample, especially one involving a social problem, is in some respects atypical of various factors and forces that might be relevant to the issues sought to be illuminated by the inquiry. Unless one included all the juvenile delinquents and non-delinquents in the world and their detailed make-up and background (not to stress the history of the universe), he would, by such facile criticism, be wasting his time. It is particularly difficult to obtain absolute similarity in respect to the myriads of factors and forces in any area from which delinquents and non-delinquents may be drawn.

Some critics fail to fulfill the burden of proving in exactly what respects the samples compared in *Unraveling* are atypical. It would

---

[4] Rubin (1951), *Unraveling juvenile delinquency*, I: Illusions in a research project using matched pairs. *Amer. J. Sociol.* **57**, 107. Reiss (1951), *Unraveling juvenile delinquency*, II: An appraisal of the research methods. *Amer. J. Sociol.* **57**, 115.

[5] '. . . there are occasions on which sociologists can unite—and this exemplifies the sociological principle that attacks from an external enemy tend to unite an in-group that is at conflict within itself.' Hartung (1958), *A critique of the sociological approach to crime and correction. Law & Contemp. Prob.* **23**, 704. (They will no doubt unite to attack the present article.) 'Edwin H. Sutherland may be said to have entered the lists against *Unraveling Juvenile Delinquency* in advance.' 'One of the great values of (Terence) Morris's book is his lengthy historical chapter on research during the nineteenth century, which helps to establish the legitimate claim of sociology to the field of criminology.' Hartung, id., 707, 726. In addition, Hartung several times quotes approvingly expressions of great regret by Sutherland at the way nonsociologic criminologists have been able to get research funds from foundations, even quoting the word 'seduced'. For the record, let it be said that the Gluecks have always had to work hard to obtain subsidization of their researches and they have never used seduction, deception or highway robbery to obtain this hard-won financial aid.

seem that they should wait until at least one study similar to ours—employing the same definitions and verifying the raw data with equal care—was done; then there would be much more substantial basis for judgment of typicality of the samples than the mere *ipse dixit* of the critics.

In the meantime, let us examine the more specific criticisms advanced with reference to the samples compared in *Unraveling*:

It has been urged that the *areas* from which the delinquents were selected were not absolutely similar to the areas from which the non-delinquents were chosen. In taking both delinquents and the non-delinquents from economically and culturally deprived regions, our aim was to 'control' major underprivileged area influences and thus set the stage for more detailed comparison of the two groups in respect to a great many more specific traits and factors—anthropologic, medical (health), psychiatric (temperament), personality-character structure (Rorschach test), and various social-psychologic factors of what we call the *under-the-roof culture* of the home and school, as well as certain influences and conditions in the boys' neighborhoods.

Professor E. N. Burgess supports his claim that the regions from which the delinquent and non-delinquent boys came were not similar by emphasizing *Table VIII–1—Type of Neighborhood in Which Boy Lives* (*Unraveling*, p. 79).[6] In that table we present a breakdown of the neighborhoods in terms, largely, of *Blighted slum tenement area* (*deteriorating socially and economically*) and *Interstitial area* (*merging of business and residential*). The table shows that 55 per cent of the delinquents' families lived in the first-mentioned type of neighborhood, while 34 per cent of the non-delinquents' did; and 31 per cent of the former lived in the second type of neighborhood, while 49 per cent of the latter did.

However, this is but one type of subclassification of the neighborhoods. Professor Burgess unfortunately fails to call attention to the other, more significant, comparisons in the book, those of a nature much more relevant to the central aim of the control of the general culture for our expressed purpose of comparing delinquents and non-delinquents in respect to more specific characters. For example, he fails to mention *Table IV–2* (p. 36) in which the *delinquency rates* of the two sets of areas compared are demonstrated to be remarkably similar. Nor does he allude to *Table IV–3* (p. 36), presenting the results of a very careful field appraisal by trained researchers, who knew the regions thoroughly, in terms of defined 'good', 'fair', and 'poor' neighborhoods (from the points of view of the presence or

[6] Burgess (1951), Symposium on the Gluecks' latest research. *Fed. Prob.* **15**, 52.

absence of vice, crime, gangs, etc., on the one hand, and the presence or absence of reasonably convenient facilities for wholesome recreation, on the other). This expert assessment, like the similarity of the delinquency rates, demonstrates that the crucial neighborhood influences existing around the homes of our delinquents were very similar to those of the non-delinquents.

Moreover, while for certain theoretical sociologic purposes it may be helpful to classify regions into 'blighted slum areas' or 'interstitial areas', etc., the sociological area-criminologist himself does not make this the significant distinction when he gets down to the study of delinquency in the field. He first defines his areas in terms of the *rates of delinquency* (as we did), then he compares the incidence of certain *economic and social factors* existing in areas or zones of different delinquency rates (as we did). He analyzes the situation in low income areas as opposed to high income areas[7] and relates the other factors to that distinction rather than to whether he is dealing with a blighted or interstitial area. The well-known works of sociologist Clifford Shaw and his associates, for example, do not differentiate between areas on the latter basis for the purpose of ultimate analysis of delinquency causation. Their familiar spot-maps and circular zonal maps cut across regions part of which may be termed either 'blighted slum areas' or 'interstitial areas', or both. Shaw and McKay emphasize economic status as one of the most generative and pervasive of the conditions under which 'the conventional forces in the community become so weakened as to tolerate the development of a conflicting system of criminal values'. They say:

'It may be observed, in the first instance, that the variations in rates of officially recorded delinquents in communities of the city correspond very closely with variations in economic status. The communities with the highest rates of delinquents are occupied by those segments of the population whose position is most disadvantageous in relation to the distribution of economic, social, and cultural values. Of all the communities in the city, these have the fewest facilities for acquiring the economic goods indicative of status and success in our conventional culture' (p. 437).

Applying such a relevant yardstick, then, as economico-cultural status, our non-delinquents have unquestionably been chosen from areas relatively similar to those of our delinquents, so like in fact that not a few delinquents lived within the same city block or two as the non-delinquents and sometimes even in the very same tenement house.

[7] C. R. Shaw & H. D. McKay (1942), *Juvenile delinquency and urban areas* (Chicago: Univ. of Chicago Press), 435 *et seq.*

It happens that Shaw and McKay had plotted *delinquency rates* in Boston shortly before we began our research for *Unraveling*, and their geographic distribution of various delinquency rates is very similar to our own. One of their conclusions was: 'Considering the area [of Boston] as a whole, heavy concentrations are noted in old Boston, especially in the areas north and northeast of the Common, known locally as the West End and the North End; and in Charlestown, East Boston, and South Boston. Only slightly less concentrated are the clusters in Roxbury' (p. 222). Both our non-delinquent group and our delinquent group came very largely from these same regions and, in very similar proportions, from the same census tracts. (See *Unraveling*, *Table IV–2*, p. 36.)

As we pointed out in *Unraveling*,

'Since it was our purpose to draw the boys only from neighborhoods in which the environmental conditions were deleterious to the wholesome development of youth, the fact that fewer delinquents than non-delinquents . . . were found to be living in so-called interstitial areas (merging of business or industrial and residential elements) and a larger proportion in blighted tenement areas has no significance. What is of importance for our purposes is the extent to which the general neighborhood environments were alike in both groups' (p. 35).

It is amusing to find certain sociologic criminologists insisting upon the ultra-precision of the physical and chemical laboratory in this type of comparison.[8] We should be grateful to have our attention

[8] Taft says: 'Second, the delinquents and non-delinquents were paired in the neighborhood by physical proximity only. Because of this neglect of social influences in the neighborhood, it is not possible to accept the Gluecks' claim that the two groups in the study were actually paired by identical social influences of the neighborhood.' Taft (1951), Implications of the Glueck methodology for criminological research. *J. crim. L., Criminol. & Police Sci.* **42**, 300. It is perfectly obvious that absolute identity of the myriads of influences involved in neighborhoods is impossible, nor did the Gluecks claim that. Reiss's view that 'the study largely ignored the influence of primary groups in guiding behavior and in enforcing conformity to sets of norms', the familiar sociological formula in familiar sociological jargon, is a convenient attempt to explain away some of the disturbing findings of *Unraveling*; but nobody has defined these supposed narrow-area and extremely subtle differences in the locales from which our two groups of boys were taken; nor has any critic shown exactly how these minute differences could have been determined and how they would affect the outcome. Besides, the argument is quite irrelevant because we found that the great majority of our boys (90 per cent) were already delinquent at under eleven years of age, long before the alleged influence of 'primary groups' in supposedly 'enforcing conformity to sets of norms' of a delinquent type could make itself felt. A similar comment can be made with respect to the more penetrating suggestion put forth by Gault to the effect that areas may differ in terms of the leaders of a community. Gault (1951), *Unraveling juvenile delinquency*—a symposium of reviews. *J. crim. L., Criminol. & Police Sci.* **41**, 734. The method used in selecting the neighborhoods is discussed in *Unraveling*, p. 30.

directed to even one study by them which achieves such absolute and detailed identity in a matching of two culture-areas. Certainly the 'proof' of the favorite sociologic theory of 'differential association' is notoriously imprecise.[9] One cannot help being reminded in this connection of poor little Brother Juniper's burning belief (in Thornton Wilder's delightful novel, *The Bridge of San Luis Rey*): 'It seemed to Brother Juniper that it was high time for theology to take its place among the exact sciences, and he had long intended putting it there.'

In this connection I should like also to advert to a criticism by a reviewer who confuses our aim to control the *general* neighborhood-cultural complex of influences for statistical purposes with the finding of differences in various detailed sociologic factors which could only have been, and which were, in fact, brought out by our factoral comparisons of the delinquents with the non-delinquents. This critic seems to imply that we were engaged in some deep-dyed plot to banish sociologic influences.[10] This is sheer nonsense. Just as we did our utmost to match each delinquent with a non-delinquent for age, I.Q., and ethnic derivation, so did we control the general cultural area situation in respect to delinquents and non-delinquents as a basis for the subsequent detailed comparison of the incidence of the psychologic and socio-cultural traits and factors in the home, school, and neighborhood.[11] As to many of these characteristics, statistical comparison proved the status of the delinquents to be significantly

[9] See Ch. 16 of this volume.

[10] 'In place of a study which sought steadfastly to eliminate environmental factors as well as to eliminate them from a causal law, *the force of social* (*or environmental*) *causation of delinquency proves irrepressible.*' Rubin, op. cit. *supra* note 4. Hartung repeats this misconception. 'First, although the Gluecks sought steadfastly to eliminate environmental influences, the great influence of social causation proved to be irrepressible in their data.' Hartung, op. cit. *supra* note 5. The Gluecks neither 'sought steadfastly to eliminate environmental factors' from the research nor to 'eliminate them from a causal law'; nor does 'the force of social (or environmental) causation of delinquency prove irrepressible' from analysis of our materials, which establish a *multicausal* influence neither exclusively social nor exclusively biologic.

[11] '*Socio-cultural level.* A primary approach to the analysis of crime causation is the exploration of the forces and circumstances of the family background and the physical and social environment of the home; for character and conduct may be said to consist of the result of the interplay between innate constitution and environmental forces. The selection of the delinquents and the non-delinquents from similar neighborhoods of underprivilege carried with it, of course, no necessary assumption that poverty and its correlates or the cultural forces of urban delinquency areas play no role in the causation of delinquency. However, just as the matching of delinquents with non-delinquents on the basis of general intelligence permits us to examine the constituents and patternings of intelligence, so matching by residence in underprivileged neighborhoods makes it possible to control the general factor of area culture and to determine whether subtler differences exist in respect to the more intimate socio-cultural factors of home and school and the attitudes and practices of parents, teachers, and companions as bearers of the home and school culture.' *Unraveling*, p. 16.

different from that of the non-delinquents. The differences were very clearly brought out, taking full account of the possible influence of chance, and they established factually the point we made in the introductory chapter of *Unraveling* (p. 5) with respect to the difference between the typical sociologic 'area' or 'subculture' study of delinquency and our own eclectic approach—a point which forms a major aspect of our conception of etiology:

> 'The area-studies establish that a region of economic and cultural disorganization tends to have a criminogenic effect on people residing therein; but the studies fail to emphasize that this influence affects only a selected group comprising a relatively small proportion of all the residents, They do not reveal why the deleterious influences of even the most extreme delinquency area fail to turn the great majority of its boys into persistent delinquents. They do not disclose whether the children who do not succumb to the evil and disruptive neighborhood influence differ from those who become delinquents and, if so, in what respects. Until they take this factor into account, they cannot penetratingly describe even the culture of the delinquency area. For to say that certain bacteria have a fatal effect on some individuals but no such effect on the majority, without describing or explaining the differential influences, is to describe that infective agent inadequately.'

How do some sociologic critics answer this? By the following *reductio ad absurdum*: 'First, it is generally recognized that there is a gap of unknown size between "actual" and "known" delinquency. Some students think that *few if any adolescent boys in high-rate areas escape delinquency*.'[12] It will be seen below that, where convenient, these critics assume that only 10 per cent or less of slum area boys are delinquent (that is, those supposedly subjected to 'differential association' with delinquent persons or patterns); but when necessary to mount what they conceive to be a really devastating attack on the kind of basic argument presented in the quotation above, they conclude that *all* boys in high delinquency areas are delinquent!

B. The sample of the delinquents (*and of the non-delinquents*) *is atypical, because: It did not include all ethnic groups.* Our samples dealt largely with matched representatives of such ethnico-racial derivation as Italian, Irish, English, and Slavic. (See *Table IV–6*, p. 38, and Appendix

---

[12] Hartung, op. cit. The specific reference is to Hartung's reply to criticisms of A. Cohen's theory of a delinquency subculture and hypothesis that 'middle-class' male delinquency is 'a consequence of the middle-class adolescent boy's anxiety concerning his masculine role'. But the quotation in the text would apply equally (and I have several times heard the argument seriously advanced) to the specific point made in the text.

B of *Unraveling*.) The results have been criticized in some quarters because the samples did not include representatives of other ethnc groups and because the number of Jews was small. The reason for our sample not including more Jewish boys is the very simple one that it was exceedingly difficult to find enough Jewish delinquent boys in the areas in question. As for the other complaint, our samples do not include Chinese, West Indians, Hottentots, Eskimos, etc., although there may well be a few boys descended from these ethnic groups in Boston. If the objection be made that then we had no right to 'generalize' about a 'tentative causal law' of delinquency, we invite the reader's attention to Chapter II (especially p. 15) and Chapter XXI (especially p. 272) of *Unraveling*, where we fully recognize the limitations of our conclusions arising out of the necessity of controlling, at the outset, certain generalized sets of variables (including ethnic derivation). The extent to which our findings will ultimately prove to hold good for other samples of cases (ethnic, economic, etc.) can only await testing through further research. But, as will be shown below, our social prediction table based on certain sociocultural factors of family life has proved to have very high prognostic force when applied to samples of Jewish, Negro, French, Puerto Rican, and Japanese delinquents.

C. The sample of delinquents is atypical because: The boys selected were largely those who had been committed to an industrial school and who were, thereby, presumably 'institutionalized'. On pages 13–14 of *Unraveling* we give our definition of delinquency for the purposes of the research in question. We have spent a great many years in the investigation and study of delinquents and criminals, and on the basis of that experience we point out (p. 13) that children who, once or twice during the period of growing up in an exciting *milieu*, steal a toy in a ten-cent store, sneak into a subway or motion picture theatre, play hooky, and the like, but *soon outgrow* such peccadilloes, are not true delinquents even though technically they may have violated the law.[13] We state that 'in order to arrive at the clearest differentiation of disease and health, comparison must be made between the unquestionably pathologic and the normal.'

Certainly, if a laboratory technician is studying cancer, he must first make sure he is dealing with a malignant and not a benign growth. It is for that good reason that we decided to include in our

[13] 'Indeed, it is now recognized that a certain amount of petty pilfering occurs among many children around the age of six or seven and is to be expected as part of the process of trying their wings. Children appear to be no worse for very occasional and slight experimental deviations from socially acceptable norms of conduct. Since they voluntarily abandon such behavior, their misconduct or maladaptation cannot be deemed either habitual or symptomatic of deep-rooted causes.' *Unraveling*, p. 14.

sample only boys whose misbehavior could be said to be truly delinquent in that it was persistent, rather than either accidental or very occasional and followed by early abandonment of misconduct. And it is precisely for this reason that we have grounds to believe that our prediction tables, designed to 'spot' probable future delinquents at school entrance, will be able to differentiate *true* prospective delinquents showing difficulties of adjustment in the early years from pseudo-delinquents who display *similar external behavior* but whose future is in fact more promising.

One severe critic makes a great to-do about the 'institutionalization' of our delinquents as invalidating the findings with reference to delinquents in general, findings he nonetheless is quick to accept in another part of his critique as proof of his claim that, despite our supposed ruling out of sociocultural influences, 'the force of social (or environmental) causation proves irrepressible'. He produces no proof for his contention about 'institutionalization'.[14]

Here are the relevant facts:

Our boys spent, on the average, 7·12 months in correctional institutions, 61·8 per cent having been there less than six months (*Unraveling, Table A–10*, p. 296). By contrast, they had had an average of 10·84 months on probation, over half of them six or more months (*Unraveling, Table A–9*, p. 296). The institutions to which they were committed are open industrial schools with a regime of education, athletics, recreation, religious guidance, etc. No lockstep and bars are involved. Surely nobody with even an elementary first-hand knowledge of psychology or the conditioning of delinquent attitudes and behavior could seriously claim that the brief stay in such an institution would crucially overbalance all the other experiences of a young lifetime gained in the home, school, and community! We solemnly assure this critic that our delinquent lads did not have the 'prison pallor', did not talk out of the corner of the mouth, did not glance apprehensively over the shoulder.[15] Besides, the vast part of our data concerns the personal make-up and early conditioning

---

[14] Rubin, op. cit. 'Two outstanding facts emerge from *Unraveling Juvenile Delinquency*: . . . (2) Institutionalized children differ from children who have not been institutionalized.' A similar criticism, made in more temperate terms, is that of P. P. Lejins (1951) in the Symposium in *Fed. Prob.*, **15**, 58.

[15] Rubin pontificates: 'The most elementary caution in criminological research is the recognition that an examination of institutionalized offenders (or delinquents) will provide information about *institutionalized offenders* and *not* about offenders in general. An institutionalized offender is characteristically, in great part, an institution product.' Rubin, op. cit.; Symposium in *Fed. Prob.* **15**, 55. Rubin confuses an institutionalized delinquent with a delinquent who happens to have been sent for a brief time to a correctional school. Besides, 80 per cent of the boys were twelve years or older by the time of their first commitment to an institution, and their basic character structure was by then quite firmly fixed. *Unraveling*, Table A–5, p. 294.

factors operative *years before* these boys were 'institutionalized'.

To the extent that relevant factors exist for comparison, we have found little difference between the general run of delinquents who appear in a juvenile court and our sample. Strong inferential proof of this fact, by neutral investigators, is to be seen in a study significantly entitled *The Close of Another Chapter in Criminology*, by William Healy, Augusta E. Bronner, and Myra E. Shimberg.[16] Another sample of juvenile delinquents had been used by us in an investigation prior to *Unraveling*, and that research involved a follow-up of delinquents who had passed through both the Boston Juvenile Court and the Judge Baker Guidance Center (Clinic). The findings of recidivism reported in that investigation, *One Thousand Juvenile Delinquents*[45], had been questioned on the ground that, since the cases were those that had been sent by the judge to the clinic, they must have been the most *serious* ones and this must have accounted for the high failure rate we discovered in tracing these boys during a five-year follow-up period after court appearance. On the basis of a check group of a thousand *other* cases—*the general run of the mill* of the same court (*i.e.* those who 'passed through the . . . court, but were not referred . . . to the' clinic)—the authors of the above-named check study (two of them at that time directors of the clinic in question) concluded, after their own careful follow-up of these cases, that 'the results of the two studies [the Gluecks and theirs] are amply corroborative'.

It is further significant on the issue of sampling, a point worthy of repetition, that many prediction-validation studies (see below) on samples of boys of a variety of ethnic derivation, religion, culture, etc., are also 'amply corroborative' of major findings in *Unraveling*.

II. THE TECHNIQUES OF INVESTIGATION AND TESTING

A. Interviewing and investigating

Some critics claim that the facts we were able to obtain through interviewing the parents of non-delinquents are very probably not similar to those we could obtain through interviewing those of delinquents, on the ground that the latter are under compulsion to give information, the former not.[17] While this view is understandable,

---

[16] Healy, Bronner & Shimberg (1935), *The close of another chapter in criminology*. *Ment. Hyg.* **19**, 208.

[17] Taft (1951), Implications of the Glueck methodology for criminological research. *J. crim. L., Criminol. & Police Sci.* **42**, 305. See also Gault & Anderson (1951), *Unraveling juvenile delinquency*—a symposium of reviews. *J. crim. L., Criminol. & Police Sci.* **41**, 734, 746.

we believe these critics to be mistaken. Neither set of families was under compulsion to give *us* information. We are not officials, and our field investigators made their special research interest and non-official status very clear to the parents. There is a technique, carefully developed over many years of experience with this type of research, that enables us to obtain data both intensive and verified; the method is described in the first chapters of *Unraveling* and in an unpublished (mimeographed) account of the building up of a typical case history by our two chief investigators.[18] Long experience in investigating families, the scrupulous care with which parents and relatives were interviewed, and, especially, the intensive search for verifying data through *pre-existing records* (in private social agencies and public offices, and made by others for purposes entirely different from those of our research) render it most unlikely that the intensity and range of the investigations were significantly different in the case of non-delinquents from that of delinquents. It must further be borne in mind in this connection that the same syllabus of data to be gathered and verified, and the same statistical schedules, were used for non-delinquents as for delinquents.

B. Reliability of tests and measurements

1. The method of anthropometry and the Sheldonian technique of somatotyping are supposedly not reliable. Taft first admits he is no specialist in anthropology, then presumes to question the validity of the anthropometric and somatotyping work performed by the two highly experienced physical anthropologists who did the measuring and morphologic classification of types for *Unraveling*. Another critic[19], also not an anthropologist, attacks the anthropological work in reviewing *Physique and Delinquency*[176]. Why? Because the late Professor Edwin H. Sutherland, whom both critics admire greatly, 'with his wonted thoroughness, gave the Sheldon contribution to criminology a terrific going over'. However, Sutherland, also, was no anthropologist. Moreover, the 'going over' referred to a book by William Sheldon in the field of criminology, which had nothing whatsoever to do with our own work. We ourselves had criticized Sheldon's book, *Varieties of Delinquent Behavior*,[20] because, although

---

[18] McGrath & Cunningham, *The Case of Henry W., Illustrating Method of Social Investigation.* Copies of this mimeographed statement, too bulky to have been included as an appendix to *Unraveling*, as originally planned, have been distributed to principal libraries. Since the above was written, this case history was published in *Family Environment and Delinquency*[245], App. A, pp. 169–204.

[19] Hartung (1958), Review of *Physique and delinquency* in *J. crim. L., Criminol. & Police Sci.* **48**, 638.

[20] Sheldon (1950), *Varieties of delinquent behavior* (New York: Harper). Our review appears in *Survey* (1950), **86**, 215.

the somatotyping is excellent, the sociologic data and interpretations are, in our opinion, questionable. But this is irrelevant to the employment of (and the basic improvement upon) Sheldon's categorization of somatotypes (in turn an improvement over Kretschmer's) in our study. We are convinced that the anthropometry and analysis of the somatotype data in *Unraveling* are exceptionally meritorious. A distinguished authority in the field, who *is* a trained anthropologist, Professor C. Wesley Dupertuis, is lavish in his praise of this work.[21]

Hartung attacks the *statistical* basis of *Physique and Delinquency*, which employed the somatotype findings of *Unraveling* in intercorrelating morphologic types with numerous traits and factors. He is concerned with the fact, for example, that careful anthropometry, by experts, showed that 60·1 per cent of the delinquent group compared to 30·7 per cent of the non-delinquents are *mesomorphic* (with 'relative predominance of muscle, bone and connective tissue') and, at the other extreme, 14·4 per cent of the delinquents compared to 39·6 per cent of the controls were found to be *ectomorphic* (with relative predominance of linearity and fragility and, in proportion to their mass, with 'the greatest surface area and hence relatively the greatest sensory exposure to the outside world') (*Unraveling*, pp. 54, 193, 344). After correctly stating that we presented 109 tables 'in an effort to ascertain which traits and factors supposedly exert a significant differential influence on the delinquency of four body types', he incorrectly concludes that the statistical treatment is questionable. The argument is that 'There are at least forty-six tables in which the number of delinquents, or controls, or both is less than 100', and that 'None of the 109 tables deals with the entire sample of delinquents and non-delinquents' (op. cit. *supra* note 5).

This is a fallacious argument. Of course none of the 500 delinquents and 500 non-delinquents had *all* the traits and factors embraced in *Unraveling*[22]. To have made that possible it would have been necessary to match myriads of thousands of cases in respect to over 400 items included in the study. But apart from this, the purpose of the comparisons in both *Unraveling* and *Physique and Delinquency* was to determine the traits and factors in respect to which the incidence significantly differed between the delinquents and the controls, *in the cases where those traits and factors did exist*. If, as was true of many characters, the incidence was found to vary significantly among the two groups compared, this certainly did not indicate that, because a

[21] Dupertuis (1951), Physical anthropology. *Harv. L. Rev.* **64**, 1031.
[22] '. . . it is rare indeed in the social, as in the meteorological field, that we can find an attribute or small group of attributes invariably associated in the past with occurrence or non-occurrence of the phenomenon whose future behavior we wish to predict.' Wilson (1951), Prediction. *Harv. L. Rev.* **64**, 1040.

particular trait or factor was not present in *all* 500 cases of the delinquents and in *all* 500 of the control group, it should be eliminated.

When, for example, it is found that, in relation to all twelve sociocultural factors of the home contributing selectively to delinquency, mesomorphs had the lowest incidence in comparison with the three remaining body types but especially in contrast to ectomorphs, and this response is exactly what one would expect of the solid bone-muscle mesomorphic type as opposed to the fragile, sensitive ectomorphic type of person (*Physique and Delinquency*, p. 240), are we to be told that because the factors in question did not exist in all 500 delinquents and all 500 non-delinquents the result should be ignored or is due to pure chance?

In all this it should be borne in mind that where necessary we have consulted statistical authorities.[23]

And as to the anthropologic soundness of *Physique and Delinquency*, which is based on *Unraveling*, not only the anthropologist Dupertuis but also one of the world's leading biologists, Julian Huxley, made this judgment: 'This is an interesting and indeed important book . . . as demonstrating beyond any doubt the importance of specific and readily detectable genetic factors determining psycho-physical type, in predisposing boys to delinquency.'[24]

Under the circumstances, can we be blamed for preferring the judgment of those with expertise in the relevant fields to that of those sociologists who are neither recognized anthropologists nor statisticians?[25]

In fairness it should be pointed out that not all sociologists have gone off the deep end in an attack on somatotyping. For example, Professor Albert Morris, a sociologist and cultural anthropologist who is both well read and experienced in criminologic research, has

[23] It should be mentioned that, unlike the critics, our statistical consultants, Edwin Bidwell Wilson, Jane Worcester, Carl R. Doering, and Rose Kneznek, with whom it has been our practice to discuss statistical problems from time to time, *are* highly experienced in statistical theory and technique. See 'Explanation of the Statistical Method' by Carl R. Doering, Professor of Biostatistics, Harvard University, in *Unraveling*, and 'Explanation of Statistical Method' by Jane Worcester in *Physique and delinquency*.

[24] Huxley (1957), Review of *Physique and delinquency*. *Int. J. soc. Psychiat.* 3, 71. A recent study in England confirms the presence of excessive mesomorphy among delinquents in a Borstal institution. See Gibbens (1960), *New forms of juvenile delinquency*, 13, 50 (WHO mimeograph).

[25] Taft refers to the fact that when he sent the authors of *Unraveling* a draft of his proposed review, 'Professor Glueck properly chides me with failure to explain the basis of my questioning the validity of these methods and failure to name the critics'; yet Taft adds: 'I leave the brief comment unchanged, because as indicated I am no specialist in these matters.' Op. cit. *supra* note 17. It would seem that this fact is a pretty good reason why Taft (and Hartung and the other nonexperts in the fields involved) should *not* have dogmatized on the anthropologic and statistical aspects of *Unraveling*.

said, after setting forth a perceptive appraisal of the difficulties involved in the types of research we are doing:

'These difficulties, usual in research in the behavioral sciences, have been understood and intelligently met. The techniques for doing this have elsewhere been clearly discussed. The result, of course, falls short of perfection; but, perhaps, only those who love certainty more than truth will be misled by unawareness that the statistician has been given only the opportunity to develop precise summaries of good approximation. . . . They [the authors] wisely recognize that the soundness of their effort is best judged by the clinical "good sense" and the internal consistency evidenced in the integrated result.'[26]

2. The Rorschach test is supposedly invalid. Another criticism of a field in which the sociologic critic is no authority has to do with the Rorschach test. Taft announces that 'an eminent psychologist tells me that the Sheldon and Rorschach techniques have both been demonstrated to be invalid.'[27] The unreliability of the criticisms of the Sheldonian somatotypes has been discussed. As to the other, I should like to be informed by whom and just how the Rorschach test has been 'demonstrated to be invalid'; and invalid for what? Nobody claims that the Rorschach test (or for that matter, any 'projective' test or any intelligence test) is perfect. Yet nobody with even an elementary acquaintance with psychology and psychiatry would seriously assert that the Rorschach test has been 'demonstrated to be invalid'.

As a matter of fact, until *Unraveling* nobody had made a systematic study of a large sample of true delinquents as compared with a carefully matched control group of non-delinquents; nor had the Rorschach results been previously systematized into a rational clinical set of categories as they have been in *Unraveling* (Appendix E). It is to be emphasized that the boys in that research were subjected to the tests by different psychologists (in Boston) from those who interpreted the tests (in New York). Taft glides over, *en passant*, the fact that the New York experts on the Rorschach test (Dr Ernest Schachtel and the late Dr Anna Hartoch Schachtel) were not informed by us which of the 'protocols' sent them for interpretation were the test-responses of delinquents and which were those of non-delinquents. He then unwarrantedly proceeds:

'Delinquents were assumed and then discovered to have less

[26] Morris (1957), Review of *Physique and delinquency. Harv. L. Rev.* **62,** 753.
[27] The use of the Rorschach test was also questioned by Rubin and Monachesi, among others. See Symposium in *Fed. Prob.* **15,** 55.

fear of authority and dependence upon it than "non-delinquents". . . . Delinquents were assumed, and then discovered to be, more unstable and impulsive in their behavior. . . . Delinquents were assumed and then discovered to be more aggressive and destructive. The logical relationship of these characteristics to delinquency is so obvious that a cynic might add that delinquents might be assumed to be law-breakers and then proven to be such by elaborate Rorschach devices!'

This is patently prejudiced as well as absurd. In the first place, Rorschach responses cannot be successfully manipulated by a subject taking the test. In the second place, there are certain standards of interpretation of the Rorschach results. In the third place, the Rorschach experts who interpreted the protocols in New York were not the same psychologists who had given the tests in Boston; as pointed out, the interpreters did not know which protocols came from delinquents, which from non-delinquents. In the fourth place, this critic is silent about the Rorschach traits in respect to which it was found that delinquents do *not* differ from non-delinquents (*Unraveling*, pp. 223, 226, 228, 233, 238, 272). Finally, any expert in Rorschach psychology can testify that the traits and factors brought out in the Rorschach materials of *Unraveling* are there in the protocols completed by the testees; they certainly were not 'assumed and then discovered' by either the Rorschach experts or the authors of *Unraveling*.

One could turn the tables on this critic by saying that he assumes the predominance of general cultural influences, and then finds them to predominate; except that, contrary to his insistence that cultural forces are all important in delinquent etiology,[28] he now discovers that the various psychologic traits he cites bear an 'obvious' and 'logical relationship to delinquency'—something he evidently did not know until he read the findings of *Unraveling*.

But another critic, Reiss, seizes upon the Rorschach aspect of *Unraveling* to prove that, far from its being bad, it is the best part of the study! This generous judgment fits in neatly with his misconception of a statement by Dr Schachtel, one of the experts who in New York interpreted the Rorschach test protocols of the boys who had been tested in Boston. He says that Schachtel

'particularly emphasizes the importance of class culture and the *milieu* in which the delinquent lives as important factors in delinquency. Specifically, in making his judgments he states: "The

[28] Taft's textbook on criminology attempts 'to integrate a strong *cultural emphasis* with a *synthetic approach*'. (The italics are his.) Taft (1942), *Criminology, an attempt at a synthetic interpretation with a cultural emphasis* vii (New York: Macmillan).

judgments would have been different if the socio-economic back-ground had been different." For the judgments were made by "asking myself whether *his character structure, as I saw it on the basis of the Rorschach test*, was of a type likely to resist the induce-ments toward becoming delinquent offered by poor socioeconomic circumstances and by the neighborhood."' (Emphasis added.) (Op. cit. *supra* note 4.)

This critic's interpretation of the quotation is amusingly typical of the way a few sociologists, eager to place their discipline at the head of the procession in the interpretation of the etiology of delinquency (and indeed denying there is any procession), misinterpret the findings of others to suit their preconceptions.[29] This critic omits altogether the crucial statement regarding *character structure* and speaks exclusively about the general culture. The significant thing in the above quotation is not culture but the *variations in character* which bring about a *differential response* to a similar *milieu*. (The role of culture is discussed below.)

Another criticism of the sample from the point of view of the Rorschach test has recently emerged: It is insisted that to list indi-vidual traits is all wrong; that the Rorschach is a 'holistic technique, the entire pattern of responses is what is significant, not one response factor alone', and that the Schachtels evidently did not know their business in checking on individual traits.[30] To show that contradic-tory criticisms do not prevent the critics from being mutually wrong, it should be pointed out that not only did the Schachtels list traits but before doing so they interpreted the Rorschach protocols in terms of whole character structure (the 'psychogram'), taking into account the 'test situation'. This is what enabled them to make such a good record in deciding, without being told in advance, which of the protocols came from delinquents, which from non-delinquents. Appendix E of *Unraveling* describes the Schachtel method of analysis in detail and presents sample records and trait analyses.

When it is considered that, despite the fact that the psychiatrist and the Rorschach test interpreters, although neither was permitted

[29] One reviewer of the most recent Glueck work has this diagnosis about the attitude of certain sociologists: 'Since the foreign experience demonstrates these critics to be so wrong, the question arises as to whether major portions of their criticisms may not be traced to damaged professional pride due to the failure of the Gluecks to include a sociologist on their research staff.' Fox (1960), Review of *Predicting delinquency and crime. B. U. L. Rev.* **40**, 157.

[30] Datta (1955), *Sociological Theory in Contemporary American Sociology* (unpub-lished thesis in University of West Virginia Library), quoted by Hartung, op. cit. In contrast to this student's amateur status, it is not altogether irrelevant to point out that the Schachtels, whose work she criticizes so cavalierly, had had many years' experience with the Rorschach test and were trained by Rorschach himself.

by us to see the results of individual examinations by the other, achieved a very high incidence of agreement in diagnoses (we found what seemed to be inconsistencies between the two sets of diagnoses in only seventy-four out of some 1,000 cases and in only six was there continued disagreement after the two experts went over the cases and straightened out semantic misunderstandings (p. 242)), it must be conceded that both the Rorschach test and the psychiatric interview yielded extraordinarily reliable results.

So much, then, for the criticisms of the samples from the point of view of the Rorschach test.

3. The psychiatric interview was inadequate. It has been pointed out that, since the psychiatrist interviewed most of the boys only once, there may be some weaknesses in the psychiatric findings. We anticipated that this criticism would be made. We ourselves would have preferred more contacts (p. 60);[31] but who can say how many more interviews would have been sufficient—two, ten, or a complete psychoanalytic technique requiring years? Moreover, it must be borne in mind that the aim of the psychiatric interview was diagnostic rather than therapeutic.

The psychiatrist of the research, Dr Bryant Moulton, is an expert with long experience in interviewing maladjusted children (he had been for twelve years with the Judge Baker Guidance Center) and with a special gift of winning *rapport* with boys. But apart from this fact there is an internal test of the reliability of the psychiatrist's findings; that is, the evidence thrown up by a very significant aspect of the design of the research, namely, the fact that care was taken to avoid infection of the findings of one scientist by those of another investigator. Thus, as already pointed out, the psychiatrist was not given access to the Rorschach test findings, nor were the Rorschach interpreters aware of the psychiatric diagnoses. Yet when we compared the diagnoses on the boys as determined by these single psychiatric interviews with the findings evolved through independent interpretation of the Rorschach test protocols, a remarkable similarity emerged (pp. 242, 252). So, also, when we compared the highly predictive factors (that is, those most markedly differentiating delinquents from non-delinquents) which resulted from the psychiatrist's interviews with those derived from the Rorschach tests, they were, taken as a pattern, quite consistent.[32]

[31] Criticism of the single psychiatric interview was made, among others, by J. Satten, a psychiatrist, in the Symposium in *Fed. Prob.* **15**, 55.

[32] *Psychiatric*: Adventuresomeness, suggestibility, stubbornness, extroversion in action, emotional instability; *Rorschach*: social assertiveness, suspiciousness, defiance, destructiveness, emotional lability.

III. CAUSATIVE ANALYSIS

A. Hartung, citing Reiss, claimed that, since our investigation 'was eclectic and not guided by any theory', the interpretations of the findings 'were necessarily *ex post facto*'. We have several things to say about such a judgment:

In the first place, no unilateral theory advanced by sociologists— whether culture conflict, the 'ecologic characteristics of the interstitial area', 'differential association', or 'delinquency subculture'—is sufficiently comprehensive, sufficiently specific or sufficiently close to the realities of both individual and social psychology and the actualities of behavior to have been used as a guide to our research. Differential association, for example, is a very thin and distant abstraction without capacity to guide practical research. (See Chapter 16 of this volume.) And the delinquency subculture did not fall from the heavens; it was made, and is being sustained, by delinquent people, and to attribute etiologic exclusiveness or priority to it is to reason in a circle.

In the second place, our eclectic approach, broad and comprehensive as it is, was much better designed than any existing sociologic theory to get at the specific facts that differentiate delinquents from non-delinquents. In this connection, no research, either before or after *Unraveling*, has so comprehensively and pointedly dug up traits and factors that are very probably etiologic.

In the third place, there was nothing *ex post facto* about the interpretations; on the contrary, every precaution was taken to avoid 'reading in', and any careful student of *Unraveling* will find this to be so. The process was the familiar scientific one of comparison of a representative and substantial sample of true delinquents with an equal sample of true non-delinquents. (The charge of *ex post facto* reasoning is, by the way, an interesting illustration of the psychoanalytic concept of 'projection'; it is certain sociologists, not we, who, desirous to 'prove' their theories, manage to *omit* factual data running counter to their preconceptions, such, for example, as the biologically-rooted changes in interests, attitudes, and behavior that tend to occur with changes in age-spans no matter what the general culture or subculture may be.)

Discussion of the etiologic implications arrived at, not through pre-existing preconceptions about this or that individual theory, cause, or discipline, but inductively, on the basis of the evidence emerging from comparison of over 400 factors at different levels of inquiry, is given in pages 281–82 of *Unraveling* and developed further in Chapter XV of our more popular book based on *Unraveling*, *Delinquents in the Making*[153].

279

B. Our position as to *etiology* may be stated in these terms:

At the outset we had to re-examine the implications of the entire history of the study of the problem of crime causation, especially the causes of juvenile misconduct; for as Dostoevsky long ago shrewdly observed in his famous novel, *The House of the Dead,* 'With ready-made opinions one cannot judge of crime. Its philosophy is a little more complicated than people think.' The same may be said of ready-made theories.

It is well known that throughout the centuries there have been favorite, unilateral explanations—call them facts or theories—of criminalism. Some insight into the causation of delinquency or crime can be obtained from almost any approach that may seem to bear a relationship to the problem. Even meteorology can contribute; investigations have been made which show seasonal and climatic variations in crime and delinquency. Numerous studies have been conducted, especially in Europe, of fluctuations in various indexes of economic conditions (prices of basic commodities, business activity, and the like) as related to the ups and downs of crime or delinquency. Many researches have been made, especially in Chicago, on the relationship of neighborhood conditions to crime. Numerous investigations have studied specific factors of environment and culture, such as the conflict of cultures between foreign-born parents and native-born children or between residents of different sections of the same region, the effect of bad companions, the dearth of adequate recreational facilities, and the like. More recently, old wine has been poured into new bottles under such general titles as the 'differential association theory', the 'delinquency subculture', etc.

There have also been many biologically-oriented investigations of the causes of delinquency and crime, from the famous and now questionable works of the Italian anthropologic criminologist, Lombroso, involving variations on the theme of the 'born criminal', atavism or hereditary 'throwback', or degeneration, and certain forms of epilepsy, to the traditional psychiatric studies which emphasize psychoses, 'psychopathic personality', and psychoneuroses. Finally, in more recent years, there have been a few psychoanalytic investigations, and numerous studies (based on inadequate samples and lack of comparable control groups of non-delinquents) of various individual psychologic, emotional, or characterical elements or patterns alleged to be causal of a tendency to criminalism.

Examination of existing researches in juvenile delinquency disclosed a tendency grossly to overemphasize a particular science or explanation. Proponents of various theories of causation still too often insist that the truth is to be found only in their own special fields of study. Like the fabled blind men examining the elephant, each builds the entire subject in the image of that piece of reality which he happens to have touched.

Obviously, then, a *many-sided approach* to this highly complex problem of human nature—a problem which has puzzled philosophers, scientists, parents, and clergy for hundreds of years, and judges and probation officers more recently—is, we were and are convinced, the only type of first step that gives promise of yielding useful insights leading to inductively arrived at theories and hypotheses which can then be subjected to more fruitful tests.

It is such a many-sided study, and for the reasons noted, that we attempted in *Unraveling*.

To avoid as many pitfalls as possible, we designed an investigation in which we compared numerous persistently delinquent boys, ranging in age from eleven to seventeen, with as many truly non-delinquent boys, matching them, boy for boy, by age, by ethnic (racial) derivation, by general intelligence (I.Q.), and by residence in underprivileged 'slum' areas of Boston. This matching was necessary because the factors that had to be analyzed in order to dig closer to the roots of delinquency are so numerous that a way had to be found to avoid confusion. In order to study a large enough sample of variables, certain other sets of factors had first to be 'held constant'. In deciding which such factors to equalize among the two groups, through the pairing off of delinquents with non-delinquents as a preliminary to their later detailed study, we were guided by several methodologic aims: First, it was felt that since the ultimate comparison ought to deal with subtle processes of personality and environment, the more general or cruder factors should be kept as nearly as possible alike in the matching; second, those traits which typically affect a whole interrelated range of factors could also usefully be held constant; third, those general characteristics which had already been explored sufficiently by other investigators and about which there was considerable agreement (such as the partial, indirect role of poverty, or of residence in a socially deteriorated urban area) could also be usefully held constant in the matching, to the extent possible in such an inexact field.

It was only after this careful matching of persistent delinquents with true non-delinquents that the two sets of boys were systematically and minutely compared in respect to the percentage-incidence of numerous traits and factors, measured or assessed at the following levels:

1. Family and personal background. This is a comparative picture of the kinds of homes and families these two sets of boys came from, based on home visits and on the reconstruction, from numerous recorded sources, of the history of delinquency and criminalism, alcoholism, intellectual and emotional deficiency, physical ailments, economic and educational conditions and achievements, not only of the members of the boys' immediate families but also of grandparents, uncles, and aunts. The aim was to determine the conditions under which the parents of the two groups of boys had themselves been raised, a situation that must have influenced the ideals, attitudes and practices which they, in turn, brought to the task of child-rearing so far as our boys were concerned.

The cultural, intellectual, and emotional conditions in the homes of our boys were of course likewise subjected to intensive study.

2. Boys' habits and use of leisure. Attention here was especially directed to the age at which deviating behavior began and the nature of the earliest signs of antisocial conduct. There was also secured a detailed history of each boy's progress in school, as well as an assessment of the various forms of school misbehavior.

3. Physique types. The bodily structure and form of the boys was determined by the use of photographs and their anthropologic measurement and classification in respect to fundamental physique patterns or somatotypes. After various measurements, the boys were classified anthropologically according to the predominance of one of the three root-components that entered into their development: *endomorphy*, in which softness and roundness of the various regions of the body predominate; *mesomorphy*, in which solid muscle, bone and connective tissue, and bodily compactness predominate; and *ectomorphy*, characterized by the relative emphasis of linearity and fragility of body form. A *balanced* type (relative similarity of all three components) was also identified. The importance of comparing delinquents and non-delinquents in terms of physique-type lies in the fact that the dominance of one or another of the three root components of body form may well imply basic variations in energy output, temperament, affect, and differential *response* to 'differential association'.

4. *Health.* A meaningful comparison of delinquents with non-delinquents obviously had to include a medical examination, since poor health is often alleged to be a significant causal factor in delinquency. Through this we got a comparative picture of the general health and of the gross evidence of various diseases in the two sets of boys.

5. Intelligence. It is commonly believed that the hows and whys of human behavior are largely governed by the degree and quality of intellectual power. One of the bases of original matching was *general* intelligence as summarized in the I.Q. This equating of global intellectual capacity gave us a chance to compare the delinquents with the controls in respect to various constituent elements of intelligence; two boys of like I.Q. can have quite varying intellectual qualities in terms of specific traits, talents, and deficiencies.

6. Temperament and character structure. In recent years, those who have studied the human mind and behavior have concluded that the temperamental and affective life of the individual, and especially the feeling-laden experiences and trauma of the first few years in the home, have a great deal to do with the development of personality, the structuring of character, and the channelling and habituation of behavior-tendencies. To reach the main features of character-structure, various 'projective' tests have been evolved. The Rorschach (or ink-blot) test, which the psychologists applied to both sets of boys, is one of the most revealing of such probers of the foundations of personality and character.

As pointed out, there was also an interview by a skilled psychiatrist with each boy. This revealed the more obvious personality traits of the boys, uncovered their many emotional stresses and conflicts and how they resolved them, and provided some clues to the reasons for the persistency of misbehavior of the delinquent lads and the conventional conduct of the control group.

Such an extensive and intensive exploration at so many levels involved years of careful investigation, tireless verification of data from many sources, entering of the numerous factors on statistical schedules according to carefully prepared definitions, and meeting many delicate problems of public relations. Several chapters in *Unraveling* render full account of these various techniques, so that the interested reader can judge for himself the reliability of the raw materials that went into the numerous tables and statistical computations from which the basic conclusions of this comprehensive study were derived.

Such, oversimplified in the above description, are the philosophy and technique of *Unraveling Juvenile Delinquency.*

C. How do these fit into our practical view of '*causation*'?

1. There has been altogether too much seemingly profound but essentially superficial writing on the theme (borrowed from the pure sciences) that one must never use the term 'cause', but only such evasive expressions as 'associated factor', or 'decision theory', etc. But

the issue is a pragmatic, not a semantic, one. Where a considerable number of factors that 'make sense' from the point of view of common and clinical experience are found to characterize delinquents far more than non-delinquents (the difference not being attributable to chance) it is highly probable that what is involved is an etiologic *connection* between them; in other words, the delinquency not only follows the traits and factors that have been found to precede it, but follows *from* them. The soundness of such a conception of 'causation' from a practical point of view is provable by (*a*) the fact that the concatenation of different traits and factors yields high predictive power in the sense of identification of delinquents and non-delinquents when applied to a considerable variety of populations, and (*b*) the fact that when such patterns of assumedly criminogenic traits and factors are absent from or are eliminated from a situation, delinquency usually does *not* exist or is greatly diminished.

The possibility that some day variations in the behavior of people may be explainable largely in the more ultimate terms of differences in, say, endocrine gland function, or of microscopic physico-chemical reactions, does not, in the meantime, prevent effective action on the basis of existing cruder assessments of reality, any more than the recent development of nuclear science prevented effective coping with many problems of nature through employment of prenuclear chemistry and physics. In the meantime, it can serve no useful purpose for criminologists to keep wringing their hands about the inadequacies of the etiologic researches thus far produced. Medicine made therapeutic strides in several fields long before the specific etiologic agents in certain diseases were discovered (in the treatment of malaria, for example).

Nor should too much time and energy be expended in the armchair search for some grand, all-unifying theory. Fruitful theories and hypotheses usually spring only from soundly gathered facts which suggest clues or influences leading to further investigations. The multidisciplinary evidence of our comparisons of delinquents with non-delinquents convinces us that, taken in the mass, if boys in the underprivileged urban areas have in their make-up and early conditioning certain identifiable traits and factors found markedly to differentiate delinquents from non-delinquents, the boys are very likely to turn out to be delinquent. In this general sense of *high probability* of persistency of antisocial conduct related to the presence of a sufficiently weighty combination of differentiative characteristics of person and *milieu*, a rough etiologic relationship was established.

2. It should be emphasized that throughout the work in analyzing the data for *Unraveling*, we insisted on the fundamental importance of *sequence in time*. That is why we ruled out gang membership (frequently emphasized as a cause of delinquency) and other influences which were found to have occurred long after definite proof of antisocial behavior. The onset of persistent misbehavior tendencies was at the early age of seven years or younger among 48 per cent of our delinquents, and from eight to ten in an additional 39 per cent; thus a total of almost nine-tenths of the entire group showed clear delinquent tendencies before the time when boys generally become members of organized boys' gangs. The leading authorities on the subject recognize the gang as 'largely an adolescent phenomenon'; for example, of some 1,200 cases of gang membership studied in Chicago, only 1·5 per cent of the boys were six to twelve years old, while 63 per cent were classified as adolescents.

3. We further decided that 'cause' (we would have preferred to use a less controversial term) involves a *totality* of conditions necessary to bring about the delinquency result; individual traits or factors are only parts of the total cause. That is why our *non-delinquents* sometimes had in their make-up and background *some* of the traits and factors found among the delinquents. Not all the characteristics arrived at inductively and included in our general etiologic formulation will be found in all delinquents and be absent in all non-delinquents.

Consider, for example, the fact that twice as many delinquents as non-delinquents were found to be of the closely knit, muscular, athletically inclined (mesomorphic) type. The very fact that 30 per cent of the *non*-delinquents were also of this physique immediately contradicts any conclusion that *mesomorphy* inevitably 'causes' persistent delinquency. Or, consider such a trait as *defiance*, which one would naturally regard as closely related to delinquent behavior tendencies. True, 50 per cent of the delinquents had this characteristic, but 12 per cent of the non-delinquents also had it; and the very fact that half the delinquent group did *not* display this trait further reveals the inadequacy of conclusions about causation derived from a single factor.

Thus, a single factor (or even a small group of factors) may be involved, and even frequently involved, in delinquent behavior and yet will not, of itself, have sufficient weight or potency to tip the scales among boys who remain non-delinquent. In any realistic sense, the cause of an effect is that *totality* of conditions sufficient to produce it. The fact noted that as many as half of the delinquents did *not* have the trait of *defiance* is but one illustration of the absence among a considerable group of delinquents of characteristics which are present in some other large group of delinquents. It reveals the usually unrecognized truism that persistent delinquency is not the potential result of only one specific combination of factors which markedly differentiates delinquents from non-delinquents, but of each of several *different* combinations. Just as death, although always the *same terminal event*, may be the result of *various preceding sequences* of conditions, so the terminal event of persistent delinquency may be the result of a variety of different sequences. For we are dealing with a complex aggregation of internal and external conditions which are associated with socially maladjusted, unlawful behavior, and not all of them are indispensable to the result in any single case.

In criminal conduct, as in most other forms of human expression, every person has his individual breaking point. It is difficult for all members of any society at any one time to conform to the requirements and prohibitions of socially desirable behavior,because this involves a subordination of the natural impulses of sex expression, aggression, and the like, to those conduct norms which the law has declared necessary to the general welfare. But most persons are able (through various combinations of numerous factors of native endowment and elaborate conditioning in home, school, church, neighborhood, and supportive elements in the general culture) to meet the requirements of the major legal standards of the age and place wherein they live. If a boy persists in delinquency, it means that his power of resistance to natural impulse, or his desire to obey socio-legal mandates, has been overbalanced by the strength of the other circumstances that incline to antisocial behavior.

4. Closely related to the preceding concepts is the concept of *probability*. Nowadays, even the physical sciences state their generalizations in terms not of absolute inevitability but only of high probability. The statistical method of comparing delinquents, as a group, with non-delinquents, as a group, is not designed to bring out any point-to-point causal sequence that will always hold good for each and every case. It is rather intended to disclose whether or not a group of boys having a certain cluster of factors in its make-up and background will much more probably turn out to be delinquent than a group not so loaded down; or, to put it differently, whether the 'typical' delinquent is likely to be the result of such a concatenation of factors.

5. The intellectual fruitfulness of our etiologic conceptions compared

to the unilateral theory of the sociologist is shown by an example to be found in *Predicting Delinquency and Crime*[212]. Our Social Prediction Table (discussed below) is effective in about 90 per cent of the new cases to which it is applied. Why does it not also select potential delinquents and non-delinquents in the remaining 10 per cent? The answer is that there are cases in which the etiologic-predictive nexus based on the factors of family life shown to be highly discriminative in most cases is not adequate to identify delinquents and non-delinquents among the 10 per cent because in those cases *certain other characteristics* are sufficiently potent to counteract the family influences. In other words, there is a *core type* of delinquent from an etiologic-predictive point of view, and there are one or more *fringe types*. If we examine the characteristics of the 10 per cent who were not successfully identified by the Social Prediction Table, it turns out that these *atypical* delinquents, although many come from *wholesome* families, differ from the typical (core) group in respect to many characteristics, particularly those derived from the Rorschach test and psychiatric examination (id., pp. 263–73). Some of these traits suggest a quite consistent pattern of neurotic attributes (e.g. marked submissiveness, enhanced feelings of insecurity, fear of failure and defeat), together with a *low* incidence of such characteristics as destructiveness and adventurousness which were found to be highly differentiative in the core-type of delinquent. Other traits suggest the possibility of there existing still another fringe type. We felt justified in calling this pilot analysis 'From Prediction to Etiology', because it is by this method of inductive analysis, imperfect as it still concededly is, that one approaches the determination of true etiologic involvements.

So much for our conceptions of causation.

D. We are convinced that the *criticisms* of our tentative etiologic formulation are unsound:

1. One critic points out that the etiologic 'law'[33] is untested.[34]

---

[33] 'The delinquents as a group are distinguishable from the non-delinquents: (1) physically, in being essentially mesomorphic in constitution (solid, closely knit, muscular); (2) temperamentally, in being restlessly energetic, impulsive, extroverted, aggressive, destructive (often sadistic)—traits which may be related more or less to the erratic growth pattern and its physiologic correlates or consequences; (3) in attitude, by being hostile, defiant, resentful, suspicious, stubborn, socially assertive, adventurous, unconventional, non-submissive to authority; (4) psychologically, in tending to direct and concrete, rather than symbolic, intellectual expression, and in being less methodical in their approach to problems; (5) socioculturally, in having been reared to a far greater extent than the control group in homes of little understanding, affection, stability, or moral fibre by parents usually unfit to be effective guides and protectors or, according to psychoanalytic theory, desirable sources for emulation and the construction of a consistent, well-balanced, and socially normal superego during the

One thing at a time. It was clearly presented as tentative; and no claim whatsoever was made that it is final or perfect. On the contrary, the entire discussion made clear the need of testing the general conclusion by further researches. We should be pleased if a team of specialists similar to those who worked on *Unraveling*, but aided by the presence of a relatively unbiased sociologist, were to make a study similar to ours, benefiting from our mistakes.

---

early stages of character development. (For footnote to this, see *Unraveling*, p. 283.) While in individual cases the stresses contributed by any one of the above pressure-areas of dissocial-behavior tendency may adequately account for persistence in delinquency, in general the high probability of delinquency is dependent upon the interplay of the conditions and forces from all these areas.

'In the exciting, stimulating, but little-controlled and culturally inconsistent environment of the underprivileged area, such boys readily give expression to their untamed impulses and their self-centered desires by means of various forms of delinquent behavior. Their tendencies toward uninhibited energy-expression are deeply anchored in soma and psyche and in the malformations of character during the first few years of life.

'This "law" may have to be modified after more intensive, microscopic study of the atypical cases. For example, there are instances in which the delinquents are more ectomorphic than mesomorphic in constitution, and cases in which the delinquents are of the introverted, psychoneurotic temperament. There are also some *non*-delinquents who have been reared in immoral and criminalistic homes. While all these groups are relatively small in number, they deserve further study, and their more intensive consideration may result in modification of the basic analysis. "A scientific law must always be considered as a temporary statement of relationships. As knowledge increases this law may require modification. Even the natural sciences state all their generalizations in terms of probability." ' (The quote within the quotation is from Sellin, *Culture conflict and crime*.) *Unraveling*, pp. 281–82. The summary is preceded by a careful analysis of the findings of the research. See *Unraveling*, Ch. XXI.

[34] Rubin, op. cit. *supra* note 4. He quotes the Gluecks as saying 'physical anthropologists have not yet answered a major question, namely, whether or not the somatotype remains constant and, if it does, whether, in the formative years of growth around the age of six or seven, when children normally enter school, the physique type is as yet reliably distinguishable', and asks 'what justification is there to include physique in the law?' He overlooks the fact that the boys were much older than six or seven when somatotyped for *Unraveling*, their average age then having been about fourteen and a half years. Rubin then points out that we rejected physique for predictive purposes. The reason for this (as plainly indicated in the quotation focused upon by Rubin) was that we were not as yet confident that the physique type was reliably distinguishable at age six or seven, when prediction is attempted. There is thus no inconsistency between our use of somatotypes on the boys in our samples (at about fourteen and a half) and our failure to use them for prediction (at about six or seven).

It should be noted that since publication of *Unraveling* Mrs Glueck has worked out a prediction device using somatotype data, because evidence was beginning to appear that somatotyping can in fact be made early in life (at age seven, for example). (See Chapter 11 of the present work.) In an English study, 'It has been shown that the somatotype can give some indication of the kind of behavior to expect in different individuals, and that exact measurements support what has for centuries been appreciated in less precise form, namely, that physical constitution plays an important part in shaping people's lives.' Davidson, McInnes & Parnell (1957), *The distribution of personality traits in seven-year-old children; a combined psychological, psychiatric and somatotype study. Brit. J. Educ. Psychol.* 27, 48. See also, Parnell (1959), *Physique and family structure. Eugenics Rev.* 51, 75.

2. This critic further points out that the 'law is not limited as to place, age, or administrative policy, to accord with the limitations of the sample'.[35]

On page 272 of *Unraveling* the limitations of the general sample are set forth. However, we are now able to say that the results of a number of gratifying applications of the Glueck Social Prediction Table would seem to indicate the likelihood of the findings being essentially repeated on other samples of delinquents compared with non-delinquents. (See Chapter 8 above.)

3. This critic also calls attention to the fact that some of the differentiative factors affect only small groups of delinquents and non-delinquents.

This matter has already been discussed in connection with a similar criticism of the tables in *Physique and Delinquency*. It should be re-emphasized that the fact that certain differentiative factors affect relatively small groups of delinquents and non-delinquents is proof of the existence of fringe types in which the etiologic syndrome differs, in whole or in part, from that which characterizes the core type of delinquent.

The formulation suggested by the facts of our research yields a point of view toward causation equally applicable to urban and rural regions, to crime in primitive systems and in developed cultures, to 'white collar' and 'black collar' crime, to crime in 1960 and in George Washington's day, etc., because it recognizes a variety of etiologic patterns and takes account of the continuous conflict between the individual's tendencies toward the gratification of his urgent egoistic desires, on the one hand, and sociocultural taboos and prohibitions on the other. Until the sociologists can produce a more fruitful and realistic formulation than they have thus far developed, we prefer to adhere to our multicausal analysis than to have our revealing factual findings, in Tennyson's words, 'Veneer'd with sanctimonious theory'.

E. The same critic protests that 'none of the law goes beyond mere correlation'. He has a naive conception of causation, especially in the biosocial field. High intercorrelation is of the very essence of etiologic implication, provided the factors found to be greatly interrelated with delinquency and not with non-delinquency are those that 'make sense' from the point of view of clinical experience and provided it is possible to test the influence of the etiologic factors by removing them (or enough of them) from the personal-social

[35] Rubin, op. cit.

289

situation in a series of cases and noting whether or not the behavior changes.[36]

IV. THE ROLE OF CULTURE

A. Almost all the sociologic critics claim that we have ignored what they conceive to be the most significant, if not indeed the *exclusive*, source of delinquency—the cultural *milieu*. Our view as to this (already touched upon above in discussing the control of neighborhood as a prerequisite to the detailed comparison of the delinquents with the non-delinquents) is that individuals differ with reference to the elements of culture that affect them. They tend to choose, or to succumb to, those aspects of a culture which are naturally more congenial. Individuals vary in constitution, temperament, strength of innate drives, and degree of integrative and inhibitory capacity. These differences are the result not only of early conditioning, but also, to an extent as yet unmeasurable, of heredity. Especially when the educative and supportive social agencies are inadequate or in process of rapid change does the reaction of different individuals subjected to a similar culture vary. Some find it impossible to inhibit their primitive impulses in the absence, or even in the presence, of the deterrent influence of external force; others have so efficiently 'internalized' the psychologic accompaniments of various forms of authority that they have an efficient superego (conscience) which, despite major changes in cultural controls, still enables them to 'toe the mark'.

But apart from the evidence of general experience as to nature and nurture, there are several crucial statistics that cast serious doubt upon the view held by some sociologists that such cultural entities as the gang, or the 'delinquency subculture', or the 'working-class subculture', or the wider general culture comprise the most potent (if not the exclusive) 'cause' of delinquency.

1. As to *gang membership*, as previously pointed out, it has been established in *Unraveling* that almost nine-tenths of the delinquent youths had already shown clear signs of antisocial behavior when

[36] This type of approach, and not adherence to some *a priori* theory through thick and thin, is the method of science. 'The main cause of this unparalleled progress in physiology, pathology, medicine and surgery has been the fruitful application of the experimental method of research, just the same method which has been the great lever of all scientific advance in modern times.' Dr William H. Welch, Argument against Antivivisection Bill, S. Doc. No. 34, 56th Cong., 1st Sess. (21 Feb. 1900), quoted in 1 Cushing, *Life of Sir William Osler*, 521. Of course, in the field under discussion experiment must take a less precise and more humane path than in the laboratory.

they were under eleven years of age; and the typical 'gang age' is well beyond that period, in adolescence.[37]

2. As to *neighborhood culture*, even in the most marked 'delinquency areas' or delinquency subcultures of our cities, not more than a small fraction of the boys (say 10 to 15 per cent) become delinquent. It is unreasonable, therefore, to emphasize the role of neighborhood influences on the small percentage of boys who become delinquent and utterly ignore the fact that the vast majority of the boys in the same neighborhoods somehow manage *not* to follow a persistent antisocial career.

3. As to the wider *general culture*, the New York City Youth Board has established that in America's leading urban center no fewer than 75 per cent of the delinquents are contributed by only 1 per cent of the families.[38]

If the neighborhood subculture and the general cultural patterns are as permeatively and inevitably criminalistic as they are said to be, and if the values they represent are as powerful in their criminogenic influences as claimed, how account for these statistics?

B. It will not be amiss to say a few words about the relationship of culture to the individual differences of those subjected to it, a crucial matter which certain sociologists either ignore or explain away very unconvincingly:

Suppose ten youths go out in a boat on a lake. The boat springs a leak and fills with water. Two boys drown; the other eight successfully reach shore. It happens that one of the drowned boys did not know how to swim, and the second could swim but had a weak heart which could not stand the excessive exertion; the other eight were good swimmers in fine physical condition.

[37] The charge that 'the Gluecks ignored their own finding that almost all of the delinquents were members of gangs and that only three of the non-delinquents belonged to gangs' (Hartung, quoting Clinard, op. cit. *supra* note 5) is simply not true. In the first place, not almost all delinquents were found to belong to gangs, but 56 per cent (*Unraveling*, Table XIII–16). In the second place, as pointed out in the text, the reason for excluding gang-membership in the *etiology* of delinquency is the fact that gang-membership is an adolescent phenomenon and nine-tenths of our delinquents were already manifesting clear signs of delinquency at age ten or less. 'Factors that come into play after persistent antisocial behavior is established can hardly be regarded as relevant to the original etiology of maladaptation, except as they may reflect deep-rooted forces which do not make themselves felt in a tendency to dissocial behavior until puberty or adolescence is reached.' *Unraveling*, 272. See also, *Delinquents in the making* (based on *Unraveling*), 166.

[38] The basic importance of family life has been confirmed in Japan: '(*e*) family circumstances are more important prediction factors than neighborhood circumstances.' *Juvenile delinquency as seen in the family court of Japan*, 15 (Ministry of Justice, Japan, 1957).

Under the circumstances, what is the more rational procedure: to focus primarily and (according to some even exclusively) upon the composition of the water in the lake or, while not ignoring the lake as the setting of the deaths to be explained, to concentrate on the relevant *varying* characteristics of the individuals subjected to the very same hazard but with such widely differing results?

What was the chief 'cause' of the drowning of the first two boys? Was the water the cause? This cannot be so because, despite the fact that two of the youths drowned, eight others, subjected to the same hazard, managed to survive.

The eight youths were saved not because the water, in their case, was less deep or less wet, but because they could swim and were in good physical condition. The first boy was drowned, not because the water, in his case, was different from that of the others, but because he could not swim. The second lad was drowned, not because the general 'cause' inevitably would result in people drowning, but because, although he could swim, he did not have the necessary strength to swim the required distance to shore.

Now the water is equivalent to the 'delinquency subculture'; of ten persons subjected to a like external influence, only two succumbed. The condition that affected them is *general*. It is equivalent to the existence of the institution of property and of laws against theft: *all* men are subject to such a uniform situation, but the vast majority of them do *not* commit larceny.

Now suppose this same little drama were enacted on the high seas, where the background forces are much stronger than in a lake. *All* youths are by this *force majeure* reduced to an almost similar state. True, the first two boys probably drown earlier than the others; but the general environmental condition with which all the boys have to struggle is now so overpowering as to make virtually irrelevant any difference in *individual* capacity or equipment.

Of course, the analogy is not perfect; the characteristics of a culture-medium are much more subtle and complex than are the properties of a lake, as is also the dynamic interplay between the culture and the human organism. But the basic principle illustrated by the foregoing example is similar, as an explanatory device, to the principle involved in assessing the role in criminogenesis of the special subculture of gang membership, or the interstitial area, or the working or middle class subculture, or the process of differential association—favorite explanations of delinquency advanced by certain criminologists.

It cannot be denied that despite the many unwholesome and antisocial features of our culture the great majority of people are, in normal times, relatively law-abiding. In the very research under review, we were able to find 500 boys, living in high delinquency areas of Greater Boston, whom extremely careful investigation showed to be non-delinquent. In times of exceptional crisis, such as widespread economic depression, some persons who have been treading a precarious zone between law-abidingness and criminalism go over, or are pushed over, into antisocial territory; but even in such times the great majority remain law-abiding. Yet they have been living and making decisions and acting in the same malign culture as those who become delinquent or criminal. To insist, therefore, that in such a situation cultural influences are the most satisfactory explanation of the incidence of delinquency and crime is seriously to distort the actual picture.

Antisocial aspects of culture are only *potential* or *possible* causes of delinquency; persons of varied innate nature and early parent-child relationships respond to those elements of the culture which they wish, or are impelled, to *introject* and thereby transform into antisocial motives. In brief, certain sociologists, in their eagerness to promote their profession and its assumedly deserved leadership in explanation of delinquency and crime, forget that environment—'culture'—plays no role in conduct unless and until it is, as it were, emotionally swallowed, becoming part of the motivating force against the taboos and demands of the prevailing culture. This oversight, among others (including a defective conception of the learning process and of motivation), accounts for the superficiality and puerility of the differential association theory (see Chapter 16 of this volume). To those who cling to the theory, there seemingly are no such realities as the gene and the germ plasm or individual differences in bodily morphology, temperament, intelligence, etc.; nor is there much significance to them in that most crucial of all cultural influences, parent-child relationships during the first few years of life. To these theorists it is all the peer-group, the gang, the regional subculture, the general culture, the *Massenmensch*. How they can reconcile their extreme overemphasis of environmental conditioning with actual differences among human beings from birth is a question they do not deign to answer.

C. The critic whose misinterpretation of Schachtel's Rorschach statement I have mentioned also claims, it will be recalled, that the Gluecks ignore culture completely. With certain loyal sociologists it is all or nothing. Although all experience, in botany, zoology, biology, medicine, proves daily that the resultant product is the outcome of the interplay of the seed and the soil, they write as if nothing counts but the soil.[39] But in point of fact, the Gluecks do *not* ignore culture. In stating their views in the opening chapter of *Unraveling*, and in the close of their summary of the dynamic etiologic pattern arrived at inductively, they say:

'In the exciting, stimulating, but little controlled and culturally inconsistent environment of the underprivileged area, such boys readily give expression to their untamed impulses and their self-centered desires by means of various forms of delinquent behavior.'

But they add, on the basis of carefully assembled, verified, and as nearly as possible measured data, that the

'tendencies toward uninhibited energy-expression are deeply anchored in soma and psyche and in the malformations of character [compare Schachtel's misinterpreted statement] during the first few years of life' (p. 282. See also p. 15.).

V. THE PREDICTION METHOD

Ever since the publication of *Unraveling*, a few critics have attacked that work on the ground that the prediction tables could not possibly forecast efficiently because they are based on equal proportions of delinquents and non-delinquents (500 : 500), whereas the proportion of non-delinquents to delinquents, even in the most extreme 'delinquency area', is only about 9 : 1.

We have avoided taking issue with these critics, although from the beginning we believed them wrong and certainly premature in their theorizing, because we felt that the most effective answer would have to be the pragmatic one of the 'proof of the pudding'[40] through actual experience.

Sufficient evidence has now been accumulated in various validation experiments of one of the tables (known in the literature as the Glueck Social Prediction Table) to enable us to give careful consideration to these criticisms.

The basic objection is entered, for example, by Reiss, who states

[39] There are of course many exceptions; the names of Paul Tappan, Thorsten Sellin, Albert Morris, Peter Lejins, Marvin Wolfgang and, in Europe, Hermann Mannheim and Wolf Middendorf, come to mind.

[40] 'In their present work, after a long and careful analysis of a large number of physical, psychological and social characters attributable to 500 delinquents and to an equal number of controls (non-delinquents matched pairwise with the delinquents in respect to age, ethnic origin, intelligence and type of area of residence), the Gluecks set up a series of proposed prediction tables based on attributes common among delinquents and uncommon among the controls, or vice versa. I do not see how they could have done better, but the proof of the pudding can come only with its eating.' Wilson (1951), Prediction. *Harv. L. Rev.* **64**, 1040.

dogmatically that 'unless this [50 per cent] is the actual rate in a similar population for which the predictions are made, the tables will yield very poor prediction.'[41] Reiss recomputed the Glueck Social Prediction Table, taking account of an assumed 9 : 1 ratio of non-delinquents to delinquents, and purports to prove that, by his figures, the original table can show very little predictive capacity:

'It can be seen in Table 2 that, so far as prediction of delinquency or non-delinquency is concerned, the table has a low predictive efficiency when the rate of delinquency is estimated at 10 per cent. For example, in the score 250–99 the chances of delinquency were 63·5 in the Gluecks' table, while the chances are only 16·2 per hundred in the table which assumes a rate of 10 per cent habitual delinquency.'

Reiss and similar critics have not clearly explained just why the adjustment to a supposed actual proportion of 9 : 1 is necessary; or, why differences in the incidence of delinquents and non-delinquents in any population should and would have a serious distorting influence on the distribution of scores of the predictive factors as presented in our 50–50 table.

If their point is, simply, that where the proportion of non-delinquents to delinquents in a population is far higher than one-half, one can just as readily 'predict' by *assuming all* boys to be non-delinquent as by going to the trouble of examining the families to see which boys possess the deleterious categories of the predictive factors in their background and which do not, then the point is insignificant. *Of course* one can assume that in a population in which the proportion of non-delinquents to delinquents is 9 : 1 *all* boys are non-delinquent and thereby triumphantly point out that one has guessed wrongly in only 10 per cent of all cases, which is alleged to be as good as the Glueck table is able to do.[42]

But that is not the issue.

The issue is whether one can *identify*, individually, the future delinquents and the future non-delinquents; otherwise one is not

[41] Similar criticisms have been made by Shaplin & Tiedman (1951), Comment on the juvenile delinquency prediction tables in the Gluecks' *Unraveling juvenile delinquency. Amer. Sociol. Rev.* **16**, 544; Stott (1960), The prediction of delinquency from non-delinquent behaviour. *Brit. J. Delinq.* **10**, 195; Duncan (1960), Review of *Predicting delinquency and crime. Am. J. Sociol.* **65**, 537.

[42] Indeed, one critic rushed into print in the New York City press (claiming, incidentally, that he represents a society of some 2,000 psychologists and thereby implicating them) with the assertion that by 'pulling names out of a hat' he could do just as well as can be done by the Glueck table!

really predicting at all but asserting what was known, *ex hypothesi*, beforehand.

It may be, however, that what the critics have in mind is the possibility that there could be factors involved in distinguishing delinquents from non-delinquents *other* than the ones used in the Glueck table, which express themselves in the result that in the community to which a 50–50 table is to be applied the proportions are really 90 : 10.

This raises certain important issues. There are seemingly three problems involved in the criticism under discussion:

(*a*) Will the Glueck table's distribution of scores for samples of *delinquents*, as found in the original Boston study, reproduce itself in other communities?

(*b*) Will the table's distribution of scores for *non-delinquents* reproduce itself in other populations?

(*c*) Even assuming that the distributions of new populations of delinquents and non-delinquents are identical with the Glueck table, will the table prove to be an effective predictive instrument in a population in which the proportion of non-delinquents is much higher than one-half?

It seems to us that in respect to all three of these questions the critics are confusing the counting of heads with the *weighing* of heads; a blind census with a device for *pinpointing* delinquents and non-delinquents; the percentage-incidence of non-delinquents and delinquents in a particular region with the incidence of certain criminogenic factors in a representative sample of delinquents compared with a representative sample of non-delinquents. To put it differently, they are confusing the effect of differences in the size of two statistical 'universes' with differences in the size of substantial, representative *samples* drawn from those two universes. By confusing the concept of universe with that of sample, the critics are begging the very question at issue, which is: Will the factors embodied in the Glueck table actually identify prospective delinquents and potential non-delinquents with a high degree of accuracy, irrespective of other influences, *including the differences in the size of the universes from which the original samples were drawn and to which they are applied?*

Our prediction table is not designed to forecast the probable chances of a boy's delinquency if he lives in Boston or a city like Boston; but rather the chances of his becoming delinquent if he happens to have in his make-up and background the crucial factors which have been shown, in comparing numerous delinquents with numerous non-delinquents, to be highly associated with persistency in misbehavior.

The use of equal numbers in the samples originally compared is not only legitimate but important for the accurate determination of the incidence of the factors under comparison. It is, for example, a frequent technique in medical research. The difference in the proportion of the *pools* from which samples of non-delinquents and delinquents were drawn can affect the outcome only if influential factors other than those embraced in the samples are omitted or included; and this is to be determined, not *a priori*, by manipulating the original table to reflect a 90 : 10 proportion, but only empirically, by the application of the table to other populations. Assuming that the sample of delinquents and the sample of non-delinquents are fairly representative of the populations from which the cases were derived, the fact that the *total* group of non-delinquents in the general population is nine times as numerous as the total group of delinquents can have little to do with the outcome when comparing the two samples; and it should, equally, have little to do with the outcome when applying the table to new populations.

If one were making a study comparing the incidence of blood pressure, pulse, certain chemicals in the blood and urine, etc., of persons with a malignant disease, with their incidence among healthy persons, would it make any difference whether the *general* incidence of such diseased persons in the particular community amounted to 10 per cent or 50 per cent? And, assuming that in the city in which the original experiment was done the population proportions of the well and the ill were 50–50, would this fact interfere with the predictive capacity of a table of indications and symptoms when applied to a city in which the proportions were 90 : 10?

Our own view has been and is that the variation in the proportion of non-delinquents to delinquents as between the original population and the new one to which the table is applied should have very little to do with the capacity of the table to 'spot' the delinquents and the non-delinquents. The reason is that the characteristics inductively arrived at as most markedly distinguishing the two groups were selected from among more than 400 factors as to the incidence of which the 500 pairs of matched delinquents and non-delinquents had been compared at levels of study ranging, widely, from anthropometric and psychiatric to social. It should be borne in mind, too, that by chi-square calculation we regarded as statistically significant only those factors in which the probability of the difference found between the delinquents and the controls being due to chance or random sampling was less than one in a hundred.[43]

We are aware of the fact, however, that, despite all this, empirical evidence might disprove our hypothesis as to the high identifying capacity of the prediction table. But one should not dogmatize at the outset that the influence of differences in proportions will seriously affect the outcome; one must await the proof of the pudding. The 'proof of the pudding' is turning out to be very satisfactory, as indicated by two important recent follow-ups. (See Ch. 8 above.)[44]

It should be pointed out that the tables reflecting the experience in these check-ups resemble *not* the adjusted tables of Reiss and others, but the original Glueck table. Thus, for example, the report by the New Jersey Department of Institutions and Agencies on delinquent boys on parole says: 'It will be observed that the closeness of the findings on the basis of the New Jersey data with the original findings in the study of *Unraveling Juvenile Delinquency* is rather noteworthy, since the New Jersey boys were selected at random, and no attempt was made to match the individual characteristics of the New Jersey delinquent boys with the delinquent boys included in the Harvard Law School study.'[45] The resemblance of the distribution of scores for samples of non-delinquents and delinquents in such a study as, for example, the New York City Youth Board's, suggests that, had the adjusted table of Reiss or other critics been used instead of the original, the utility of our table would have been seriously reduced, the predictions would have greatly miscarried, and there would have been many more 'false positives' (a concept discussed below) than turned up through the use of the original table.

On the basis of the check-up studies thus far made, we may now consider the first two questions posed at the outset of this section:

Does the Glueck table's distribution of scores for samples of *delinquents* reproduce itself elsewhere?

Nobody can read the evidence marshalled in the paper by Eleanor

[43] See 'Explanation of Statistical Method' by Carl R. Doering in *Unraveling*, p. 75.
[44] Several more follow-up studies have been called to our attention since Chapter 8 was written. For a more recent summary of prediction validation studies in Japan which confirm the earlier findings in regard to the validity of the Glueck Social Prediction Table, see Juhei Takeuchi, 'Juvenile Delinquency in Japan—Characteristics and Preventive Programs', a speech prepared for the Second United Nations Congress on the Prevention of Crime and the Treatment of Offenders, London, 1960, especially notes 24–32 (mimeographed). Those interested in the growth of Japanese prediction studies are invited to write to the Criminological Research Division of the Research Training Institute of the Ministry of Justice, 1–1 Kasumigaseki, Chiyoda-ku, Tokyo, Japan.
[45] *Predicting juvenile delinquency* (1955), Research Bulletin No. 124 (Trenton, N.J.: State Department of Institutions & Agencies).

Glueck (Ch. 8 above) without acknowledging that the answer can already safely be *Yes*.

Does the Glueck table's distribution of scores for new samples of *non-delinquents* reproduce itself elsewhere?

While it is true that only two of the validation studies so far carried out are prospective, the evidence is already reasonably persuasive that the answer will again be *Yes*.

Before turning to the final question posed above, I should like to point out that not only do the various check-up experiments embrace a variety of potential and actual delinquency, ethnic derivation, economic status, religion, cultural background, and even sex, but—something especially pertinent to the claim that, to have predictive power, the table must be applied to a population similar in the *proportion* of delinquents to non-delinquents to that of the original table—the check-ups also covered populations presenting a variety of proportions of non-delinquents to delinquents.

Thus it can reasonably be vouchsafed, on the basis of the empirical evidence so far adduced, that the Glueck table will tend to reproduce its distribution of scores for both delinquents and non-delinquents when it is applied to other populations.

The essential support of the table's pattern of factor-scores as related to behavior-outcomes by its application to a variety of samples elsewhere is very important to criminology; for as emphasized by the distinguished biostatistician, Professor Edwin Bidwell Wilson, 'Science advances by broadening the base upon which empirical uniformities are established; indeed, it is only by this broadening that we come to know that the descriptions of our samples are uniformities.'[46]

This brings me to the third question involved in the issue raised by the critics: *To what extent is the Glueck table an 'efficient' predictive instrument*; that is, to what degree does it improve on a 'prediction' made by simply calling every boy in the community non-delin-quent?[47]

Since no prediction device can reasonably be expected to forecast accurately in *all* cases, there will inevitably be some 'false positives', that is, some persons wrongly forecast as future delinquents and some wrongly spotted as future non-delinquents. To be sure, true prediction, especially in this field, cannot be 100 per cent accurate; but the Glueck table is indubitably much more correct in identifying potential delinquents and potential non-delinquents than the method suggested by the critics which does not *identify* any child but supplies

---

[46] Wilson (1951), Prediction. *Harv. L. Rev.* 64, 1040.
[47] See Chapters 9 and 10 above.

only the proportion of non-delinquents to delinquents that was estimated at the outset.

The 'false positives' aspect of the problem is not a scientific one but an issue in social ethics and social policy. In this connection, it is very important to point out that mistakes in *not* spotting future *delinquents* can be very costly to society, while mistakes in assuming a few persons to be potential delinquents (ten out of the 186 in the New York study, for example) who nevertheless ultimately turn out *not* to be delinquents can do little harm and might even do considerable good. Professor Samuel Stouffer, a social scientist for whom we have high respect, has suggested that if, for example, the Glueck table accurately 'spots' seventeen out of twenty potential delinquents but does so at the cost of predicting, say, eighteen non-delinquents to be delinquents,

'the answer might be that the eighteen "false positives" may not be hurt by the extra close watching we give them, for many of them may really be borderline or incipient delinquents. Furthermore, in view of the specific social factors used in prediction, these kids may be really in need of some help *in loco parentis*. Hence, the answer from the point of view of social ethics might be that the social gain in spotting the seventeen correctly more than justified any damage which might be done to the eighteen spotted incorrectly, If everybody scoring above 250 were to be sent to an institution, society would scream. But if the kind of watchful and helpful treatment which the "false positives" might get, along with the true delinquents, would not hurt them or would actually be good for them, you would have a most convincing case' (letter to authors).

It should be added, first, that the New York City Youth Board's validation study still has several years to run, and if it proceeds along its present lines the chances are that the percentage of 'false positives' will be very small indeed.[48] Secondly, Professor Lloyd Ohlin, who has had both theoretical and practical experience with prediction methods, has rated the *efficiency* of the Glueck Social Prediction Table very high in comparison with others:

'An analysis of published results shows that the predictive efficiency of the experience tables in follow-up samples varies from an efficiency of 25 per cent to a loss of 41 per cent in efficiency over what could be achieved with a simple prediction of success

[48] Since this was written, a definitive report of findings on 224 cases has been published by the New York City Youth Board. See Chapter 13.

for all cases,' a 'notable exception to these modest prediction results' being the predictive efficiency of the Glueck Social Prediction Scale from *Unraveling Juvenile Delinquency* which has been computed by Ohlin as 55 per cent.[49]

There is a related aspect of social policy to be considered—the question whether, assuming a high predictive potency of the Table, it is desirable to apply it in public schools as the basis of a prophylactic program, when this might entail 'stigmatizing' a few children. It has been claimed that such a procedure would 'label' such children as predelinquent and by that very process turn them into delinquents to live up to the role thus assigned them.[50] Apart from the superficial conception of child psychology revealed in such a dogmatic claim, it cannot be supposed that trained social workers would typically force themselves into a home and dramatically announce, 'Your child has been predicted as a delinquent!'; nor would the child be told this. In the New York City experiment, neither teachers, nor parents, nor children have been told which boys are probably potential delinquents and which are not. If that experiment should be followed by a program of delinquency prophylaxis, it is presumed that trained social case workers will be entrusted with the job, and they can be expected to be more perceptive and tactful than to 'stigmatize' a child as a predelinquent. It must be remembered, also, that, typically, the families involved are already the clients of social agencies for all sorts of problems other than delinquency.

If the argument of those who oppose the use of identification techniques to disclose which children are vulnerable were sound, we should logically close all of our child guidance clinics, dismiss our school counselors and visiting teachers, and sit back complacently (as, unfortunately, we too often do today) until the child has developed into a true delinquent or gang member and then haul him into court with the usual far from satisfactory result.

The choice presented to a community is whether its citizens prefer to let potentially delinquent children ripen into persistent offenders or to intervene, prophylactically, at a stage which gives the greatest promise of changing their dangerous attitudes and behavior, by

[49] Report by L. E. Ohlin to Third International Congress of Criminology, London, 1955; *Predicting delinquency and crime*, p. 150.

[50] 'No magic formula exists for identifying boys and girls who will later commit delinquent acts except by stigmatizing as "pre-delinquent" many who will never come before a court.' Report to the Congress on Juvenile Delinquency, U.S. Department of Health, Education, and Welfare, Children's Bureau. It is submitted that in the light of the discussion in the text, the quotation expresses a superficial interpretation and an unwise social policy. We have never claimed any 'magic formula'.

aiding parents to modify their damaging disciplinary and non-affectional attitudes and practices which have been found, in thousands of cases, to be potent influences in inclining children to delinquency. Our follow-up researches have consistently shown the tragic role of deep-rootedness in rendering antisocial behavior impervious to the usual methods of treatment thus far invented by society.[51] Finally, it should be pointed out that the application of the table might be limited to cases reported by teachers as presenting difficulties in class, in order to distinguish true delinquents from pseudo-delinquents, or the services offered the parents of a child found vulnerable can be voluntary, not compulsory; but it is hoped that with the passage of time parents will learn to welcome aid in the behavioral field as they have in the medical.

CONCLUSION

I have attempted to give due consideration to all the major criticisms leveled at *Unraveling Juvenile Delinquency*.[52] Naturally, the authors

[51] In *Predicting delinquency and crime*, p. 82, it is shown that in eighteen out of thirty prediction tables dealing with adult offenders and three of ten concerned with juvenile delinquents, during all forms of sentence-treatment and for fifteen years thereafter, the factor of *age at onset of antisocial behavior* had to be included as a differentiative indicator because of its strong predictive influence as between successes and failures. In all but four of the tables dealing with adult offenders, the *earlier the onset* of the delinquency, the higher the failure-score under one or another form of peno-correctional treatment and thereafter; or, to state it differently, the deeper the roots of childhood maladjustment, the smaller the chance of adult adjustment.

[52] There is a criticism by psychiatrists typified by the following statement, which I have not attempted to go into thoroughly because it would require a separate and lengthy paper: 'A truly dynamic approach . . . recognizes that any individual's behavior is the result of the interaction between internal and external forces, and can be understood dynamically not in terms of his membership in any class, but only in terms of his unique life situation—what he is reacting to and expressing in his behavior.' Satten in the Symposium in *Fed. Prob.* 15, 53. There is some truth in this, of course; but there is also the danger of the dynamic psychiatrist 'individualizing' quite inaccurately. To take account of all the influences of a single person's 'unique life situation' is something that only God can do. The criticism under discussion has been largely directed against the use of predictive devices in aid of clinician and judge. Here I can only say that it springs from a misconception of both the aims of *Unraveling* and the prediction tables developed therein. It is of course not intended that either clinicians or judges should make their decisions mechanically, exclusively on the 'odds' presented by the prediction device. The aim is not to substitute mechanical gadgets for either clinical or judicial expertise based on much experience but rather to furnish psychiatrist and judge an instrument reflecting *organized experience* based on the follow-up of numerous cases that have gone before. This is clearly superior to exclusive reliance on 'clinical experience' or judicial 'hunch'. Nor does it counteract such individualization as is possible. As the Illinois experience with a prediction device used in parole has shown, 'the net result of the use of the tables has been to challenge the application of mechanical formulas at every point and to force more detailed examination of the unique merits of the individual case'. Ohlin, quoted in *Prognosis of Recidivism*[(173)].

of that work are convinced, and I trust I have convinced the reader, that the theories advanced by the critics are essentially unsound. With ill-advised Olympian *hauteur*, two of our severest critics call attention to the literature on actuarial work which they claim we should have read.[53] In the light of the foregoing analysis, I trust they will forgive me if I too call attention to several bits of 'literature'.

First, I would call attention to the prescient judgment of Professor Edwin Bidwell Wilson: '*A priori* argument will not get far, howsoever it be extended. What one needs is trial and observation.'[54] And in this connection, some advice on the relation of theory to fact, offered by two distinguished scientists of the past, is not without relevancy:

In the wise bequest left by the eminent Russian physiologist-psychologist, Ivan Pavlov, just before his death in 1936, he said: 'Perfect as is the wing of a bird, it never would raise the bird up without resting on air. Facts are the air of a scientist. Without them your "theories" are vain efforts.'

And the distinguished physiologist Claude Bernard laid down this safe rule to follow: 'When you meet with a fact opposed to a prevailing theory, you should adhere to the fact and abandon the theory, even when the latter is supported by great authorities and generally adopted.'

[53] 'But then there is a technical literature on the technique of prediction' (Reiss). 'The relevant literature is so voluminous and lucid that ignorance can be no excuse for failure to meet criteria of acceptable research design. . . . It is supererogatory to publish an introduction to the book [*Predicting delinquency and crime*] by the Chief Justice of the United States Supreme Court [sic] calling for "unbiased consideration" of the authors' prediction tables on the part of "people of open minds, minds that are open to accept or reject the thesis solely on reason" ' (Duncan). Ah, we pure scientists!

In the light of the analysis in the text, I believe I can confidently leave it to the reader to judge for himself with whom the charge of supererogation might more fairly be lodged.

[54] Wilson (1951), Book review. *Harv. L. Rev.* **64**, 1039.

CHAPTER 18

Wanted: A Comparative Criminology[1]

SHELDON GLUECK

I

AT THE First International Congress on the Prevention of Crime and the Treatment of Offenders, held at Geneva in 1955, a basic suggestion was embodied in the final recommendation of that Congress in words which I quote:

'Comparative, co-ordinated, and interdisciplinary research should be carried out to determine the relative effects of programs in different countries' and 'through cooperation between researchers from different countries . . . to develop a highly promising new field of comparative criminology', in order to determine 'uniformities and differences in causal influences, in predictive factors, and in results of preventive and treatment programs' and to develop 'a true science of criminology'.[2]

I regret that the development of a Comparative Criminology—a project designed to uncover etiologic *universals* operative as causal agents irrespective of cultural differences among the different countries—has not proceeded more systematically and more rapidly. If Criminology is ever to deserve the name of science, its practitioners and researchers must employ the techniques of science. A basic technique of science is *replication*—the controlled repetition of an experiment to see if it yields results comparable to those in the original experiment. Criminology has made so little progress precisely because, instead of experimenters building on reliable pre-existent researches, they have usually insisted on carrying on investigations of their own in many directions, with little or no regard to what has gone before. The result has been that in various countries we have fragments of research structures, scattered helter-skelter, instead of a coherent texture built logically and strongly on a solid and ever-widening foundation.

---

[1] Lecture delivered at the Fourth International Congress on Criminology, The Hague, 8 September 1960.
[2] Ch. 15 of this volume.

304

It is the purpose of this lecture to specify some of the basic issues with which a Comparative Criminology might concern itself. These examples are drawn from the researches which have been conducted by my wife and myself, only because they are the findings with which I am most familiar; there are of course other fundamental researches which have been conducted by scholars in various lands. To mention but two which come to mind, the concepts of Sellin regarding the role of culture-conflict[3] and the extroversion-introversion 'dimension' of personality as related to delinquency-proneness and recidivism, presented in the report to the present Congress by Bartholomew,[4] deserve further exploration.

II

As to the researches by my wife and myself which might usefully be duplicated, first may I discuss a series of intensive *follow-up* investigations to check the post-institutional careers of various classes of offenders. We have made such check-up investigations during many years, beginning with *500 Criminal Careers*, a report published in 1930, continuing in 1934 with *One Thousand Juvenile Delinquents* and *Five Hundred Delinquent Women*, and embracing later investigations of the male offenders, juvenile and adult, which spanned a fifteen-year period.[5] This type of project is continuing with the follow-up of the 500 delinquents and the 500 non-delinquents who were the subjects of *Unraveling Juvenile Delinquency*.[6] The tracing of these youths until the age of twenty-five was completed two years ago and the findings have been tabulated; but we are continuing the check-up of the two groups until they reach thirty-two years of age. It is too early to be specific about the findings; but it may be said that the changes that have taken place in the criminal history of the delinquents appear to follow the general pattern established in our various prior researches, which have all indicated that, with advancing years (and especially in the early thirties), there is a slowing up of criminal activity with a reduction in recidivism. It might be pointed out also

---

[3] T. Sellin (1938), *Culture, conflict and crime*, Bull. 41, Social Science Research Council, New York. See also Culture conflict and delinquency[73].

[4] Allen A. Bartholomew, Prediction studies and personality factors. Fourth International Criminological Congress, The Hague, 1960, Preparatory Papers M.

[5] The follow-up studies thus far published by Sheldon and Eleanor Glueck are: *500 criminal careers*[26], *One thousand juvenile delinquents*[45], *Five hundred delinquent women*[44], *Later criminal careers*[71], *Juvenile delinquents grown up*[85], *Criminal careers in retrospect*[102], *After-conduct of discharged offenders*[119]. The follow-up study of the 500 delinquents and 500 non-delinquents embraced in *Unraveling juvenile delinquency*[138] is still in process.

[6] See also Ch. 17 of this volume.

that the vast majority of the boys originally selected as true non-delinquents to be compared with the delinquents, when setting up the research reported on in *Unraveling*, are still, after ten years, in fact not delinquent.

This audience hardly needs to be persuaded of the importance of follow-up studies. Let me, however, remind you of a few of the values derived, apart from the construction of a substantial arc of the life-cycle of offenders which may have an important bearing on under-standing the life experiences of law-abiding persons as well.

First, as many of you know, we found that the incidence of *recidivism* among juveniles and young-adults who have passed through the portals of the courts and industrial schools and reforma-tories is very marked. It was established, through intensive tracing of the after-careers of large samples of delinquents and criminals in the Commonwealth of Massachusetts (an American state with average or better than average agencies for the administration of criminal justice) that there is far more repetition of crime among offenders subjected to various forms of peno-correctional treatment than had previously been claimed. While it had frequently been announced, in official reports and at congresses of penologists, that some 80 per cent or more of the 'graduates' of juvenile courts and young men's reformatories are 'successes' in the sense that they never commit crimes again during a reasonable period of time thereafter, intensive, unbiased investigation proved that the true picture is practically the reverse.

Thus, of a group of 905 (out of a total of 1,000) *juvenile* delinquents appearing in the Boston Juvenile Court (and committed to industrial schools for correction) who were examined (but not treated) by a well-known clinic, some 88 per cent continued to be delinquent during a five-year test-span thereafter.[7] Similarly, during a five-year period following completion of sentence to the Massachusetts Reformatory, some 80 per cent of 422 of 510 *young-adult* offenders about whom relevant information could be obtained continued to commit crimes.

[7] The 'typicality' of the delinquents embraced in this study had been widely doubted and it was claimed that the high failure-rate was attributable to the supposed practice of the judges of this court to send to the clinic for investigation and report only the more seriously recalcitrant cases. However, William Healy, Augusta E. Bronner and Myra E. Shimberg, taking another sample of a thousand Boston delinquents who were the general run of the mill of the Juvenile Court (i.e. those who 'passed through the . . . court, but were not referred . . . to the' clinic), and following them up, in a study significantly entitled 'The close of another chapter in criminology', concluded that 'the results of the two studies [the Gluecks' and theirs] are amply corroborative'. Healy, Bronner & Shimberg (1935), The close of another chapter in criminology. *Ment. Hyg.* **19**, 208.

In the United States, these findings helped to shatter the hopeful illusion that the traditional régimes of industrial schools and reformatories are in fact very effective in preventing the further development of criminal careers, and to start movements for intensive re-examination of fundamentals in the administration of criminal justice as well as a search for *preventive* programs, instead of an emphasis on corrective efforts.

The question I would put to this audience is: What would the picture be in your countries? So far a few follow-up studies have been made in England and a beginning has been made in Japan; but systematic, objective appraisals of the efficacy of reformative, corrective, and punitive systems in other countries, in terms of the proportion of former prisoners who recidivate, and through which age-spans they do so, still wait to be made. If they were indeed made accurately, and with a serious attempt to follow the techniques found useful in the American studies, a great step forward would be taken toward a Comparative Criminology.

Let me give a few illustrations of the topics with which such a multinational follow-up program might be concerned:

(*a*) In comparing the criminality of the young-adult offenders who passed through the Massachusetts Reformatory, during three stages —pre-reformatory period, parole[8] stage, and five-year post-parole span[9]—it was found that there were measurably fewer 'total failures' (that is, continued serious offenders) and more successes (that is, non-offenders) during the parole stage than during either the pre-reformatory period or the post-parole span.[10] Claims for the great success of the parole process too frequently ignore the distinction between adequate response of parolees *during the period of active supervision* and their avoidance of criminal behavior *during a reasonable test period*, say five years, thereafter, when they are completely on their own. The proposed multinational studies might take this basic distinction into account in countries where parole, or some

---

[8] Parole is the release of an offender from prison to serve part of his original sentence in the community with some sort of supervision and under conditions imposed by the releasing agency.

[9] The average age of the ex-prisoners at the end of the first five-year check-up following expiration of their sentence to the Massachusetts Reformatory was thirty years; they were thirty-five, on the average, at the close of the second five-year follow-up, and forty at the end of the third.

[10] *500 criminal careers*, p. 190. It is sometimes said that since it is impossible to check on all crimes actually committed, it is futile to make follow-up studies. In answer to such a nihilistic point of view I would remind the reader that it *is* possible, through conscientious checking on all official and non-official records, to obtain a reliable appraisal of the true picture. The reader is invited to consult the chapters on method in the works listed in note 5.

equivalent provision, is in force. And a similar distinction should be made of behavior during a period of pre-institutional probation granted by a court, and a reasonable post-probation test period.

(*b*) Again, in our investigations we studied not merely the changes in behavior so far as the commission or non-commission of crime is concerned, but also alterations in *conduct other than criminal*. To obtain a fair assessment of the efficiency of a reformatory or a parole system it is not enough to ascertain merely the criminal history; for antisocial behavior is typically not something detached from the personality as a whole and does not operate as a thing apart from a person's other attitudes, values, and activities. As a consequence, the institution's and parole agency's techniques of reformation and rehabilitation cannot afford to ignore these other intertwined aspects of conduct, personality, and character, if they expect to get relatively permanent results in reducing recidivism. The processes of reformation and rehabilitation involve the teaching of trades, the inculcation of habits of industry, the introduction of the offender to wholesome means of self-expression in recreational matters, the provision of the aid and comfort of religion, and other such activities intended to make it easier and more attractive for him to lead a law-abiding life than to continue in criminalistic ways.

Let me give a few illustrations of the expressions of character which we studied in addition to criminalistic behavior:

1. The research published under the title of *500 Criminal Careers* had revealed that the work habits of the young-adult offenders under investigation had been *good*[11] (by standard definition, in terms of steadiness of employment and devotion to duty) in only 19·8 per cent of the cases during the pre-reformatory stage (based on 378 cases as to which reliable information on this point was available) and rose to the appreciable proportion of 33·6 per cent during the post-parole five-year test period (based on 399 cases); the work habits had been *fair* in 27·7 and 24·5 per cent within the respective periods, this category remaining virtually unchanged; and *poor* in 52·5 and 41·9 per cent during the periods under comparison, an appreciable reduction (p. 193).

2. Again, as to *industrial capacity*, 13·8 per cent of the men had been *skilled* workers during the pre-reformatory stage (based on 505 cases), and 17·5 per cent during the post-parole period (434 cases); 32·1 and 41 per cent, respectively, were *semi-skilled*, and 54·1 and

[11] Where detailed definitions of terms in the text are not given, the reader is referred to the books listed in note 5.

41·5 per cent, respectively, were *unskilled* (p. 194). Here too, then, there is some improvement, albeit modest.

Information of this type is of course related to the definition of the tasks presented to a reformatory in its efforts to strengthen the equipment of its charges so as to make it easier for them to get along in society without committing crimes.

3. Throwing light on the relationship between the rehabilitative efforts of the Massachusetts Reformatory and their effect upon the inmates after they left the institution is the finding that although 397 men had been engaged in the reformatory's industries long enough to learn at least the rudiments of the trades taught therein, only 131 men (33 per cent) actually used the occupations taught at the reformatory, at some time during the parole or post-parole periods, while 233 men (58·7 per cent) never used the reformatory-taught occupations at all when returned to freedom. Moreover, in 325 cases (or 63·9 per cent of the total) there was no relation between the trades and skills taught in the reformatory (and not known by the men before they entered the institution) and those at which they worked during the parole or post-parole period (p. 198). (It must be remembered in this connection that many years have elapsed since the follow-up studies were made, and no doubt there has been some improvement in the situation.)

4. Classifying the men into categories of success or failure in the *meeting of their economic obligations* to their dependents, it was found that none of the group could be designated '*good*' in this respect during the pre-reformatory stage (based on 396 cases) and only 11·5 per cent could be so judged during the post-parole period (366 cases) (p. 201).

5. Similar analyses were made of the marital and family relationships of the men during the periods in question.

For example, during the five-year post-parole period, there occurred an appreciable increase in the number of men whose relationship to the family could be designated '*good*'.[12] Thus, of a

[12] The standard of socially acceptable conduct in family relationships was the following: The man must not be harming his family in any injurious way; that is, if married, he must not neglect or desert wife or children and must not be separated or divorced from his wife, not have illicit relations with other women, nor be abusive to wife or children or continually away evenings. If single and living away from home, he must be in touch with parents or nearest relatives. If single and living at home he must have given evidence that he considers home more than merely a convenient place to sleep and eat in; for example, he must not be continually out evenings, or living at home only when in need of funds. If a man's relationship with his family in the above noted respects was especially wholesome, he was classified as '*good*'. If he just met the standard, he was classified as '*fair*'. If he failed to meet it, he was classified as '*poor*'.

total of 377 known post-parole cases, 20·2 per cent could be called *good* in their post-parole family relationships, 34·2 per cent *fair*, 45·6 per cent *poor*, compared to none good, 31·6 per cent fair and 68·4 per cent poor during the stage prior to the men's sentence to the Massachusetts Reformatory (p. 205).

6. Again, in respect to use of leisure and to habits, there was improvement as between the pre-reformatory and post-parole stages. In the former, none of the young men could be classified as '*constructive*'[13] in this regard; and while only 3·5 per cent could be designated constructive in the post-parole period, the harmful category fell from 96·5 to 61·8 per cent, and the negative group increased from 3·5 per cent in the pre-reformatory stage to 34·7 per cent in the post-parole (p. 210).

There were similar evidences of improvement in other matters apart from criminal activity; but space does not permit of their setting down here.

The foregoing illustrations suggest the importance of analyzing *contrasts* between the stage prior to an offender's conviction for a crime and the stages of parole and at least a brief period thereafter. Further follow-ups, during two subsequent five-year periods— making a total of fifteen years since the men left the reformatory— disclosed very significant changes both in criminalism and in other aspects of behavior.

7. For example, while, during the first five years after completion of sentence only 19·9 per cent of the young-adult former inmates of the reformatory about whom information was available remained nondelinquent, the proportions of non-offenders during the second and third five-year spans rose to 30·1 per cent and 30·8 per cent, an obvious though static improvement with the passage of time.[14] The former juvenile delinquents as a group also improved with the passage of the years, the amelioration as between the first and second period being, however, much greater than thereafter.

8. So, also, the investigation over the three post-institutional periods

[13] For a man to be classified in the '*constructive*' category he had to be a member of a well-supervised social group for youth, such as the Y.M.C.A., he had to utilize his leisure to further himself culturally or vocationally (as by attendance at nightschool), and he had to be free from conspicuous bad habits of the kind indicated below. To be placed in the '*negative*' group he must at least not have been engaged in harmful activities, even though not utilizing his time constructively. Further, he must have had no marked bad habits. Those who were using their spare time harmfully, who had pronounced bad habits and associations, who were indulging in forms of recreation which might lead to criminal conduct (such as membership in gangs, association with bootleggers, prostitutes, and loafers, drug addiction, excessive drinking or gambling, sex immorality), were classified in the '*harmful*' category.

[14] *Criminal careers in retrospect*, p. 350.

showed some improvements—though not very marked—in family relationships and in certain aspects of the economic status of the men. For example, the moral standards of the home had to be classified as poor in 37·1 per cent of the families in a second follow-up period of five years, but fell to 29·1 per cent in the third period; and while the 'good' category remained essentially unchanged, there was a rise from 22·8 to 32·7 per cent as between Periods II and III in the 'fair' category (ibid., p. 331).

9. As one aspect of the economic situation, good work habits rose from 19·8 per cent in the pre-reformatory stage to 35·1 per cent in the first follow-up five-year period, to 41·2 and 42·9 per cent in Periods II and III (p. 339). So, also, there was ultimate improvement in respect to steadiness of employment, the average length of time a job was held having been 14·7 months in the first follow-up period, 10·7 in the second and 18·1 in the third (p. 340).

Without going into further detail about other indices of change in economic status, it might be said that on the whole the men at least retained, during the third follow-up span, many of the gains they had achieved in the second, although they did not make further substantial progress.

In a report we submitted to the Congress[223] we mentioned other follow-up studies we have been conducting over the years; and when their results are analyzed we hope to be in a position to say which features are *universal* (or at least quite general) so far as American urban culture is concerned.

Findings of this kind are of great importance in leading to an assessment of both institutional and post-institutional efforts in any region under study; and a comparative analysis of such findings in different countries would enhance knowledge of the influences involved and of the types of programs best suited to regions of differing cultural traditions, economic resources, and political systems. Moreover, by comparing outcomes on the basis of recidivism or non-recidivism in countries with penal-code emphases on the retributive and deterrent objectives of the law in contrast with those adhering largely to the reformative and rehabilitative aims, important clues might be obtained as to the actual value, in terms of social defense against recidivism, of the different peno-correctional philosophies as implemented by institutions and régimes.

III

Let me next consider another problem worthy of comparative research; especially in view of the recent tendency in a number of countries to develop their industrial potential as a means of raising the general standard of living. I refer to the fact of the increasing mobility of the residents in cities and the enticement of many farmers and an increasing number of housewives into urban industrial occupations. The neighborhood turnover of population is one of the marked social phenomena which have accompanied the tremendous growth of urban communities and the continuous acceleration of industrial activity in modern America and in certain other lands. This has had an influence on the quantity and nature of delinquency and crime, largely, I believe, through its direct effect on family life. The extent to which and the manner in which industrialization and urbanization have enhanced the incidence not only of delinquency but of various other societal problems in countries undergoing rapid social transformation might well be a topic for systematic comparative multinational research, employing, as nearly as possible, uniform standard techniques and definitions.

But it is time that I pointed out that these complex problems do not lend themselves to so-called research by means of questionnaires sent out to governments from some distant bureaucrat. They must be done carefully and objectively by trained scholars and experts in research methods. It is self-evident that such researchers must not be put in any position which makes it likely that they will be influenced by political or propagandistic motivation.

IV

Another field for much needed comparative research of a multi-cultural character is the study of *causation*.

Lawyers are familiar with the conception that at the basis of 'criminal intent' or '*mens rea*' is the generally accepted assumption that adult human beings are normally possessed of a 'free will'. If, therefore, they violate the penal law, it is deemed to be just to punish them, since they could, *ex hypothesi*, have avoided such violation. This procedure is also deemed efficient, on the assumption that the infliction of punishment is both a preventive of repetition of crime on the part of the person punished and a deterrent to prospective offenders. Thus, in a sense, the substantive-criminal law proceeds on a very simple unilateral theory of causation. However, criminologic research has indicated that there are many traits and factors involved in the motivation and conditioning of antisocial behavior, and that such biologic and environmental influences are much more capable of study, and afford much more concrete and manageable data regarding causal sequences, than does philosophic or theologic speculation as to whether Man, in the abstract, possesses free will or is wholly governed by a deterministic chain of cause-and-effect.

This does not mean, as has been assumed by some, that there is no trace whatsoever of conscious, purposive self-guidance in behavior. It means, merely, that just as individuals vary in physique, temperament, and intelligence, so also do they vary in the degree to which they are able to manifest freedom of conscious choice. Unfortunately, science is not yet able to measure the extent of this capacity in individuals as it can, roughly, measure the degree of intelligence; but it can, more or less, measure and weigh the specific and obvious *interferences* with the capacity for free choice in individuals. The more that the correctional system of the future has as its aim the removal of the *handicaps* to efficient and happy yet law-abiding life, handicaps under which most offenders have been shown to labor, the more will it be able to release and increase the adaptive capacity of conscious, purposive self-direction within limits laid down by natural endowment in individual instances, and thereby enhance the preference for lawful, as opposed to criminalistic, conduct.

A *transnational* study, employing as nearly as possible standardized methods and uniform definitions, might well contribute to a more reliable *multi-causal* approach to the understanding and treatment of criminal behavior than at present exists. In this way, it might also contribute to the development of more realistic penal codes, to a redesign of techniques of treatment of the convicted offender, and to the setting up of more pointed programs of prophylaxis and prevention.

In this connection may I call your attention to such studies as *One Thousand Juvenile Delinquents* and *Unraveling Juvenile Delinquency*. It would take too long to give specific findings or clues of real significance that these two studies (especially the latter) have yielded. Let me however urge that they are the type of researches which deserve careful *repetition* by other investigators, using similar definitions and techniques but applying them in regions with a different culture from that of urban America. A beginning in this direction has been made in Japan; and it would contribute greatly to the establishment of a true science of Criminology if the techniques of *Unraveling* were replicated by competent researchers elsewhere. The keynote of this type of research is the *multidisciplinary approach*, which, despite the skepticism of certain criminologists,[15] has yielded a richer harvest of knowledge and understanding of causation than any other method. I will speak later of one of the fruits of this approach—the technique of prediction.

---

[15] See Ch. 17 of this volume.

V

Another important topic that might be pursued in multinational investigation is a check-up on the concept of *maturation* which has emerged from some of our researches. In earlier works we gathered a general impression that a substantial proportion of our offenders, both male and female, presented a picture suggestive of the delayed or persistent adolescent—a person mature in years but immature in respect to *affective* development and to the harmonious integration of emotional, intellectual, and physical aspects of the total personality. In the research we published under the title *Later Criminal Careers*, in which a follow-up span of two five-year periods beyond completion of the sentence to the Massachusetts Reformatory was involved, this impression of immaturity and lack of integration among a large proportion of our offenders was enhanced. By a process of analysis in which we compared the incidence of non-recidivism among the former prisoners during the first and the second five-year follow-up spans as related to the presence or absence of one or another of numerous factors included in the research, it was found that while many of these factors bore no significant relationship to the decrease of recidivism with the passage of time up to the age-span of thirty-one to thirty-five years, and others were but slightly related, the factor of *aging* was apparently of considerable significance.

However, closer examination of the evidence led us to the conclusion that it is not the reaching of the age of thirty-one to thirty-five years *per se* that is important, but rather the *stage in the course of an offender's criminalistic career* at which he reaches that age-span; that is, whether he becomes thirty-one to thirty-five years old at a time in his career that is still *close to the origins* of his delinquent tendencies or reaches that age relatively late in his criminalistic career, when he is already many years beyond the early childhood beginnings of his delinquent tendencies.

This fundamental conception led us, in *Juvenile Delinquents Grown Up*, wherein we dealt with *three* five-year follow-up spans beyond the end of the offender's contact with the juvenile court, to go more thoroughly into the *content* of age. A man's age, as measured by the calendar, denotes merely that he has been alive a certain number of years; it gives no indication of the nature of his life so far as biologic development is concerned. This fact, of course, is seen most strikingly among the feebleminded, some of whom are of middle or even older age chronologically, yet at the stage of infancy or childhood intellectually or emotionally.

To test whether it is aging *per se* or the content of aging that is the significant influence, we developed, in *Juvenile Delinquents Grown Up*, a series of tables comparing the incidence of criminalism among former delinquents in various age-spans during *three* five-year follow-up periods. Comparing the results with those of the prior investigation, we concluded more confidently that the tendency to abandon criminalism is not attributable to arrival at any chronologic age-span; but that it is the *maturation* process, which often but not always occurs with the passage of time, and which is sometimes delayed, or uneven, in development among different individuals, that in considerable measure accounts for the giving up of aggressive behavior expressed in criminalism. The two groups of offenders, studied independently of one another and at different stages of society's official apparatus for coping with criminalism (that is, juvenile court and industrial school, on the one hand, and criminal court and reformatory for adults, on the other), were found to have been very similar in the extent of abandonment of recidivism at the *same average distance away from the original onset of their criminal careers.* Therefore, it seems reasonable to infer that, despite the varying external influences to which these two groups had been subjected, there must have been some underlying biologic process in their lives, related to their development from the time of the onset of their delinquent behavior, which exerted a fundamental influence on the evolution and devolution of their criminal careers.[16]

At any rate, here is another important concept—both biologically and from the point of view of a more rational and realistic determination of the average length of sentence which will most probably keep offenders out of harm-dealing circulation—that deserves testing through Comparative Criminology; the idea, namely, that it is not so much the peno-correctional efforts thus far devised which bring about a reduction in recidivism as it is the combined influence of Father Time and Mother Nature as related to the time at which delinquent behavior began.

VI

I turn next to another concept that requires testing on diverse ethnic samples. In *Unraveling*, one of the most interesting yet controversial findings was the presence of the *mesomorphic* constitution (the closely-knit, muscular, athletically inclined type) in some 60 per cent of our delinquents (who had previously been matched with their

[16] Père Dr Maurice Verdun, a distinguished French anthropologist, has recently made a contribution to defining the physical-psychiatric attributes of maturation. See, M. Verdun, Anthropo-Biométrie et Mâturation, Extrait des *Rapports au Premier Congrès Européen de Pédo-Psychiatrie*, Paris, September 1960.

non-delinquent opposite numbers in respect to ethnico-racial derivation) compared to only 30 per cent of the non-delinquent control group; and, contrastingly, a far lower incidence of *ectomorphy* (the thin, fragile type) among delinquents than among non-delinquents. The importance of comparing delinquents with non-delinquents in terms of physique-type lies in the probability that the dominance of one or another of the three root components (the third is *endomorphy*, in which softness and roundness of the body predominate) may well involve basic variations in energy output, in temperament and in affect, as well as differential response to similar sociocultural stimuli.

In a book entitled *Physique and Delinquency*[176], we presented proof of the importance of body-type in influencing the relation to various criminogenic traits and factors. For example, in comparison with other physique-types, and especially in contrast to the fragile, linear ectomorphs, boys belonging to the muscular, mesomorphic physique-type were found to possess such characteristics as greater strength, less sensitivity, less submissiveness to authority, less emotional instability and other such traits—a picture of daring and enterprise together with the dynamic tendency to unrestrained action which add up to a higher *delinquency-potential* among mesomorphs than among the other body-types. The ectomorphs, on the other hand, were found to be more inclined to phantasy, more sensitive, less stable emotionally, more prone to emotional conflict, more inhibited in motor responses to stimuli, tending rather to 'bottle up' their impulses than to resolve their tensions in action as do the mesomorphs. As pointed out, such differences in characteristics of these two most contrasting physique-types were reflected in the finding that in a random sample of 500 true delinquents taken from the underprivileged areas of Boston and matched by ethnico-racial origin, 60·1 per cent of the boys were classifiable as mesomorphs while only 14·4 per cent were ectomorphs, these figures contrasting with 30·7 per cent mesomorphs and 39·6 per cent ectomorphs among the 500 *non*-delinquents with whom the delinquents were compared.

Correlatively to the contrasting traits of the mesomorphs and ectomorphs, there were also dissimilar responses to such influences of family life as broken homes, emotional disturbances in parents, mothers working outside the home, lack of family cohesiveness, inadequate maternal supervision of child, parental incompatibility, and many others. Such factors of home and family life have more of an effect on the anti-social behavior of ectomorphs than of mesomorphs, in contributing selectively to their delinquency; over-reactivity is the keynote to the response of this more fragile and sensitive physique-type. However, the great majority of ectomorphs respond to deleterious home influences by neurotic symptoms instead of delinquency.

Here, then, is another field of research in which replications of our investigation might be helpful. I believe a beginning in somatotype-study among delinquents has been made in England, where Borstal youths examined anthropometrically were found, as in our sample, to show an excess of the mesomorphic physique type. Italian researchers, such as Professor Benigno Di Tullio of the University of Rome, are also interested in somatotype investigations. It is hoped that in other countries this type of research will be stimulated, also, as part of the broader interdisciplinary design employed in *Unraveling*.

VII

I come, next, to what is perhaps the most important aspect of our researches—the prediction device. We believe that the idea and the technique of prediction comprise the most fruitful and promising 'break-through' in the entire history of criminology.

This is so for several reasons:

In the first place, some device has long been needed to render manageable the numerous, varied, and complexly interrelated traits and factors which at one time or another were deemed to be involved in the etiology of delinquency. It would be superfluous to review, before this audience, the various theories and 'causes' which, at one time or another, have been given special etiologic significance, beginning with the theories of the forerunners of Lombroso, carrying on with the views of the outstanding investigators of the Italian and French Schools, and continuing, in our day, with the findings of the sociologists, psychiatrists, and psychologists.

What has long been needed is some way of reducing this not always consistent multiplicity of traits and factors to the few that have been proved, in fact, to make a *significant difference* in terms of behavior.

This is what the carefully constructed prediction table does at psychologic, psychiatric, and sociocultural levels. On the basis of statistical correlation of numerous traits and factors with delinquency on the one hand and non-delinquency on the other, with recidivism and with non-recidivism as related to each of the existing forms of sentence and peno-correctional treatment, with post-institutional conduct while offenders are on parole, and during a reasonable period thereafter, only those traits and factors are retained for use in prediction tables which have in fact proved themselves to be most

317

extensively related to varieties of behavior and which have thereby established themselves as the influences—direct or indirect—that are truly *relevant*, and hence etiologic in a realistic sense.

In *Predicting Delinquency and Crime*[212] we present an entire system of prediction devices based on over thirty years of research. These include tables to be used in identifying potential delinquents at the early age of five or six, when they first enter school; tables to aid juvenile court and adult court judges in choosing among alternative types of sentence on the basis of those traits and factors which have, in the past, in fact characterized successes. as opposed to failures under each form of sentence and accompanying treatment; tables to be used by parole boards in connection with the release of prisoners; tables involving male offenders and those concerned with female offenders.

From this variety of predictive instruments it can be seen that it is not only in contributing to the better management of the etiologic problem that prediction devices are of prime significance, but also in giving to judges and parole authorities practical instruments for a more realistic sentencing and releasing program. Prediction tables place before the judge and the releasing authority the organized experience with many hundreds of cases that have gone before, and in respect to which the relationship of various traits and factors in the make-up and background of different types of offenders has been systematically correlated with varieties of behavioral response. In the light of these tables, then, the judge and the releasing authority (and the same is true of the clinician) can assess the individual case before them. This is done by comparing the instant case with the tabulated results in respect to hundreds of similar cases about which past experience can illumine the case under immediate consideration.

This does not mean, as those who persist in misunderstanding or misstating the nature of prediction devices claim, that tables will replace judges, parole officials, and clinicians; quite the contrary, predictive devices will enrich the decision-making function of these authorities and render it much more realistic.

We are well aware of the fact that until such tables have been validated successfully on samples of cases other than those on which the prediction devices have been constructed, such tables are only theoretical; and in *Predicting Delinquency and Crime* we present the results of several validation experiments, including a sixteen-year follow-up of the boys involved in *Unraveling* to whom the prediction table indications presented in the prior study of *One Thousand Juvenile Delinquents* were applied with marked success in forecasting their varied responses to ordinary probation and probation with suspended sentence; to commitment to a boys' industrial school, sentence to a young men's reformatory, sentence to jail, to house of correction, and to prison; to release on parole; and to the events of life during many years after the offenders had passed through the processes of criminal justice.

Predicting Delinquency and Crime also reports on several validation experiments dealing with the table based on five parent-child relationships and designed to identify *future* delinquents at an early age; and Chs. 8, 13 above set forth in greater detail the results of these check-ups not only in the United States but in France and Japan. Those of you who heard the interesting address, at the recent United Nations-sponsored Congress in London, by Juhei Takeuchi, Director, Criminal Affairs Bureau, Ministry of Justice, Tokyo,[17] must have been persuaded of the great importance attached by Japanese scholars and practitioners to systematically organized prognostic devices for identifying potential delinquents and recidivists. Indeed, the Japanese are also working on prediction tables designed to aid prosecutors and police officials to exercise their discretion more meaningfully.

I am, of course, fully aware that the prediction method has been subjected to criticism. In the book, *Predicting Delinquency and Crime*, we devote an entire chapter to considerations of objections raised to prediction. I invite your attention to that chapter as well as to my article, 'Ten Years of *Unraveling Juvenile Delinquency*—An Examination of Criticisms' (Ch. 17 above). In the meantime, I wish to emphasize the great promise of predictive research in the development of a Comparative Criminology and Penology.

VIII

There is yet another field in which a Comparative Criminology would prove illuminating; and that is the subject-matter of much of the present Congress, which includes the relationship of legal definitions and procedures to psychiatric and psychologic diagnostic patterns. The specific topic has been touched upon by Professor Paul Tappan in his workmanlike general report to this Congress.[18] If time permitted I would enlarge upon this highly significant area of cross-disciplinary conceptions and approaches to the serious social issues presented by groups of offenders—defective delinquents,

[17] Juhei Takeuchi, Juvenile Delinquency in Japan—Characteristics and Preventive Programs, *Second United Nations Congress on the Prevention and Treatment of Offenders*, London, August 1960.

[18] General Report II², Sexual Offences, by Paul W. Tappan, *Fourth International Criminological Congress*, The Hague, 1960, pp. 16–18.

psychopaths, and others—who present special psychiatric and psychologic problems as well as problems of legal definition, lawful court procedure designed to protect the rights of such offenders, and the relationship of the limits of effective legal action to the limitations of psychiatric diagnosis and therapy. Let me just briefly mention one example out of my own experience:

Some ten years ago I had two students in my Seminar on the Administration of Criminal Justice at the Harvard Law School examine, realistically, the situation of the so-called defective delinquents, from the points of view of the statutory provisions, the actual commitment procedures which were being used, the institution to which the defective delinquents were sent by the courts, and the corrective-therapeutic measures actually employed in that institution. Massachusetts is one of the first American states to have provided special law, procedure, and facilities for defective delinquents. The students found that the statute was too loosely drawn both in definition of 'defective delinquent' and in provisions of procedure; that not a few prisoners had been committed for periods without upper limit—which could mean for life—and had served many years, on the basis of proceedings that were open to serious question from the point of view of legal rights and remedies; that the place to which they had been committed by summary proceedings and without thorough prior psychiatric and psychologic examination was not a special hospital for mental and emotional defectives but rather an antiquated prison, a 'dumping ground'; and that little or no psychiatric, psychologic or educational treatment facilities had been provided. Partly as the result of the publication of the students' report, many inmates of the institution for defective delinquents had to have their cases re-heard—sometimes after long imprisonment, not a few of them had to be released, and the spotlight of public opinion was played on a very swampy area of the relationship of law to psychiatry.[19]

The tragedy, however, was not merely that of these men who had been imprisoned under less than desirable legal proceedings, but also that of some pioneers in psychiatry and psychology at whose

[19] 'The body of our study has been concerned with the abuses which are the inevitable consequence of a statute so loosely drawn that the roles of judge, lawyer, psychiatrist and administrator are undefined.' E. A. Gordon & L. Harris, An investigation and critique of the defective delinquent statute in Massachusetts (1950). *Boston Univ. L. Rev.* **30,** 459. Since 1 June 1953, nearly 250 male defective delinquents have been discharged after hearings by the Superior Courts of Massachusetts, because their original commitments were found to be procedurally improper. Upon further psychiatric examination, eighty-eight were recommitted because found to be dangerous or a menace to the public; seventeen were recommitted, after hearing on habeas corpus, on adjudication that the original commitments were proper.

initiative and after years of hard work the defective delinquent statute had originally been enacted as a great reform. This is an illustration of the indispensability of disciplining desirable reform—that is, the substitution of scientific therapeutic measures for retributive penal sanctions—by the rule of law. Legal protections must go hand in hand with psychiatric, psychologic, and educational advances. Here, then, is a field in which comparative research in a number of key countries might yield fruitful clues to a sounder definition of statutory terms; a more just procedure for commitment, periodic reassessment of status, and release; and more realistic therapeutic experimentation.

There are several other fundamental areas in which comparative research might yield rich harvests. But this chapter is already too long.

Let me, then, close with a warning that I mentioned previously. Research is one thing; propaganda another. The type of research which will expand the borders of knowledge cannot be done by the questionnaire method, or by pontifical speeches, or by untrained investigators. It requires day-to-day imaginative, informed, steady, and objective investigation, devotion to the ideals of science in assembling and verifying the raw materials, and caution in their interpretation. Even in the pure sciences, the best investigators can make mistakes in technique. One is reminded of the great Japanese-American bacteriologist, the late Dr Hideo Noguchi, working in the laboratories of the Rockefeller Institute. When he announced the epoch-making discovery of the spyrochete of syphilis by means of his development of a method of staining brain sections and of a culture-medium for breeding the spyrochete, skeptical bacteriologists attacked his findings, claiming that by following his method they did not achieve his results. Noguchi was able to show that these critics had in fact not exactly followed his techniques; and when he corrected their method they too arrived at his findings.

Even more necessary is it, in the discipline of criminology, to be accurate and objective in method. In an enterprise dealing with human nature, the achievement of these ideals is especially difficult. But we must keep them ever before us; and by the comparison of experience among researchers in different countries we can at least reduce egregious errors.

Let me repeat what I said at the outset to the effect that the illustrations I have given of the types of fundamental findings and conceptions that might lend themselves to *transnational* research and thereby enhance the area of Comparative Criminology are of course not limited to the investigations I happen to be most familiar with.

They do, however, point up one basic fact; and that is *the need to build upon pre-existing foundations.*

One final matter: In building a science of Comparative Criminology all of us must strive our utmost not to be hypnotized by authoritative or pseudo-authoritative opinions; and that includes the opinions expressed in this paper.

For, as Dostoevsky long ago penetratingly observed in *The House of the Dead*, 'With ready-made opinions one cannot judge of crime. Its philosophy is a little more complicated than people think.' Bearing this fact in mind, I hope you will do me the honor of reflecting upon the opinions I have expressed.

CHAPTER 19

A Decade of Research in Criminology: Stock-taking and a Forward Look *

SHELDON AND ELEANOR GLUECK

I

WE have been impelled to prepare this paper by the fact that we are now rounding out a decade of support from the Ford Foundation, which has not only been generous in funds but has given us the cherished freedom to pursue our researches in any direction that seemed promising to us. There is no greater encouragement than this to the researcher.

Before we focus on the last ten years, we should point out that our joint research endeavors began in 1925 with a comment by Sheldon Glueck in a seminar at Harvard University conducted by the late Dr Richard Clarke Cabot, entitled 'The Kingdom of Evils', that it is high time for an evaluation of the effectiveness of peno-correctional treatment. For fifteen years thereafter we devoted ourselves to follow-up studies of three groups of offenders—500 'graduates' of the Massachusetts Reformatory for Men, 500 'graduates' of the Reformatory for Women, and 1,000 juvenile offenders who had passed through the Boston Juvenile Court and been referred to the famous Judge Baker Guidance Center for diagnosis and for recommendations regarding treatment. The first follow-up investigation covered a five-year period; we did not go further in the case of the women offenders. We followed the two groups of males for a total of fifteen years.

In 1940 we launched into the comprehensive study of 500 young delinquents and 500 matched non-delinquents which resulted in the publication in 1950 of *Unraveling Juvenile Delinquency*[138]. Some researchers might have ceased their work at this point, but we saw so many facets in the data emerging from *Unraveling* that we were impelled to continue; and, fortunately, this became possible with the financial assistance of the Ford Foundation supplemented for

* Address delivered at the Annual Banquet of the Harvard Voluntary Defenders, Harvard University, Cambridge, Massachusetts, 15 April 1963.

five years by the National Institute of Mental Health and several small private foundations.

While the investigations cannot be said to comprise a completely coherent system, we think it fair to say that they at least approximate the scientific tradition in spirit and method. This dictates that investigations should grow systematically, building on preceding work, and thereby contributing more and more to the construction of a unified factual and theoretical structure.

II

When the recent decade of our work began we had already published *Unraveling*. The grant from the Ford Foundation made it possible for us to follow up the 500 delinquents and 500 non-delinquents of *Unraveling* until age twenty-five and, later, until age thirty-two. When they were originally included in the inquiry these boys ranged in age from ten to seventeen, with an average age of about fourteen and a half years. Much has of course happened to them during the subsequent years. Now a tremendous task awaits us; the analysis of the numerous follow-up materials gathered on these thousand boys, the inter-correlation of the materials with the rich background data of *Unraveling*, and the interpretation of the findings.

III

In addition to the follow-up project, we carried on a number of other studies and activities that will now be summarized briefly, to give some insight into their individual value as parts of our overall research endeavor.

The first of the researches growing out of the findings of *Unraveling* is recorded in the volume *Physique and Delinquency*[176]. This investigation uncovered a significant relationship between anthropologically determined physique-types and delinquent as opposed to non-delinquent behavior mediated through temperamental and psychologic traits which were found to be differentially related to the various body structures (*mesomorphic, ectomorphic, endomorphic*, and *balanced*). While of course fully recognizing the influence of various social forces, we have long been of the opinion that American criminologists, in their preoccupation with the sociocultural 'causes' of delinquency and crime, have tended to overlook or minimize the crucial fact that such influences are *selective*. In *Unraveling* we had found that 60 per cent of the delinquents as compared with only 30 per cent of the non-delinquents (both groups having been previously matched in terms of ethnico-racial derivation) were *meso-morphs* (the closely-knit, bone-and-muscle, energetic type); while only 14 per cent of the delinquents in contrast with 39 per cent of the non-delinquents were *ectomorphs* (the thin, linear, fragile type).

We followed these clues further in *Physique and Delinquency*, the *leitmotiv* of that inquiry being indicated in the opening words of the volume:

'From time immemorial—in folklore, philosophic speculation, and literature—there have been attempts to link forms of bodily structure to traits of temperament, character, and conduct. The vigorous antics of Shakespeare's energetic shrew-tamer, Petruchio, the jealousy and envy of the "lean and hungry" Cassius, the indolence and gluttony of the fat knight Sir John Falstaff, the compensatory villainies of the "deformed, unfinished" Richard III —these are among the more familiar illustrations from literature.'

We regard *Physique and Delinquency* as important to Criminology because it is a serious attempt systematically to interrelate body structure with temperamental and psychologic traits; and it may therefore account for the *differing responses* of various types of persons to quite similar environmental stimuli. While the findings must of course be regarded with caution until replicative studies are made,[1] the clues appearing in *Physique and Delinquency* are already of value to clinicians. Two illustrations must suffice:

1. In respect to *mesomorphs* (the closely-knit, bone-and-muscle type), the following clues, among others, emerged. Such traits and characteristics as *susceptibility to contagion, feelings of not being taken care of, feelings of inadequacy, destructiveness, emotional instability,* and *emotional conflicts* were found to be relatively infrequent in the mesomorphic constitution. But, when they did occur in mesomorphs, they were seen to play a special criminogenic role in that physique habitus where they normally do not exist in excess. In such cases it becomes important for the clinician and his aides (social workers, probation officers, etc.) to take such mesomorphically *atypical* traits into account in the treatment-plan in order to provide satisfying emotional support and physical outlets for the youths involved.

2. The special *sensitivity* of *ectomorphs* (the thin, linear, fragile type),

---

[1] It might be said that two American studies indicate that the essential somatotype differences between delinquents and non-delinquents reported in *Unraveling* and in *Physique and Delinquency* have been found to exist in other samples of cases. See W. Sheldon (1950), *Varieties of delinquent behavior* (New York: Harper), and J. B. Cortez (1961), *Physique, need for achievement, and delinquency*, a doctoral dissertation in the Social Relations Department, Harvard University.

their excessive inclination to *emotional conflict*, their tendency to keep their *affective tensions bottled up* inside, and the *relative deficiency* among ectomorphs generally of an *outflowing motor tendency*, gives to this class a significantly lower delinquency *potential* than that of mesomorphs. To lessen the chances of this potential becoming an actuality may often require intensive psychotherapy as well as special instruction of parents and teachers. Clinically, a history of *extreme restlessness* in early childhood and excessive *receptive* ('oral') *trends* must be noted as particularly related to delinquency in boys of this body type. On the other hand, the delinquency of ectomorphs is not especially associated with those traits which operate with excessive force on mesomorphs.

The interested reader is referred to other illustrations in *Physique and Delinquency* (Ch. XIV), and to various hypotheses which emerged from its intensive analyses (Ch. XV).

IV

Of course it was recognized that *Physique and Delinquency* emphasizes but one side of the nature-nurture controversy, and from the outset it was planned to analyze the other side as well. This has been accomplished in *Family Environment and Delinquency*[245], a work correlative to the preceding volume. In the analyses embodied in this book an attempt was made to determine the probable essential orientation of various physiologic and psychologic traits in terms of their relative position at one or another end (or toward the center) of a postulated *biosocial continuum*. This was a major effort dealing with the age-old problem of heredity and environment. While here, as in the prior work, the findings must be viewed with reasonable caution, they emerged, in systematic analysis, much like those which clinicians have from time to time noted when working with individual cases, but as to which the essential orientation of individual traits in constitution or environmental conditioning has heretofore been far from clear.

In *Family Environment and Delinquency* it was established (*a*) that certain sociocultural factors contribute to the formation of traits which, in *Unraveling*, had been found to be significantly associated with antisocial behavioral tendencies; (*b*) that certain malign social influences operate to render criminogenic some traits which, in the absence of such influences, are etiologically neutral; and (*c*) that other sociocultural factors operate within the total complex of criminogenic forces quite apart from the influences of various delinquency-linked physiologic, neurologic, and psychologic traits.

It was also discovered in *Family Environment and Delinquency* that it is in the *interaction* between certain traits and certain sociocultural influences that the significant dynamism of etiology is to be found; and that, standing alone, most traits and factors are not likely to induce deviant behavior, but in combination and interaction the probability of such behavior is considerably enhanced. For example, not all mesomorphs become delinquents; many become successful athletes, soldiers, and businessmen. Thus a major conclusion which emerged is that it is not the sociologist's 'differential *association*' with delinquents that is at the root of deviant behavior (for, obviously, the great majority of boys even in the most criminogenic regions do *not* become delinquents), but rather differential *contamination*; and this depends not only on *exposure* to delinquency patterns (which is only part of the etiologic process) but also on the *immunity* or *non-immunity* of the particular individuals so exposed. We have found that it is in the *direction-inducing* influence on boys of the different body-types possessing the accompanying trait-patterns that the various sociocultural forces operate to incline particular individuals toward deviant or toward conventional behavior. These forces are to be found largely in what we have called the under-the-roof situation, and especially the parent-child relationships in terms of affection, discipline, and family cohesiveness.

In *Family Environment and Delinquency*, as well as in *Physique and Delinquency*, in addition to important theoretical insights leading to fruitful hypotheses, valuable clues of practical clinical significance have emerged. Space permits only a few illustrations.

Certain aspects of the *father-son* relationship were found to be influential in inclining a boy to delinquency. The impact of the unacceptability of the father as a symbol or pattern for emulation (a fact found to exist significantly more frequently among delinquents than non-delinquents) is much heavier on boys characterized by such traits as *stubbornness*, and/or a tendency to *uninhibited motor responses to stimuli*, and/or *acquisitiveness*. The obvious remedial approach is to provide a substitute adult model with whom the boy can identify, such as a teacher, Boy Scout leader, Big Brother, clergyman, athletic director; but, while such a person would gradually get to know the boy, he would be in a much better position if he knew that one of the delinquency-related traits, *stubbornness*, does *not* vary among boys of the different body-builds; so that whether a boy is meso-morphic, at one extreme, or ectomorphic, at the other, would make little difference. But it would also be useful for the parent-substitute to know, for example, that, while a father's unacceptability as a pattern for emulation does not in itself contribute to the formation

327

of the criminogenic trait of stubbornness, its presence does enhance a boy's delinquency *potential*. It would also be useful to know that stubbornness is probably constitutional in orientation though not varying in incidence among the body-types. Such knowledge would preclude any head-on attempt to modify this trait but would, rather, suggest the need of guiding a stubborn youngster into socially acceptable expressions of the trait. His stubbornness might, for example, be modified into *perseverance* in socially acceptable tasks.

Again, such a trait as the tendency to *uninhibited motor response* to stimuli is not attributable to a father's unacceptability by the son; it, like stubbornness, is probably of constitutional orientation. Its presence in a boy should encourage a father substitute to guide his charge into socially acceptable uses of this tendency.

What can the clinician or boys' worker do about a situation in which a pre-delinquent or delinquent boy is being reared in a home with an *alcoholic father*? Such a father can, in his sober interludes, be an affectionate and loving parent. Here too, therapeutic strategy can be aided by the clues turned up in *Family Environment and Delinquency*. For example, such delinquency-related traits as *hostility*, *feeling of not being appreciated*, and *feeling of isolation*, found to enhance the son's delinquency potential, are probably modifiable through well-directed, patient effort by the father-surrogate.

Suppose a boy has a father who is *seriously disturbed emotionally*. Examining the impact of such a social-relational influence on the relevant characteristics of the boy, it was found that it tends to develop in the son certain traits which are themselves, in turn, related to delinquent behavior tendencies, such as an inclination to escape reality through *excessive flight into phantasy*, and/or *marked dependency* attitudes, and/or a *feeling of inadequacy*. As might be expected, paternal emotional disturbance more generally affects ectomorphic than mesomorphic boys.

The therapist can be effectively guided by such findings of the impact of a father's emotional disturbance on his son. Thus, for example, he need not despair of being able, through motivated reconditioning, to reduce the boy's marked inclination to escape into the make-believe world of *phantasy*. Again, a trait such as a *feeling of inadequacy*, in the presence of which a tendency to deviant behavior is enhanced among boys with an emotionally disturbed father, is also susceptible of reconditioning.

There are many other clues in *Family Environment and Delinquency* —those, for example, pertaining to the *mother-son* relationship— which the clinician, social worker, counselor, or probation officer might take into consideration in the effort to modify the attitude and behavior of boys of varying body-type and trait-pattern. But enough has been said to indicate that the kind of research out of which such findings have emerged is of value not only as a contribution to knowledge but, practically, in the day-to-day work with pre-delinquents and delinquents.

V

We have also during the last decade prepared a volume entitled *Predicting Delinquency and Crime*[212], the Foreword to which was written by the Chief Justice of the United States, Honorable Earl Warren. In that book all our prediction tables (over fifty in number) have been systematically assembled. The work also contains the results of a check-up of our series of prediction tables for use in juvenile courts. These encompass the delinquents' behavior on probation, on probation with suspended sentence to an institution, in correctional schools and in a reformatory for young adults, on parole, and during a span of five and fifteen years after first appearance of the delinquents in a juvenile court. The check-up consists of the application of these tables to a sample of cases other than those on which the predictive instruments had been originally framed.

In addition to this volume setting forth our various prediction tables, we have prepared articles dealing with different aspects of the sentencing problem (with special reference to the utilization of predictive devices) and others having to do with the early recognition of *potential* delinquents, focusing especially on sharpening and perfecting a device for such identification originally published in 1950 in *Unraveling*. Among the more important of these articles are 'Pathways to Improved Sentencing'[238] and those that appear as Chapters 9 and 10 of this volume.

VI

Through the years we have been called upon, as is usual in scientific endeavor, to answer various criticisms of our work. Perhaps the two major contributions toward meeting them are 'Crime Causation'[92] and the articles that appear as Chapters 16 and 17 of this volume.

At this point it might be well to advert to two aspects of growth in research thinking that are beginning to assume considerable importance among a small group of informed investigators of social problems. The first is the recognition that there has been too much emphasis on the need to build a single theory of delinquency, and the resultant recognition of the prerequisite of careful empirical

329

investigations as the basis for any sound theoretical construct; the second is the recognition that the fundamental techniques of pure science are just as relevant in an attempt to win understanding of the nature of delinquency and criminalism as they are in exploring the nature of Nature. It will not be amiss to cite one example of each of these forward-looking intellectual movements.

One consequence of a more recent subtle change of attitude toward the value of empirical research as indispensable to the building of scientific theories is the growing recognition that the previously-claimed radical differences in theoretical point of view of the more outstanding researches in delinquency are not as extreme as had been hastily assumed. An example of this is the following statement by Professor Daniel Glaser, of the Department of Sociology of the University of Illinois, in a recent letter to us from which he has permitted us to quote:

> ' I see much convergence in criminological theory from your work, that of Reckless, and some of my own work with adult offenders, despite the differences in our initial orientations. It will be a good thing if our efforts can be more closely co-ordinated, since they all are pursued as means to further crime prevention, an end which we all share.'

The second example we would cite, and which recognizes that the methods of pure science ought (with unavoidable but not fundamental modification) to be followed also in the social sciences, is the recent emphasis on the basic technique of comparing an experimental group with a control group. It is encouraging to find such an expression of a sound approach to research into social problems as in the following recent statement by Professor Harold Fallding:

> 'Evaluating social arrangements as functional or dysfunctional is equivalent to classifying them as normal or pathological. This is a necessary preliminary to the search for causal explanation. A physiologist cannot arrive at the function of the liver by generalizing directly from a random collection of livers which contains some diseased specimens. He distinguishes between the diseased and healthy organs at the outset and, setting the diseased ones aside, generalizes from the healthy ones. Certainly, by contrast, he gains some understanding of healthy functioning from an examination of the diseased cases, but can only do so if he first sets them in opposition by classifying them apart. His account of the liver would be altogether confounded if it simply averaged the properties of the whole collection. Distinguishing normal from

pathological cases is one of his first assignments, and precedes causal knowledge of the conditions of normal or pathological functioning. Social systems are more complex than livers, of course, but the two things are alike in this respect.' [2]

It is in this spirit that in *Unraveling* we compared 500 persistent delinquents with 500 boys whom intensive investigation showed to be non-delinquent. Our point of view is expressed in the statement that 'In order to arrive at the clearest differentiation between disease and health, comparison must be made between the unquestionably pathologic and the normal', and in this connection we said:

'Children who once or twice during the period of growing up in an excitingly attractive *milieu* steal a toy in a ten-cent store, sneak into a subway or motion picture theatre, play hooky, and the like, and soon outgrow such peccadilloes, are not true delinquents even though they have violated the law. Indeed it is now recognized that a certain amount of petty pilfering occurs among many children around the age of six or seven and is to be expected as part of the process of trying their wings. Children appear to be no worse for very occasional and slight experimental deviations from socially acceptable norms of conduct. Since they soon voluntarily abandon such behavior, their misconduct or maladaptation cannot be deemed either habitual or symptomatic of deep-rooted causes' (p. 13).

VII

In addition to the various commitments to paper of our research findings and ideas about certain theoretical and practical aspects of the delinquency problem, we should make reference to the scope of international activities which have grown tremendously during the past ten years. We have both been active members of the International Society of Criminology and have attended several important gatherings in various parts of Europe where the influence of our work and thinking has grown far beyond our expectations.

During the last ten years we were present at two United Nations Congresses on Juvenile Delinquency (one in Geneva and one in London), three Congresses of the International Society of Criminology (Paris, London, The Hague), a Congress on Social Defense (Stockholm), a World Mental Health Congress (Paris), an Annual Meeting of the British Royal Medico-Psychological Association (London), and also the XIIth International Course in Criminology

[2] Harold Fallding (1963), Functional analysis in sociology. *Amer. sociol. Rev.* **28**, 1.

(Jerusalem). We have participated actively in all of these international gatherings through preparation of source materials or lectures or discussions.

In addition to these summer activities we spent five weeks in Japan (28 May to 3 July 1960) at the invitation of the Japanese Ministry of Justice. Here we conducted a joint Seminar on our prediction work and on certain problems of juvenile delinquency, and delivered lectures in various parts of Japan, largely in law schools.

VIII

There still lies ahead of us the vast task of coordinating the data that have emerged from the follow-up study of the 500 delinquents and 500 non-delinquents of *Unraveling* to age thirty-two. These data should provide the basis for developing a *typology* of delinquents and recidivists.

In recent years a number of workers in the field of delinquency have been emphasizing the fact that to treat all offenders as a single class tends to blur distinctions which may be significant not only in understanding etiology but in varied therapeutic and preventive programs. A great many forms of deviant behavior—ranging from truancy to murder—are, compendiously, included in statutes and procedures dealing with 'delinquency', and the same variety is to be found in respect to the age-range of young offenders. There is evidence, also, that among delinquents, as among ordinary persons, there are wide variations in personality and temperament. It may well be that these differences of anti-social act, age, and personality-character make-up are susceptible of inductive integration into meaningful patterns or *Gestalten*, and that these combinations of hereditary-environmental human structure require differing forms of treatment, for the purpose of reducing both the number of youngsters who drift or are impelled into delinquency and the number who develop into adult criminals.

During the many years of our researches at the Harvard Law School we have accumulated a unique mine of materials which we now propose to subject to computer-analysis in order to ascertain whether they will inductively yield several more or less distinct types of delinquents from the points of view of etiology, recidivism, and preventive indications. Our data are replete with materials dealing with criminal records, with somatotypes, psychological and psychiatric findings, early parent-child relationships, school history, typical deviant behavior, and so on.

In addition, we have a unique quarry of information based on many years of intensive follow-up of both the delinquents and the non-delinquents in respect not only to their criminalistic activities but also to their socioeconomic status, physical and mental health, family life, industrial history, recreational outlets, ambitions. This follow-up material will be intercorrelated with the background data of *Unraveling* to provide a truly pioneering exploration. We also have materials on several previous follow-up investigations on other samples of offenders—1,000 juvenile delinquents and 500 graduates of the Massachusetts Reformatory—whose careers were studied in the 'thirties, and the data from such investigations can, at various points in the projected analysis, be compared with the more recent investigation to age thirty-two of the 500 delinquents of *Unraveling*.

Our search for etiologic, recidivistic, and treatment types becomes more feasible by the fact that Harvard University has installed an IBM 7090 computer, enabling us to follow through a great many intercorrelations and computations which would be virtually impossible without this time-saving device. Of course several preliminary 'test-runs' of various segments of the data are necessary in connection with the sound ultimate programming of the entire project; and we are now engaged in this preliminary experimentation.

This comprehensive project is bound to present some intricate problems, especially because of the longitudinal (historical) nature of some of the follow-up data; but the technical issues can be resolved only as we move step by step toward the ultimate goal. Any such intensive and extensive multiple-factor analysis must necessarily proceed in this way. It obviously involves interim analyses and the pursuit of various 'leads' that may be suggested during the continuous examination of the statistical data.

This study is the core of our research program for the next five years. Toward support of this aspect of our work an appropriate grant has recently been made by the National Institute of Mental Health.

IX

There are also some specialized and specifically focused studies flowing from the basic data of *Unraveling*, which we have been tabulating and which are in fact almost ready for writing. They may be referred to as 'Aspects of Delinquency'. We mention them now only in passing, because the large research just mentioned will occupy most of our time and thought. Ultimately, however, these intensive monographic studies will constitute a volume to be called

Some Aspects of Delinquency. Among these projected monographs are the following:

Differences Between 'Serious' and 'Minor' Offenders;
Differences Between Younger and Older Delinquents;
Ethnic Origin and Delinquency;
School Retardation and Delinquency;
Family Misconduct and Delinquency;
Delinquents from Wholesome vs. Those from Unwholesome Family Background;
Types of Character-Structure among Delinquents.

There are some twenty of these monographic studies, each one of which will require statistical processing beyond the present stage of descriptive tabulation.

X

Another project that we have in mind and on which we are already engaged in a preliminary way is the preparation of a volume, *Nature and Nurture in Delinquency*, based largely on trait-and-factor *clusters* or patterns that are found to result in the highest delinquency *potential*. The aim is to bring the analysis well beyond the scope of the data encompassed in *Physique and Delinquency* and *Family Environment and Delinquency*.

XI

Still another project challenges our attention. The carrying out of this is dependent upon a sufficiency of unrestricted funds. The plan concerns the *comparison and cross-interpretation* of the findings of our various follow-up studies and the extraction from the multifarious data of all the clues derived on etiology, treatment, and theoretical formulations. We have in mind, for example, a comparison of the age at first delinquency and of intelligence level, health, family life, school history, recidivism, and many other factors involving the variety of samples of delinquents and criminals investigated by us over the years. Perhaps influences of a *general* nature will be found to run through these groups of cases, which had been assembled and studied at different times, some of them, for example, during the depression years and some during the early post-war years. Perhaps, through comparison of these separate groups of offenders and their vicissitudes in and out of the courts and correctional institutions, more light can be shed on the successes and failures of criminal justice and on the extent to which the outcomes are attributable to the original make-up of the offenders; to their varying family life in childhood homes and in the households which the offenders themselves later established as adults; to the shortcomings of the peno-correctional system.

We are already proceeding with the preliminary work on this far-flung inquiry, confining ourselves at present to setting down in juxtaposition the findings of the various follow-up studies concerning those factors which are strictly comparable because of uniformity of the categories and definitions throughout the studies. In designing the series of studies (*500 Criminal Careers*, *Five Hundred Delinquent Women*, *One Thousand Juvenile Delinquents*, *Later Criminal Careers*, *Criminal Careers in Retrospect*, *Juvenile Delinquents Grown Up*, *Unraveling Juvenile Delinquency*, and, more recently, the two follow-up studies of the cases of *Unraveling Juvenile Delinquency*) we kept in mind the possibility of a later comprehensive comparison of the findings.

XII

We turn now to the important topic of *Prediction*. During the last ten years a number of prediction-validation experiments checking on the Social Prediction Table published in *Unraveling* have been carried out. These checkings have been made not only in the United States but also in Japan, England, France, Israel. But probably the most significant validation experiments are those which have been going on for many years in New York City under the auspices of the Youth Board (a municipal agency) and in Washington, D.C., under the auspices of the Commissioners' Youth Council. (This latter prediction-validation study is known as the Maximum Benefits Project.) The New York study consists of the follow-up of the behavior of 302 boys to whom the prediction table was applied when they first entered the public school system at age five and a half to six; the latter deals with 179 youngsters (boys and girls), a somewhat older age-group, who had been referred by teachers to a school behavior-clinic in Washington because they were causing serious difficulties in the classroom.

The New York City Youth Board's Research Department have published the results of their study in the July 1963 issue of *Crime and Delinquency*;[3] the Washington researchers have reported on the interim results of their prediction-validation study in the *American*

---

[3] Maude M. Craig and Selma J. Glick, Ten years' experience with the Glueck Social Prediction Table.

Journal of Psychiatry, November, 1963.[4] The findings indicate that potential delinquents *can be identified.*

Experience with use of the device has suggested modifications of the original five-factor table to enhance its practical utility (see Chs. 8, 9, and 10 of this volume). It must be borne in mind that the original Social Prediction Table in *Unraveling* was constructed on information pertaining largely to English, Irish, Italian, and Slavic boys. In the validation experiments, of a prospective as well as a retrospective nature, it has been applied to children of very different ethnic origin. This is assuredly a most rigorous test of a predictive instrument.

It should be obvious that in the testing of the efficacy of a device intended to distinguish delinquents from non-delinquents, it is inherently impossible to obtain the absolute point-to-point precision regarding each case as was done, for example, in the kind of experiment conducted by Pasteur. He vaccinated, with his attenuated virus, a number of sheep showing the symptoms of anthrax and left an equal number of such sheep without inoculation, permitting the results to prove his point. In the experimental group the vaccinated sheep recovered their health; in the control group they died.[5] Obviously, human beings are much more complex; to a varying extent individuals among them are not sheep but self-managing organisms. In the human field, therefore, the most that can be done is to rely on high probability, as in the case of predicting longevity in the field of insurance. This has been successfully achieved with our prediction table.

One cannot exaggerate the great potentialities of a device which permits of the identification of delinquency-prone children at an early stage in the development of personality and character. However, from *anticipating* the future to *mastering* the future requires a great leap. It is hoped that the demonstration of the validity of our predictive device will stimulate psychiatrists, psychologists, teachers, and other practitioners of the behavioral and motivational arts to develop effective methods for the salvaging of endangered children.

In view of the success of the two major efforts to check the screening device for the identification of delinquents and non-delinquents, it is not unlikely that there will be some demands upon us to give stimulus and direction to other experiments and specific uses of the tables initially developed in *Unraveling* for the identification of potential delinquents. It is not our intention to seek such

---

[4] Drs E. F. Hodges, Jr. & C. D. Tait, Jr., A follow-up study of potential delinquents.
[5] R. Vallery-Radot (1925), *The life of Pasteur* trans. by Mrs R. L. Devonshire (New York: Doubleday), 323, 367–68.

opportunities but rather to fulfill those demands that may come and then only to the extent that they would further our research interests in the field of prediction. It is rather our hope that both the New York City Youth Board and the Commissioners' Youth Council of Washington, D.C., will be in a position to provide the guidance that may be necessary to those wishing to explore the use of the screening device.

Our interest is not limited to the early identification of delinquents. There is the related problem of instructing judges and their probation officers in the use of prediction tables designed to improve the sentencing practices of juvenile and adult courts. We were asked for aid by a juvenile court judge (Judge Holland M. Gary of Zanesville, Ohio) a few years ago; and we gave it through one of our assistants, Mr George McGrath (now Commissioner of Correction of Massachusetts); and other judges have expressed interest.

XIII

In Chapter 18 above reference has been made to our interest in sponsoring and participating in the development of a *Comparative Criminology*. This has been a concern for many years and has been partly stimulated by the fact that some of our Japanese colleagues are interested in replicating the study *Unraveling Juvenile Delinquency*.

It would be desirable to carry out a replication of *Unraveling Juvenile Delinquency* in one of the European countries. We are considering the possibility of projects in Rome and Puerto Rico.

One of the major difficulties in replicating *Unraveling* in other countries is the matter of definition. To quote from an editorial in the *British Journal of Criminology*, there is a need for 'a handbook of working paraphrases of the technical terms employed by psychiatrists and sociologists respectively'; but we may add that there is also need of a *multilingual* set of technical definitions, so that relative uniformity of meaning will exist among the workers abroad and those in the United States. Something like this was worked up by a committee appointed by the Research Section of the Supreme Court of Japan, in preparation for translating *Unraveling Juvenile Delinquency* into Japanese. A group of outstanding scholars (a judge, a psychiatrist, a sociologist, a statistician, etc.) met frequently over a period of a year to formulate the word-signs in Japanese that were deemed by the group to be equivalent to the terms used in *Unraveling*. Only recently this group published a revised version of the Japanese translation of *Unraveling* in which certain word-symbols were corrected because experience had taught that some of the concepts as they appeared in English had been initially misunderstood.

We hope very much that it will be possible to proceed with replications of *Unraveling* in Japan, Italy and perhaps in other countries, as this would serve as a beginning of a *Comparative Criminology*.

The systematic determination of which traits of personality and which sociocultural influences significantly differentiate persistent delinquents from true non-delinquents is a *sine qua non* to the development of a science of Criminology. If repeated investigations of samples of delinquents and non-delinquents reared in a variety of cultures should reveal that certain influences exist irrespective of ethnico-racial and cultural contexts, these influences could then be legitimately regarded as *etiologic constants*. As was pointed out above, there are a few straws in the wind—the revelatory results of the application of the factors of the Social Prediction Table in such varying contexts as New York, Washington, France and Japan— that would seem to justify a multifaceted study of delinquency in various countries, employing the definitions and techniques used in *Unraveling Juvenile Delinquency*.

This does not of course mean that the repetitive studies would be limited to the methods and findings of *Unraveling*; there are other impressive pieces of criminologic research in the United States, England and elsewhere which, as time goes on, ought to be duplicated in places of differing cultural and ethnic backgrounds. But, because of the variety of disciplines that comprise *Unraveling*—ranging from anthropometric, medical, psychologic and psychiatric studies to factors of the under-the-roof culture, as well as data from school and neighborhood—a beginning of replicative studies based on the definitions and techniques of *Unraveling* seems the most immediately promising.

Nor does the proposal mean that such studies ought not to include investigative channels not embraced in even the wide-ranging *Unraveling* study. For example, in designing it, we had hoped to include electroencephalograms of each boy; but, while a beginning was made in the early 'forties, this was abandoned both because of the practical problem of convincing parents that their children are not being 'electrocuted' and the theoretical fact that electroencephalographic diagrams had not as yet been sufficiently standardized to be usable with a special group such as delinquents. Similarly, although we used the Rorschach Test to determine personality-character structure, it may be that this test should be supplemented by such instruments as the Thematic Apperception Test.

338

At all events, it seems to us that the time is ripe for the systematic development of a Comparative Criminology.

XIV

The contributions made possible by the researches have of course not been confined to publications of the kind discussed above; indirect values in the enrichment of teaching are also to be attributed to the investigations.

For many years much has been said about research in Criminal Law as related to the behavioral disciplines. It is perfectly clear that while book-research can contribute to improvement of the internal logical consistency of the Criminal Law through the familiar techniques of the legal scholar, it can hardly be expected to bring about fundamental improvement of the ultimate processes and crime-preventive attributes of the administration of criminal justice. On the plane of law-decision research, investigation into the Criminal Law largely yields improvement of the law in its major aspect as a normative and logical discipline. This is of course very necessary and important; but it is not the type of research that will materially reduce crime and recidivism. Hand-in-hand with traditional legal research, two conditions are indispensable to the development of a more realistic and just administration of the Criminal Law: first, the planful absorption of the insights of the relevant non-legal ('behavioral' or, preferably, *motivational*) disciplines into the law's social policy aspects; secondly, and relatedly, creative field-and-fact research.

That this is now being recognized by outstanding legal scholars may be inferred from Professor Edwin W. Patterson's recent book, *Law in a Scientific Age*.[6] We may be pardoned for expressing satisfaction that among his three examples of 'scientific method in legal empiricism' he includes our researches:

'. . . The first one, the studies by Professor Sheldon Glueck and Dr Eleanor Glueck of the treatment of offenders and the prediction of juvenile delinquency or crime, came closer to discovering causal relations than did the others. . . . For more than thirty years Professor Glueck and his wife, with the aid of an able staff of assistants and consultants, carried on at the Harvard Law School and in its vicinity the most comprehensive and sustained investigations thus far made into the explanation and prediction of juvenile

[6] New York and London, Columbia University Press, 1963.

delinquency and crime. The published reports of these studies are so voluminous that one can, in a brief space, only sample rather than summarize them. Their conclusions are, for the most part, contained in tables showing percentages of frequency. They have no formulas equivalent to a scientific law of causation. Yet, out of the sixty-three factors that they used as variables in their well-planned programs of inquiry, five, all aspects of the juvenile's relations to his family, were found to give the highest "delinquency scores" for use in the prediction of delinquency.

'. . . In view of their wide-ranging and dispassionate search for significant factors, one may say at least that their Prediction Tables provide valuable clues for the judge to use in exercising his discretion with respect to the treatment of juvenile delinquents' (pp. 65–66, 70).

We have long engaged in an endeavor to implement the administration of criminal justice through the application of 'scientific method in legal empiricism'. There is evidence that, in addition to basic contributions to the etiology of delinquency, crime, and recidivism, some 'practical good' has resulted from our investigations in different parts of the world. There is also evidence that promising leads—such as the concept of *delayed maturation*[7]—to more fundamental general research have been contributed by our investigations in three separate follow-ups covering different samples of delinquents and criminals investigated at varying periods.

But our researches have also made possible some basic work in fields more directly related to substantive and procedural Criminal Law. Throughout the teaching of Criminal Law, Administration of Criminal Justice, and the Problem of Delinquency, there has been a systematic endeavor to bring to the attention of students the relevant aspects of the behavioral disciplines. This was begun with the publication of *Mental Disorder and the Criminal Law*[7] and has proceeded through such works as *Crime and Justice*[120] and, most recently, *Law and Psychiatry: Cold War or Entente Cordiale?*[246], as well as numerous articles in legal and criminologic journals.

Probably the most comprehensive plan to bring to law students the insights of the relevant behavioral disciplines is the volume

[7] Proof that recidivism tends to continue until the late twenties and early thirties of the life-span, after which there is a marked drop in its incidence. See *Juvenile delinquents grown up*[85], pp. 268–9; *Criminal careers in retrospect*[102], pp. 39, 64, 250, 292. Preliminary examination also suggests the same phenomenon among the 500 delinquents originally studied in *Unraveling*; but definitive details await the analysis of the vast amount of materials involved.

entitled *The Problem of Delinquency*[213][8]. Since there is so much discussion nowadays of the indifference of lawyers to the contributions of the behavioral sciences, it will not be amiss to present here a précis of the table of contents of this volume:

PART ONE—Incidence and Causation: Sec. I, Incidence and Measurement of Delinquency. Sec. II, Theories and Findings regarding 'Causes' of Delinquency (Cause and Effect in Biosocial Problems involving Delinquency, Anthropologic-Biologic Aspects of Delinquency, Psychologic Aspects of Delinquency, Family Life and Delinquency, School Influences and Delinquency, Sociocultural Aspects of Delinquency, Theories of Delinquency Causation).

PART TWO—The Juvenile Court and the Law: Sec. I, History and Organization (The Juvenile Court: Historical Background, Philosophy and Organization). Sec. II, Basic Legal Issues (Constitutional Protections, Jurisdictional and Related Problems, Problems of Proof, Problems of Disposition, Custody, Neglect, Dependency; Suggested Procedural Reforms; Youths Beyond Juvenile Court Age). Sec. III, Detention, Investigation, Sentencing (Intake, Detention, Clinical Examination, Investigation, Hearing, The Sentencing Process).

PART THREE—Treatment: Sec. I, Types of Disposition and Treatment (Forms of Treatment: Probation and Its Adjuncts, Foster Home Care, Institutional Care, Hospital Care, Institutional Personnel). Sec. II, Treatment Devices (Techniques of Treatment: Casework, Individual Psychotherapy, Group Therapy [Group Therapy Proper, Work with Gangs, Camp Work], After-Care: Punishment or Treatment of Parents of Delinquents, Post-Treatment Behavior).

PART FOUR—Prevention of Delinquency: Sec. I, Early Recognition of Potential Delinquents (Prediction of Delinquency). Sec. II, Preventive Action (Preventive Philosophy, Programs, Devices).

Each Section is introduced by a comprehensive Note, and the Sections contain many carefully selected articles and judicial decisions.

That the class discussion of delinquency as a multifaceted and not merely a legal problem has been effective may perhaps be judged in

[8] The publication of this work, intended to introduce considerations of the delinquency problem into law school curricula, was made possible by supplementary financial assistance from the Ella Lyman Cabot Trust and the Field Foundation, as well as another foundation and a public-spirited friend both preferring to remain anonymous. Because of its considerable bulk the price to students would otherwise have been prohibitive.

part from the titles of some student-papers in the Seminar on Juvenile Delinquency:

The Use of Medicine, Psychology and Psychiatry at the Warwick State Training School, New York;

The Phenomenon of 'Transference' in the Treatment of Juvenile Delinquents, with Special Attention to the Contributions of Orthopsychiatry;

An Analysis of the Program and Accomplishments of the Massachusetts Youth Service Board;

The Legal Precepts involved in the Institutional Treatment of Juvenile Delinquents;

The Juvenile Delinquency Subcommittee of the United States Senate;

Problems in the Structure of the Juvenile Court;

The Approach of the Catholic Church to Juvenile Delinquency;

A Brief Historical Outline of the English Juvenile Court System and an Assessment of Certain Selected Features in the Light of American Practice;

A Community Program for the Penetration of Juvenile Delinquency;

Milieu Therapy: New Hope in the Treatment of Delinquents;

Problems in the Evaluation of Community Efforts to Control Delinquency;

The Pros and Cons of Statutes punishing Parents for their Child's Delinquency; and an Appraisal of the Judicial Attitude toward such Statutes;

A Challenging Approach to Juvenile and Youth Delinquency: The Scandinavian System;

A Comparative Study of Some Aspects of Juvenile Delinquency Control in California and in the Philippines;

A Therapeutic Summer Camp for the Treatment and Rehabilitation of Delinquent Boys;

The Role of the Schools in the Prevention of Delinquency;

The Legal Problems of Family Therapy;

The Social Worker, the Lawyer, and the Juvenile Court;

Proof of Facts in Delinquency Proceedings;

Aspects of Cooperation between Law Enforcement Officials and School Officials in dealing with Problems of Delinquency;

The Child Criminal in Two Environments: A Comparative Study of the Treatment of Child Offenders in the Bombay State and Massachusetts;

The Administration of Criminal Justice and the Control of

Juvenile Delinquency in the State of Massachusetts and in the State of Sao Paulo (Brazil): A Comparative Study;

A Critique of Recent Congressional Activity relating to Juvenile Delinquency;

Vandalism;

Constitutional Problems of Summary Commitment of Juvenile Delinquents;

The Child Welfare Committee System in Denmark: A Study of Laws and Authorities dealing with Juvenile Delinquents and Other Socially Maladjusted Children;

The Quiet Rebels: The Problem of Drug Use among Adolescents;

Ganging and the New York City Youth Board;

The Psychopath: What's Behind the 'Mask of Sanity'?;

Obscenity, Censorship, and Juvenile Delinquency;

The Relationship of Body Chemistry to Juvenile Delinquency;

An Attempted Rationale for the Age Jurisdiction of the Juvenile Courts;

The Right to Counsel in Juvenile Courts;

The Problem of Juvenile Delinquency in the Republic of China;

The Role of Organized Religion in Preventing Juvenile Delinquency;

The Effects of the Mass Media of Communication on Juvenile Delinquency;

Juvenile Courts in the United States and in the Netherlands;

A Critique of Two Sections of the Standard Juvenile Court Act;

Conflict in the Family and the Delinquency Problem.

No attempt has been made in this presentation to classify these topics. Many more titles might have been included. It is believed that the thesis-subjects sufficiently illustrate the rich variety of work done by the students in the Seminar on Juvenile Delinquency—a variation characterized both by the juxtaposition of legal and extra-legal materials and by comparisons of American with foreign thought and practice.

XV

In conclusion, it seems appropriate to point to the *acumulative* nature of our inquiries and findings. A major weakness of criminologic and criminal law research is its fragmentary and disconnected status—a special piece of investigation here, another special piece there—without any systematic follow-through of root problems into their developed stages with a view to building a coherent, structured theory and derivative hypotheses for further inquiry. Mere theorizing *per se* has not produced any marked growth of knowledge of etiologic involvements, results of correction and rehabilitation, prognostication of conduct. In our investigations we have tried to follow the example and pattern of scientific endeavor in the purer disciplines. For example, both *Physique and Delinquency* and *Family Environment and Delinquency* grew naturally and logically out of the findings and resultant clues, queries and hypotheses of *Unraveling Juvenile Delinquency*. Similarly, the follow-up investigations of the postparole careers of the youthful offenders reported on in *500 Criminal Careers*[26] led to a like technique in the tracing of the 1000 juvenile delinquents described in the book *Juvenile Delinquents Grown Up*[85]. These, in turn, suggested the importance of tracing the *after-conduct* of the 500 delinquents and 500 non-delinquents first examined in *Unraveling Juvenile Delinquency*—a study still to be reported on. This process of natural evolution of one research from a preceding one promises to be even more fruitful in the years ahead.

We cannot close this résumé of a decade of research in Criminology without expressing our appreciation not only to the Foundations and Governmental agencies which have made the work possible, to Harvard University and to Dean Erwin Griswold of the Harvard Law School, but also to Professor Glueck's students, past and present, and our many colleagues around the world who continue to be keenly interested in our researches and who encourage us to go on with our work which is to us an ever-exciting adventure into the unknown.

CHRONOLOGICAL BIBLIOGRAPHY
1923 – 1963

SHELDON GLUECK
ELEANOR T. GLUECK

Harvard Law School
Cambridge, Massachusetts

Publications 1923-1963

1923

ARTICLES

(1) GLUECK, s. Ethics, psychology and the criminal responsibility of the insane. 14 *J. Crim. Law* 208; 58 *A.L.Rev.* 641 (1924).

1924

BOOKS

(2) ——, s. *Criminal responsibility of the mentally abnormal.* Thesis. Harvard University.

ARTICLES

(3) ——, s. New trends in criminology. *National Conference Social Work* 196–201.

(4) ——, s. State legislation providing for the mental examination of persons accused of crime. 8 *Mental Hygiene* 1–19.

(5) ——, s. State legislation providing for the mental examination of persons accused of crime. 14 *J. Crim. Law* 573.

MISCELLANEA

(6) ——, s. Rational bases of the law. 8 *Mental Hygiene Book Review Supplement* 306–315.

1925

BOOKS

(7) ——, s. *Mental disorder and the criminal law.* A study in medicosociological jurisprudence, with an appendix of state legislation and interpretive decisions. Boston, Little Brown. XXII, 693 p. 24 cm. Bibliography 645–61.

ARTICLES

(8) ——, s. Mental examination of persons accused of crime. *American Review* 336–47.

(9) ——, s. Reformers and crime. 44 *New Republic* 120–23.

(10) ——, s. Some implications of the Leopold-Loeb hearing in mitigation. 9 *Mental Hygiene* 449–68.

(11) ——, s. A tentative program of cooperation between psychiatrists and lawyers. 9 *Mental Hygiene* 686–98.

1926

ARTICLES

(12) ——, s. The ministry of justice and the problem of crime. 4 *American Review* 139–56.

MISCELLANEA

(13) ——, s. Book review: Lenroot & Lundberg, *Juvenile courts at work.* 39 *Harvard Law Review* 1109–10.

1927

BOOKS

(14) GLUECK, E. *Community use of schools.* Baltimore. XIV, 222 p.

(15) ——, S. *Mental disorder and the criminal law.* A study in medicosociological jurisprudence, with an appendix of state legislation and interpretive decisions. Boston, Little, Brown. 693 p.

ARTICLES

(16) ——, E. Extended use of school buildings. 5 *U.S. Bureau of Education Bulletin* 1–80.

(17) ——, S. Psychiatric examination of persons accused of crime. 36 *Yale Law Journal* 632–48.

1928

ARTICLES

(18) ——, S. Perennial puzzle: crime. 60 *Survey* 333–34.

(19) ——, S. Principles of a rational penal code. 41 *Harvard Law Review* 453–82.

(19a) ——, S. Psychiatry and the criminal law. 14 *Virginia Law Review* 155–81; 12 *Mental Hygiene* 569–95.

MISCELLANEA

(20) ——, S. Book review: Toulemon, A., *Le progrès des institutions pénales.* 41 *Harvard Law Review* 931–34.

1929

BOOKS

(21) ——, S. (Ed.). assisted by Edna Mahan, *Harvard crime survey; handbook of illustrative cases.* [n.p., 1929] 2 p. 1., V, XXIX, 211 numb. 1. 29 cm. Reproduced from typewritten copy.

ARTICLES

(22) ——, S. & E. Predictability in the administration of criminal justice. 42 *Harvard Law Review* 297–329; 13 *Mental Hygiene* 678–707.

(23) ——, S. Redl: No ivory tower. 4 *Children* 79.

MISCELLANEA

(24) ——, S. *Massachusetts. Department of Education. Division of University Extension. Penal Institution Administration and Routine.* Oct. 5 1928–May 24 1929. Boston, 1928–29. 3 pts. in 1 v. 28 1/2 cm. Various pagings. A series of 29 lectures. Reproduced from typewritten copy. Contents: Pt. I. Criminal law and procedure. Pt. II. The administration of penal institutions. Pt. III, Social problems in penology.

(25) ——, S. & E. *Tables used in address on scientific method in the administration of criminal justice* (n.p., 1929). (1), 4 numb. 1 tables. 28 cm. National Conference of Social Work, Division of Delinquency, San Francisco, July 3 1929. Reproduced from typewritten copy.

1930

BOOKS

(26) GLUECK, S. & E. *500 criminal careers.* New York, A. A. Knopf. XXVII, 365, XVI p., 11. 24 1/2 cm. The Harvard Milton Fund supplied the means for the present study.—Pref.

ARTICLES

(27) ——, s. Criminal justice at the crossroads. 8 *Ohio Woman Voter* 8, 11.

(28) ——, s. Significant transformations in the administration of criminal justice. 14 *Mental Hygiene* 280–306.

MISCELLANEA

(29) ——, s. Book review: Leonardo Bianchi, *Foundations of mental hygiene.* 21 *Journal of Criminal Law & Criminology* 305–08.

(30) ——, s. Book review: Smoot, George A., *Law of insanity.* 43 *Harvard Law Review* 518.

1931

ARTICLES

(31) ——, s. International prison congress of 1930. New York City. 15 *Mental Hygiene* 775–90.

(32) ——, s. Status of probation. New York City. 15 *Mental Hygiene* 290–98.

MISCELLANEA

(33) ——, s. Book review: Franz Alexander & Hugo Staub, *The criminal, the judge and the public.* Trans. from the German by G. Zilboorg. 44 *Harvard Law Review* 1316–19.

1932

ARTICLES

(34) ——, s. Individualization and the use of predictive devices. 23 *Journal of Criminal Law & Criminology* 67–76.

(35) ——, s. Mental hygiene and crime. 19 *Psychoanalytic Review* 23–35.

(36) ——, s. Mental hygiene and crime. 19 *Indian Association for Mental Hygiene Quarterly Bulletin* 1–13.

(37) ——, s. The significance and responsibilities of probation. American Bar Association, *Report of 55th Annual Meeting* 618–27.

MISCELLANEA

(38) ——, s. Book review: Louis N. Robinson, *Should prisoners work: a study of prison labor problem in the United States.* 1931. 46 *Harvard Law Review* 183–85.

(39) ——, s. et al. Housing and delinquency. In *Housing and the Community*, The President's Conference on Home Building and Home Ownership, Washington.

(40) ——, s. Insanity—criminal law. 8 *Encyclopaedia of the Social Sciences* 64–68.

1933

BOOKS

(41) GLUECK, S. (Ed.) *Probation and criminal justice;* essays in honor of Herbert C. Parsons. New York, Macmillan. VIII, 344 p., 22 1/2 cm.

ARTICLES

(42) ——, S. On the causes of crime. 29 *American Mercury* 430–36.

(43) ——, S. The social sciences and scientific method in the administration of justice. 167 *Annals of the American Academy of Political and Social Science* 106–18.

1934

BOOKS

(44) ——, S. & E. *Five hundred delinquent women.* Introduction by Roscoe Pound. New York, A. A. Knopf, XXIV, 539, X p. 11, 24 1/2 cm. First edition.

(45) ——, S. & E. *One thousand juvenile delinquents; their treatment by court and clinic.* Introduction by Felix Frankfurter. Cambridge, Harvard University Press. XXIX, 341 p. 24 cm. (Half-title: Survey of Crime and Criminal Justice in Boston, conducted by the Harvard Law School, vol. I.)

(46) ——, S. & E. *One thousand juvenile delinquents; their treatment by court and clinic.* Introduction by Felix Frankfurter. Harvard University Law School: Survey of Crime and Criminal Justice in Boston, 1. 2nd ed. 341 p. Tables 8 vo. Cambridge.

ARTICLES

(47) ——, S. Professor Glueck's reply to Judge Eastman. *National Probation Association Year Book* 90–98.

(48) ——, S. & E. A reply (to critics of *One thousand juvenile delinquents*). 18 *Mental Hygiene* 553–74.

(49) ——, S. A thousand juvenile delinquents, some facts and inferences of a recent survey. *National Probation Association, Year Book* 63–75, 90–98.

MISCELLANEA

(50) ——, S. *The delinquent boy* [n.p., 1934], I, p. 1, 12 numb. 1. 28 cm. Address delivered at the 28th Annual Convention of the Boys' Clubs of America, Pittsburgh, Pa. Reproduced from typewritten copy.

(51) ——, S. *The future of correctional work.* Massachusetts Department of Education, university extension course in penal institution administration and routine offered in cooperation with Massachusetts Department of Correction. Nov. 13 1934–May 28 1935, Boston. 3 pts. in 1 vol. 36 cm. Various pagings.

(52) ——, S. *The place of proper police and prosecution in a crime reduction program;* address delivered at the Attorney General's Conference on Crime, Memorial Continental Hall, Washington, D.C., Dec. 11 1934. Multigraphed. (1) × 18 fol. 4to. At head of title: For release on delivery about 11.20 a.m., Tuesday, Dec. 11, 1934. Department of Justice.

MISCELLANEA

(53) GLUECK, S. *The place of proper police and prosecution in a crime reduction program* (cont.). In Attorney General's Conference on Crime, Washington, D.C., Dec. 10–13 1934, pp. 52–63.

(54) ——, S. Book review: John Barker Waite, *Cases on Criminal Law and Procedure*. 1931. 43 *Yale Law Journal* 512–16.

1935

ARTICLES

(55) ——, S. Crime prevention. 1 *Vital Speeches of the Day* 41–57.

(56) ——, E. Family, the school and crime. 1 *Vital Speeches of the Day* 50–61.

(57) ——, E. The family, the school and crime. (2) × 11 p. *Harvard Teachers Record*, April 1935.

(58) ——, S. Future of American penology. 2 *Vital Speeches of the Day* 96–101.

(59) ——, S. The future of American penology; the call for more discriminating law enforcement. 7 *Quarterly Bulletin*, N.Y. State Conference on Social Work 15–29.

(60) ——, E. Mental retardation and juvenile delinquency. 19 *Mental Hygiene* 549–72.

(61) ——, S. Prison and community. 1 *Prison* 38.

(62) ——, S. Psychiatry and the criminal law. 2 *Current Legal Thought* 84–91.

MISCELLANEA

(63) ——, S. *Crime prevention;* address at annual meeting of the Big Brother and Big Sister Federation, New York, April 15 1935. [n.p., 1935] 23 numb. 1. 28 cm. Reproduced from typewritten copy.

1936

BOOKS

(64) ——, S. *Crime and justice*. Boston, Little, Brown. VIII p., 2 1., [3]–349 p. 21 1/2 cm.

(65) ——, E. *Evaluative research in social work*. IV. 27 p. Columbia University Press

(66) ——, S. & E. (Eds.) *Preventing crime, a symposium*. Contributions by Henrietta Additon, Meta L. Anderson, David W. Armstrong . . . [and others]. 1st ed. New York & London, McGraw-Hill. XI, 509, p. diagrs. 23 1/2 cm.

ARTICLES

(67) ——, S. Contributors to correctional science. *Yearbook of the National Probation Association* 325–44.

MISCELLANEA

(68) ——, S. Book review: L. W. Fox, *Modern English Prisons*. 1934. 52 *Law Quarterly Review* 130.

MISCELLANEA

(69) GLUECK, E. Book review: Courtland C. Van Vechten, *A study of success and failure of one thousand juvenile delinquents*. 26 *J. Crim. Law* 985–89.

(70) ——, s. *Probation and parole in Greater Boston*, in collaboration with Frank Loveland and Hans Weiss, assisted by Abraham Kaminstein and Sidney Spear, With a monograph on The Pardoning Power, by Norman D. Lattin. Cambridge, Mass. ? 1 v. (various pagings), tables (part fold.), diagrs., 28 cm.

1937

BOOKS

(71) ——, s. & E. *Later criminal careers*. New York, The Commonwealth Fund; London, H. Milford, Oxford University Press. XI, 403 p., 24 cm.

ARTICLES

(72) ——, s. A criminologist looks at social work; an address. 11 *Social Service Review* 247–62.

(73) ——, E. Culture conflict and delinquency. 21 *Mental Hygiene* 46–66.

(74) ——, s. Sex crimes and the law. 145 *The Nation* 318–20.

MISCELLANEA

(75) ——, s. Future of American penology: The call for more discriminating law enforcement. 14 p. Albany.

(76) ——, s. Book review: Harry Soderman & John J. O'Connell, *Modern criminal investigation*. 1936. 25 *Georgetown Law Journal* 532–35.

(77) ——, s. Book review: August Vollmer, *Police and modern society*. 1936. 31 *American Political Science Rev*. 132–36.

1938

MISCELLANEA

(78) ——, s. *Criminal law syllabus*. Prepared for the use of the first year class in Criminal Law at the Harvard Law School, Cambridge. With L. Hall.

(79) ——, s. & E. *Women and girl offenders in Massachusetts;* report of the committee formed by Mrs R. F. Herrick for the study of the problems presented in *Five hundred delinquent women* by Sheldon & Eleanor T. Glueck. Boston, Massachusetts Child Council. 8o (2)+48 p., Tables and diagrams.

1939

BOOKS

(80) ——, s. & LIVINGSTON HALL, *Cases and materials on criminal law*. Temporary ed. St Paul, Minn., West Publishing Co., XVI, 502 p., 25 1/2 cm.

ARTICLES

(81) ——, s. Crime and justice. *American Journal Medical Jurisprudence* 1: 217–27; 2: 25–26, 59, 115–33, 178–86, 193–222. December 1938–April 1939.

ARTICLES

(82) GLUECK, E. Newer ways of crime control. 9 *Harvard Educationa Review* 184–202; 14 *Social Science* 104–16.

MISCELLANEA

(83) ——, S. Introduction to *John Augustus—first probation officer.* Reprint of the original report of John Augustus, published in Boston in 1852. New York.

1940

BOOKS

(84) ——, S. & LIVINGSTON HALL, *Cases and materials on criminal law.* St Paul, Minn., West Publishing Co., 1 p. 1, VII–XXI, 556 p. 26 cm. (American Casebook Series; W. A. Seavey, general editor). Table of cases: p. XIII–XXI.

(85) ——, S. & E. *Juvenile delinquents grown up.* New York, The Commonwealth Fund; London, H. Milford, Oxford University Press. VIII p., I 1, 330 p., incl. form., 23 1/2 cm.

MISCELLANEA

(86) ——, S. *Administration of criminal justice.* Syllabus of assigned readings and cases (1940–1941) [n.p., 1940?]. 6 numb. 1. 28 cm. Caption title. Reproduced from typewritten copy.

1941

ARTICLES

(87) ——, S. Indeterminate sentence and parole in the Federal system; some comments on a proposal. 21 *Boston University Law Review* 20–32.

(88) ——, S. Parole and juvenile delinquents. 37 *Proceedings of the National Conference of Juvenile Agencies* 49–62.

(89) ——, S. John H. Wigmore; Pioneer. Editorial. 32 *J. Crim. L.* 267–68.

1942

ARTICLES

(90) ——, S. Causas que promueven el crimen. 12 *Archivos de Medicine Legal* 347–66.

(91) ——, E. Coping with wartime delinquency. 16 *Journal of Educational Sociology* 86–98.

(92) ——, S. Crime causation. New York, National Probation Association 80 25 p. Reprinted from *National Probation Association Year Book* 1941.

(93) ——, E. Juvenile delinquency in wartime. 78 *Survey* 70–72.

(94) ——, E. The morals of youth in wartime. 26 *Mental Hygiene* 210–17.

(95) ——, S. Of crime, probation and cognate matters. 6 *Federal Probation* 53–60.

(96) ——, S. Trial and punishment of the Axis war criminals. 4o (8) p. Reprinted from *Free World* vol. 4.

(97) ——, E. Wartime delinquency. (An address). 33 *J. Crim. Law* 119–35.

MISCELLANEA

(99) GLUECK, S. *Report of Committee on Crime Prevention of the American Prison Association.*

(101) ——, S. *Report of the Committee on Crime Prevention of the American Prison Association*, October 1942. S. Glueck, chairman.

1943

BOOKS

(102) ——, S. & E. *Criminal careers in retrospect.* New York, The Commonwealth Fund, XIV, 380 p. 24 cm. (Half-title: Harvard Law School. Studies in Criminology.)

ARTICLES

(103) ——, S. By what tribunal shall war offenders be tried? 56 *Harvard Law Review* 1059–89.

(104) ——, E. Moral goals for modern youth. 9 *Social Action* 6–39.

(105) ——, S. Punishing the war criminals. 109 *New Republic* 706–09; and 110 *New Republic* 243–44 (1944).

MISCELLANEA

(106) ——, S. *Administration of criminal justice.* Syllabus of assigned readings and cases (1943–1944). 7 numb. l. 28 cm. Caption title. Reproduced from typewritten copy. With manuscript notes.

(107) ——, S. Book review: *Report to the Judicial Conference of the Committee on Punishment for Crime* by Judges Parker, Hand, and others. 1942. 56 *Harvard Law Review* 839–42.

1944

BOOKS

(108) ——, S. & E. *After-conduct of discharged offenders.* Upon invitation of the Faculty of Law of the University of Cambridge, England. London, Macmillan.

(109) ——, S. *War criminals.* Brochure prepared at invitation of American Historical Society and published in edition of 200,000 by the War Department.

(110) ——, S. *War criminals, their prosecution and punishment.* New York. A. A. Knopf, VIII, 250, XII p., 1 l. 22 cm. 1st ed. Bibliographical references included in Notes p. 187–250.

(111) ——, S. *What shall be done with the war criminals?* Washington, U.S. Government Printing Office. 2 p. l., 44 p. illus. 19 cm. War Department education manual EM 11, G.I. Roundtable series. Cover-title.

ARTICLES

(112) ——, S. Board vs. sentencing judge. 1 (N.F.) *The New Era*, Leavenworth, 57–58.

(113) ——, S. Bringing the Nazis to book. 27 *Sat. Rev. Lit.* 9–10.

(114) ——, S. & E., CAPTAIN ALEXANDER J. N. SCHNEIDER & LIEUTENANT CYRUS W. LA GRONE. Prediction of behavior of civilian delinquents in the armed forces. 28 *Mental Hygiene* 456–75.

ARTICLES

(115) GLUECK, S. & E. What do we know about delinquency? 80 *Survey Midmonthly* 91–92, 103–04.

MISCELLANEA

(116) ——, S. Introduction to *Boys in men's shoes: a world of working children* by H. E. Burroughs, New York.

(117) ——, S. & E. Introduction to *Rebel without a cause,* by R. Lindner.

(118) ——, E. *Let's take stock of our children. Reader's Digest,* program service no. 5.

1945

BOOKS

(119) ——, S. & E. *After-conduct of discharged offenders, a report to the Department.* Foreword by Dr Felix Frankfurter, Preface by Professor P.–H. Winfield. London, Macmillan. XVI, 114 p. 22 cm. (Half-title: Department of Criminal Science, Faculty of Law, University of Cambridge. English studies in criminal science. Vol. V.)

(120) ——, S. *Crime and justice.* Cambridge, Mass. Harvard University Press. VIII p., 2 l., [3]–349 p. 21 cm. Based on eight lectures delivered to a lay audience at the Lowell Institute, Boston, Spring 1935. Notes: p. [281]–337.

(121) ——, S. *Penologic program for Axis war criminals.* II, 69 numbered leaves.

ARTICLES

(122) ——, S. By what tribunal shall war offenders be tried? 24 *Nebraska Law Review* 143–81.

(123) ——, S. It's Allies' duty and right, as victors, to try and punish Axis war criminals. *P.M.,* January 29 1945, p. 7.

(124) ——, S. Justice for war criminals. 60 *The American Mercury* 274–80.

(125) ——, S. War criminals; their prosecution and punishment. The record of history. 5 *Lawyers Guild Review* 1–10.

MISCELLANEA

(126) ——, S. Book review: David Abrahamsen, *Crime and the human mind.* 1944. 28 *Saturday Review of Literature* 12.

1946

BOOKS

(127) ——, S. *Criminales de guerra, su proceso y castigo.* Buenos Aires, Editorial Anaquel. 4 p. l., 11–250 p., 3 l. 23 cm. Traduccion de Carlos Liacho. Bibliographical footnotes.

(128) ——, S. *The Nuremberg trial and aggressive war.* New York, A. A. Knopf, XV, 121 p., 1 l. 19 cm.

ARTICLES

(129) ——, S. Needed: a world university. This Week Magazine, *Boston Herald,* May 12 1946.

(130) ——, S. The Nuremberg trial and aggressive war. 59 *Harvard Law Review* 396–456.

ARTICLES

(131) GLUECK, S. Ist der Nurnberger Prozess illegal? *Amerikanische Rundschau.* Zweiter Jahrgang 1946 Neuntes Heft 3–15.

1947

MISCELLANEA

(132) ——, S. *Administration of criminal justice.* Syllabus of assigned readings and cases. 7 numb. l. 28 cm. Caption title. Reproduced from typewritten copy.

1948

BOOKS

(133) ——, S. *The Nuremberg trial and aggressive war.* Translated into Japanese under the auspices of the Department of the Army Special Staff. Tokyo. Trans. by Shoyo Shoin.

1949

ARTICLES

(134) ——, S. Causal bases. 1 *Virginia Law Weekly Dicta Compilation* 16–18.

(135) ——, E. Comments on Coulson paper. 45 *Proceedings of the National Conference of Juvenile Agencies* 49–51.

MISCELLANEA

(136) ——, S. Follow-up studies. Encyclopedia of Criminology, edited by V. C. Branham and S. B. Kutash, New York. 167-741.

(137) ——, S. *Social work in a troubled world.* Address at New York School of Social Work, November 4 1949.

1950

BOOKS

(138) ——, S. & E. *Unraveling juvenile delinquency.* Foreword by Erwin N. Griswold. New York, The Commonwealth Fund, XV, 399 p., 28 cm. Harvard Law School. Studies in Criminology.

ARTICLES

(139) ——, S. The new course in criminal law. 12 *Harvard Law School Bulletin* 6. With L. Hall.

(140) ——, S. & E. Preventing delinquency. 36 *Newsweek* 56.

(141) ——, S. Purpose and design of a multi-discipline study of the causes of juvenile delinquency. *L'Enfance délinquante,* 262–77.

(142) ——, E. Techniques of the research. *L'Enfance délinquante* 278–91.

(143) ——, S. What makes a bad boy? 53 *Harvard Alumni Bulletin* 167.

MISCELLANEA

(144) ——, S. & LIVINGSTON HALL. *Criminal law,* 1950–51—Harvard Law School—all sections. Cambridge, Mass. 33, 234 numb. l. 28 cm. Caption title. Reproduced from typewritten copy.

MISCELLANEA

(145) GLUECK, S. & E. *Introduction to case of Henry W*. Cambridge, Mass. [1], 51 numb. l. tables. 27 1/2 cm. Caption title. Reproduced from typewritten copy.

(146) ——, S. *Is a pre-sentence examination of the offender advisable?* Report to the 12th International Penal and Penitentiary Congress, The Hague.

1951

BOOKS

(147) ——, S. & LIVINGSTON HALL, *Cases on criminal law and its enforcement*. St Paul, Minn., West Publishing Co. XXIV, 883 p., 25 1/2 cm. American casebook series.

ARTICLES

(148) ——, S. & E. Plans for further unraveling juvenile delinquency. 41 *Journal of Criminal Law & Criminology* 759.

(149) ——, S. Pre-sentence examination of offenders to aid in choosing a method of treatment, The Hague, 1950. 41 *Journal of Criminal Law & Criminology* 717.

(150) ——, S. Twelfth International Penal and Penitentiary Congress (The Hague) and Second International Congress of Criminology (Paris). 107 *American Journal of Psychiatry* 551.

MISCELLANEA

(151) ——, S. *Criminology*. Assignments. Cambridge, Mass. 1 v. 28 cm. Caption title. Various pagings. Reproduced from typewritten copy.

1952

BOOKS

(152) ——, S. *Crime and correction: selected papers*. Cambridge, Mass. Addison–Wesley Press. X p., 2 l., 273 p., 23 cm.

(153) ——, S. & E. *Delinquents in the making; paths to prevention*. New York, Harper. VIII, [2], 214 p., 21 cm.

(154) ——, S. (Ed.) *The welfare state and the national welfare; a symposium on some of the threatening tendencies of our times*. Introduction, by Sheldon Glueck. Cambridge, Mass., Addison–Wesley Press. IX, 289 p., 21 1/2 cm.

ARTICLES

(155) ——, E. Predicting juvenile delinquency. 88 *Survey* 206–9; 2 *British Journal of Delinquency* 275–286.

(156) ——, S. (Ed.) The welfare state and the national welfare. Book condensation. 2 *U.S.A. the Magazine of American Affairs*.

MISCELLANEA

(157) ——, S. Book review: L. E. Ohlin, *Selection for parole*. 66 *Harvard Law Review* 368–73.

(159) ——, S. (Ed.). Introduction to *The welfare state and the national welfare*. Cambridge, Mass.

MISCELLANEA

(161) GLUECK, S. *Special commission on the laws relating to the sentencing, treatment and release of prisoners in the penal institutions.* Report of the special commission, under Chapter 59, Resolves of 1951, and Chapter 102, Resolves of 1952. Cambridge, Mass. At head of title: The Commonwealth of Massachusetts. Cover-title, 4 p. l., 2–54 numb. 1, 28 1/2 cm. Typewritten corrections in text. Bibliographical footnotes. Reproduced from typewritten copy.

1953

BOOKS

(163) ——, S. & E. *Dal fanciullo al delinquente.* Traduzione di Ernesta Vacca, presentazione di Guido Colucci. Firenze, Editrice universitaria. XI, 233 p., 1 l., 21 cm. (Collezione psicologica, diretta da Alberto Marzi). At head of title: Sheldon and Eleanor Glueck.

(164) ——, S. & E. *Shonen hiko no kaimei. Unraveling juvenile delinquency,* trans. by Chuo Seishonen Mondai Kyogikai. Tokyo, Okurasho Insatsu Kyoku. 2 p. 1, 14, 3, 408, 21 p., 1 l., 26 cm.

ARTICLES

(165) ——, S. Home, the school and delinquency. 23 *Harvard Education Review* 17–32.

MISCELLANEA

(166) ——, S. *Special commission on the laws relating to the sentencing, treatment and release of prisoners in the penal institutions.* Report of the unpaid special commission relative to prisoners, appointed under Chapter 59, Resolves of 1951. Boston, Wright & Potter Printing Co., 62 p. 23 cm. Massachusetts General Court. House Doc. No. 2198.

1954

ARTICLES

(167) ——, S. & E. Etude sur la délinquance juvénile. *Sauvegarde de l'enfance* 472–89.

(168) ——, S. & E. L'énigme de la délinquance. 35 *Revue de Droit Pénal et de Criminologie* 3–22.

MISCELLANEA

(169) ——, S. & E. Harvard University Law School. *Research project into the causes, treatment, and prevention of juvenile delinquency. Progress report.* Cambridge. 28 cm. Report year ends June 30. Reproduced from typewritten copy.

1955

ARTICLES

(170) ——, S. & E. Détection anticipée des futurs délinquants. *Revue de Science Criminelle et de Droit Pénal Comparé* 639–51.

(171) ——, S. In memoriam: George H. Dession. 5 *Buffalo Law Review* 6.

MISCELLANEA

(172) GLUECK, S. & E. *A preview of physique and delinquency.* Prepared for Plenary Session, Third International Congress of Criminology, London, England.

(173) ——, S. Prognosis of recidivism. *Third International Congress on Criminology,* London, General Report, sect. IV. Cover-title, 25 p. 21 1/2 cm.

(174) ——, S. & E. Harvard University Law School. *Research project into the causes, treatment and prevention of juvenile delinquency. Progress report* 1954–1955. Cambridge.

1956

BOOKS

(175) ——, S. & E. *Délinquants en herbe; sur les voies de la prévention.* Tr. de l'américain par M. Verdun. Lyon, E. Vitte, 274, [2] p. 19 cm. (Animus et anima, 7). At head of title: Sheldon et Eleanor Glueck. Trans. of *Delinquents in the making.* Bibliographical footnotes.

(176) ——, S. & E. *Physique and delinquency.* New York, Harper. XVIII, 1 l., 339 p., 1 l., tables 22 cm.

ARTICLES

(177) ——, S. & E. Early detection of future delinquents. 47 *Journal of Criminal Law, Criminology & Police Science* 174.

(178) ——, S. & E. Detection anticipada de futuros delinquentes. 2 *Revista de Criminologia* 95–107 (Uruguay).

(179) ——, E. Identifying juvenile delinquents and neurotics. 10 *Mental Hygiene* 24–43.

(180) ——, S. Mental illness and criminal responsibility. A radio lecture. 2 *Journal of Social Therapy* 134–57.

(181) ——, S. Kei no ryotei no mondai. The sentencing problem, trans. by Haruo Abe and Takaki Kobayashi. Tokyo, Teikoku chiho gyosei gakkai, 29–33 p. 25 cm. Reprint from 9 *Horitsu no Hiroba.*

(182) ——, E. Spotting potential delinquents: can it be done? [7]–13 p. 28 cm. Caption title. Reprinted from *Federal Probation Quarterly* June 1949 [i.e. Sept. 1956].

(183) ——, E. Status of Glueck prediction studies, 18–32 p. 26 cm. Reprinted from 47 *Journal of Criminal Law, Criminology & Police Science.* Bibliographical footnotes.

(184) ——, S. Theory and fact in criminology. 7 *British Journal of Delinquency* 92–109.

(185) ——, S. Two international criminologic congresses: a panorama. 40 *Mental Hygiene* 384, 599. See Appendix B.

MISCELLANEA

(186) ——, E. Guideposts to crime prevention, 4 p. 28 cm. Caption title. Condensed from an address given at the annual dinner of Family Service of Cincinnati and Hamilton County, Ohio, April 11 1956. Reprinted by permission, 17 *Family Service Highlights,* June 1956.

MISCELLANEA

(187) GLUECK, E. *Guideposts to crime prevention.* Address given at the Annual Dinner of Family Service of Cincinnati and Hamilton County, Ohio, April 11 1956.

(188) ——, S. *The nature of predictive techniques, Part I, Predictive techniques in the prevention and treatment of delinquency.* Address at Conference of National Council of Juvenile Court Judges, Boston, Mass. June 19 1956.

(189) ——, S. *The nature of predictive techniques, Part I, Predictive techniques in the prevention and treatment of delinquency. Salute to American youth,* p. 47. Boston Conference, National Council of Juvenile Court Judges, National Juvenile Court Foundation, Pittsburgh, Pa.

(190) ——, S. & E. *Predictive techniques in the prevention and treatment of delinquency.* 47–66 p. 21 1/2 cm. Caption title. At head of title: Boston Conference.

(191) ——, S. & E. Harvard University Law School. *Research project into the causes, treatment, and prevention of juvenile delinquency. Progress report 1955–56.* Cambridge.

(192) ——, S. *The sentencing problem,* 1 p. l., 32 p. 28 cm. Address delivered at Judicial Conference of Third Circuit, United States Courts, Atlantic City, New Jersey, Sept. 12 1956. Reproduced from typewritten copy. Bibliographical footnotes.

(193) ——, E. *The workability of predictive techniques, Part II, Predictive techniques in the prevention and treatment of delinquency.* Address at Conference of National Council of Juvenile Court Judges, Boston, Mass., June 19 1956.

(194) ——, E. *The workability of predictive techniques, Part II, Predictive techniques in the prevention and treatment of delinquency. Salute to American Youth,* p. 57. Boston Conference National Council of Juvenile Court Judges, National Juvenile Court Foundation, Pittsburgh, Pa.

1957

ARTICLES

(195) ——, S. But et orientation générale de l'enquête. l'ère Partie, les rapports entre les caractéristiques physiques et la délinquance. *Revue de Science Criminelle et de Droit Pénal Comparé, janvier-mars 1957,* 73.

(196) ——, E. Directives pour la prévention du crime. 11 *Revue Internationale de Criminologie et de Police Technique* 77.

(197) ——, S. Further comments on the sentencing problem. Washington, Administrative Office of the United States Courts in Cooperation with the Bureau of Prisons. 47–54 p. 28 cm.

(198) ——, S. & E. Physique and delinquency. *Mental Health* July 1957, 449.

(199) ——, S. Les rapports entre les caractéristiques physiques et la délinquance; exposé de l'ouvrage 'Physique and Delinquency'. Paris, Librairie Sirey. Cover-title, [73]–83 p. 24 1/2 cm.

(200) ——, S. The sentencing problem. 20 *Federal Probation* 15.

ARTICLES

(201) GLUECK, S. & E. Working mothers and delinquency. 41 *Mental Hygiene*, 327–52. XVIII tables.

MISCELLANEA

(202) ——, S. & E. Harvard University Law School. *Research project into the causes, treatment and prevention of juvenile delinquency. Progress report 1956–57*. Cambridge.

1958

BOOKS

(203) ——, S. & LIVINGSTON HALL, *Cases on criminal law and its enforcement*. 2 ed. St Paul, West Publishing Co., XXIII, 699 p. 25 1/2 cm. American casebook series.

ARTICLES

(204) ——, E. Body build in the prediction of delinquency. 48 *Journal of Criminal Law, Criminology & Police Science* 577.

(205) ——, E. La conformation somatique dans la prévision de la délinquance. Paris, Librairie Sirey, cover-title, [81]–85 p. 24 cm. Extrait de la *Revue de Science Criminelle et de Droit Pénal Comparé, janvier-mars* 1958. Bibliographical footnotes.

(206) ——, S. Internationelle ou ungdomsbrotts-lighet. *Jurist Nytt*, November 1958 292.

(207) ——, S. Predictive devices and the individualization of justice. 23 *Law & Contemporary Problems* 399 at 461–76.

(208) ——, S. Techniques de la prévision et le traitement de la délinquance. 12 *Revue Internationale de Criminologie et de Police Technique* 241–47.

MISCELLANEA

(209) ——, S. Foreword to *Alexander Maconochie of Norfolk Island*, by J.-V.-W. Barry. [6] p.

(210) ——, S. & E. Harvard University Law School. *Research project into the causes, treatment and prevention of juvenile delinquency. Progress report 1957-58*. Cambridge.

1959

BOOKS

(211) ——, S. *Cases on the criminal law and its enforcement*. With L. Hall. St Paul, Minnesota.

(212) ——, S. & E. *Predicting delinquency and crime*. Cambridge, Mass., Harvard University Press, XXII, 283 p. tables. 25 1/2 cm. Bibliographical footnotes.

(213) ——, S. (Ed.). *The problem of delinquency*. Boston, Houghton, Mifflin. XVI, 1183 p. 25 cm. Includes bibliographies.

MISCELLANEA

(214) ——, S. & E. Harvard University Law School. *Research project into the causes, treatment and prevention of juvenile delinquency. Progress report 1958-59*. Cambridge.

1960

ARTICLES

(215) GLUECK, S. Criminal law, criminology and crime causation. Trans. by Prof. R. Hirano. 77 *Hogaku Kyokai Zassi* (Journal of the Jurisprudence Association) No. 1.

(216) ——, S. Criminogenesi: Teoria E. Fatti. 1 *Quaderni di Criminologia Clinica*, Rome 1–19.

(217) ——, E. Efforts to identify delinquents. 24 *Federal Probation* 49. Reprinted in 6 *International Journal of Social Psychiatry* 206–17.

(218) ——, S. Book review. *Manual of correctional standards.* 1959. 22 *American Journal of Correction* 18.

(219) ——, S. Philosophy and principles of delinquency prevention. Trans. by Shinichiro Michida. 67 *Kyoto Law Review* 1–23.

(220) ——, S. & E. Reflections on basic research in juvenile delinquency. 12 *World Mental Health* 6.

(221) ——, E. Role of the family in the etiology of delinquency. *Bulletin de Société Internationale de Criminologie* 13; 7 *Alabama Correctional Journal* 63. Trans. by Takeo Hayakawa. 9 *Kobe University Law Journal* No. 3.

(222) ——, S. Ten years of unraveling juvenile delinquency. An examination of criticisms. 51 *Journal of Criminal Law, Criminology and Police Science* 283.

(223) ——, S. & E. Progress report to members of Fourth International Congress of Criminology. The Hague. Issued by the Secretariat to the Congress.

(224) ——, S. The meaning and management of delinquency. Part I, Crime causation: theory and fact. Trans. by Katsuhiko Nishimura. 32 *Horitsu Jiho* (*The Law Times Journal*) 111–125. (Tokyo.)

(225) ——, S. The meaning and management of delinquency. Part II, Methods of coping with delinquency and crime. Trans. by Katsuhiko Nishimura. 32 *Horitsu Jiho* (*The Law Times Journal*) 81–93. (Tokyo.)

(226) ——, S. Predictive techniques in the management of juvenile delinquency. Part I, The nature of predictive techniques. Trans. by T. Miyamoto and H. Abe. 13 *Horitsu no Hiroba* (*The Law Forum*) 34–39. (Tokyo.)

(227) ——, E. Predictive techniques in the management of juvenile delinquency. Part II, The workability of predictive techniques. Trans. by T. Miyamoto and H. Abe. 13 *Horitsu no Hiroba* (*The Law Forum*) 39–43. (Tokyo.)

(228) ——, S. Philosophy and principles of delinquency prevention. Trans. by Shinichiro Michida. 67 *Tokyo University Law Review*, No. 5.

MISCELLANEA

(229) ——, S. Foreword to *Reaching the fighting gang*, by the New York City Youth Board.

(230) ——, S. & E. *Basic researches into the causes, management and prevention of juvenile delinquency being carried on at the Harvard Law School.* Spring 1960.

MISCELLANEA

(231) GLUECK, S. & E. Harvard University Law School. *Research project into the causes, treatment and prevention of juvenile delinquency. Progress Report 1959–60.* Cambridge.

1961

BOOKS

(232) ——, S. & E. *Unraveling juvenile delinquency.* Trans. by Shigemitsu Dando et al.; edited by Haruo Abe. (Rev. Japanese ed.) Ministry of Justice of Japan, Tokyo.

ARTICLES

(233) ——, S. Ten years of *Unraveling juvenile delinquency*: An examination of criticisms. Trans. by Shunji Ifukube; edited by Haruo Abe. *Horitsu no Hiroba (The Law Forum)*, Tokyo, June–October 1961.

(234) ——, S. Philosophy and principles of delinquency prevention. Trans. by Shinichiro Michida. Reprinted in *Comparative studies on American and Japanese business law*, Shinichiro Michida (Ed.). Tokyo, Yushindo Publishing Co.

(235) ——, S. Wanted: a comparative criminology. Trans. by Akira Tanigawa. *Jurist* (Tokyo), February 25 1961. Also in *Bulletin de Société Internationale de Criminologie*, 2ème Semestre 1961.

(236) ——, S. Theory and fact in criminology. Trans. by Armand Mergen. *Kriminologie—Heute*, Armand Mergen (Ed.), Kriminologische Schriftenreihe aus der Deutschen Kriminologischen Gesellschaft. Hamburg, Kriminalistik Verlag.

(237) ——, E. A preview of *Family environment and delinquency*, prepared for the Sixth International Congress on Mental Health, Paris, September 1961.

(238) ——, S. Pathways to improved sentencing. Address delivered before the American Society of Criminology, Denver, Colorado, December 1961.

(239) ——, E. Toward improving the identification of delinquents. Address delivered before the American Society of Criminology, Denver, Colorado, December 1961.

(240) ——, S. & E. Méthodes pronostiques para-cliniques dans le domaine de la délinquance juvénile et des troubles émotionnels de l'enfant. *Hommage à George Heuyer. Pour un Humanisme Médico-Social.* Paris, Presses Universitaires de France.

MISCELLANEA

(241) ——, E. Book review: Clara Chassell Cooper, *A comparative study of delinquents and nondelinquents.* 25 *Federal Probation.*

(242) ——, S. & E. Publications, 1923–1960: Bibliography. Compiled by Harvard Law School Library. *Bulletin de Société Internationale de Criminologie*, 1ère Semestre 1961, 207–19. Bulletin, Library of the Ministry of Social Welfare, Israel. Jerusalem, 1961.

(243) ——, S. & E. Harvard University Law School. *Research project into the causes, treatment and prevention of juvenile delinquency. Progress Report 1960–61.* Cambridge.

1962

BOOKS

(244) GLUECK, E. *The Gluecks' adventure in Japan, May 28–July 2 1960.* From a diary kept by Eleanor T. Glueck. Tokyo, Obun Printing Co.

(245) ——, S. & E. *Family environment and delinquency.* London, Routledge & Kegan Paul; Boston, Mass., Houghton Mifflin.

(246) ——, S. *Law and psychiatry: Cold war or entente cordiale?* Baltimore, Johns Hopkins Press; London, Tavistock Publications.

ARTICLES

(247) ——, E. T. A preview of *Family environment and delinquency.* 8 *International Journal of Social Psychiatry*, No. 2; *International Annals of Criminology*, 1ère Semestre, 1962; Trans. by M. Shikita, 15 *Horitsu no Hiroba* (*The Law Forum*) 44–48.

(248) ——, E. T. Toward improving the identification of delinquents. 53 *Journal of Criminal Law, Criminology & Police Science*, No. 2.

(249) ——, S. Toward improved sentencing. In *Essays in jurisprudence in honor of Roscoe Pound.* Prepared by the American Society for Legal History, Editor, Ralph A. Newman. Indianapolis, Bobbs-Merrill, pp. 410–38.

MISCELLANEA

(250) ——, S. & E. Harvard University Law School. *Research project into the causes, treatment and prevention of juvenile delinquency. Progress Report 1961–62.* Cambridge.

1963

BOOKS

(251) ——, S. & E. *Jugendliche rechtsbrecher: wege zur vorbeugung.* Trans. by Dr Helga Gilbert of *Delinquents in the making: paths to prevention.* Stuttgart, Ferdinand Enke Verlag.

ARTICLES

(252) ——, E. Toward further improving the identification of delinquents. 54 *Journal of Criminal Law, Criminology and Police Science*, No. 2.

(253) ——, S. & E. Family environment and delinquency in the perspective of etiologic research. *International Annals of Criminology*, 1ère Semestre, 211–18.

(254) ——, S. Probation and social agencies. 8 *Utah Law Review*, No. 3.

(255) ——, S. Law and the stuff of life. 14 *Harvard Law School Bulletin*, No. 6.

(256) ——, S. On the conduct of a seminar in the administration of criminal justice. 16 *Journal of Legal Education*, No. 1.

(257) ——, S. & E. A decade of research in criminology: stock-taking and a forward look. 3 *Excerpta Criminologica*, No. 5.

MISCELLANEA

(258) ——, S. & E. Harvard University Law School. *Research project into the causes, treatment and prevention of juvenile delinquency. Progress Report 1962–63.* Cambridge.

INDEX